COLLECTED POEMS & PROSE

Freddy Anderson

Dedicated to the memory of JIM FRIEL (1941-2020) —a true and stalwart comrade of Freddy and a trusted and generous friend. He was straight, principled and stood for working class unity, socialism and internationalism.

And to the memory of JANETTE MCGINN (1930-2020) and WILLIE GALLACHER (1940-2020)—both staunch friends and advocates of Freddy's work.

COLLECTED POEMS & PROSE

Freddy Anderson

with a preface by Paul Anderson and
an introduction by Ian Spring

First published 2020
by Rymour Books
with Hog's Back Press
45 Needless Road,
PERTH

© the estate of Freddy Anderson

ISBN 978-0-9540704-7-2

supported by the

Scottish Poetry Library
Bringing people and poems together

Cover design by Ian Spring
Typeset in Garamond
Printed and bound by
Imprint Digital
Seychelles Farm
Upton Pyne
Exeter

All rights reserved. No part of this publication may be reproduced, stored in a retrieval system, or transmitted, in any form or by any means, electronic, mechanical, photocopying, recording or otherwise, without the prior permission of the publishers.

The paper used in this book is approved by the Forest Stewardship Council

ACKNOWLEDGEMENTS

Many thanks to the many people who have provided their comments, thoughts, manuscript materials and various other forms of support. These include Gavin Paterson, Davie Foy, Elspeth King, Stephen Coyle, Jeanette Hill, Michael Donnelly, Jim Ferguson, Fred Crayk, Joey Simon, Jim Dey, Susan Lynch, John Gagahan, Chris Lytton and others.

Meg McGuinness, Ruby McCann, Carol Jamnejad and Calum Smith took on the onerous task of proofreading parts of the book for which the editor is grateful.

Willie Gallacher, Jim Friel and Janette McGinn, great friends and supporters of Freddy, sadly passed away shortly before the publication of this volume.

The Freddy Anderson Archive is located in the library at Glasgow Caledonian University and we acknowledge the University and the Head of Special Collections, Carole McCallum, for their assistance with this volume. The collection was first catalogued by John Fowles with the help of Joe Fodey and Philip Wallace (who also wrote an introduction to the published edition of *Krassivy*). A more detailed catalogue was leter compiled by Carole McCallum assisted by Simon Docherty.

This edition is supported by Glasgow Caledonian University, home of the Freddy Anderson Archive, Cheeky Besom Productions, a Glasgow arts and literary collective, the Scottish Poetry Library and FARE: Family Action in Rogerfield and Easterhouse. Freddy was closely involved with the community in Garthamlock and Easterhouse and the east end of Glasgow in general. On behalf of the Anderson family and the publisher, all profits from this edition of the book go to FARE to help with their work in providing opportunities for young people in the area.

Freddy Anderson was no ordinary poet. The epithets 'folk poet' or 'poet of the people' merely hinted at the fact that he was one of (or the last of) a long line of Scottish balladeers or chapmen hawking their broadsheets and chapbooks and reciting their poems in pubs, markets or on the street. This offers the poet a very personal connection with the people and a status within the community which is testified to by the many personal recollections and appreciations of the poet contained within this volume. It also complicates the task of the editor, as many of the poems existed in ephemeral form, xeroxographic and even handwritten copies circulated by hand. Nevertheless, thanks to the efforts and contributions of several people, this collection presents a substantial representative sample of the completed work of Freddy Anderson over six decades.

CONTENTS

Foreword: Paul Anderson — 11
Introduction: Ian Spring — 13

POEMS AND BALLADS

A British Soldier Foresees his Death in South Armagh — 43
A Parody — 45
A Poem for all Peoples — 46
Aberfan — 48
Atom Bomb Blues — 49
Bonnymuir — 51
Children of the Night I — 52
Children of the Night II — 53
Elegy on a 'Great Man' — 55
Elegy to Churchill — 56
Free Scotland in the Dawn — 58
Glen Masson — 59
Hitler Meets Franco in Hell — 60
Holy Cliff's Prayer — 61
In Comedie Lane, Garthamlock — 63
John Bull's Lament — 64
John Cairney's Prayer — 66
Midnight of the Century — 68
National Affront — 70
Near William Blake's House — 71
Neither Red Nor Dead — 72
Nuclear Fision — 74
On Balladier Bridge — 76
On Churchill's Death — 77
On W B Yeats — 78
Ora Pro Nobis — 79
Poison Pen — 81
Poppycock — 82
Shy Couple — 84
Song of a Spud — 85
Song of the Duke — 86
Song of the Scab — 87
Strontium Ninety-Three — 88
The Atomaniacs — 89
The Billionaire's Wife — 91

The Blackberry Man	92
The Calton Martyrs of 1787 I	93
The Calton Martyrs of 1787 II	94
The Colours of Ireland	95
The Connolly Ballad	96
The Dawning of the Day	97
The Green Hills of Monaghan	98
The Kirk's Alarm	99
The Lark	100
The Lord's Lament	101
The Love Ballad	102
The Malapropist	103
The Millionaire's Prayer	104
The Moonlighter	106
The Orra Man	108
The Polis o' Argyll	110
The Red Herring	111
The Scabs of Nottingham	113
The Spectre Inspector	114
The Stash Me Father Wore	115
The Statue of Liberty	116
The Sunbright Flower of Peace	118
The Sword of Damocles	121
The Wee Folk	122
The Workers Millennium	123
These Are My Friends	124
To An Erstwhile Friend	125
To the Scabs	126
Transmutation	127
Trees of Liberty	128
Via Dolorosa	129
Wake (on the Occasion of the Irish 'Republic') 1949	130
War Fever	131
Waukrife—a Pectoral Encounter with Nessie	132
When After Armageddon	135

GLASGOW POEMS AND SONGS

A Ballad of Red Clyde I	139
A Ballad of Red Clyde II	141
A Peculiar Stranger on Glasgow Green	143
A Song for the Glasgow Irish	144
A Song of Paddy's Market	145

At Glasgow Cross	147
Glasgow Street Characters	149
Johnny and the Starlings	152
Let Glasgow Flourish!	154
Lines on the Ramshorn Kirkyard	156
Old Scotia	157
Pioneerville. Ha! Ha!	161
Rab's Impression of the First Sunday Opening of the Victoria Bar	163
Song of the Vicky Bar	165
The Back Streets of Glasgow	166
The New Jail in Carlton Place, Glasgow	167
Where is the Glasgow That I Used to Know?	168
Ya Bass	169

POLITICAL VERSE

A Letter from an American Convict to President Reagan	173
Georgy Porgy	174
Haxks and Doves	175
How Dare You, Alex Kitson!	176
Maggie Meets Her Match	178
Pat Lally's Golden Ghain	180
Squibs, Skits and Epitaphs	182
The Hero of Hospitality Inn	191
The Knighting of Sir Harold Wilson	193
The Labour Crocodiles	194
The Mean Devil—Maggie!	195
The Old Lag's Ambition	197
The Real Terrorist	198
The Red Flag	199
The Workers Prayer	201
Two of a Kind	202

ILLUSTRATIONS 203

OINEY HOY 209

SHORT STORIES

The Banshee in the Corn	291
A Legend of Saint Mungo	297
The Rose and the Thorn	300

PLAYS

Krassivy	307
The Calton Weavers	363

NOTES TO THE POEMS & PROSE	413
INDEX OF NAMES	417

FOREWORD

I have delayed writing this until today—my 60th birthday. My father and mother—Freddy and Isobel—met Paul Robeson on May Day 1960 and said that if their first child were a boy, they would call him 'Paul.' and that is my name. This will be very much a family day for us. My sister Isobel will be speaking to us from Galway on a video conference app. My brother Dermot is staying with me because of the current lockdown due to the coronavirus.

We can't wait to see everyone when we can—all our friends, acquaintances and loved ones. Many of them are well aware of Freddy and his writings and political and cultural activities have impacted their lives in different ways and in different proportions. Our recent birthday party for Freddy featuring many Glasgow singers, musicians and poets, reminded us how well he was loved and admired by many of the great talents in our literary and folk community who have dedicated themselves to keeping our independent traditions alive.

Freddy was steeped in these traditions and was an avid connoisseur of international literature and folk culture. His understanding of this inspired him to become a peace activist. He was proud of the folk movement's involvement in the struggles against Polaris and later Trident. This, along with the writings and deeds of John Maclean (whom Freddy wrote the the award-winning play *Krassivy* about), brought him to Scottish socialist republicanism. This, above all, is our family agenda and is the biggest theme of our family conversations still. This is why we are extremely grateful to Ian Spring for putting this collection together.

We hope that this collection will prove to be a joy, and spread the spirit of joy and mirth that was at the heart of Freddy's personality. Moreso, we also hope that this collection leads to greater recognition of Freddy's stature in world literature. His original use of magical realism, political satire and celtic story-telling in his novel *Oiney Hoy* is exceptional. His efforts in poetry and short stories are also of a high standard and reflect his varied interests. His many plays were performed and received critical acclaim.

Salute.

Paul Anderson,
June 9th 2020

INTRODUCTION

Until I was about 30 years old I [was] a 'wild rover'—Tipperary, Dublin, Belfast, London, Liverpool, Bombay, Calcutta, Mandalay, Rangoon and finally Glasgow. I had been through some unique adventures and I really wanted to settle down... Glasgow kindly provided that opportunity and despite the food rationing and housing shortage at the time, Glasgow had the richest score of warm-hearted people I ever met in my many travels.

So Freddy Anderson recounts his early days leading to what was to become the major part of his life in the city of Glasgow and his writing career which was largely posited on an engagement with that city. 1951 was the year that he identified as the fulfillment of his desire to settle down; the year he met and married Isobel Foy: 'It brought a great companionship and stability into my life, a necessary basis, I think, for sustained literary output'.

Anderson's personal odyssey, of course, also reflected a general migration, in the period after the war, of the Irish to Scotland and, particularly, Glasgow. He later fictionalised it in a short prose piece:

I came in from the west with the wet rain filling the tarpaulin with mountain pools, up the Clyde to Glasgow town, with the harvesters glumly on green chests as old as the hills of Donegal, a drunken soldier groggy as the white swirl of the wake, a little lass of two, red ribboned and lonely... God, how we cattle stank in the close foul hold.

If this was pleasant I would make a rhyme for you all. I would bring in the birds, the stretching beaks of the gulls out of a white cloud down to the shadowed water with the chance of a bite swooping down from the hungry circus keen eyes on a salt soaked crust... I would mention the waves, riders with dancing plumes and the old man aft with a stick watching it with deep eyes, deeper than the sea, on his way home.

Don't let the picture cards deceive! It was cold, like a wet post in a wintry lane with the thin pine of Scotland on either side as the snail ship wearily crawled up to the womb of the Clyde.

Anderson's literary career was to be established on both sides of this divide. Forward to his life in Glasgow, and backwards to his reminiscences of his childhood in Ireland.

Freddy Anderson was born on September 11th 1922 in Lower Main Street, Ballybay, County Monaghan, one of four children of Fred and Minnie Anderson. Ballybay is a small town on a crossroads near the border between the Republic of Ireland and Northern Ireland. Once noted for linen manufacture, it is now frequented by anglers and birdwatchers attracted by loughs in the proximity. It is the subject of a song: *In the Town of Ballybay*, by Tommy Makem. A noted native of Ballybay (who attended the same school as Anderson) was Fergal O'Hanlon, a member of the Pearse Column of the Irish Republican Army, who died at the age of 20 in a raid on a Royal Ulster Constabulary barracks. O'Hanlon is commemorated in Dominic Behan's *The Patriot Game*.

Educated at the Cistercian College in Roscrea in County Tipperary and the Christian

Brothers School in Monaghan, Anderson progressed to University College, Dublin to study architecture, but didn't complete the course. He became interested in writing and the theatre, joining the Dublin Writers Circle and performing briefly at The Olympia Theatre where his mentor was Sheila Richards, one of the original cast of *The Plough and the Stars*. Subsequently, he left Dublin for Belfast, the city of his father's birth, and worked as a wages clerk in the Harland & Wolff shipyard in Belfast (unusual for a catholic) prior to joining the RAF in 1943. He served as a radar operator in Crossmaglen and then Burma, as past of 'the forgotten army'. Very little is known of this period, but in a lecture on Burns delivered to the Bangla Centre in 1996 he notes: 'In the many months I spent in Bengal and Burma during the war against Fascism... I saw great kindness and goodness among the Bangla people even to the extent of one young Bengali saving me from a scorpion bite.' In 1946 he was medically discharged due to a duodenal ulcer from the rank of leading aircraftsman with a 'very good' conduct record.

After the war ended, Anderson settled in Glasgow and in 1951 married Isobel Foy. whose family were from County Mayo. They had three children together—Paul, Isobel and Dermot. Paul was the first born, in 1960, and was named after Paul Robeson, who Anderson had met when he visited Glasgow and led the May Day parade in Queen's Park that year.

Anderson's involvement in theatre stimulated in Dublin continued in Glasgow with the Glasgow Unity Theatre post-war which resulted from a meeting with the Scottish actor Roddy McMillan. Anderson's acting skills were limited (he often said his biggest part was as a typewriter salesman in *Juno and the Paycock*) and Jim Friel recorded an amusing story from his time at the Olympia when he was called in at short notice for a role: 'He was a bit nervous wondering if he could cope with the situation. He spied a bottler of what he thought was whiskey in the corner of the dressing room and took a swig before going on stage. Unfortunately, the 'whiskey' was turpentine! The actors on stage had to say 'The church is on fire! The church is on fire.'When Freddy made his entrance he roared: 'And I'm on bloody fire too!'.'

He soon discovered that his talents were better directed towards writing. It is recorded that his play, *Thirty Three Years*, a pageant of the Bolshevik revolution, was produced by this company between 1947 and 1950 and played to packed houses in the St Andrew's Halls, but no script survives. At this time, Anderson's political stance was developing and he had joined the Communist Party.

During this time Anderson was also writing poetry, and, in 1949, his work was published in the volume *Fowrsom Reel*, along with three other Scottish poets: Morris Blythman—the folksinger who wrote under the sobriquet Thurso Berwick—John Kincaid and George Todd. Apart from Anderson, all the poems were in Scots. The book came with a foreword by Hugh MacDiarmid and was generally well received, but was perhaps a little peripheral to the Scottish literary scene in general. It was published in a limited edition and Anderson noted himself in 1985: 'Chris Grieve wrote a very good introduction... in fact it has made the little book quite a collector's item and very occasional copies that appear on the market fetch quite a price!' In 1959, Hamish Henderson and Hugh MacDiarmid were involved in a dispute regarding the contributors to a volume of poetry in honour of Robert Burns and Henderson wrote: 'Does he [MacDiarmid] really think that there was no place in 1959 under Burns' 'honour'd shade' for a single one out of the eight poets of *Fowrsom Reel* and *Four Part Song*?' Henderson was a champion of Anderson's work and notes of the poems in *Fowrsom Reel* that they were '…magical atmospheric evocations of his Irish childhood, written in a distinctive Monaghan-accented English [employing a] seemingly artless but actually highly accomplished style. The landscape and the 'props' are those of Patrick Kavanagh's early poetry—he also was a Co. Monaghan man!—but the voice and the rhythm are quite individual… the man who had written these lines had learned to good effect from Yeats' later ballad style.'

There are two clear influences on Anderson's work at that time. Firstly, as Henderson states, his childhood memories of Monaghan, exemplified, for example, in *The Love Ballad*:

> Come gently round me, town bred folk
> and listen to my tale
> I was born in Monaghan of the little hills and vales
> My mother kept a fruit shop, my father he ran wild
> and I became in a village street an anxious daring child.

This also informs one of his best known works, *The Blackberry Man*. The key to this poem is the move from the specific to the general in the last two lines, reflecting on the innocence and wonder of childhood.

> All the lanes of Monaghan are heavy with blackberries,
> And the children carry cans:
> They fill them in the summer sun
> And sell them to the blackberry man.
> The blackberry man has beady eyes
> That ripen with the bee:
> He packs the fruit to the brim in barrels
> And sends it over the sea.
>
> Now the blackberry man is a happy man
> With his house upon the hill,
> With his pony and trap and bright tweed cap,
> And men to run the mill.
> But happier far are the children there
> Whose laughter greets the morning air
> In the dew-grass lanes of Monaghan,
> Who fearing neither God nor man,
> Find the world in the rim of a blackberry can.

Secondly, his interest in Irish history and politics. *The Connolly Ballad* is based on a local Irish legend about a daft lad, Oiney Hoy, who gains a local reputation after he performed a supposedly prodigious jump:

> Oiney Hoy stands the day long swearing
> at the gawking gapes of Carricktee
> that he'll drown himself in a six-foot bog hole
> and set all holy Ireland free…

The conclusion develops this story to make a generic point about the political situation in Ireland:

> …But where's the word for Connolly
> in the tolling Angelus bell,
> with cream-faced traitors sanctified
> and Ireland's saints in hell?

The Connolly Ballad is a powerful series of images from the Irish revolutionary years. James Connolly was, of course, born in Scotland, but his parents were from County Monaghan, so there is a indirect connection with Anderson.

A poem in the same lyric tradition but with a Scottish setting is *Glen Masson*, written after Anderson heard of the tragic fate of an orphaned boy from Mull whose bones were found in an Argyll glen. Hamish Henderson notes: 'Glen Masson is in Cowal; like Glen Etive and Glendarnel it is mentioned in the Irish tale of The Sons of Uisneach, of which the well known Gaelic song 'Deidre's Farewell to Scotland' forms a part. The very name, therefore, recalls this old Scottish-Irish connection; using it as a springboard, Freddy has written a poem which encompasses the closely-related, but non-identical twin tradition. Indeed, it's a poem which could easily have been composed on either side of the Moyle.'

Perhaps, as Henderson suggests, a comparison can be made between these poems and some of the early works of Patrick Kavanagh, such as his poem *Peace*:

> And sometimes I am sorry when the grass
> Is growing over the stones in quiet hollows
> And the cocksfoot leans across the rutted cart-pass
> That I am not the voice of country fellows
> Who now are standing by some headland talking
> Of turnips and potatoes or young corn…

However, Henderson is quite correct that, in general, Anderson's voice is distinct, somehow more youthful and innocent.

During the fifties and sixties Anderson wrote articles and short stories for the BBC, Radio Eireann and *The Irish Press* and had a variety of jobs: tram conductor, lamp lighter, museum attendant, night porter, telephone operator and a spell selling books from a barrow in the Glasgow streets. However, there is a hiatus in his poetic output and, arguably, the next substantial poem to be penned wasn't until 1970. This time the subject is not Irish but Scottish political revolt and the style of the work is obviously influenced by the folk tradition and the folk revival in Scotland spurred by Morris Blythman, Hamish Henderson and others. The poem is *Bonnymuir*, focused on the weavers' rebellion of 1820:

> I am a Calton weaver and simple is my plea,
> Not to be tied forever to four posts of poverty;
> The grim dark days o' Castlereagh have settled with their blight,
> Though the sun shines down on Glasgow town, it seems eternal night.
>
> We tried to make a union then, our scanty rights defend;
> The cotton and tobacco lairds its ruin did intend:
> They hired an informer—Richmond was his name,
> And bribed with gold our cause he sold to misery and shame.
>
> 'Twas early in the April and the Springtime o' the year,
> As I went down the Ladywell, a great crowd did appear;
> They read a notice on the wall: 'Tae Arms! Tae Arms!' it cried,
> 'Twas there that Andra Hardy stood and Tyranny defied…

Henderson notes: 'By the time he wrote this splendid ballad, which never fails to gain warm applause when he declaims it, Freddy had mastered the 'feel' and the rhythms of Scots traditional ballad-poetry; this means that he had effectively bridged the idiomatic divide between his Ulster poetry and the kindred but separate literary tradition of his adopted country.' Anderson's interest in Scottish radical history was also to spark a play about the 1820 rebellion and two poems about the Calton Weavers' Strike of 1787.

A version of *Bonnymuir*, set to a tune based on *The Smashing of the Van* by John Greig can be found in Ewan McVicar's collection of Glasgow songs, *One Singer, One Song*, and, although it should be noted that Anderson was not himself a singer or a songwriter, he was influenced by the folk song movement. During the anti-Polaris protests of the early sixties as part of the Glasgow Song Guild, he penned *The Polis o' Argyll* as a contribution to the *Ding Dong Dollar* song collection edited by Morris Blythman:

> You may talk about your Nelson, and Francis Drake as well.
> And how they blew the Spaniards and pirates all to hell,
> But they've nothing on the Yankee subs that sneaked past Arran Isle,
> And left the Battle o' Dunoon to the polis o' Argyll
>
> These worthy sons of Robert Peel are trained to keep the law,
> And any danger they'll confront, providin it is sma';
> In naval operations they specialise in style,
> But the Holy Loch proved quite a shock to the Polis o' Argyll.
>
> With only frogmen to assist and 'specials' by the score.
> The Polis proved they're gallant men, all heroes to the core:
> With Proteus squat behind them and nuclear missiles, too,
> They did the near impossible and captured a canoe.
>
> Now all you Russian astronauts who navigate the globe

> Stay far away from Scotland in your Cosmo-Rocket probe,
> For should you land near Gourock, you'll be conquered in line style
> By the Yanks combining forces with the Polis o' Argyll.

On 4th January 1999, in a letter to Hamish Henderson, Anderson details a recording of songs he intended to prepare including the following singers and songs:

> John Greig, *Bonnymuir, Ballad of the Clyde*
> Gordeanna McCulloch, *The Woods of Eaglesham*
> Frank McCulloch, *Glen Masson*
> Ian Campbell, *Aberfan, the Polis of Argyll*
> Gerry MacGregor, *The Lark, Poppycock*

(He also intended to record *The Old Man's Farewell* and the following poems recited: *The Blackberry Man, On William Butler Yeats, On Nan Milton, These Are My Friends, Let Glasgow Flourish, Ballad of Paddy's Market*.)

The production did not appear in this form but *The Lark*, Anderson's poem about Bobby Sands was subsequently recorded on an album by the republican folk singer Gerry MacGregor. The mother of Bobby Sands heard this recording and praised it. MacGregor sang this song at Anderson's funeral in 2001. Anderson also made a personal contribution to a folk album when he appeared on the topic album *The Streets of Glasgow* in 1972 reciting *Let Glasgow Flourish*. Towards the end of his life, Anderson was planning an album in collaboration with his friend, the uilleann piper Pat McNulty, author of *The Piper's Dream*.

From the late sixties onwards, Anderson's spiritual home was in Stockwell Street (reputedly named after William Wallace stocking a well with the bodies of dead Englishmen) near the river Clyde, at the Scotia Bar (and latterly the Victoria Bar and The Clutha Vaults across the road—popularly amalgamated to form the 'Stockwell Folk Village'). At that time, the Scotia (once called the Old Scotia Inne; now commonly The Scotia) which stood on the site of the old Scotia Music Hall was populated by a range of writers, artists and folk singers including Billy Connolly, Danny Kyle, Jon Martyn, Mick Broderick, Cy Laurie, Tam Harvey, Hamish Imlach and the members of noted folk bands such as The Clutha, Molendinar and The Whistlebinkies. Along with Willie Gallacher and Jimmy Blackburn, Anderson edited a periodic broadsheet, *Scotia Folk*, which recorded the comings and goings of the folk scene.

There was a burgeoning folk scene at this time; politicised and keenly aware of Glasgow and Scotland's historic and literary traditions. This was an ideal environment for Anderson to develop his political ideas, angage in activism and to hawk his poems, usually as sheets printed on a xerox copier. These days are recorded in possibly the longest poem Anderson ever wrote, *Old Scotia*. Prophetically, perhaps, the poem imagines a return to the bar in a future when the characters inhabiting it are gone:

> For where is Clydebank's bearded Mick, regaled us a'
> wi' mony a trick, fantastic hoverin's in mid-air
> that made even strangers stop and stare, an' then

applaud. The Scotia's heroes he gi'e fame gif in
the act himself became a kind o' God?

Or Campbell huggin' his guitar, elbow leanin' on the
bar, speers John the Host—lain just back frae Germanie,
causin' new perplexity 'twixt truth an' boast?

Or where is Grimes' dark, rollin' eye, could raise
the subject to the sky, still be mundane?
Where are they now? Stockwell Street no langer
echoes wi' their feet—I search in vain.

Ah, gone those names we used recite in early days
with ardour bright as though tae light the gloom
o' night wi' saints an' sages.

But frae the shadows o' the mist, tho powers o'
dree my plan resist, I'll dip my pen an' mak a
list, my Book o' Ages.

Where is that young minstrel pair, Harvey Tam an'
Connolly there? What feasts o' music we wad
share—twa Humblebums? Your party try in vain
tae guard, you'd find them in your ain back-yaird come
doon the lum!

In the mid seventies, The Scotia Bar had been partly taken over by a crowd of bikers called the Blue Angels resulting in the folk fraternity decamping to the Victoria Bar across the road. Shortly afterwards, Scottish licensing laws changed to allow Sunday opening, prompting Anderson to pen a piece entitled *Rab's Impression Of The First Sunday Opening (Of The Victoria Bar)*:

> I thocht the law wad ne'er be passed,
> but help me, God, it's come at last,
> an' take perdition we gang fast,
> a skelping rate—
> we'll save the unco-guid declare
> wi' prattlin' prate.
>
> Puir Holy Willie staunin' by,
> wi' blasted wunner in his eye,
> an' whether he should laugh or cry
> he's fair perplexed,
> but by the way he bites yon lip,
> I'd say he's vexed.

> John Knox and Calvin fume an' glower,
> oh, wad tae God they had the power
> tae be amang ye at this hour,
> alas, alas.
> Oh, why can't Paisley raise the stour
> or Pastor Glass...

'Rab' is, of course, Robert Burns, and Anderson has convincingly embraced the style of the bard. The stanzas are based on a form known as 'standard habbie', often employed by Burns. Another good satirical piece in this style is titled *Waukrife: A Poetical Encounter With Nessie* in which the eponymous monster laments the failings of modern society:

> The lanely loch we waukrife nicht
> I saw an eerie, eldricht sicht
> And heard strange things
> That gart me think
> O' Mankind hovering on the brink,
> O' hell's perdition,
> And I became maist fashed indeed
> For oor condition.
>
> I saw this creature lang an' laigh,
> Whiskin' tail an' gapin' craig,
> Wi' scaly skin and glow'rin' even
> That amaist lit the mirky scene:
> Frantic feart I wad hae ran
> Had no the puir lane beast began
> A plaintive lay;
> It couldna fail tae mak me bide
> An' hear her tale...

Burns remained central to Anderson's poetic ambition and he spent a great deal of time mapping Burns's travels in and around Glasgow, resulting in a short book produced by the Mitchell Library funded by the Glasgow New Opportunites Millennium Awards Scheme, and another pamphlet called *Glasgow Burnsiana*. In an interview given shortly before his death, Anderson responds to the question 'If you could meet one famous person, living or dead, who would it be?' as follows: 'Rabbie Burns—without a doubt. Even his great political rival, Sir Walter Scott, had to admit that he had never seen such lustre glowing in the dark eyes of any other human being... He was just that rare thing—a genius. He was a super-genius.'

It should also be noted that Anderson shared his familiarity with Burns with the idioms of folk poetry. On a couple of occasions he employs the well known folk tale type, sometimes known as *The Carle of Kellyburn Braes*, in which a scolding wife proves too much for the devil to cope with. One of his best political poems is *Maggie Meets Her Match*:

> ...Poor Maggie took her bags and climbed,
> climbed down the golden stair,
> but Old Nick stood with his pitch-fork
> and stopped her coming there.
>
> 'Oh, Maggie, we have heard of you
> from every kind of source,
> and though our hell's a wicked place,
> you'd make it ten times worse'...

Another aspect of this period is that Anderson could be volatile, especially in his cups. He had an on-off relationship with Brendan McLaughlan, proprietor of the Scotia and laterally the Clutha Vaults, himself a poet and songwriter. In a form of flyting, Anderson would pen fake letters or press reports referring to those he was in disagreement with. For example, he believed that McLauglan was inventing some Glasgow 'tradition':

Two world famous archaeological finds in Stockwell Street
Stone of Destiny found in Scotia
Blarney Stone found in Clutha
If anything is lacking in your city's history 'I will make it up'

Donald Anderson (no relation) recalls in an obituary for Anderson: 'One angry Scotia batman had to go outside and buy up all of Freddy's poems lampooning him and immediately lift his ban. Across the road in the Victoria Bar, he was barred after asking his fare home, ending his night entertaining all and sundry at the barman's expense. when giving his bus fare he threw the change over the bar, demanding a taxi—and was immediately barred again.'

He had a similarly difficult relationship with the Irish writer and folksinger Dominic Behan (who he had met at the Sheffield Youth Festival in 1953) who could be equally beligerent at times. There is a short prose piece preserved in the Anderson archive which recalls this uneasy relationship:

In the Marland pub in George Street after closing time I sat in the corner of the room, while Behan talked to young Eric Bogle...
  As a prelude to boasting about his own successes, Behan shouted over to me:
'Have you been doing any writing yourself lately, Freddy?'
'No,' I replied gruffly, not wishing to impart any information to him.
That was all the launching pad he needed.
  'What a pity! You know of course about my novel *Teems of Times*, and then my song *Liverpool Lou*, and, of course, *The Patriot Game* and...'
He went on and on until I could bear it no longer.
  'Dominic', I said, 'I'm going to add to your fame. In fact I'm writing a book about you.'
  He turned his conceited delight towards Eric Bogle.

'Well, what do you know about that. Freddy's writing a book about me.'

'Oh, I haven't got very far with it, Dominic. In fact I've only got its title at the moment, and your old man gave it to me in Dublin. It's to be called THE MACHIAVELLIAN BASTARD!

On this occasion Anderson's ire actually resulted in an interesting short poem, *To An Erstwhile Friend*:

> Darken not my door again, you false unfriend,
> Squint not your malice at me, this is the end!
> A foil you thought to serve your needs,
> Proceed your wriggling way,
> But what you thought my night, to build,
> May prove the day!
> A Dublin man? God help us now,
> Did Emmett walk those streets?
> And who would trade his triumphs all
> For one of his defeats?
> Farewell, goodbye, I'm glad we met,
> For after all the revel,
> Having borne you so long
> I will not fear the Devil!

Friends were dear to Anderson and the other side of the coin can perhaps be seen in another short poem *These Are My Friends*:

> These are my friends—the dear ones of a day
> Of whom I sing with spirit in my voice;
> These are the ones who on my winding way
> Arise like the sun and make my heart rejoice…

The personal and the political become one in Anderson's aversion to Norman and Janey Buchan who, along with their involvement in the folk scene, were serving Labour politicians and were lampooned in various squibs that Anderson produced. Anderson's left wing views prompted splenetic dismissals of Tory politicians but his greatest contempt was reserved for Labour politicians who had betrayed the socialist cause. These included members of the government such as George Brown, Harold Wilson, Clare Short and (in the last few years of his life) Tony Blair, as well as Scottish figures: the Buchans, Jimmy Reid (who he had earlier praised), Donald Dewar, and—especially—Pat Lally, the Glasgow council leader, despised by the Scottish left, who was nicknamed Lazarus with reference to his many political comebacks. And not only politicians were subject to the sharp end of Anderson's pen if he could scent hypocrisy. Cliff Richard and the actor John Cairney are also the recipients of his ire. Of course, this type of verse is contained within a long satirical tradition; James Young of Stirling University (comparing Anderson to Woody Guthrie) states 'he had kept the tradition of the broadsheet alive, his own efforts mercilessly lampooning those that James Connolly called 'the Labour fakirs full of guile'.'

With regard to the political verse preserved in section three of this collection, it is in the nature of the type of poet that Anderson was that many of the poems here have no great longevity, written for the moment and circumstances of their time. Nevertheless, they are reproduced here as, at least, a record of social history. It is with this in mind that the body of work as a whole can give us an indication of many of the political and social concerns of the period of the second half of the twentieth century during which Anderson was active. Interestingly, the period from the end of the eighties into the nineties which produced the Workers City group led by James Kelman and Farquhar McLay among others, which met in the Scotia Bar, has recently attracted fresh interest and a Radical Glasgow archive has been set up in the Mitchell Library. One of Anderson's contributions to this period is the poem *Trees of Liberty* which deals with the protests led by Colin MacLeod (aka The Birdman of Pollock) to prevent a motorway being built over public parkland.

Anderson regarded his poetry as a form of political intervention and, in his preface to a pamphlet titled *Epitaphs and Squibs on Political Chancers Living or Dead or Both*, he writes:

> I hope my verse
> helps to disperse
> ignorance
> and lets folk see
> both the anger and love
> in me,
> by no means unique or alone,
> they may find my thoughts
> very often akin to their own.

For some time during the seventies and eighties, Anderson had been keen to publish a new selection of his poems. His original idea was to title it *Poems With a Punch*, with a cover featuring Mr Punch. The emphasis was to be on his political poems. However, a volume finally materialised in 1987, published by Fat Cat Publications and titled *At Glasgow Cross And Other Poems*. The title poem and some others take Glasgow as their subject but there is a representative mix of poems from different periods and on different topics.

It is fair to say that the poems are of varying quality. It is often thought that Anderson over-valued some of his political poems. Before the volume was published, Hamish Henderson wrote to him on this matter suggesting that he ditches one intended poem, *The Red Herring*:

> The latter—in my opinion—is too simplistic and 'overstated' even to make an effect as propaganda. I'm all in favour of hard-hitting polemic poetry, but it *has* to have a 'dialectical' element in it. Most of Europe political poems are too dualistic for my liking: they say 'we're right and they're wrong'. Nobody—no reader of poetry, at any rate—really believes this. The complexities of life are too great. Alright, I'm 100% against Thatcher and Reagan—and have tried to show it—but that doesn't mean that

I don't see blemishes… on the Russian side.'

In his otherwise effusive introduction to the collection, Henderson hints at this unease: 'Some may consider his world-view too perfervid to take in, and put into focus, all the deep paradoxical complexities of our present human situation on this beleagured planet.' In a review, Carl McDougall also notes ' …quality is not consistent, and there are times when form and content combine to cancel each other out, or when the less engaging subject fails to summon up writing of the same standard his other pieces have led us to expect.'

However, the socialist and working class traditions of Glasgow were dear to Anderson's heart and he characterises the history of the city as a voyage akin to the journey of the river Clyde in *A Ballad of Red Clyde*:

> Come all ye strange historians,
> and hiders of the truth,
> my story I will tell the world
> from days of tender youth;
> high in the mossy Lowther hills
> my rivulets begin
> their windings to the Lanark glades
> and doon by Corra Linn…

And similarly in *Let Glasgow Flourish*:

> Brave city on the Clyde, thorn of the tyrant,
> And famed the far world wide
> For gallant deeds wed to a homely hospitality!
> I'll trace your course with Clyde and Molendinar
> To its source, and from the infant stream
> Of ancient days, wind down the shadowy maze of history…
>
> …Slowly then from a sparse inland burn,
> To where the mighty waves in tumult churn,
> An arduous channel scooped by industry,
> 'Til Glasgow made her marriage to the sea.

Anderson is unswerving in his devotion to his adopted city, but some of his Glasgow poems have been accused of over-sentimentality; as one reviewer states: 'Anderson is at his best when aiming at the rich, the right, their dupes… But he is prone to the weakness of writers from the oral tradition—sentimentality and over-the-top idealism. Among other things I have had my fill of 'the warm-hearted folk… on the banks of the Clyde' idea.

If this is indeed true, there is one avenue in which the love of Glasgow working class history, the political idealist and the literary craftsman come together to great effect, and that is Anderson's work as a playwright. As noted, Anderson had scripted a play for the

Unity Theatre and in 1974 penned a children's pantomime, *Wee Willie Winkie*, for the Close Theatre, annexe of Glasgow Citizens). However, his major theatrical achievement came when *Krassivy*, his play about John Maclean, was performed at the Edinburgh Festival Fringe in 1979, the year of the centenary of Maclean's birth. It was widely and enthusiastically reviewed and and won a Fringe First prize. Subsequently it was successfully performed at various venues in and around Glasgow including Barlinnie Prison. It was performed by the Easterhouse Summer Festival Company with Anderson taking a small part as Lenin! Gary Stevenson (later Lewis) was Maclean. Lewis went on to achieve critical acclaim in movies such as *Shallow Grave, Orphans, Billy Elliot, Gangs of New York* and the television series *Outlander*.

The play is extremely well scripted, juxtaposing the main characters with a variety of Glasgow types of all classes and, cleverly, using Glasgow street characters, who were recorded as interesting eccentrics of their time, to add atmosphere and humour. Anderson had previously penned several short verses about some of them and Ewan McVicar notes his use of established lore:

Well known old street characters have been revived in Glasgow song. Auld Hawkie was a famous singer and seller of ballads. Freddie Anderson wrote about him:

O gather round and I'll tell you my tale
O' the times I was jovial an' hearty an' hale,
But this prick-the-louse tailor's attention was such
That I limp round the town on this tattered auld crutch.

Another modern songwriter whose name is mislaid wrote about the same man:

Gather round all you fine folk, in your silks and your laces.
Gather round here and listen to me.
I was the last man who spoke to the prisoner
Before he was hung on yon auld gallows tree.

Funny how both writers chose the same opening. Both of them have written songs about another character, Hirstlin Kate, who had lost the use of her legs altogether. The unknown writer begins, to a tune from Newfoundland:

Kate, you're bonny, Kate you're sweet.
It's a shame you canny use yer feet
As you go bauchlin up the street,
Hirstlin on yer way-oh.

While Freddie says:

See Hirstlin' Kate o' the town
On her brushes go sweepin' round,

Some heads may be high
Perin' into the sky,
But Katie's is fixed on the ground.

Anderson also suggested, in a letter to Hamish Henderson, that another Glasgow character, Blind Alick, a poet and fiddler, may have inspired William MacGonagall when he lived in Glasgow in the 1830s. The nineteenth century street characters were first recorded in Peter Mackenzie's *Reminiscences of Glasgow* (Mackenzie himself appears as a character in Anderson's play *The Weaver Lads*).

His favourite character, however, was Alexander Petrie, aka The Clincher, who produced a newssheet and pestered the city authorities with his opinions on various matters. Anderson scripted a radio documentary on him and a couple of short poems:

> A braw auld man,
> A dandy in his day,
> The only Glasgow man wi' proof
> His heid was not astray.
> Sauchiehall Street was his pitch—
> He often dandered there;
> At times he took a longer route
> Doon tae St Enoch's Square.
> He wrote an' sold his ain newssheet,
> 'The Clincher' it was called,
> An' mony's the time afore the Court
> The brave auld chap was hauled.
> Some know their Royals, some their luck
> An' some a load o' corn,
> But if the Clincher ye did miss
> Ye werenae Glesca born!

Anderson scripted other plays during the 80s and 90s when he was involved with community theatre groups variously called The Greater Easterhouse Theatre, The Provan Players Theatre Group and The Doon the Dunny Theatre Company. In May 1986, he writes to Hamish Henderson, 'I have just finished a quite unusual play… *Mungo Was a Merry Saint*, the title from a Sandy Rodger's song.' Other plays completed or drafted in this period are recorded as *The Provan Spirit*, *The Witch of Provan*, *The Lucky Midden* and *Wandering Aengus*, based on the poem by Yeats.

The most substantial subsequent production was *The Calton Weavers*, for the 200th anniversary of the Calton Weavers' Strike. As reported in the *Evening Times*: 'August 1987: 200th anniversary of the Calton Weavers: 'the Calton Weavers industry is in full swing. At lunch time there was a commemoration service to the early trade union martyrs at Calton burial ground. Tonight there's the unveiling of a mural to them at the People's Palace, and tomorrow night, Freddy Anderson's play about them is giving a one night airing at the Riverside club in Fox Street.'

The play had previously been performed at the Edinburgh Festival Fringe by Alien Theatre and was reviewed in the *Scotsman*: 'This up-and-coming community theatre group from Glasgow, directed by Billy Marshall, presents some excellent ensemble playing in a script by Freddy Anderson. The actors are the spiritual if not the actual descendants of those 'low-born idle conspirators' who suffered and died. And this lends the peace an added poignancy.'

Anderson's reputation had soared through the success of his plays, but possibly his finest literary accomplishment was to come in 1989 with the publication of his only novel *Oiney Hoy*. Oiney Hoy, of course, featured originally in *The Connolly Ballad* published in 1949, forty years earlier and is revived as the progenitor of amusing adventures satirising historical and contemporary Ireland. A comparison could be made with Dominic Behan's *The Public World of Parable Jones*, published in the same year, but the eponymous hero of that, the world-weary writer Parable Jones is the opposite of the eponymous green fool of Oiney Hoy, and the style more literary than folkish.

The novel, in fact, was partially based on a play of the same name performed in Glasgow and Edinburgh previously and reviewed by Mario Relich: "Jonny Crayton, as the broth of a boy, carried off his role with earthy aplomb, always in the thick of comic mayhem, yet always suggesting unshakable integrity, and a stubborn will to plough his own furrow in a venal, incredulous and intolerance society. Despite all the bare-knuckle criticism however a full, wide awake house at the Mandela Theatre delighted in the positive, even nostalgic, aspects of Ireland portrayed.'

On publication, the novel immediately received enthusiastic reviews. Brian McCabe wrote in the *Scotsman*: Iit shows none of the faults of the average first novel… He uses Oiney Hoy as a passive and receptive medium through which to show us Ireland in all its cruelty, bigotry and hypocrisy.' Benedict Brogan notes in the *Glasgow Herald*: 'It is funny. Funny because it plays with Irish myths and stereotypes, shakes them out, exposes their weaknesses but rejoices in their accuracies.'

Various comparisons were mooted. Ellen Mitchell in the *Irish Democrat* compares *Oiney* to *The Good Soldier Svelk*, Anderson's satire to Swift and to *Holy Willies Prayer*. Another reviewer notes it is reminiscent of 'the Flann O'Brien of *The Third Policeman* and *An Beal Bocht*. And not that far in the background I spied a shadow of James Joyce.'

It is summed up by Seán Damer as follows 'This is a truly delightful book whose lightness of tone camouflages wit, humour and a mordant satire of Ireland's Holy Cows. else, it is very funny; a short review simply cannot do justice to the many hilarious episodes… Freddy Anderson is a master of his craft, who has written a quite exceptional first novel. It will be greeted with delight by all those who appreciate the long Irish tradition of satirising the pompous and the pratitudinous. Freddy Anderson has another novel nearly finished. Power to his elbow, as the man said. Apart from anything but the ability to make us laugh out loud. I can hardly wait for more.'

Oiney Hoy, as suggested above, follows a long tradition of satirical works, echoing Voltaire, Cervantes, Sterne, Swift and others. The initial setting is clearly based on Anderson's home town of Ballybay: 'Creevan, in the very heart of Ireland. I was about to call it a God-forsaken wee place, but that would be a lie. Nature endowed Creevan, which is the Gaelic word for twig or little branch, with two lovely lakes surrounded by frail reeds and three small hills, one of which, with its mantle of bluebells and green ferns reflected in the still waters, is like a vision of fairyland.'

Creevan is the background for the novel's eccentric characters:

No! Creevan was not forsaken by God or Nature, but by the rich landowners of Ireland, so that for centuries the poor had to leave home and search for work in foreign lands. Oiney Hoy's grandmother, however, was able to remain in Creevan, where she sold apples and oranges and bananas. She had a fruit stall in the Market Square, and woe betide you if you passed without buying some of her goods. She would hurl sharp stinging invective after your retreating figure and even lambast your poor dead ancestors. It was a tongue like hers put the curse on Cromwell that his warts would bleed venom and a restored monarch dance on his grave. On the three braes of Creevan she was known to every man, woman and child as 'The Holy Terror'... The original Oweney Hoy, pronounced 'Oiney Hoy' in Creevan, was a poor, old amadhaun, or green fool, of the Carrick Hills to the south of the village. A tall, thin, bony man, like Don Quixote, and strange enough in his own way, he lived about a hundred years ago in a tumbledown, thatched shed on a bleak hillside. Of his many eccentric deeds, one is especially remembered for its quaintness in that remote countryside. Oiney spread the word around the Carrick Hills that, on a coming Sunday, he was going to die for Ireland. The event, he said, would take place in the Long Meadow below the chapel after second Mass [then follows Oiney's famous leap over the bog mentioned in *The Connolly Ballad*].

The green fool is an Irish tradition (Patrick Kavanagh, another Monaghan writer titled his autobiographical novel such) and is a thematic ploy in the novel in which Oiney's naïvety provides the lens through which comings and goings of contemporary Ireland are evaluated. At the end of Oiney's travels, however, Anderson sardonically returns him to his starting point in Creevan:

The train moved slowly into Creevan and he had a great view of the Bluebell Hill in full bloom above the lovely calm lough. A thrill of excitement ran through his veins, despite his sadness, to see his native fields and surrounds again. As the train drew to a halt, he looked out on the platform. My God, he thought, what am I seeing? He could not believe his eyes. Nor was it her ghost but her wee sturdy plump self, standing with the little brown jug in one hand while with a smile on her face she shook the other gnarled fist of welcome at Oiney. On either side of her stood those grinning pair of rogues, Jemmy McGurk and Jonjo, who had joined her conspiracy to send the fake telegram to lure him back to Creevan. Who in the world but herself would connive such a plan? And Creevan itself wasn't it splendid that day, none but a fool would leave it with its loughs and rivers and lush green fields and winding blackberry lanes in the hidden hills of Monaghan! Overhead on the tapering chapel spire above Jonjo's belfry the famous weathercock still had pride of place and Oiney smiled too remembering the tale and many others of his home in these little Ulster hills, tales that will endure in a world of peace, still to be won, aye, even a million years ere Ireland dreams of sinking in the wild Atlantic.

So Oiney returns actually and symbolically to Creevan, which perhaps contains both Heaven and Hell, but Anderson never returned to Ballybay, although his childhood there inspired his finest work. Were his feelings perhaps akin to those of Paddy Kavanagh: 'Back once again in wild, wet Monaghan/ Exiled from thought and feeling/ A mean brutality reigns'?

Anderson had been presented with an *Irish Post* Award in 1991 (shortly after it had been awarded to his friend, the piper Pat McNulty) and a society of British Authors Award in 1992. However, even in his seventies, he still had plans for further publications. One of his great literary heroes was Jonathan Swift and he often reminded friends that he wrote *Gulliver's Travels* in his sixties. Janette McGinn, the widow of Anderson's friend, the songwriter Matt McGinn, encouraged him in his endeavours, There was a prolonged but unsuccessful attempt to have *The Calton Weavers* produced on television, with the script sent to Scottish Television and to Tom McGrath at the Royal Lyceum, and a plan, supported by Nan Milton, the daughter of John Maclean, to publish *Krassivy* (it was eventually published by Clydeside Press four years after Anderson's death). But despite encouraging responses, neither was realised. Of course, for Anderson, as with many writers, financial reward was irregular and frugal (although it is recorded, for example, that around this time he received £16 for appearing on the Jimmy Mack Show on radio).

Another uncompleted project was an anthology of various pieces in different forms on Glasgow revealed in his own notes:

Book suggestion for Mitchell Library:
What about having the Calton Weavers as the final item in a Glasgow book which included the following:
1. Robert Burns and Glasgow
2. Patrick MacGill
3. The Glasgow Clincher
4. The Martyrs (the story of the 1820 rebellion in prose)
5. Essays: my Contemporaries
Roddy McMillan
Matt McGinn
Hamish Henderson
Harry Keir
The Old Scotia Inn
6. Glasgow poems
At Glasgow Cross
Bonnymuir
In the Ramshorn Cemetery
Waukrife
A Ballad of Old Scotia
Glasgow Folk
7. Wee Willie Winkie

How Wee Willie Wilkie enlists Hawkie, etc. to find the golden key in Glasgow Green that will enable the fish to swim, the bell to ring, the tree to grow and the bird to fly.
8. The Calton Weavers (play).

Among those not previously mentioned are Patrick MacGill, the Irish author of *Children of the Dead End* and *The Rat Pit* (Anderson is recorded as giving a lecture on him to the Irish in Scotland History Group in 1993) and Harry Keir, the artist, who Anderson remembered in a piece in *West Coast Magazine* shortly after his death in 1977.

In his last years, Anderson still occasionally frequented the Scotia Bar although the back room, where Ewan McVicar remembered him, had been incorporated into the rest of the bar: 'the first time I entered the Scotia Bar, it was a quiet early evening. I went in and sat in the Wee Back Room. Already looked across at me and said 'Hullo. You look like a man that could sing a song.' Freddie has friends all around the globe, and enemies very few.'

In July 2000, he gave his last interview to the *Evening Times* and responded to the question 'How would you like to be remembered?' with 'For my dedication to the cause of world peace and human happiness… for any of my writing that future generations think worth preserving… for being a bold yet somewhat anxious pilgrim of the twentieth century.' Anderson's own favourite among his poems was *The Sunbright Flower of Peace*:

> I see an international crowd
> Of colours, faces, garments, creeds,
> Place hatred in its burial shroud
> And end the reign of greed;
> I see them linked from land to land
> Across the seven seas,
> Whilst in their midst the petals glow
> The sunbright flower of peace,
> The shining flower, the lovely flower,
> The sunbright flower of man,
> With roots enriched by selfless deeds
> Since history began;
> That blossom grows in every land
> It decks the earth with grace,
> Entwining now the human heart
> To save the human race.

Anderson was a long-time activist for peace and disarmament—'I see sense in Bertrand Russell's fear of nuclear war arising by sheer accident, owing to the great number of missiles already in existence; and these numbers will greatly increase, as the industrialisation of the world continues. I do not believe that the nuclear bomb is a deterrent. I think the only real deterrent is disarmament'—and his uncompromising stance marks not only his poetry but his whole life. He would not hesitate to stand up for the rights of the working man and also, when required, for his friends; a key example being his support for Elspeth King when she was ousted from her post as curator of the People's Palace for purely political motives. Throughout this collection, each piece of poetry or prose can be read not only for its intrinsic merits but also as a commentary on period and place.

Up to his final days Anderson had plans for more works including an autobiography which he intended to title *From the Green Hills of Ulster*. In October 2001 he is noted as 'putting the finishing touches to *Oiney Hoy in Glasgow*… a follow up to *Oiney Hoy*. And also working on a play set in Monaghan, *Slievegullion Brae*.' Here we see again an interesting conjunction of the theme suggested at the beginning of this introduction: the conjunction between his childhood in Monaghan and his later days in Glasgow. Oiney Hoy's further adventures was never completed. However there are tantalising glimpses of parts of it preserved in the Freddy Anderson archive:

Two years after Oiney's return to Creevan from his grand tour of Ireland, the Holy Terror began to see her grandson in a different light. She now saw him as a sensible, intelligent and responsible member of that quaint little village Creevan In other words his poor granny had begun to dote.

There were the frightening times too that she imagined Oiney to be Finn MacCool or Brian Boru, Daniel o' Connell or Dr Valera. Oiney had no idea of the physical dimensions of Finn, Brian or Dan but he was certain that he had not the faintest resemblance to that skinny bean pole, Dev, who imagined that speaking Gaelic on the radio was ample proof of his patriotism. Oiney only knew about 9 or 12 words in the native language but he was quite certain that he was more Irish than Mr de Valera or the blue shirt, General O' Duffy, or any of the oddballs much stranger than himself who walked the Green Fields of Ireland in the days of his early youth.

Isobel Anderson died in the year 2000. Anderson's poem *The Dawning of the Day* was read at her funeral:

> I'll love my lass forever,
> The rainbow of my heart,
> As sure as sun and moon there be,
> I know we'll never part.
> The shadowed city wandering,
> I went my lonely way,
> Until I fell for Isobel,
> At the dawning of the day…
>
> 'Twas in the woods of Eaglesham,
> That May morning we met.
> Those lovely honest eyes of blue,
> They still are shining yet.
> O, desolate this world would be,
> This life turned dull and grey,
> Could I forget that lass I met.

> At the dawning of the day.

Freddy himself followed her on December 10th 2001. His funeral, at Daldowie Crematorium, was attended by a range of friends, political allies and writers such as Alasdair Gray and James Kelman. The party adjourned to Lynch's Bar in the Calton where many tributes were offered. Gerry MacGregor penned a valediction which sums up many aspects of Anderson's career:

> Auld Glasga hings her heid in grief
> And cooncillers smile in quiet relief
> The rapiered edge o' justice's quill
> In vacuumed silence is all astill...
>   'Richmond's spawn ah curse ye aw'
>
> Borne fae the dust o' Cuchulain's banes
> Bred in Monaghan's berried lanes
> Hibernian migrant of sweat and toil
> And settled sound on auld Scotia's soil...
>   'Great architect we thank ye'
>
> You told us o' the blackberry man
> And the inhuman waste of Aberfan
> An orphan's failed Bunessan flight
> And the Calton weavers' bonny fight...
>   'For which we're grateful'
>
> You gave us stories o' Glasgow Cross
> Like pullin' the tail aff Billy's horse
> Things that were done and things that were hid
> Like the Scotia being built fae a pyramid...
>   'And it wis says Brendan'
>
> And tales fresh brocht fae Germanie
> O' Grimes and Harvey's teutonic revelrie
> And Broderick's life himseelf did dangle
> By callin' ye a dirty, wee, obtuse triangle...
>   'Jist ask Mickey Donnelly'
>
> But onto a much more serious plain
> Whatever did he do of acclaim
> Is asked by a mob of no' many pairts
> The feted Glesga Cooncil o' Airts...
>   'Thank God ye's irnie chocolate'
> Well listen here and listen well

Afore ye join auld Nick in hell
Krassivy wisnae o' yer taste or size
But it fuckin' took Auld Reekie's prize…
 'So hell scud it intae ye'

But mair, much mair, than this aside
Ye spiered o' and kept alive the Clyde
And like oor hero great John McLean
Ye said what ye meant and meant what ye were sayin'…
 'All hail the Scottish Workers Republic'

I mind ye tell o' the Tontine dance
Ere the weavers were put to sword and lance
O' there's little changed in Glesga toon
As in the chambers Machevalian's gather roon…
 'O come all ye faithful'

You sang of Bobby, known as the Lark
Murdered by Britain in a prison dark
But his spirit will come again to rise
Exposing perfidious Albion's lies…
 'The fools, the fools, the fools'

Frae yer poisoned pen nae cuiff wis spared
Wee Peter Mac and his Arabian sword
Or e'en the infallible Lazerus Lally
Wi' his safe full o' videos and boattles o' swally…
 'Honestly they were only gifts'

Alang wi' auld Hawkie, Burns and McGinn
It's no' the museums o' Glasgow, but oor hearts yer in
It's the folk o' auld Scotia fir
Wi' the best o' auld Scotia ye lived and ye died…
 'Up the rebels'

Freddy Anderson belonged to and exemplified a long-standing, anti-establishment counter culture in Glasgow which is expressed in a piece he wrote for the *Evening Times*:

> The real Culture of Glasgow has existed not in the upper echelons but in the heart of Glasgow among the tenement dwellers. These created the bands to lead the unemployed during the Hunger Marches of the '30s. It lay in people like John Maclean and the Clydeside Workers' Committee who defied both the Glasgow and the London bosses in the fight against War and the exploitation of the poor. This is the real Culture; though suppressed and hidden by the authorities it survived underground

and was orally transmitted from parents to children from the early 19th century in the Glasgow tenements. It was not from the teachers in the schools or the Glasgow Herald journalists that folk learned to seek out the Calton Weavers' grave of 1787 in Abercrombie Street, or the Sighthill Monument of 1820. It was from their grannies and fathers and mothers, cousins and aunts... The real culture of Glasgow lay in the poets and writers like Sandy Rodger, James Macfarlan, William Miller, Joe Corrie; in artists like Harry Keir and Tom MacDonald etc., in agit-prop theatres like Unity Theatre Workshop and Wildcat. In recent days it has existed in the great rallies against the Poll Tax. It exists in the proud defiant songs of Matt McGinn and Hamish Henderson and dozens of others. It lies in the growing fight against injustice imposed by a Tory-elected English Government in London.

It is important to recognise that this tradition voyages on, even in the more hazardous waters of post-truth politics. Anderson's *Bonnymuir* inspired Michael Donnelly to set up the 1820 Society and there has recently been growing interest in that period of Scottish history. Regarding more recent radical events, the Mitchell Library has supported the Radical Glasgow History Project and set up an archive: Spirit of Revolt—Archives of Dissent. And the publication of this volume is part of that tradition also.

In the run-up to this publication, friends were asked to submit their own memories of Freddy Anderson. Here are some:

I first met Freddy Anderson in March 1989 at a fundraiser in Bairds Bar in the Gallowgate for the dependants of Irish republican prisoners. We found we had much in common and struck up an enduring and rewarding friendship over the next decade. We both had roots in County Monaghan and were active in the city's vibrant Irish community where Freddy was very much part of the cultural scene. He wrote short stories for Radio Eireann and *The Irish Press* and in recognition of his literary skills he was given an award by *The Irish Post*. I recall organising a memorial lecture in Govanhill in November 1993, at which Freddy spoke with expertise on the Donegal poet and writer Patrick MacGill, who is the historian's chief witness to Irish immigration to Scotland at the start of the twentieth century.

Freddy had the same socialist vision for Ireland as James Connolly, and supported the struggle for Irish unity and independence leading ultimately to a workers' republic. Freddy was a familiar figure at Irish solidarity meetings and fundraisers organised by groups like the Connolly Association. I remember introducing him to a leading figure in Sinn Féin Poblachtach from South Armagh, who was in Glasgow to address a public meeting in 1994. The speaker was entertained afterwards by Freddy's stories of working at a radar station for the Royal Air Force in Crossmaglen in 1942, where his skills as a smuggler were much in demand. I used to meet Freddy and a mutual friend and comrade Jim Friel (former Scottish President of the Graphical, Paper and Media Union) in the Scotia, Victoria and Clutha Bars, where we would convene the 'Provisional Government in Exile' and resolve how best to right Ireland's wrongs. Freddy was of course just as committed to the freedom of his adopted country as he was for the land of his birth. Like the songwriter, singer and novelist Dominic Behan, he broke with the Communist Party of Great Britain, over the national chauvinism it displayed towards the Scottish national question. We were both members of the John Maclean Society which was formed to commemorate the great man's life and work. I recall Freddy being a regular attender and contributor at meetings. He did more than most to promote Maclean through his writing and production of his tour-de-force play *Krassivy*. Freddy will always be an inspiration to me. He broke with untruth wherever he found it and could be neither purchased or intimidated by the establishment. He would surely be heartened by the unstoppable march of Scottish democracy and the renewed prospect of a united Ireland. As *The Irish Post* stated in its 16 March 1998 edition, 'Freddy Anderson is Monaghan's gift to Glasgow—an endowment to his adopted city.' (Stephen Coyle)

I was a cop on the beat in the east end of Glasgow. I would be about 27 years old by this point and had been trusted to tutor brand new polis from Tulliallan.

Exactly a year before I had got into the folk scene via the Glasgow International Folk Festival. (Top of the bill was The Ideal Band and 20 years later I was a part of the same band).

Anyhow, it's around one in the morning and I'm showing this brand new, fresh face polis around the exterior of The People Palace when I sees Freddy stumbling his way through Glasgow Green. I thinks, 'I can have a bit of fun.' I says to Freddy 'Excuse me, Sir' and he looks up at me with a look that I can only assume he reserved for Polis. 'Freddy' says I. He looks a bit more unsure now... 'Freddy, gie's *The Weavers*'. With perfect timimg he drew himself to his full hight and proclaimed 'I am a Calton Weaver and simple is my plea.'

I'm not sure how many verses he gave but I believe it was the lot. I told him I knew fine who he was, made sure he was OK and bid him goodnight. I said to the cop not to judge a book by the cover. He told me decades later that he never forgot it. (Gavin Paterson).

Anderson has also been an inspiration for scholars of a younger generation:

I have followed the red thread of Freddy's *Krassivy* for the past year, a play about the great socialist John Maclean. It was first performed by the Easterhouse Summer Festival Drama Company at the Edinburgh Fringe Festival in 1979, with Freddy in the role of Lenin and a young Gary Lewis as Maclean. The ESF Drama Company was described in that year's Fringe guide as 'the talented offspring of a community arts festival in one of the most deprived areas of Britain. Its shows are brash, committed and built to stand the test of playing to enthusiastic audiences normally deprived of theatre as well as most other social and cultural activities.' The show played to packed houses and rave reviews, with the *Glasgow Evening Times* declaring 'Easterhouse could quite easily take over the world the way they're going…'

As I dug into the story behind *Krassivy*, layers of the city slowly began to be unearthed, layers seemingly lost when the grime was scraped off the tenements and Glasgow presented its shiny new face to the world. Fragments of what Freddy had called 'the real culture of Glasgow' were still swirling around in the wind and began to come together to form something concrete out of the asbestos-laced dust. In chance encounters on the backs of buses, in libraries, pubs and theatres, at parties and funerals and on the street, mention of Freddy's name provoked memories, stories, long-forgotten feuds, letters, books, pamphlets and suggestions from drinkers, writers, archivists, activists, actors, trade unionists, booksellers, janitors and poets (some famous, others not) as well as from work colleagues, friends (some former, others not) and family members. Random asides and conversations kept leading to new connections, to Freddy, *Krassivy*, Easterhouse, Unity Theatre, Maclean, Red Clydeside and beyond and often back to myself personally. New questions kept emerging too as I read and learnt and listened. Certain parallels in the process of forgetting and fighting for history also began to emerge. John Maclean was, after James Connolly, the greatest revolutionary yet produced by Scotland. After years of poverty, persecution and prison, he died in 1924. Fifteen thousand people attended his funeral, the procession led by the Clyde Workers' Band. In 1947, the annual marches in MacLean's memory ceased and his name, never mind his political thought and practice, was almost forgotten…

The Easterhouse Summer Festival Drama Company production of Freddy's play was not just a piece of theatre but an intervention in the struggle to reclaim, rediscover and re-popularise a knowledge of working class history without which the fight to change social conditions was impossible. As John McGrath wrote in connection with 7:84's own play about MacLean (*The Game's a Bogey*, 1979), the point was to relate Maclean's words to their historical context, but pointing them, by way of their defeat at that time, through to the consequences of their non-fulfilment today.' The thread which connects Maclean to the Unity theatre through to 7:84, the Easterhouse Summer Festivals, the Workers' City group and others needs to be picked up… but how and by whom?

…The other point for me is that the ideals which motivated Freddy and generations of artists and writers in Glasgow was inseparable from the lives they led and the work they produced, where it came from and what it aimed at. This seems a major difference to the cultural environment in Glasgow today. Freddy and others were for sure not misty eyed about socialism and could laugh at themselves and their comrades; as Dominic Behan wrote: 'About forty years ago in Ruchill, me and Freddie Anderson and Matt McGinn were waiting for the revolution. It was a favourite pastime of the 'dissident' mind… Within the tenement closes, most decent working men, weighed down, one could perceive, with the dignity of Labour, came to their doors, eyed us and our fraternal message, and promptly told us to 'fuck off'.

Yet they believed fundamentally in the power of ordinary people to organise and change the social conditions which crushed their potential, and the role of culture, in the broadest sense, was crucial to this. In the 1982 documentary *Easterhouse: People and Power,* one Easterhouse resident eloquently states the ideas which have motivated my own search:

> I didnae know what the word socialism meant, y 'know, till I wis late teenager. But I want to know and I want to learn, I want to know about these people that are controlling my life and I want to take that control off them and I want to have it. And I want my children to have it. But the one thing that I can teach them that I think parents didnae teach me was the history of my area and why I'm here. And about I am a member of the working class and my children are working class and they've gottae learn, through learning about their area, the structure of their area, the history of their area, why it was built and learning more about, y know, where the buck actually stops. When you learn about where the buck actually stops you can start changing it. And I've gottae bring my children up to want to change the people that are in control of their lives.

I have discovered my own connections to this story. The Unity Theatre's premises on South Portland Street in the Gorbals were round the corner from my grandparents' house. My gran used to go regularly to see plays by Maurice Blythman there, and knew Ida Schuster, the 90 year old member of Unity and the Jewish Players who spoke, and sang, at a Scottish Theatre Archive event which I attended last year. I have discovered a great great uncle from Russia who worked as a miner in the Lanarkshire coalfields where MacLean organised and was interred in 1916 in a POW camp as a 'pro-German sympathiser with revolutionary tendencies' according to a 1930 police report. A thousand such threads connect people in Glasgow to their history and one another, threads broken and frayed but still extant and capable of being knitted back together. (Joey Simon)

And a contribution from the editor, from the book *Real Glasgow:*

Walking down through Garthamlock there is only one person that comes to mind round this neck of the woods. Freddy Anderson, once resident bard of the Scotia Bar and Glasgow's premier folk poet, lived here, and I frequently came to visit him and his family. Freddy was often short of a bawbee or two and would hawk broadsheets of his poems in the local pubs with a famous line of patter: for example, 'the only thing that exceeds your generosity is your good looks!'. In 2001 I was living in England and hadn't seen Freddy for some time but had heard that his wife, Isobel, had died. Then I met him in the Clutha Bar. I didn't at first recognise him. He looked very frail and was staring into a bowl of soup which had been delivered with only a knife and fork. But after a moment he greeted me with a smile. 'Ah, Ian, it's yourself. Can you get me a spoon?' The funeral service itself, at Daldowie Crematorium was quite an occasion. Writers—Alasdair Gray, Jim Kelman—and folksingers were there

(Arthur Johnstone concluded the service with a rousing singing of *The John MacLean March*) and a great many old lefties. If the ghost of Lenin had turned up himself it would have surprised no one. Afterwards, upstairs at Lynch's, one of his haunts in the Calton, a traditional funeral meal of steak pie and tatties was served (no pastries or curled-up sandwiches—at a Glasgow funeral; you get properly fed). The family bought a round of drinks then, one by one, the landlords of all the pubs that Freddy drank in and had sometimes been barred from—as Brendan McLaughlan, of the Scotia, pointed out: 'if you hadn't fallen out with Freddy, you didn't really know him.' Several people gave informal tributes and Freddy's son Paul sang Joe Hill's gospel parody 'Pie in the sky when you die'.

As Brendan had noted, Freddy had a fierce tongue, especially when in his cups. Many moons ago, local residents, including Freddy, had worked hard to ensure the construction of a social club in Garthamlock. Within no time at all it was reckoned that it had been taken over by the local hard men. One night, Freddy, with little concern for his own safety, stood up and harangued them one by one. (Ian Spring).

It was the editor's, perhaps naïve, intention to contain within this volume all, or nearly all, of the existing work of Freddy Anderson. This soon proved impossible for various reasons. Firstly, material that is recorded as existing seems to have been lost (this is compounded by the fact that some pieces may have been recorded that were in a planning stage rather than extant). Secondly, some material in the Archive—mostly plays and short stories—exist in fragmentary form: some are incomplete and some in different versions. More research and editing work would enable these to be put together, but that would be a daunting task on top of the considerable work already undertaken. For example, the plays *The Witch of Provan* and *Saint Mungo* are not contained here as, although there are substantial sections contained within the archive material, no complete playscript is available. An interested scholar could reconstruct them. Another major omission is the various essays, mainly on Scottish history and Robert Burns, some of which were partially published. All these remain in the archive at Glasgow Caledonian University awaiting other scholars to continue the exploration of Anderson's work.

The source materials for this collection come from three main sources: the editor's own collection, the collection of the late Willie Gallacher, and the collection in the Freddy Anderson Archive at Glasgow Caledonian University. A few additional materials have been provided by friends of Freddy Anderson (all of the material gathered by the editor of this volume is now deposited in the archive). Whereas this consists of a large accumulated mass of materials, the disparity between the three main sources only serves to suggest that additional material may still be available or indeed that some of the word ephemeral work may have been lost.

Nearly all the poems discovered by this process are contained here with the exception of a few that were largely personal. Dramatic works are represented by the two major plays written by Anderson. These are reproduced from, firstly, the published version of *Krassivy* printed by the Clydeside Press in 2005 and an electronic archived copy of *The Calton Weavers* produced by Janette McGinn. There are three short stories and the entire text of the novel *Oiney Hoy* originally published by Polygon in 1989.

Regarding the poems, it would have been interesting to publish them in this collection in chronological order. However, so many are undated that it was decided that this was not practical. They have been divided into three inexact categories. *Poems and Ballads* is the most generic of these. *Glasgow Poems* deal directly with the city or the city's history. *Political Verse* uses the term political to refer narrowly to actual UK party political events and personalities largely in the 80s and 90s.

Due to the rather haphazard gathering of the material in various different forms from handwritten notes to complete published work, and also to the lack of consistent punctuation and capitalisation (and sometimes spelling), in the poems especially, the editor has used his own discretion in editing the final versions.

It is intended that this representative selection will encourage more interest in the work of Freddy Anderson which stands not only in its own right as a body of Scottish/ Irish literature but also as a testament to the vitality of the folk and political traditions of Glasgow at the end of the last century. As editor, I am pleased to leave this collection not as a final account of the work of my friend Freddy Anderson, but as a stimulus for further scholarship.

Ian Spring 2020

SOURCES:

Freddy Anderson Archive, Glasgow Caledonian University
Hamish Henderson Archive, University of Edinburgh
Freddy Anderson, *At Glasgow Cross and Other Poems*, Fat Cat Publications: Glasgow (1987).
Freddy Anderson, *Poems of a Glasgow Worker*, Caledonian Press:: Glasgow (1952).
Freddy Anderson, *Poems of an Irish Rebel*, privately printed (ND).
Freddy Anderson, *Epitaphs and Squibs on Political Chancers Living or Dean or Both*, privately printed (ND).
Freddy Anderson, *Oiney Hoy*, Polygon: Edinburgh (1989).
Freddy Anderson, *Krassivy*: a play about the great socialist, John Maclean, Glasgow Caledonian University: Glasgow (2005).
Contributions to *Cencrastus* and *West Coast Magazine*.
Hamish Henderson, *The Armstrong Nose*, Polygon: Edinburgh (1996).
Ewan McVicar, *One Singer One Song*, Glasgow City Libraries: Glasgow (1990).
Reverend R Ferguson (ed.) *The Writing on the Wall*, privately printed (1977).
Ian Spring, *Real Glasgow*, Seren Books: Bridgend (2017).
NB 'Freddy' is used, as opposed to 'Freddie' throughout this volume. However, the editor was surprised to discover that Anderson used both spellings himself as evidenced by signed works!. Indeed, both spellings are employed in Hamish Henderson's introduction to *At Glasgow Cross and Other Poems*.

NB The more common 'Freddy' is used throughout as opposed to 'Freddie' although the editor was surprised to find that Anderson had used both spellings on signed works!

POEMS
AND BALLADS

A BRITISH SOLDIER FORESEES HIS DEATH IN SOUTH ARMAGH

By an ex-RAF chap who served there to his shame in the light (darkness, rather) of Brit and RUC thuggery since 1996

'Twas not the love of dearest England,
White cliffs of Dover or Big Ben,
That's sent me crawling in these dark,
Spine-chilling lanes of Crossmaglen.

I know it in my inmost soul,
That this is Irish, not English soil,
And I've been sent by politicians,
To serve here as the Orangemen's foil.

This base, low cause has brought me hither,
Among these ancient fields of Erin,
And this night I feel as false,
As the camouflage I'm wearing.

I see deep anger in the eyes,
Of all who wish their Ireland free,
And even little boys and girls,
Detest the very sight of me.

For I'm the terrorist to them,
A British bandit on the prowl—
I know that's true, but my pay is due,
And I just vent a brutal scowl—

I joined the army out of boredom,
They promised me I'd get around,
Sunny skies and sweet warm breezes—
But never six feet underground.

They'll lay me in a coffin drab,
And drape it was the usual flag,
Loyalists love their Union Jack,
But to millions it's a pirate's rag.

This epitaph place o'er my grave,
'Stop traveller, stop and pause!
Here lie the bones of another fool,
Who died to serve the Orange cause.'

Oh God, make dark this night with clouds,
Weave o'er these fields a foggy quilt!
But Lord, your densest smog can't hide,
My sense of bloody shame and guilt.

A PARODY

I'll never see though far I roam
a tree as lovely as a poem,
a poem where beauty can outpour
her bounty in rich metaphor,
a poem whose soaring imagery
looks down upon the tallest tree
and whose grandeur is not lost
in forest fire and winter frost,
but where the soul's in woven rhyme
beats harmony with boundless time
and stanzas of enduring verse
embrace the magic universe.

Mankind's spirit makes poetry
sure, any fool can plant a tree!

A POEM FOR ALL PEOPLES

In ten million years to come, this small green world may join the boiling sun,
And all the twinkling stars in high, vanish from the neighbouring sky!
Ten thousand years, the frost may creep, embrace Mankind in our last sleep,
And nowhere in the void be heard, the voice of man or warbling bird.
Thus Nature may the final curtain draw, transform our joys to scenes of grief and awe,
Whilst we, poor humans, have but a passing glance,
And ebb with the cruel tide of lost significance.

And yet we rose
From shaping crude rough stone
To polished marble in perfection;
From drawings on the wall of some dark cave
To rich engravings and great portraiture,
And with astonishing creation,
Endowed the countless generations,
Made ships of steel to sail the seven seas.
Harnessed mountain streams for electricity,
Walked on the moon and probed the Milky Way,
Brought worlds unknown into the light of day;
Music, Art and Medicine revealed their first vast store of Mankind's brilliant deeds
With slightest thought of self or long-consuming greed.

Out of the caves we came,
Out of the forests and the mountain slopes,
And down upon a world we might well tame,
And founded there together our tribes
In earnest wish to find a better day,
Never dreaming much about tomorrow,
Though often grieving for our women's sorrow and our own,
And even in our poor stupidity made gods;
Even then caught up in a captive fraud,
We sailed upon a sea of senseless shame.
When priests and chiefs were made,

We had no notion of democracy,
We never dreamed from this that Pharoahs would arise,
That Buddhas would be raised on our own backs,
That all the Earth's religions would soon be used
To progress fossilise.
We never dreamed the deep-down cunning wise

Would throw the evil sands back in our eyes for innocent mistakes;
We dearly pay for our slow consciousness.

Yet now we know, yes now we know
When Capitalism presents its ultimatum,
When all the evil there ever was
Conspires at the cross-roads,
With bombs and rockets holds the world in terror,
Combining now the shameful errors of our history—
How we enslaved our fellow negro,
Committed the sacrilege of war in the name of God
And with a thousand frauds
Nigh sealed the ruin of our inner self.
We now have reached the point of total destruction
Or the liberation of the beauty in us.

ABERFAN

The clouds of grief roll down the vale
To the town of Aberfan,
And silent are the narrow streets
Where bright-eyed children ran
In play and mirth the live-long day
Of many a summer span,
Heard songs and tales of ancient Wales
In the vale of Aberfan.

O brave, courageous mining-folk,
What cruel sacrifice!
In lowly homes amid the hills,
You pay a bitter price—
Disaster's roll at Pontypridd,
Newport and Brynamann,
But we little dreamed how the tears would stream
In the vale of Aberfan.

'Twas in the year of sixty-six,
The children were at school,
When suddenly the mountain slag
Became a raging pool;
It blotted out the sun and sky,
The school-house over-ran
And our children fair lay buried there
In the vale of Aberfan.

The ghost of Tonypandy looms
High over Rhonnda Vale,
And from the midnight of the mine
Ascends an anguished wail;
By Aberdare and Mountain Ash,
It echoes o'er the land,
the coal's black silt made the flowers wilt
In the vale of Aberfan.

Curse the cruel hand of greed
No gold can satisfy,
Nor innocence not laughter spare,
It heeds not children's cries;
By callous profit's plan,
And mothers weep as their young ones sleep
In the vale of Aberfan.

ATOM BOMB BLUES

Oh, I'm fed up living in a shelter,
Oh, I'm fed up being a bleeding gnome:
Instead of joining CND protesters,
I ended up in my wee place at home.

I lent my ears to bare-faced Tory liars,
Who from war profits daily grow more fat,
I didn't realise their propaganda
Was merely numskulls talking through their hats.

Now Ethel's dead through H-leukæmia fever,
Poor grandpa got no further than the hall,
When a rocket bound for Moscow quickly rebounded
And left dear grandpa's shadow on the wall.

Now all the earth around is radioactive,
Bacteria and clouds of gases fell,
Uncle Bert sought refuge 'neath the table,
Now the table's gone—and uncle Bert as well.

I shaved myself in nuclear fission water,
And suddenly small problems quick arose,
My teeth fell out and strangely then my right ear
Decided to change places with my nose.

Better dead than red, smart asses told us,
To heed them was the silly thing to do,
For now I'm not just red with radiation,
I'm orange and green and purple, black and blue.

The tourists swore we were defending freedom,
I look around remembering those words,
And yes, we're free indeed of children's laughter
And the sky above is free of singing birds.

I used to hear some idiot politicians,
Declare that nuclear bombs were a deterrent,
I doubt if even now the lying scoundrels
Would tell the truth admitting that they weren't.

But I'll reveal the reason why our brass hats,

Have no cause to suffer common fears and dreads,
They are so thick a megaton great H-bomb
Would bounce back off their solid plated heads.

BONNYMUIR

A Tribute to the Brave Men of 1820

I am a Calton weaver and simple is my plea,
Not to be tied forever to four posts of poverty;
The grim dark days o' Castlereagh have settled with their blight,
Though the sun shines down on Glasgow town, it seems eternal night.

We tried to make a union then, our scanty rights defend;
The cotton and tobacco lairds its ruin did intend:
They hired an informer—Richmond was his name,
And bribed with gold our cause he sold to misery and shame.

'Twas early in the April and the Springtime o' the year,
As I went down the Ladywell, a great crowd did appear;
They read a notice on the wall: 'Tae Arms! Tae Arms!'
It cried, 'Twas there that Andra Hardy stood and Tyranny defied.

As we went up by Carronside, ah, what a sad, brave sight,
A little band o' marching men to match a nation's might:
With only pikes and staves half-armed, a weavers' poor platoon,
But hearts so brave to stand the waves of sabre and dragoon.

Oh, there's dancing in the Tontine now, the bells toll our defeat,
And the rich who cowered with their gear now strut the open street,
And saintly ministers thank God how he preserved the state,
Gave it relief though bowed with greed the poor o' Gallowgate.

As we came in by Stirling, you'd hear the clanking chain,
The poor gaunt Calton weaver lads at Bonnymuir were taken;
They hanged two in the castle, Baird and Hardy were their names:
Though turned to mould is Richmond's gold, untarnished lives their fame!

The remainder were in irons clamped and banished o'er the waves,
'Neath the Southern Star in a land afar, you'll find their patriot graves,
And Jamie Wilson o' Strathaven Vale, a man advanced in years,
Nigh Glasgow Cross his life he lost among the people's tears.

Farewell bold Calton weaver lads! On Castlereagh my curse!
His end in bloody suicide had murder as its source;
Farewell brave lads o' Glasgow who died your lands to save!
Auld Scotia's rose in blossom grows aboon the weavers' grave.

CHILDREN OF THE NIGHT I

Life can be such a lonely road
In this the starry great wide universe,
With goodwill so abundant
Yet it's fulfilment scarce.
The road is long and winding
And no end in sight is there,
And a list of night can pall and plight
This road to God knows where.
They have no home to call their own
In a cardboard city site,
Not even a Christmas stable shields
The children of the night.

From family strife in which they played
No part in its creation,
They wander now upon a road
That has no destination.
A desolate road beneath the stars,
That once were gleaming bright.
Oh, where are the saints to pity for
The children of the night?

Ah, may you never have to walk
That endless thoroughfare;
Heartache and grief without relief
On the road to God knows where.
They have no home to call their own
In a cardboard city site,
Not even a Christmas stable shields
The children of the night.

CHILDREN OF THE NIGHT II

They wander lonely deserted streets,
These children of the night,
Or huddle in a fitful sleep,
To wait the morning light.

They are no tramps or hobos brave,
Who bitter wins endure,
These are the lonely souls of grief,
the children of the poor.

From broken homes or parents harsh,
Uncaring for their plight,
Forsaken now by God and man,
These children of the night.

The pious clergy chant their woes,
The papers seek the blame,
The rich folk stuff their faces fat,
Which should be red with shame.

No conscience moves those hearts of brass,
No helpful hand of pity,
Nor clamour from above to house
The homeless of the city.

With weary legs and aching heart,
A doleful wretched sight;
Not even a Christmas stable rests
The children of the night.

(To be put to music)

There's nothing wicked in my heart,
Nothing terribly wrong;
I was just born in a family,
To which I couldn't belong.
And so I wandered lonely streets
And great bleak office blocks,
Then join my group in the queue for soup,
And sleep in a cardboard box.
And sleep in a cardboard box.

How would you be if you lived like me,
To wander 'neath the stars,
And see rich folk laugh and joke
In posh hotels and bars.
A social leper, call me that,
Or any damn name you choose,
You've stripped me down,
To a bare park bench,
And what have I left to lose?
What have I left to lose?

I'm coming on my eighteenth year,
With neither home nor hope;
Do you wonder at me on your big TV,
Taking my kind of dope?
Shutter your doors in housing schemes!
Give me no place to live!
Pray God you're saved on Judgement Day,
But my Christ, I won't forgive!

ELEGY ON 'A GREAT MAN'

Behold the sycophantic crew
all their dead-leaf laurels strew
around his funeral bier!
Deceit despite expressions wry:
in their calculating eye
no genuine tear.

He was not great,
but one vast compound
of hate and vanity,
a ponderous tongue
which made inanity seem profound
to servile minds.

They saw in him
a bulwark for their kind,
not just survival, but power's sway
that damned the nation
to a long, long day
of grief and corruption

He was their God,
replacing truth by fraud
and vile dexterity:
he may be gone,
but all the maggots bred in him
live on.

ELEGY ON CHURCHILL

Amplify the voice of a dwarf!
Set him on a mountain peak!
The ignorant folk of the valley
Will have the god they seek.
When the powers-that-be conspire
To raise a vast image of stone,
'Tis the role of a canting priest
To invest it with flesh and bone.

The people return to the ploughshare
To toil in the wind and the rain;
In that moment of servile homage,
The powers and priests all gain,
And they smile at your humble folly,
Their greed and their fame increased;
Thus clothed in the robes of deception,
They sit to the sumptuous feast.

And so, with Churchill's death,
The ancient frauds all gathered round
And hope by whooped-up acclamation
To lay you prostrate on the ground.
Dukes and generals, kings and lords
A puppet host with dangling swords.
Money, mighty magnates too
And all that low lickspittle crew.

Disguised as 'Labour' to deceive,
Join with their Tory friends to grieve
This propped-up fraud,
And Churchill hoist to heaven high
Just next to God.
The trumpets of a crooked state
Blare out the myth that he was great;
Hack journalists and white-robed liars
Try to raise him even higher.
And scoundrels now of all degrees
Are everywhere upon their knees;
To praise this man who merely meant
The evil which they represent,
Who to himself to credit for
The millions slaughtered in the War,

And full of phrases, pomp and pride,
Betrayed the cause for which men died.

Oh, grim John Bull,
In-year declining, dithering days,
Is this the idol which you raise,
Shakespeare compare?
Dollards! fools! Gaze not up!
If he's in heaven, no saint is there.

FREE SCOTLAND IN THE DAWN

We love the lore of Scotland,
Our ballads and our song,
An' that braw tale o' Wallace
Wha righted a' our wrongs.
Bruce and Bannockburn's great hour,
We fondly think upon,
But what is foremost in our minds,
The sight for which we long,
Frae Wick tae Berwick, Fife tae Carrick,
Free Scotland in the dawn.
  Chorus (rousing pipes and drums)

Free Scotland in the dawn,
Free Scotland in the dawn,
For now we feel
It can be real.
Free Scotland in the dawn.

We love the bonnie Highlands
And the glens sae rich in song.
We love the hundred islands
That to our folk belong.
The Hebrides and Orkneys fair,
We proudly gaze upon,
But what is foremost in our minds,
The sight for which we long,
Frae Wick tae Berwick, Fife tae Carrick,
Free Scotland in the dawn.
  Chorus (kettle drums and pipes)

Then peace will weave a rainbow
Above the happy throngs,
And Clydeside build her ships again
And right a thousand wrongs.
The mist of tyranny dispersed,
The passing years wind on,
And what wis foremaist in our minds
We can now gaze upon,
Frae Wick tae Berwick, Fife tae Carrick,
Free Scotland in the dawn.
  Chorus

GLEN MASSON

On the green slopes of Glen Masson
lies the lonely little boy;
the Winter snow now falls on him
away from human joy,
and far below him in the glen
a phantom window gleams;
he ne'er shall see his home again,
Bunessan of his dreams.

Cold and cruel are these hills,
there moves no living thing,
you'd never dream this bleak white waste
could feel the breath of Spring;
and in the grip of Masson's arms,
the little boy lies still,
and every blade of Summer green
turns white upon the hill.

Then slowly weary Winter glides
unwilling to the Spring
and all the valley now awakes
in nature's blossoming:
the flowers peep and sparkling streams
cascade the pebble stones,
as Masson sings a song of life
around his whitened bones.

HITLER MEETS FRANCO IN HELL

'Sieg Heil! And so you've come at last!
You've found the way!
But then I always knew you would some day'.
A bit of news;
I've ousted Satan from his official post
And you and I and Mussolini's ghost
Can run the show down here—
It's just a piece of cake—
Like burning Reds and Jews for old time's sake,
Gouging and garrotting without a word of fuss,
Which makes this hell a heaven for the likes of us.'

The old bastard, Franco he took so long to die.
Some say the Man above prolonged his agony,
And stayed his end that in his final pain,
Brave souls might praise the murdered sons of Spain.

Said Franco, 'Adolf, dear, Führer and friend!
Your hari-kari drove me round the bend!
What a delight to see you in your own,
Unseat the very devil from his throne,
And welcome me, one of that vile spawn
Of European fascists, and last great holder-on!
For my chances, when you left, I would not give a damn,
But reprieve was soon forthcoming from dear old Uncle Sam.
I gave him atom-bases, and he covered up my crimes
(He had sins himself to answer for, aye, even worse at times).
With friends like Ronald Reagan, McCarthy and Goldwater,
Sure we didn't need you, Adolf, to lead us to the slaughter.
So let's keep the fires burning, there's hope in hell as yet,
When England's Queen has forwarded her message of regret.

Epitaph:
Not even a crocodile cried
When this beast died

HOLY CLIFF'S PRAYER

O Lord, who in the heavens doth dwell,
I soon will join you there mysel',
Your right hand sit, even move you o'er a bit,
To share Thy glory,
I'm sure you're dying just to hear
Sir Clifford's story.

I was born again with Billy Graham
And joined the 'hallelujah' game,
Exploiting Thy most gracious name,
All 'Holy Willies',
One speciality was mixing hymns
And hilly-billies.

But Lord, you know when life began
You made the Snake as well as Man,
And with the former I did plan
To creep and crawl,
And show a slithering worm could rise
Above them all.

With childish pop I millions made
And daft wee souls my records played.
I flourished in the jukebox trade
And Christmas holly,
Small tribute to Yourself I pay
For so much lolly.

The video racket and BBC
Made fortunes too in plugging me,
Stick by me, Lord and I'll make thee
An almost equal.
With rock 'n' roll in heaven one day,
A perfect sequel.

How dare the Crown just dub me knight,
I should be king or queen by right,
Correct, O Lord, this oversight
And sad complaint,
And stop the envious calling me
A plaster saint.

For, Lord, a favour I have done
To boost You higher, O Mighty One,
My proudest gift to you, bar none,
Is Your own prayer,
Child's play to me—the words and tune
Were already there.

I stole the tune from a great Scot—
What other way has John Bull got,
His oil and whisky, the bloody lot,
By thieving take,
For didn't You create the World
For England's sake!

I feel not the last trumpet call,
For sometimes I doubt You're there at all,
Or else You'd smash in pieces small
The likes of me,
A smarmy conman oozing with
Hypocrisy.

IN COMEDIE LANE, GARTHAMLOCK—TO NANCY

(A decade before the housing scheme)

I came unto this land today
With lonesome heart for my lost love,
And underneath these sun-capped trees,
I softly sing of memories—
Music these fields once held,
Though unaware I walked,
Filling my heart with still vague dreams.

By my unheeding side she walked,
A queen in her own soft domain,
Drinking the beauty with her eyes.
The grass of the earth
And the swift skies gave,
And all the wonders that she saw
She added to with child-like awe,
That in its innocence was born
A kinship with the morning dew.
Her heart was glad that it should be
This realm was here
For other eyes to see.

And as I walked,
My castles turning stone,
My young love passed
Into the greenness of the grass
And I was left alone.
Solitary I search the lane,
And seek in furrows in the field,
And beg the tender earth to yield,
The secret of her hiding-place.

JOHN BULL'S LAMENT

Oh, the world is sadly changing
From the days of my renown—
It seems to be the ruddy globe
Has just turned upside down.
Where has the jolly Empire gone?
I'm hardly worth a farthing,
And I'll be lucky if I'm left—
With an English country garden.

Where are my jewels of the East?
Hong Kong and Singapore
Are all that's left to mind me of
The golden days of yore,
When sahib basked in the noonday sun,
Ah, such was my glory then,
That the orb of heaven never set
On mad dogs and Englishmen.

Where are my Fuckamee tribes,
My Zulu and Ugandan?
Treacherous brutes—to think that they
Poor John Bull would abandon!
I never dreamed my geography
In so few years would alter,
And leave me clinging like a Barbary ape
To the Rock of Gibraltar!

I once called Uncle Sam my friend
When I pawned this land at Fulton,
And I but reap what I did so—
What else could it result in?
A little Yankee atom base—
Cor blimey, what a target—
And a bankrupt partner in what's called
Oh, Christ, the Common Market!

But there'll always be an England,
And the rest may go to rot,
While they leave me with the oil wells
Belonging to the Scot!
There'll always be an England,
And I tell you, come what may,

If we only stand united,
We'll beat Iceland any day!

JOHN CAIRNEY'S PRAYER

('The Man Who Played On Robert Burns')

Oh, Lord, wha dwells ahint the moon,
And doles oot riches, wreck or ruin,
I beg tak pity on me soon,
I'm sic a creep,
A blasted scunner mair oily than
Uriah Heep!

An', Lord, I've conjured up a book,
A load o' drivel'd mak you puke,
Not worth a damn—
Mere clishmaclaver that portrays
A bloody sham.

Ah, Lord, ye ken that day langsyne,
When quoting Rabbie line for line,
Ma bardic face did fairly shine,
A gowkin' wonder;
Both god's an' stalls an' hauf-wits all
They clapped like thunder.

I ranted, raved an' played the 'poet',
(Being masel an' did I know it!)
Ma handsome mug was there tae show it,
Baith front an' side.
Could Lucifer in a' his glory
Near match ma pride?

But, Lord, yes Lord, there's aye some snag,
That lets the damned cat frae the bag,
And proves ma muse a weary hag—
Ah, Rab, forgive,
An' I'll ne'er mimic you again
As lang's I live.

The Parkheid voice ane micht abide,
But why did ma puir brain decide
Tae mash that up wi' Kelvinside,
Hae folk in tears;
The only sane ones in the hall
Had plugged their ears.

But, Lord, keep this frae public view,
I'll swear I'll dae as much for you,
I'll mak your name immortal too
An' play God fine
An' add to your old Bible text
Great words o' mine.

As God they'll see me far an' wide,
I'll tak the heavens in ma stride,
Nae saint'll match ma awful pride
An' swollen heid.
Oh, Lord, for a' ma damned conceit,
Don't strike me deid!

I ken that maist Rab's days were spent
Withoot a bawbee or a cent,
But dae ye think I'd be content
Wi' sic a deal.
Oh, Lord, I'm just an actor loon
An' far frae real.

When I meet Rab on the Last Day,
Frae his contempt I'll crawl away,
An' for a change I'll let God say
The final word,
'John Cairney thocht he looked like Burns—
The man's absurd!'

MIDNIGHT OF THE CENTURY

Nineteen-ninety-three,
Another year in the life of me,
I got a two pound rise in April,
52 giros in front to go,
And pubs galore,
Mainly the Scotia Bar.
The power of love.

The year 2000,
Revolution around the corner.
I get a two pound cut in April,
In the middle of the year,
The benefits to go I hear.
What's another homeless man,
Inside the universal time span.

Take me back to the sixties,
When I could afford the dope.
Where at last one found,
Talk of hope,
And dreamers shouted on the streets.
The power of love.

In and out of tragedies,
Homeless friends and suicides,
The Christians still give charity;
Amid the ruins hungry children,
Ask not for food but guns.
The power of love.

The power of love,
A force from below,
Rushing outside of me
Towards the day.
Let yourself be beautiful,
And give the children guns.

The state is our enemy,
Oppressing you, oppressing me.
Its time has surely come at last,
A mystic power from the past.
Make your love goal,

A sky-scraping cannon,
Aimed at Westminster,
A helicopter in the sky,
Flower-bombing ICI.

NATIONAL AFFRONT

We've crept out from the rat-holes,
We've crawled out from the sewers,
A band of racist hoodlums, thugs and evil-doers;
We march the streets of England,
Protected by strange laws
That permit a brood of Nazis
To parade a vicious cause.

We scoff the grief of mothers
Who sacrificed their sons,
Brave lads who fell at Arnhem
In their fight against the Huns;
We sneer at all the Buchenwalds,
The gassings and the rack,
For we hide the bloody swastika
Behind the Union Jack.

Where are your Burma veterans now?
Your men of Alamein,
As we scum spit on the crosses
Of your comrades who were slain?
Where is your gallant army,
Your Air Force and your Fleets
When we Fascists march through England
And desecrate your streets.

NEAR WILLIAM BLAKE'S HOUSE

In this street just by his home,
I sought the spirit of my poem,
And winged words to then express
My dark and restless loneliness.

Since Blake the long, long years have passed
To let the sunbeams in at last,
And even yet those rays that blind
May prove the furnace of Mankind.

The joys of home are sundered still
And conscience wars with heart and will;
Some smiles of friendship that we meet
Fade with the corner of the street.

Be this the price for birth anew
That grief our courage shall pursue
And make the tears this age looks on,
A dewy carpet for the dawn.

NEITHER RED NOR DEAD

Neither red nor dead, just plain duped,
Has been the people's fate
Since nineteen-forty-five,
When out of the cauldron hell of War,
The lucky ones came home alive.
The bosses' press never lies—
It never lies still, you mean.
While you're debating.

It's fabricating, frantic and furious,
Like Goebbels did,
To put the lid on peace and human progress;
These spineless hacks bend easy backs,
Howk in the cesspool of their mind
For every evil way to block
The forward movement of Mankind.

Soldiers,
You came home, glad it was over
And the home fires burning.
You landed at Dover
A faceless one then passed you in the street,
Going the other way,
His mission—to repeat the grim performance
With lies and hate and fear,
To corrupt the atmosphere,
And like a demon conjuror, weave the absurd,
Make peace a dark, despised, suspicious word,
And why?

When revolutions sweep the Earth,
And effort, not mere rank of birth
Or riches can determine worth,
When in their last citadels,
The tyrants here the tolling bells,
Then in the gloom,
The craven cowards crawl and quail,
And hope that nuclear blackmail
Averts their doom.
Pretending fear of Soviet might,
They really dread they'll lose the right

To rob the poor;
Thus they gamble with our lives,
Hoping Capitalism survives
And lies endure!

NUCLEAR FISION

Ye hypocrites, you know this well
And that is why you'd bear a hell
On earth below!
'Tis not the Russians whom you fear
But lest we might have freedom here
Your favours go!
One of your cloth arose to say
He'd press the button any day
On Mankind's fate;
Behind the cross what villains sneak
With saintly smiles and manners meek
Yet hearts of hate?
Christ was in a stable born
On a cold December morning
In lowly station,
But now some 'ministers of Christ'
Need bombs to keep a state they prize
More than salvation?
Who should a day of wrath appear
I'd give my very soul to hear
God's fury then,
Smite them with the bombs they bless
Give them a blast of war's distress
And hell! Amen! Amen!
They lifted up their hats and passed
Politely on their way,
And nothing in the world deterred
Man's anguish on that day

Chorus:
Nuclear Fission! Nuclear Fission! Etc…

Too many beings on planet Earth
Was never God's complaint,
He'd make another billion more
And every man a saint.
But science took the 'saner view'
Of over-population
And advocated mass control
And pruning devastation.
Too many Blacks, and too few Whites
And far too many Brown,

A neutron bomb placed here and there
We'll cut their numbers down.
All hell rained down, they're just survived a hundred
And not a woman in the lot—
A scientific blunder.

Chorus:
Nuclear Fission! Nuclear Fission! Etc…

ON BALLADIER BRIDGE

On Balladier bridge I stood in the Autumn,
To tarry a while and gaze down on the stream,
And a sad little songbird plaintively told me,
That the freedom of Ireland is still a mere dream.

By the waters of Dromore, my soul like a bubble,
Will float down on the Erne to the Donegal shore,
And dear friends and relations I loved in my childhood,
Like the green hills of Monaghan I will never see more.

ON CHURCHILL'S DEATH

The ancient frauds all gather round
to lay us prostrate on the ground;
dukes and generals, kings and lords,
a puppet host with dangling swords,
money-mighty magnates too
and most of that low, lickspittle crew
disguised as 'Labour' to deceive
join with their Tory friends to grieve
this propped-up fraud,
and Churchill hoist to heaven high
just next to God.

The trumpets of a crooked state
blare out the myth that he was great,
and scoundrels now of all degrees
are everywhere upon their knees
to praise this man who merely meant
the evil which they represent,
who on himself took credit for
millions slaughtered in the War,
and full of phrases, pomp and pride,
betrayed the cause for which men died.

O grim John Bull,
in your declining, dithering days,
is this the idol that you raise,
Shakespeare compare?
Doltards, fools, gaze not up,
if he's in heaven no saint is there.

ON W B YEATS

Here in the shadows of a vast city,
My thoughts return to Ireland,
And I see the Swan of Cool in her domain,
Beside her, Yeats—his bardic crown
Let wisely down in careful disarray,
His flowing shirt and quaint, curt, mimic lip.
He interests me in the manner of his poetry.

This man could hold the stage
In an island where buffoonery is great;
He could decide the fate of Letters,
And poets living and poets still unborn
Would have to pause and pick
The fairy thorn from out their feet,
He made the old Romance of Ireland so complete.

There in the Sligo hills, long will he lie,
The Horseman and the hunted pass him by,
And by the ancient sands of Lissadil,
The heirs of feud and famine are weeping still.

ORA PRO NOBIS

O Lord,
who dwellest on high,
to thy great favour we apply,
let there be peace, class compromise:
let men upon each other smile,
and custom's practice, horrid guile,
may so increase.
Let slave and master linked agree
to end their mutual emnity,
unite with love,
the slave to cease his ancient fight,
the master to maintain his right,
remain above!

Lord,
with thine strong hand put down
all disturbance in the town.
Maintain the law!
Reinforce the boys in blue,
thine own great truncheon,
use it too
on skull and jaw!
Help too thy ministers and priests
to riches, honours, fetes and feasts,
such sweet abuses—
Load them with thine high degree;
newspaper columns and BBC
put to their uses,
that preaching with their solemn faces,
their saintly, sickly, airs and graces,
they'll teach the folk
to touch the cap and bow the knee
to earthly lords as well as thee,
endure the yolk.

But, Lord,
my chief and direst woe,
to see the Soviet influence grow!
Them Russians give me such a fright,
I shake and shiver through the night—
such terror overwhelms me,

to hear them preach equality.
And why should peace my profits mar
when all my riches come from war?

O Lord,
I beg you on my hunkers,
provide us rich with deeper bunkers!
What odds the poor run helter-skelter
and find the grave their only shelter!
Let them endure the scorching blast—
were they not born to be downcast?
O gentle Jesus, meek and mild,
don't even spare one Russian child,
the old, the crippled or the blind—
leave not a single soul behind!

Lord,
give me big and bigger bombs
to smash them into wee atoms!
Prostrate them, Lord, and lay them low!
Destroy their cities in one blow!
By this, my God, you'll surely see
my caring Christianity.

But, Lord,
safeguard my dividends,
and I'll count you among my friends!
Maintain a class-divided Earth!
Mid common-folk restore our worth,
so that sweet luxury and pomp
continue on its royal romp!
Safeguard our banks!
Our coffers fill
and make it seem 'Divine Will'!
Do this, O Lord, and I shall be
thine servant for eternity,
but should you fail me in the end,
I know I've Satan for a friend!
(Supporting his determination to keep the world 'free').

POISON PEN

This malevolence which poisons the pen
And engraves its screed into the paper,
Foolishly goes its course in damning evidence
Against itself in spite of it.

It will have its say,
Then curse its own decay.

Each stabbing action of the nib on the paper
That pierces the writers unrepentant heart,
Probes in rapid succession again and again
Like picking constantly at a fresh wound.

It will malign,
But then its writers hand may never sign.

POPPYCOCK

(A song awaiting a good tune)

They boast of their battles,
The honours they've won,
And hide in their pomp,
All the slaughter's been done.
Poor soldiers and horses,
Tangled in death,
And cursing their fate,
With their very last breath

Chorus:
Poppy propaganda is the name,
Poppy propaganda is the game,
Like the old white feather trick,
Deceit and shame.
Centuries of wars we've been given,
We haven't them forgot nor forgiven.
They can stuff their propaganda
As we mock:
Poppycock, Poppycock! Poppycock!

They swagger, brag and beg us in the street
Pretend take old soldiers for a treat
While the Government spends billions
To murder us in millions
And poor pensioners get less and less to eat.
They have huge amounts of planes
And tanks and guns,
Of war reserves a hundred million tons.

They find cash for every crisis that they meet,
So why this poppy begging in the street?
I'll tell you why they take us for Joe Soap
They brainwash us to swallow all their dope
As we dither and we dodder
To them we're cannon fodder,
And will be thus forever, so they hope.
Our hope is that a lovely day will dawn
When this weary world will
Not be so forlorn
When this cruelty will cease,

And folk can live in peace,
And the vultures that prey
On us are gone.

SHY COUPLE

You were alone, so I asked politely to walk you home,
You agreed, and I paced the conversation so I wouldn't take the lead;
I took you to your door, and then I said good night,
Because I thought I'd been a bore,
I didn't want to presume, so I shook your hand
and left as you stepped into your room.

We are like so many, scared to take chances in case there aren't any,
We only say hello just to say goodbye; it's all the words we ever know,
Why must we wait, why do we come so close only to hesitate?
I only know that we grasp an opportunity, and then we let it go,
I guess I'm too polite to be able to ask you if if I can spend the night,
And you too much of a lady in every way, come right out and eventually say.

SONG OF A SPUD

I once was a common-or-garden wee bloke,
but fortune smiled on me, and then in a stroke,
I was lifted quite literally out of the mud
to become overnight, the omnipotent spud.

In the past bits of tears would fall from my eyes,
for even the cabbages used to despise
such a lowly born fellow without royal blood
and they nicknamed me Murphy and tattie and spud.

I wasn't worth tuppence, I was down at the heels,
poor tramps of the road will know how it feels
to be trampled and scoffed at and misunderstood,
but look at me now—the magnificent spud.

Of models in this there's surely no dearth,
the meek and the poor shall inherit the earth,
if I can aspire, then surely they could—
take heart and take hope from the song of the spud.

SONG OF THE DYKE

Where are the children who used to paddle
In the glory of the sun,
The bairns of the tenements
No longer have their fun,
By Calton and Camlachie,
By the looms and miners' rows.
'Midst the toiling disinherited
An angry murmur grows.
Like the ants of earth we labour,
Like the bees about the hive,
And our few and simple pleasures
Are still to us denied;
They would rob us of the sunlight,
A mighty voice declares
'Mid the glistening vaults of thunder
Where the anvil fires glare.
And a solemn pledge is sworn,
And manly lips sealed grim,
While a tyrant lords above us,
We will have revenge on him!
Far better sail to Botany,
In Tolbooth chains lie low,
To walk free in the valley
Where the green grass grows.

SONG OF THE SCAB

I'll sing you a song of the slippery scab,
a slimy creature from the first,
of all things crawling on the globe
assuredly the very worst;
a snivelling toad and creeping jesus
more spineless spunk you never met—
come across the creature once
and you'll wish to soon forget
that boss's yes-man, Judas sly,
who hopes by crawling through a crisis
that the world will pass him by!

STRONTIUM NINETY THREE

So did you see me can,
I didn't mean the man—
The one for brewing up the tea,
But me wee wee can
It's a bright orange wan,
And it's full of strontium-ninetythree.

I left it at the site,
I just left it overnight,
I thought it would be there when I came back.
But no I must sup sorrow,
For when I came back on the morrow,
It was gone and things are looking black.

THE ATOMANIACS—A PROPHECY

My poem will relate
The ultimate fate
Of the villains
Who always cause war.
Those Armament Kings
With their cartels and rings—
Everyone knows who they are.

For long, bitter years,
They've shed human tears
And blood, while they've jingled
Their pockets,
No warning they'd heed,
But wallowed in greed,
'Til now we're confronted
With rockets.

Yes, this is the tale
Of their latest blackmail,
And how they brought fear
To the world;
Not a tear in their eye,
That millions would die,
And our race to perdition
Be hurled.

No grief for the child,
So gentle and mild
Could be seen in these
Hard-bitten faces;
But a Christian pretence
That didn't make sense
As they sat in the highest of places.

For their own precious pelt
Was all that they felt,
As down to their shelters
They hurried;
On this underground trip,
Like rats from a ship,
To their atom-proof hide-outs
They scurried.

And down in the bunkers,
They sat on their hunkers,
Gorging their hoarded food;
Like beasts of the sewers,
Were these vile evil-doers,
Who had ponced on
The multitude.

The shelterless poor
Were left to endure,
And, God, how they staggered
And reeled
In stricken dismay,
'Til revenge had its day
And the lids of the bunkers
Were sealed.

Down there they are cooped
To the level they stooped,
The creatures who once posed
As men;
These debased ones of greed,
And all of their seed,
Can never exploit us again.

On the green world above,
There's joy and there's love,
And life with a radiant lease;
With the evil entombed ,
No longer we're doomed—
At last we're living in peace!

THE BILLIONAIRE'S WIFE

When he asked her to turn on the cooker,
She looked at him with a frown,
Is a cooker a household object?
Is it blue? is it black? Is it brown?

When he asked her to turn on the telly,
She was stunned by his arrogant cheek,
She called him a cad and a rotter,
And took to her bed for a week.

When he asked her to water the flowers,
At last she was forced to rebel;
She shrieked at the brute in wild fury,
'You're making our marriage a hell'.

Any genuine court in the country,
Would have scrubbed the daft case as a farce,
For the plaintive obviously didn't
Know how to wipe her own BUM.

THE BLACKBERRY MAN

All the lanes of Monaghan are heavy with blackberries,
And the children carry cans:
They fill them in the summer sun
And sell them to the blackberry man.
The blackberry man has beady eyes
That ripen with the bee:
He packs the fruit to the brim in barrels
And sends it over the sea.

Now the blackberry man is a happy man
With his house upon the hill,
With his pony and trap and bright tweed cap,
And men to run the mill.
But happier far are the children there
Whose laughter greets the morning air
In the dew-grass lanes of Monaghan,
Who fearing neither God nor man,
Find the world in the rim of a blackberry can.

THE CALTON MARTYRS OF 1787 I

A small green grave lies down by Calton
In the heart o' Glasgow town,
Men of honour, men of courage,
Their names are honoured with renown.

Two hundred years ago they suffered
For the workers' glorious cause.
They were shot defending freedom
Against the boss and Tory laws.

On Glasgow Green the weavers gathered,
For tyrants might cared not a fig,
They marched from Calton up towards the Highgate
And faced the army at to Drygate brig.

At the provost's order, the coward soldiers
Opened fire and six men were slain,
And the people's anger it spread like wildfire
From Glasgow Cross out to Dunblane.

These were the lads who wove all clothing,
Shot for upholding a scanty wage,
while the boss and soldier are damned forever,
Brave names will glow on our history's page.

In a small green grave down by the Calton,
Spare a thought and a prayer as you pass on,
These were the pioneers of freedom,
And heralds of a brighter dawn.

THE CALTON MARTYRS OF 1787 II

The scarlet-lairds of the Tron have worried looks!
Their counting-books tell the story
All the old glory and gain from America
Has passed with her Independence,
And what none of them foresaw
The ebb of wealth at Broomielaw.
Old furious Finlay whacked his drum
And begged for volunteers to come,
He'd crush America.

The pipe-dream lasted but a day,
They'd have to find some other way
To restore their losses,
These hard-faced men were never born
To carry crosses.
Some other victim must be found,
On Mungo's ancient hallowed ground,
For their assault.

The weavers' wages sank so low,
The struggle soon began to grow
And just complaint;
To see their families go bare,
Wives worn down with want and care
Would tax a saint.
In protest at their heavy load,
These angry men then took the road,
And cut the webs
Of those who would betray their fight,
And with their enemies unite,
Depised black-nebs!

The papers roared with arrogance,
'Hot-heads! Deep in League with France'
And similar lies that would ensure
The red-coats' march against the poor,
The musket's fire and carnage soon complete,
Six martyrs lie in Abercrombie Street.

THE COLOURS OF IRELAND

Green is the colour of Ireland,
The grass of her mountains and dales.
It shines in the banners of Erin,
Is sung in her glorious tales;
Ere Patrick made shamrock a symbol,
There hunted through bracken and brake,
Those comments of Finn and Cuchulain
Who fought for Mavourneen's sake.
O Caitlin, mo chroidhe, mo storeen
what sorrow, what suffering you've seen.
Each mountain bore struggle upon her
For the honour of wearing the green.

Oh, red is for heroes of Ireland,
The blood of the brave who did fall,
The many or few of a nation
Who answered a motherland's call.
Salute to the Red Hand of Ulster
And the fearless young men of the West,
Or those boys who lay dying in Wexford
By tyrant and traitor oppressed!
At our vanguard a rebel in Dublin
Raised that standard of glory on high—
Oh, red is a deer sacred colour,
True pledge of the heroes who died!

And white is the colour of Ireland,
The robes of fair Caitlin which grace
Those honest and dearest of Erin
Who never succumbed to disgrace.
This symbol of a people's conscience,
Thro fields which were gory or green
Oft carried more virtue than victory
From many a grim battle scene;
A flame that will flourish forever
When flags of the moment have gone
And the shining white spirit of Erin
Is banner enough for the dawn.

THE CONNOLLY BALLAD

Oiney Hoy stands the day long swearing
at the gawking gapes of Carricktee
that he'll drown himself in a six-foot bog hole
and set all holy Ireland free.
The men of '98 and Ulster
gather round the diddering clown,
while rifle shot and lonely cry
rise in the heart of Dublin town.

Oiney Hoy stands the day long swearing,
the sweat comes out of the clefts in his brow
in the meadows, you, James Connolly,
have wandered as a boy.

These are the men who were your brothers
linked against the Hungry Wind,
standing now in a meadow staring—
staring blind.

Oiney Hoy from the bog is turning
his empty face to the jeering crowd;
they cannot see the soft rain falling
in the clouds that drift at Carricktee.

They cannot see the heart of Irish dead still burning,
the cream of Ireland's mothers mourning
their few sons gallantry.

Oiney Hoy is a byword now
in Ballybay of Connolly's birth,
enough to set the cobbles ringing
with strange unholy mirth.

But where's the word for Connolly
in the tolling Angelus bell,
with cream-faced traitors sanctified
and Ireland's saints in hell?

THE DAWNING OF THE DAY

I'll love my lass forever,
The rainbow of my heart,
As sure as sun and moon there be,
I know we'll never part.
The shadowed city wandering,
I went my lonely way,
Until I fell for Isobel,
At the dawning of the day.

Then greener grew the dewy grass,
And azure grew the sky,
Such was my joy I hardly knew,
The years were passing by.
Come sun, come rain, delight or pain;
Our love will never stray,
When the bright rays shine that lovely morn,
At the dawning of the day.

Clouds will gather in the sky,
Lightning flash and thunder,
But nothing in the wide, wide world
Will tear our love asunder
Through tide and time the rocks we'll climb
In our undaunted way,
As with love as true that we first knew
At the dawning of the day.

'Twas in the woods of Eaglesham,
That May morning we met.
Those lovely honest eyes of blue,
They still are shining yet.
O, desolate this world would be,
This life turned dull and grey,
Could I forget that lass I met
At the dawning of the day.

THE GREEN HILLS OF MONAGHAN

An exile today in the world is no stranger,
He has brothers and sisters wherever he roam,
Whether from poverty, whether from danger,
The children of sorrow all seeking a home.
But think not in cities that loneliness lightens!
The heart in the crowd will cherish its dream,
And all the commotion may serve but to heighten
The grandeur of nature sweet childhood has seen.

Oh, green hills of Monaghan,
How lovely your boreens.

THE KIRK'S ALARM

Ye ministers and men o' God,
Is it to sustain dark fraud
Ye need the Bomb?
Are you weary of the length
God takes to show His mighty strength,
Blast us to Kingdom Come?
Your churches, manses and the rest
With comforts that Old Nick has blessed
Won't be secure?
No longer will your pious talk,
With tales of hell designed to shock
Deceive the poor?

THE LARK

(In memory of Bobby Sands, an Irish martyr 1981)

Though bound in a cage, the brave lark did sing
to herald the blossoming earth in the Spring;
high over Ireland that song it did soar
from Antrim's green hills to the banks of the Nore.
It sang of our sorrow and the bright dawning day,
but they silenced the lark on a morning in May.

For it sang out so freely of torture and pain,
of grillings and beatings, confinement and strain,
it spoke of the British once more on rampage,
cruel with anger and savage with rage,
but still it would sing of the bright coming day,
'til they silenced its voice on a morning in May.

It sang of a province divided, suppressed,
it sang of our youth unemployed and distressed,
it sang of the struggle for just human rights,
and a faith in the day when our nation unites;
but dreading the dawning of such a bright day,
they silenced the lark on a morning in May.

Demons of darkness guided your hand,
cruel England, to be such a curse to our land,
and Nature unkindly placed you by our shore
to slake your great thirst for pillage and gore,
but truth it will triumph and the wicked decay,
though you silenced the lark on a morning in May.

Our history of heroes and martyrs is long,
the singer you've killed, but you can't kill the song;
from Erin's green valleys to the wide world beyond,
the dastardly deed has created a bond,
for you showed your vile hand in the prison that day,
when you murdered our lark on a morning in May.

THE LORD'S LAMENT

The Lord gazed down from heaven
Upon the USA;
And even he who once made Hell,
Recoiled in dark dismay.

He saw the frightened cities
Where muggers stalked the night;
He heard the 'Skid Row' desolates
Decry their hideous plight.

He saw the Wall Street bankers
Swell out with endless greed.
Billions spend on war and hate,
Ignoring human need.

He heard the White House liars
Promote the bankers' plan,
Then brazenly describe their cause,
The 'Liberty of Man'.

He heard these hawks of Washington
Discard their 'Peace' disguise,
And clamouring for a war crusade,
Bombard the world with lies.

And looking down upon the bay,
He saw the dying flame,
As Liberty blew out her torch
And hung her head in shame.

And then a hideous, mushroom cloud
Enveloped night and morn
And humans cursed in agony
The hour they were born.

He heard a frenzied choir sing with 'patriotic' glee,
'God bless America—
The Land of the Free'.

The Lord, in anger, shook his head
This wickedness to see
Them asking for His hand to bless
Such vile profanity.

THE LOVE BALLAD

Come gather round me, town bred folk
and listen to my tale;
I was born in Monaghan of the little hills and vales.
My mother kept a fruit shop, my father he ran wild
and I became in the village street an anxious daring child.

With little boats lone day played upon the silver lake;
I saw the otter in the reeds chasing the screaming drake.
I heard the banshee howling—oh what a howl had she
when the night-wind whispered to the ford
among the dark beech trees.

I arose when the night wind whispered over the shallow stream
and screaming now was the child in me.
Alone in the woods and wild,
here I bide on the mountainside,
my cheek on the cheek of the grass
while you who said you were my love
riding my sky may pass.

THE MALAPROPIST

He never was to adept with common phrases
And when I asked how he got by, he replied:
'Oh, it's just slips off my back like a duck.'
A hard worker, he didn't spend much time in the works' bothy,
Even although, it was as he called it:
'A subsidised canteen'.
His wages for a hard day's graft weren't so substantial,
But he was affable and easily content with whatever he could get,
His quality was evident when he said:
'a bird in the hand is worth it's weight in gold'.
His wife had passed away a number of years ago
And when I give him my condolences he said:
'better to have loved and lost than to never have had a dull moment'.
Finally in my discourse with him he told me he was RC,
Observed the Sabbath and would stay in bed all day, it being the day of rest.
When I asked if he ever went to Mass, he simply replied:
'I'm a collapsed Catholic.'

THE MILLIONAIRE'S PRAYER

O Lord above protecting all
Thy favoured creatures great and small,
surely Thou must understand
now is the tine to show Thine hand,
for down upon this earth of ours
old Satan wields his wicked powers
poor folk to sway—
the worker will not doff his cap
and be the meek and servile chap
of yesterday!

And Lord, them nippers just left school
they have not learned that golden rule,
do what they're told;
they neither go to church or kirk
but demonstrate their right to work
and jobs to hold.
Lord God, to think it's come to pass
this spirit in the working-class
come to a head,
demanding now their wages just—
what downtight greed and selfish lust!
I quake with dread.

And women too.
Them brazen hussies take the street
with other hecklers to compete—
it makes me rue
the day we opened up the vote
and let the rule of petticoat
loom into view!

And Jesus Christ, them coloured folk!
How dare they spurn the ancient yoke
of slavery!
How dare they clamour for their rights
and claim they're just as good as whites
what utter drivel!
O for the galleys on the mains!
O for the good old whips and chains!
I'd make them snivel.

But, Lord, my chief and direst woe
to see the Soviet influence grow.!
Tham Russians give me such a fright,
I shake and shiver through the night—
such terror overwhelms me
to hear them preach equality,
and why should peace my profits mar
when all my riches come from war?
O Lord, I beg you on my hunkers,
provide us rich with deeper bunkers!
What odds the poor run helter-skelter
and find the grave their only shelter!
Let them endure the scorching blast
were they not born to be downcast?

O gentle Jesus, meek and mild,
don't even spare one Russian child,
the old, the crippled or the blind—
leave not a single soul behind!
Lord, give me big and bigger bombs
to smash them into wee atoms!
Prostrate them, Lord, and lay them low!
Destroy their cities in one blow!
By this, my God, you'll surely see
my.caring Christianity.

But, Lord, safeguard my dividends,
and I'll count you among my friends!
Maintain a class-divided Earth!
Hid common-folk restore our worth,
so that sweet luxury and
continue on its royal romp!
Safeguard our banks Our coffers fill
and make it seem 'Divine Will'!
Do this, O Lord, and I shall be
Thine servant for eternity,
but siould you fail me in the end,
I know I' ve Satan for a friend!

THE MOONLIGHTER

The postie chapped oor letterbox—
ah rubbed ma hauns wi' glee,
a Vernon's win, Ah'm sure it was
or a tax rebate for me,
but soon ma face fell forty yards
to read the sad report
which I found to be a missive
frae the sma' debt court.

Chorus:
Let poets praise the silvery moon,
but, och, ma heart grew lighter
when I saw there was nae moon tonight
we did the old moonlighter.

'Three months behind', the letter said,
'Your rent's lang owerdue,
an' we're sending oot the bailiffs,
The bailiffs oot tae you'.
I hadn't got a farden piece,
I was a worried man
'til light o' day began to fade
I lit upon this plan.

Oh, we bundled up oor furniture
wi' some fittin's werena oors,
we even took the meter
an' the haunles frae the doors;
I took ma new slot-telly
way doon the garden path
an' hid it on the wagon
in the Corporation bath.

I harnessed up the old grey mare
tae help us dae the bunk,
I harnessed up the old grey mare
we borrowed frae the junk;
I didna ken whit food we'd get
or water for to drink,
but we won't gang short o' basins
for we took the kitchen sink.

Says Annie on the wagon,
'Ah've only ain regret,
ma kettle an' ma teapot
tae take I did forget!'
Sure I put ma arm aroun' her
tae wheedle an' beguile her,
'Don't fash yoursel' ma lassie,
sure Ah took the copper biler'.

We called the old nag after Meg
that galloped frae Ayr toon,
but half a mile by Garngad,
the old grey mare sat doon,
but soon we foun' an empty hoose,
an' bothered wi' nae bill,
in a land they cry Blackhill.

THE ORRA MAN

When Adam oot o' heaven
was hounded for his sin,
he knew not where on this wide earth
his labours to begin;
to leave him thus bewildered
was never in God's plan,
so He took a pickle wad o' dirt
and made the orra man.

O, the orra man's a marvel,
the blessing o' Mankind
he serves the needs o' ane and a'
in every race and clime.
O, the orra man's essential
to fill and bile the can,
to sweep and brush and muck the byre
we need the orra man.

Your poor oul' maw is wearied oot,
she's never off her feet,
wi' making beds an' grub for all,
she seldom gets a seat;
she cleans the shoes, she polishes,
she scours the pots and pans,
she'll tell you what's it like to be
the poor old orra man.

Man launches into outer space,
and robots multiply
fantastic whigmalerie gigs
now sail the starry sky;
wonders great we will create,
but try the best we can,
there's nae machine we'll make to match,
the good auld orra man.

When climbers conquered Everest,
they made that grand ascension,
with sturdy will on hearts of oak
and an orra man called Tensing.
I'll praise the independent soul
yet show me him who can

sincerely say, he did it all,
without the orra man.

THE POLIS O' ARGYLL

(Tune: Johnson's Motor Car)

You may talk about your Nelson, and Francis Drake as well.
And how they blew the Spaniards and pirates all to hell,
But they've nothing on the Yankee subs that sneaked past Arran Isle,
And left the Battle o' Dunoon to the polis o' Argyll

These worthy sons of Robert Peel are trained to keep the law,
And any danger they'll confront, providin it is sma';
In naval operations they specialise in style,
But the Holy Loch proved quite a shock to the Polis o' Argyll.

With only frogmen to assist and 'specials' by the score.
The Polis proved they're gallant men, all heroes to the core:
With Proteus squat behind them and nuclear missiles, too,
They did the near impossible and captured a canoe.

Now all you Russian astronauts who navigate the globe
Stay far away from Scotland in your Cosmo-Rocket probe,
For should you land near Gourock, you'll be conquered in line style
By the Yanks combining forces with the Polis o' Argyll.

THE RED HERRING

We used to have natural disasters,
earthquakes and floods and the like,
an act of God, pious folk called it
whenever the lightning would strike,
but Goebbels delved deep for an answer
and McCarthy came up with the same,
that for every mishap in Creation,
the Russians and Reds are to blame.

When Atlantis sank under the ocean,
and poor Noah fished from his Ark,
when Etna erupted in cinders
and Moses got lost in the dark,
when the stoney-face Sphinx set the riddle
and the locusts in billions all came,
I'll wager a pound to a penny
the Russians and Reds were to blame.

It was Reds who burned the Armada,
not Drake, or whoever they say,
the Reds lie under our bed-springs
and my God, what havoc they play,
oil slicks and bad weather and muggings,
or any damn mischief you name,
our gangsters and crook politicians,
the Russians and Reds are to blame.

When Churchill sent tanks against miners,
and Labour MacDonald betrayed,
when fat Porgy Brown got a Lordship,
and Wilson Sir Harold was made;
don't blame it on British corruption,
we British are new to that game,
I'll give you a far better scapegoat,
the Russians and Reds are to blame.

When the millionaires pep up the Arms Race,
and swear that they only want peace,
when across the wide world they stir trouble
to ensure that their profits increase;
they will swear that a goose is a gander,

and should you be deceived by the same,
you will prove easy meat for the liars
and the Russians and Reds are to blame.

THE SCABS OF NOTTINGHAM

Deep in Nottingham Forest,
Long, long years ago,
There dwelt a kindly outlaw
A goodly man we know.
But the wealthy hounded Robin
And as penance for that crime,
Few good are seen in Nottingham
Ever since that time!

No, we aren't working miners,
We're just scabs,
And we'll take what Maggie Thatcher
Has for grabs.
We are cowards, clowns and creeps,
We're just Uriah Heaps,
We aren't working miners,
We are scabs!

Robin had feathered arrows,
And graceful was their flight,
The only feather that we own
Is the one that's coloured white.
Robin's men wore Lincoln Green,
Such colours we do lack,
Yea, all, except the yellow streak
That's running down our back.

Robin robbed the greedy rich
And helped to feed the poor
But scabs like us crawl to the rich
And of this you may be sure.
I know that deep in Nottingham,
There's miners, men o' grit,
But not a single man o' them,
goes scabbing down the pit.

THE SPECTRE INSPECTOR

The spectre inspector with nerves of steel
Goes in search of long departed souls
Who were once, to the touch, living and real.

He sleeps in graveyards at dead of night
To be weakened by the odd lost soul
Re-enacting the last moments of its plight.
He visits houses haunted by ghosts vicious and benign
Who do their rounds in the silent hours
And leave closed messages on walls as proof or a sign.

For him, these things are all in a night's work
Keeping company with the dead,
Where ghastly scenes of suicide and murder lurk.

With indifference he says: 'there is nothing to fear,
It's just a job like any other
Except that my qualifications are not evidently clear,
They are not in writing and therefore cannot be seen.
You see, since I was very young
I had always been a sensitive child in the extreme.

'Since then I've seen many a spectre in my day
Yes even one who follows me everywhere I go
And she helps by keeping evil spirits at bay'.

So here we must leave him, assured that we'll all sleep tight
While he lays those restless ghosts
Which disturb the stillness of the night,
And even if you don't believe in ghosts at all,
Don't be surprised if you hear a knock on your door in the small hours
And it is the spectre inspector who has come on call.

THE STASH ME FATHER WORE

Me father was an Orangeman
Me mother was a whore
And when the bastard drank his pay,
She'd kick him out the door;

He was a dirty bully
And rotten to the core,
but Jesus Christ, you should have seen
The stash me father wore.

It was hairy, it was ugly and
It made him look a bore.
Sometimes it swept the ceiling,
And then it swept the floor.

But every twelfth in daft Belfast,
You couldn't ask for more.
The best thing on the Orange Walk
Was the stash me father wore.

He joined the Shankill Butchers,
He ranted and he swore.
He'd kill a million Catholics
And maybe twenty more.

The Flute and Derry's Walls he'd sing
And then for an encore.
The hoarse old crow'd have a go
At the stash me father wore.

But then one drunken Saturday
Me ma could stand no more.
When him and quare oul' Paisley
Came chapping at the door.

I kicked his reverence in the balls—
'Good Christ', he yelled 'that's sore!'
And then I strangled poor old Dad
With the stash me father wore.

THE STATUE OF LIBERTY

Liberty climbed from her high plinth one day
and decided to stroll through the USA
to search for that 'freedom' which Reagan did boast,
to see was it real or merely a ghost.
The hour was quite late, it was coming on dark,
when Liberty passed thro' the great Central Park.

Had she but known its dreadful repute,
upon its pathways she would never set foot;
unaware of the dangers, she walked on her way,
and was raped and was mugged on that very day!
The medical bills were a drain on her purse,
but her subsequent fate was even far worse.

She was now down-and-out and lived in a shack
in the desolate sidings of some railway track;
her friends were poor drunks and hoboes in need,
(all this was a strange sort of freedom indeed!)
there were long days of anguish with nothing to eat
'til poverty forced her to beg on the street.

The rich and well-fed passed her by with disdain
that some folk were 'free' was abundantly plain,
but millions of jobless found no such allure,
they were free but to breathe, they were free to be poor!
Drugs, suicides, murders in plenty were rife
and the cheapest regard by far was for life.

The Mafia rule and the Klu Klux Klan return,
Still gather in droves their crosses to burn.
Old Indian tribes are deprived of their rights
And some even jailed for daring to fight;
Segregation by law is said to be gone,
But the dregs of that system still linger on!

Liberty found in the sidings and shacks,
For a handful of whites there are dozens of blacks;
Many of the drifters were ex-Vietnam
Which 'Christian' America had scorched with napalm;
Now returned home from that wicked war,
Was this the great freedom that they had fought for?

Unemployed queues, grief and despair,
All these in lavish abundance are there!
Men are 'free' to shoot presidents, gun down Luther King,
They are 'free' in that land for any darn thing.
'Protect Vital Interests' becomes their war cry,
But their cause is a sham and their slogan a lie!

In the midst of this morass, this scene of dismay,
Liberty went to the White House one day—
This millionaires' haunt where the rich reign supreme,
And a nightmare create from America's dream;
In the art of destruction they are past masters,
With Star Wars and germs and nuclear disasters!

Liberty in horror heard these 'men of state'
Plan for mass murder and call it debate.
'For shame!' she cried out, she was met with their glares,
She was battered and bruised and kicked down the stairs!
Limping and lame to New York she returned,
But Liberty's anger within her still burned!
She climbed on her pedestal and that's why to this day
You'll find her back turned on the 'free' USA.

THE SUNBRIGHT FLOWER OF PEACE

Ploughman, proud of the running furrow,
Peace will bring great fields to you,
And, oh, what bounty the earth will yield
In golden days when the sun stands high
And the sky is bright with gratitude.
The leaves on the tree your deeds will know
And shade with love the path you go,
Keen-eyed son of the soil,
And for your arduous, nurturing toil,
In days of sense there will be a world of recompense.

Miner, comrade in the deep earth,
Peace through darkness radiant gleams,
And shining yet for your hands to shape
Are Mankind's treasured, untapped seams!
They stretch to days of human glory
Here upon the earth below,
The fields of grain away far above,
The flag of truth unfurled,
And you shall walk, new kinship chasing
The passing insults fools have hurled!

Teacher, tutor, men of learning,
Guarding youth from wild-eyed fears,
Steer their innocence to goodness
And stem their apprehensive tears!
Make real the dreams which their young vision
Fashions in the summer street,
When the smiling world is a joyous promise,
A glorious garden at their feet!
Let no beast for greed or malice
Destroy those gentle dreams they weave,
Or bring a horror to their lives
The mind of Man dare not conceive!

Give peace her place in childhood's story,
The queen adored by all is she,
She walks their garden, all weeds wilting
Before her radiant modesty!
And such a queen will hold the classroom
In Summer cool and Winter warm,

And children, proud to walk beside her,
Will thank you with their young heart's charm.

Writer, artist, music-maker,
Unite with artisan and baker,
We still can save the Earth,
And all the power in our hearts
Must come to universal birth
At this most potent hour!
Then what was but a human wish
Shall be a multi-coloured flower,
A slender stem and tender leaf,
But, oh, what fragrance there,
Its blossom shall delight the heart
Of good folk everywhere.

Men and mothers of all nations,
Whatever rank whatever station,
Weave a garland o'er the globe
That peace will wear that lovely robe
Among her sons!
Men of honour, men of worth,
Sinking low, or striving forth,
Peace can prove your labour's truth,
Renew your love, renew your youth
In days that dance ahead!
This Earth can soon aspire high
Where no tears need be shed,
But those of joy the day we've seen
The heart of Man forever green,
With peace and progress wed!

I see an international crowd
Of colours, faces, garments, creeds,
Place hatred in its burial shroud
And end the reign of greed;
I see them linked from land to land
Across the seven seas,
Whilst in their midst the petals glows
The sunbright flower of peace,
The shining flower, the lovely flower,
The sunbright flower of man,
With roots enriched by selfless deeds
Since history began;

That blossom grows in every land
It decks the earth with grace,
Entwining now the human heart
To save the human race.

THE SWORD OF DAMOCLES

Fortunate children, not the starving,
Laugh and play in the sun,
And there is fun in plenty for the few,
But those of us with something more to do
Are deep concerned—
The rich have learned no lesson from the past
And stand aghast at any peace proposal.

Long, long before the Soviets arose,
Spain, France and Britain had made Imperial foes;
For centuries they plunged us into war,
While they from afar, have reaped the gain of greed,
Creating havoc and universal need
In every land.
Plundered, ravaged each corner of the globe
And donned the lying robe of innocence;
They came to 'civilise the horde'?
They came to murder millions with the sword,
'To quell the natives', use any wicked libel
To loot their lands and leave them with the Bible.

Long, long before the Soviet name was heard,
The Indian and the Negro slave both shared
The whip and chain, tormented lives to live,
Or flee their homes, poor trembling fugitives.
The tyrant has not changed
But merely re-arranged his arsenal!

Instead of whip and chain and hanging-rope,
He's found new source of hope in atom-bombs;
Yet still he fears his end,
For no true man of conscience is his friend.
Groping with rage, uncertain, blind,
His last great card—
The blackmail of Mankind.

THE WEE FOLK

In the Lower Falls Road, sure I chanced once to live,
And me hand up to God, but I'll never forgive
Mesel without arms, while the peelers had theirs,
Rifles and pistols and me wi' just prayers,
But still I did, went down on me knees,
'Oh, Lord up above, would you help us out please?'
and ere the sun rose I had weapons to fight—
Ah, the wee folk were working right into the night!

No Britannia's battalions rushed down in great load
To the fields of Fermanagh and they blew up our road,
They laughed and they cheered, creating disorder,
Sayin' 'Paddy is finished along with his border!'
I gazed at the ruins, a great gaping hole,
As bleak as their brains and as bare as their soul -
But long ere the dawnin', the road was made right,
Ah, the wee folk were workin' right into the night.

Sure, England may think that her power is great,
That Ireland enslaved must bow to her fate,
But Buckingham Palace will submerge in the sea
Ere we will submit to their tyranny.
Their Union Jack is but a skull and crossbones
For pirates to plunder what Irishman own.
Tread wary our land and beware o' the light!
The wee folk are workin' right into the night!

THE WORKERS MILLENNIUM

(A brief but true history of 2000 years)

What's happened to the working man
Since the day that Christ was born?
In every century he's endured
A life of sweat and scorn.
Even in new Christian Rome
He still was but a slave
And bore that stigma with his name
From cradle to the grave.
He built and manned the self-same ships
His master's greed to please,
With wealth and told though he himself
Oft perished in the seas.
He built them gothic churches
Designed to praise the Lord,
The Christ of peace, not battle hymns
And conquests with the sword.
But Christian king and state abhorred
Picasso's gentle dove.
They nurtured an abundant hate
But not an ounce of love.
The working man he tilled the fields
And dug coals underground,
An iron collar round his neck
And oft in shackles bound.
And should a poor man steal a loaf,
His children's wames to fill,
He could be cast in Newgate gaol
Or hanged at Tyburn Hill.
In just the last five hundred years,
What's been the course of action?
Wealth's increased a thousand-fold,
Mass murder in foul wars abound,
Corruption, drugs and porn.
Be honest now—could things be worse
Had Christ been never born?
For Christians run our papers,
And not a pagan since time began
Could match their dirty capers.

THESE ARE MY FRIENDS

These are my friends—the dear ones of a day
Of whom I sing with spirit in my voice;
These are the ones who on my winding way
Arise like the sun and make my heart rejoice.
There, first of all, a girl youthful and wise,
Kindly and brave and loved by everyone,
The shining heart that nature loans to man.
Too late the world though clouds blot out the sun.
And on the noon-day street of crowded hours
There passes one who somehow I esteem,
A homely look or friendly smile,
Or in an eye a fascinating gleam.
Such folk are too the essence of my poem—
We've met and parted not-so-silent friends
And for the sudden pause in our acquaintance,
I'm certain too that time shall make amends.
Of such I sing with rapture in each note,
Ascending high above the commonplace.
These are the ones who carry in the deeds
the same sweet virtues written on their face!

These are my friends—the dear ones of a day
Of whom I sing with spirit in my voice;
These are the ones who on my winding way
Arise like the sun and make my heart rejoice.

TO AN ERSTWHILE FRIEND

Darken not my door again, you false unfriend,
Squint not your malice at me, this is the end!
A foil you thought to serve your needs,
Proceed your wriggling way,
But what you thought my night, to build,
May prove the day!
A Dublin man? God help us now,
Did Emmett walk those streets?
And who would trade his triumphs all
For one of his defeats?
Farewell, goodbye, I'm glad we met,
For after all the revel,
Having borne you so long
I will not fear the Devil!

TO THE SCABS

Are you prepared to help bring on
Your wives and children's tears,
As rich drones drive the nation back
To bitter years?

Are you prepared to kneel and bear
Their arrogance and might,
Your wretched soul to sneak away,
Betray the workers' fight?

Are you prepared to see rents rise
And living standards fall,
And turn the yellow, coward streak,
When our back is to the wall?

And do you need the masters' press,
That mass of mindless bunk,
Out-pourings from the servile pen
Of some degenerate skunk?

Then 'twas your sort made Hitler God,
And right up to your door
Leads the dark, the crooked path
Of evils gone before.

Each time we triumph in the fight
You cowards sought to lose,
To share the fruits of victory,
Not one of you refuse.

Oh, shine a day upon this land,
When the scales are turned about,
In what cavern you may crawl,
We still shall find you out!

TRANSMUTATION

In bourgeois definition,
By 'populace' we mean
Those nice conforming citizens
Who cheer both king and queen;
Whatever be their origin,
Beggar, lout or snob,
These are our glorious 'people'—
The rest we call the 'mob'.

In every Grub Street journal
By 'citizen' they mean
The flower of Olde England
Playing cricket on the green,
Or a toffee hat at Ascot
With a dangling chain and fob—
The rest we lump together
And stigmatize the 'mob'.

In standard Oxford idiom,
By 'populace' is meant
A nation's servile silence
Against bad government,
But once we see them stirring
In angry pulsing throb—
The heigh for law and order—
      Christ save us from the 'mob'.

TREES OF LIBERTY

Burns sang the tree of liberty,
Folk rising from their knees,
And now we join a chorus for
The liberty of trees.
Rally to the Green, friends,
Rally to the Green,
A stately tree is nobler far
Than any king or queen.

Here's to the lads of Pollok,
The bonny lasses too,
My curse on brass neck Wimpey
And all his toady crew;
Down with the Glasgow polis,
Propping up bent laws,
And here's to the brave Security
Who joined our worthy cause.

The motorways are putrid, controlled by the rotten rich,
That oily shit called Major and the Tory Thatcher bitch.
A sin it is to fell one tree, destroy one blade of grass,
To let these greedy useless snobs drive in comfort past.

These ruthless vandals fell our woods,
We're late the song birds sing,
And if we let them have their way, they'll ravish everything;
But Pollock and brave Corkerhill have shown us the way—
Rally to the Green, good folk, and we shall win the day!

VIA DOLOROSA

(A Christian poet once charged me to write a better
 Christian poem than he could a Communist one.
The latter came to naught. This is my effort, such as it is)

    I made this little poem last night,
    Spindrift while the city slept—
    Was it for real men like me
    Christ in the garden wept?
    I would gather his tears from the soil,
    I would toil all my years and long
    Urged on like a monk with a sanctified song,
    Again and again
    I would rise as he rose
    Tho' wildly the wind blows a storm
    In my face,
    And glowing with grace
    In sun, street, and shadow,
    Up hill and down,
    I would carry His cross
    And my own through the town.

WAKE (ON THE OCCASION OF THE IRISH 'REPUBLIC') 1949

I came in from the west with the wet rain filling the tarpaulin with mountain pools, up the Clyde to Glasgow town, with the harvesters glumly on green chests as old as the hills of Donegal, a drunken soldier groggy as the white swirl of the wake, a little lass of two, red ribboned and lonely… God, how we cattle stank in the close foul hold.

If this was pleasant I would make a rhyme for you all. I would bring in the birds, the stretching beaks of the gulls out of a white cloud down to the shadowed water with the chance of a bite swooping down from the hungry circus keen eyes on a salt soaked crust… I would mention the waves, riders with dancing plumes and the old man aft with a stick watching it with deep eyes, deeper than the sea, on his way home.

Don't let the picture cards deceive! It was cold, like a wet post in a wintry lane with the thin pine of Scotland on either side as the snail ship wearily crawled up to the womb of the Clyde.

The lads from the thatched homes by the sea sat silently, no Crusoe among them now or man of great adventure working in brown foreign fields a year for money and back to the boosted land. We are sailing third class to Glasgow a tenth of the ship in our hands with church bells ringing in Ireland, ringing of freedom with the colleens of Ireland singing and jiving there on O'Connell Bridge with the Dublin trumpeters thriving on hot air from the Dail,

We are moving out of the parish when hunger calls.

WAR FEVER

The hollow drums are beating
And the stupid wave their flags
And a tiger-faced old General
Sticks out his chest and brags;
They don't think of the horror
Or the homes they desolate,
For their minds are filled with poison
And their hearts destroyed with hate.

WAUKRIFE: A POETICAL ENCOUNTER WITH NESSIE

The lanely loch we waukrife nicht
I saw an eerie, eldricht sicht
And heard strange things
That gart me think
O' Mankind hovering on the brink,
O' hell's perdition,
And I became maist fashed indeed
For oor condition.

I saw this creature lang an' laugh,
Whiskin' tail an' gapin' craig,
Wi' scaly skin and glow'rin' even
That amaist lit the mirky scene:
Frantic feart I wad hae ran
Had no the puir lane beast began
A plaintive lay;
It couldna fail tae mak me bide
An' hear her tale.

'I'm Nessie, famed in mony a story
An' prood as Rab o' Scotia's glory!
Tho' cuifs o' me just siller mak,
Mair halesome tent o' life I tak
An' bide alow amang the herrin's
For fear I frichten gangrel bairns.
'Twas lang lang time when first I cam
An' in these wimplan waters swam,
The coollins and Ben Nevis saw,
Ere gaelic bard or Brehon Law,
Ere pibroch mor filled brae an' lea,
Frae Campsie up to Cromartie,
On haar clad glacier I slept
Ere foot upon the bracken stept.

I may seem but an uncouth beast,
But nature's laws affect the least
O' livin' creatures—
Een the grass is altered
By whit comes tae pass
An' when Earth saw the dawn o' man
A bricht new spark o' hope began
That the stage of evolution

Fortified by resolution wad wisely steer
Oor fragile planet's future coorse
Frae year tae year.

An' sae met,
I, dinosaur, wi' wee sma' brain,
An' ye wha wad sich vantage gain
Frae alphabet,
Yet for your learning an' your art,
Our ways are no sae far apairt,
Ye war an' squabble,
An' aiblings end like us as weel,
Ae ribble-rabble!
I'll tell you this—
War's wickedness jist worsens wrangs!
Think o' a' your bonnie songs nae mair
To hear,
Nor gowden lad nor sonsie lass
An' a' the trystings in the grass
O' yesteryear!
Browse ower the folly, foul and fell,
Tae broil in havoc and in hell
Sich treasures sweet.
Tae ravage Earth's green gairden fair
Wi' nuclear waste an' poisoned air,
It gars me greet.
Ye call me 'monster of the loch',
Puir hairmless beast
Wha harbours nae unkindly thought
Within ma breist,
The whiles a brimstone beast o' savage mien
Bides in another loch upon the Scottish scene
A beast wad scorch an' singst hairst an' hame
Yuir lee-lang luves an' unfurled fame
In ashes lay;
Bairn's banes blawn like chaff o'er hill
An' heather,
That e'en God maun wonder
How he can draw the lot together
For Judgement Day.

Ye call me monster,
When a' aroond ane hears an' reads
O' murder, rape and sichlike deeds,

Colour bars an' warring creeds
An' frenzied zeal;
Ill-treated bairns an' battered wives,
The way the callous canker thrives
Wad shame the De'il
An' mak the cynic thought o' Man
Regard the Earth ane vicious den.
An' some wad turn tae war again
Tho' life wad cease—
O lord, hae they nae spark o' feeling
Sich grief tae cause stony a' healing,
Whan reason's self is aye revealing
The paths o' peace?

An' wi' these warning words
Auld Nessie left the shore,
An' cleaved the caller water
Tae the benmaist bore,
But I thocht lang on her logic tae mak it mine,
For peace I hae been waukrife frae that day sinsyne.

WHEN AFTER ARMAGEDDON

When after Armageddon
And you answer to the Lord,
'Did you ever try to convert
The ploughshare from the sword?'
Will you stand with mouth a-gaping,
Eyes rolling in the head—
'I was busy, Lord, a-busking,
I was out there, winning bread.
As the war-clouds gathered round us
And the dark'ning's storms increase,
I just couldn't see the way, Lord,
To join the fight for peace.'

But the inner voice of conscience
Will hear the children's cry,
'You left us to our fate, man,
For you didn't even try!'

When after Armageddon,
Will you snigger at the good
Who have sacrificed their comfort
For the stricken multitude,
Who when you were gleaning riches
Or merely crawling by,
Strove to make this world a garden
In a free and open sky?
Will you shrug your wretched shoulders,
And the old excuse pursue,
'With the forces lined against us,
Oh, Lord, what could I do?'

And the inner voice of conscience
Will hear the children's cry,
'You left us to our fate, man,
For you didn't even try!'

When the Lord draws back the curtain
And we gaze at planet Earth,
That is freed from poison gases
In a mantle of pure green.
A world of joy and wonder
Which could easily have been,

Had the likes of you stood upright
With a staunch, courageous mind
In the fight for human freedom
And peace for all Mankind.

GLASGOW POEMS

A BALLAD OF RED CLYDE I

Come all ye strange historians,
and hiders of the truth,
my story I will tell the world
from days of tender youth;
high in the mossy Lowther hills
my rivulets begin
their windings to the Lanark glades
and doon by Corra Linn.

I nurtured many a sylvan shade
where peasants tilled the field,
and many a glorious golden hairst
those crops of bounty yield;
where sunlight gleams on silver streams,
I roam so wild and free
'til I join the tide of the estuary wide
and dance into the sea.

I saw the cottar and his kin
their bield and biggings build,
I saw the lairds deprive them of
the fruits of a' they tilled;
I saw the poor gaunt weaving folk
ply shuttle night and day,
their travails deep, their weary sleep
and lives o' hodden grey.

In mirky mines o' Lanarkshire
I heard the wee bairns cry
in damp, dark seams where no light gleams,
nor glimpse o' sun or sky,
and smelters doon by Waukenfield
sic grievances did thole,
awakening fire in their hearts
and iron in their soul.

The haughty lairds no conscience knew,
no pity had, nor shame,
with sword an' gun at dead o' night
their hireling cowards came,
an' Glasgow soon had cause to moan

the proud old patriot's loss,
wi' Purly Wilson bound in chains
and hanged close by the Cross.

My streams were harnessed by man's skill,
my bed made deep and wide,
an' I became in sang an' fame
the bonny river Clyde;
from Lowther Hills to mines and mills
and onward to the sea—
there is no might can stem the flignt,
that yearning to be free.

And there arose upon my banks
a stalwart breed o' men,
who vowed that they would never be
poor suffering slaves again;
with dignity and courage stood,
nor did they stand in vain;
what joy to me to live to see
the likes of John McLean.

Their emblem was the banner red,
they were no craven crew,
like Clyde has served you with its streams,
they forged the path for you;
their fame shall flower with the years,
remembered aye with pride,
and history shall sing with me
a ballad of Red Clyde.

A BALLAD OF RED CLYDE II

Come all good folk of old Strathclyde
and you will hear the truth!
My wandering I'll narrate to you
from days of early youth.
Beneath the mossy Lowther hills
my rivulets begin
their winding through the narrow glades
and down by Corra Linn.

I nurtured all the sylvan shades
where peasants tilled the field
and many a glorious Autumn hairst
these crops in bounty yield;
where sunlight on silver streams,
I roamed so wild and free
'til I joined the tide,
at the estuary wide,
and danced into the sea.

I saw lean serfs upon my banks
glean riches from the soil,
and then fat lairds deprive them of
the fruits of all their toil;
I saw the poor gaunt weaver folk
tied to their looms all day,
their sorrows deep and weary sleep,
their lives of hodden grey.

I saw the Lanark Miners
a similar fate endure,
and smelters in Gartsherry forge
oppresssed like all the poor,
and when they stood against their foe,
it caused me no surprise,
I saw the iron in their soul,
the anger in their eyes.
The cruel bosses on my banks
no pity had nor shame,
with sword and gun at dead of night
their wretched hirelings came;
I wept to see the agony,

and many a brave one's loss,
with Baird and Hardy at Stirling hanged;
James Wilson at the Cross.

I gave my stream to Glasgow's needs,
they made my channels wide,
'til I became in song and fame
the bonny river Clyde.
The riveteer and caulkers lads,
they sang in praise of me,
for they too bore within their hearts

A PECULIAR STRANGER ON GLASGOW GREEN

I came to Glasgow Green one day,
In the middle of the night
And when I came to Nelson's stalk,
I spied the strangest sight—
A big tall guy a-strutting there
And how his eyes did shine,
Repeating o'er and o'er
'This Glasgow Green is MINE!'
I own each tree, each blade of grass,
I own the People's Palace
And should you dare dispute me, sir,
You'll earn my deepest malice.
I own the fields at Fleshers Haugh,
I own the birds and bees,
And should a poor old tramp sleep here
I own his very fleas.
Now should you dare to contradict,
(A scowl spread down his face)
I'll pursue and punish you,
And hound you in disgrace,
For I have toadies all around,
Silenced with cash and power,
Well trained to rush and rescue me
At any evil hour.
I looked at this strange man again,
So arrogant and odd,
And then to humour him I said—
Why, sir, you must be God.
The smuggest smile spread o'er his face,
Of pleasure, pride and mirth;
He shook his head, 'not God' he said,
'But the next best thing on Earth';
I sneaked away, but then next day,
I phoned sweet Sister Sally,
I said a man needs his brain scanned
He thinks he's Patrick Lally!

A SONG FOR THE GLASGOW IRISH

Tune: *The Mountains Of Mourne*

Oh, Mary, this Glasgow's a quare shockin' place
For the crooks on the council are a bloody disgrace:
Pat Lally for years has been givin' us hell
There's more dacint folk in a Barlinnie cell.
MacAveetie's no better, and you'd far better be
Where the mountains o' Mourne sweep down to the sea.

At Easter or Pat's shure there's no green parade
But the orange in July is fully displayed:
They bombard the streets and a soul cannot pass
Not even poor granny on her journey to Mass.
That night they get drunk an' kick bloody hell
While the police just smile, for they're Orangemen as well.
Oh there's many a time I'd far rather be
Where the mountains o' Mourne sweep down to the sea.

Now Glasgow is grand for the toffs in Bearsden,
But not the schemes or a poor single-end,
Or selling *The Big Issue* in the cold pelting rain,
Or slaving your guts for some millionaire's gain.
Ah Mary, ma darling, shure the world's upside down
With them fakes they call Labour just actin' the clown.
Shure I'd pack them in boats an' drown them with glee
Where the mountains o' Mourne sweep down to the sea.

A SONG OF PADDY'S MARKET

I'll sing you a song of the Market,
old Paddy's way down by the Green,
where Watt got his Newcommen engine
and the Wrights their grand flying machine;
there's Kilmarnock editions, old masters,
Noah's Ark and a pileful of junk,
pieces of eight and an anchor
from the year the Armada was sunk,
boomerangs, cockatoos and a gurdy,
you name it, they have it in store,
the lid of the tomb of a mummy,
or the breeks of a brave matador,
knick-knacks, bric-a-brac and fine trickets
that no other place can be seen,
are there to be had for the asking
in Paddy's way down by the Green.

Sure McAllister purchased his plaid there,
himself that danced for the Queen,
and MacPherson's most famous old fiddle,
it came from a stall near the Green!
Or maybe you'll want whigmaleeries,
or a well-chamfered bit for a pound,
and if you've run short of a chanty,
you'll find there are dozens around.
And many's the laddie's first trousers
were cut down from the polis discards,
the legs fitting fine to a frazzle,
tho' the waist was too wide—by a yard.
You may boast of your Goldbergs and Woolies,
but nothing ava have ye seen,
unless you've gone Saturday-shopping
in Paddy's way down by the Green.

Some goods they say fell off a lorry, and
swear they seen it themsel',
sure, if you're up bright and early,
they'll sell ye the lorry itsel';
'twas at Paddy's the crafty wee moocher
the Suspension Brig sold for a song,
and when the Yank paused in suspicion

he threw in for a bargain the Tron.
Naw, that's but the patter o' Glesca,
and goes by the way of a joke,
there's never a soul down at Paddy's
gets landed a pig in a poke,
for it's there that I met with my dearie,
what a bargain I got wi' my Jean,
and I helped her to carry her bundle
to Paddy's way down by the Green.

Poor Glasgow's being bulldozed to pieces,
and half of it razed to the ground,
that demolishing gang in the Chambers
want to leave nothing around,
the Met and the Queens and the Palace,
(next on the list who can tell?)
as Glasgow's transformed to a car-park
and our city a big empty shell.
But no-one can oust 'Paddy's Market',
he baffled the experts around,
yes, Paddy out-witted the planners
when he placed all his goods on the ground,
and folk will aye come from all quarters,
Tam, Dick and Harry be seen
wi' Jock Tamson's bairns as they gather
at Paddy's way down by the Green.

AT GLASGOW CROSS

At Glasgow Cross on a dreich, cold evening,
I watched some pleasured people pass,
Doctor, tailor, saint and sailor,
True love and his lass,
But each sweetened taste was tainted there
By a lonesome river-cry,
And kind folk said it was a child
The world was passing by.

At Partick Cross, my heart was sickened
In a one-side, shadowed street,
The world's distress and loneliness
In the imprint of men's feet;
Hastened I to the river-side,
I held that child as mine,
More meaningful than miracles
Of water into wine.

And I raised him in the night-sky there
With the stars above his head,
And shone those eyes, oh, brighter far
Than anything I said,
'This city, child, your fathers built!
This city's yours to own
And never bow to any man,
The pulpit or throne!

Bring down the tints of rainbow
And raise the tone of earth!
Sing gladness that our base age dies!
Be proud of Mankind's birth!
In every land across the globe,
A glorious dawn you'll see,
And live in days that usher in
the end of poverty!"

In old George Square, as the night wore on,
I heard poor beggars moan;
The marble effigies are not
The only hearts of stone.
In lieu of the pillared men I'd raise

A monument to pity—
Two tiny hands that battered on
The conscience of the city.

GLASGOW STREET CHARACTERS

I'll sing you a sang
O' nae so lang syne,
When Glasga was fu'
O' the characters fine—
Thin Teapot Man Tammy
An' Ewing the Craw;
Rab Haw the great glutton
And wee hirstlin' Kate;
Blind Alex an' Hawkie,
An' Jamie, his mate,
Bob Dreghorn the Hermit
An' Penny a Yard,
But the bravest by far
That the Trongate e'er saw,
Was the bold Glasgow Clincher,
The king o' them a'.

The Teapot Man
Familiar on the Glasgow streets
100 years ago,
His shape raised many a passing smile
In that great traffic flow.
One arm akimbo on his hip,
The other he stretched out,
Selling papers, but it seemed
A very teapot spout.
He's in the People's Palace now,
A picture on the wall
He'll make some little children smile
When we're beyond recall.

Hirstlin' Kate
See Hirstlin' Kate o' the town,
On her brushes go sweepin' around.
Some heads may be high
Peerin' into the sky,
But Katie's is fixed on the ground.
The bawbees she spies there below,
And buttons an' pins in a row,
So close to the earth,
Gives her senses more worth,

She can hear the very grass grow.

Old Malabar
One bawbee more the ball goes up,
I heard the strange, loud shout,
I aye scratched my head in wonder there
At what it's all about.
Above the crowd this heavy ball
Did in the skies ascend—
And shoot it fall upon his head,
His very life will end.
Higher, higher, higher still,
The spool went up and up,
And when it fell he caught it in
A solid leather cup.
This cup was strapped around his brow,
On each side an old scar.
Dearth may drive some folk to drink,
But not Old Malabar.

Old Hawkie
O gather around till I tell you my tale
O' the times I was jovial an' hearty and hale,
But this prick-the-louse tailor's attention was such
That I limp around the town on this tattered auld crutch.

At Glasgow Green fairings or doon by the Green,
That's where the bold Hawkie's aye tae be seen,
Wi' hundreds around him and many a fool
Come to learn what he should have been taught at the school.
They ask me conundrums about this, about that:
What is the stars, an' who belled the cat?
The craziest questions an' that sort o' kind,
Would drive a feelosopher oot o' his mind.
But they can't stump Old Hawkie, not one little bit,
To answer their riddles I'm able and fit,
If ye want come an' try me, I'm aye to be seen
Doon by Airn's Well at the foot o' the Green.

The Glasgow Clincher
A braw auld man,
A dandy in his day,
The only Glasgow man wi' proof

His heid was n ot astray.
Sauchiehall Street was his pitch—
He often dandered there;
At times he took a longer route
Doon tae St Enoch's Square.
He wrote an' sold his ain newssheet,
'The Clincher' it was called,
An' mony's the time afore the Court
The brave auld chap was hauled.
Some know their Royals, some their luck
An' some a load o' corn,
But if the Clincher ye did miss
Ye werenae Glesca born!

JOHNNY AND THE STARLINGS

The poor hungry starlings once held a convention,
and so famed far abroad was old Glasgow's renown
that is showing of cards proved a million in favour—
the Clyde was the place where they'd all settle down.

So they came with the aunties and uncles and cousins,
they came with their distant relations and friends,
the fortunate first had the Kelvin to choose from,
while the poor lonesome stranglers just got single-ends.

But they treated old Glasgow in a manner revolting,
the buildings they messed on, oh my, I declare
I never once saw such conduct outrageous,
such strange goings-on and in front of the Square.

On Bobby Peel's statue, him that founded the polis,
on no lesser than him, their droppings went home,
and how low can you get when your natural instincts
showers down disrespect on the Lord Provost's dome.

Oh, they picked out their targets with shocking abandon,
they spared not their betters in grandeur or wit;
I shudder to think if grandpapa had seen it,
his darling, Victoria, all covered in grit.

We built wire meshing to vex and torment them,
then we coaxed and cajoled them and begged them to clear
but you might have been talking to poor Paddy's Milestone,
they turned up their noses and just wouldn't hear.

Then up rose Johnny Cameron, a man by the river,
a starling Pied Piper if ever there was one,
by a power of cunning of his own machination,
he cleared out the vandals before he was done.

Some say it was witchcraft, some say it was science,
some say just a torch that in Woolies he bought,
but none will dispute the fact of contention,
'tis certain he cleared this affliction we'd got.

Oh, London may have them along with our headaches,
or Belfast, where sorrows are more than their share,

but I'll swear that St Mungo through a porthole of heaven
will not see a starling parading George Square.

'Now, pay up', says Johnny to the City Corporation,
'for many cauld nights an' me working like hell!'
But the cute City fathers, wage-paring and freezing
says, 'Johnny you've taught us so we'll do it wersels!'

Bad luck to ingratitude's snell, icy breezes,
the favours of fortune frowned dour and black,
'til he hit on a plan audacious and vengeful,
'I took out the starlings but I'll soon send them back!'

Now tenants of Glasgow, thereby hangs a story,
stand up for your rights and go forward like men.
When they increase your rates and send out your rent bills,
Like the bold Johnny Cameron, just return them again!

LET GLASGOW FLOURISH

Brave city on the Clyde, thorn of the tyrant,
And famed the far world wide
For gallant deeds wed to a homely hospitality!
I'll trace your course with Clyde and Molendinar
To its source, and from the infant stream
Of ancient days, wind down the shadowy maze of history.

Dim scenes of yore begin to flit and glide
In early morning light of old Strathclyde,
When Pict and Celt and a forgotten race
Defying time did once a legend trace
Down by the Fisher's Yett,
A thousand years ere Mungo's name was clept.
Along these streets brave Wallace led his men
'Til freedom's cry re-echoed hill and glen
In that first light'ning spark o' early morn
When Scotia's claim to nationhood was born.
And here upon the high Bell o' The Brae
Where Mercat Cross and Bishop's Castle lay,
There kindled soon that great heroic flame,
The proudest link in Glasgow's glorious name—
It shone for Bruce and brave Wiseheart the Good,
And later still a very multitude of martyr sons.

This was their town, a thousand souls or so,
Of six long centuries ago,
Prebend houses and Cathedral grey
Clustered on the legendary brae;
Whinstone and wattle, too, over-thatched with straw
Subjected to the rigours of church law.
So close to Caledonia's western hills,
Men grappled here a foe much sterner still—
The lave of ages,
Prince and prelate locked in earthly spoil,
And all the customary turmoil,
Descending clans long used to sharp conflict,
And all the rage the Southron might inflict,
We bore it here and still applied our crafts,
Made little boats and merchandising rafts,
To steer at first the shallow streams of Clyde—
Adventure's prelude to the oceans wide.

Slowly then from a sparse inland burn,
To where the mighty waves in tumult churn,
An arduous channel scooped by industry,
'Til Glasgow made her marriage to the sea.

LINES ON THE RAMSHORN KIRKYARD

Strange oasis in the city,
Neat and proud and well-preserved,
Lies in the Ramshorn kirkyard!
In it the dust of men who made Glasgow great,
Who sealed by a mighty word
The fate of some hapless weaver,
Who windward or with the breeze
Sent vast cargoes on the seas,
Or summoned armies to dispute
Both lowly cause and high repute,
Edging from the pavements grey
All lesser mortals in their way.
How low they lie!

Time, wind and weather,
Conspiring together,
Have all but effaced their name.
Their fame remains in tarnished history book
Or adorning some neuk in a seemingly heartless city.
Mostly they were without pity,
Creating their image and challenge to fame
And tears were no part of it;
They never cried 'Shame'
When Wilson's grey head hung high on his Cross,
Nor crept under darkness to Baird's distraught mother
Mourning the loss of her patriot son.

They carved out their glory in dross,
Dreaming their splendour and fame
Would remain like the story forever. How low they lie!
And under the darkening sky, the offices loom
To send them down deeper in shadow.

OLD SCOTIA

Years ahead, lets us draw the scene: An aged
man leaves Glasgow Green, and slowly then on
weary feet, stops for a breath in Stockwell Street.
Then from his eye there drops a tear, recalling
days o' folk spent here in times lang syne;
the ancient tenements are gone; wi' smeddum
still, the Clyde flows on, but all aroun' a
brighter scene where once but dark grey haunts
have been in his young day.

And from a house across the way, there sallies
forth a kindly lad enquiring why he looks so
sad. 'Young man,' the bearded one then said,
'I'm thinkin' noo o' folk lang dead. For on
this spot Old Scotia stood, and, ach, I'm in
a dreamy mood, as my wanderin' mind recalls
the merriment within its walls.

For here on many a Saturday, the low roof rang
wi' laughter gay, and, oh, how merry they could
be—these lads frae yaird an' factory. For this
was no your common pub o' boozers swillin' at
the tub, or dominoes an' flyin' darts. Here
came men o' many pairts.

Engineer and student came, an' some upon
the brink o' fame, an' some who wealth an' fame
despised lest their interest be enticed into
that web o' lure so wove, talent transforms to
treasure trove.

Here by the turn o' Howard Street, the minstrel
and the sage might meet, and in those days o'
which I dream, the lore o' music was supreme.
How the very roof-beams rang, re-echoin' many
an old Scots sang, as doon frae rugged crag an' glen
a ragged host o' Hielandmen, Cullodenmuir
made lean an' lankie, relived through strains o'
Killiekrankie, and helped restore a nation's
pride upon the busy banks o' Clyde. For here banjo,
guitar an' whistle upheld the glory o' the thistle

an' hairst upon the Lalland rig by magic's seen
at Glesga brig. Here were lads an' lassies bright,
langsyne ha'e faded frae my sight, an' that's for
why the sad tear falls, induced by memories I recall.

For where is Clydebank's bearded Mick, regaled us a'
wi' mony a trick, fantastic hoverin's in mid-air
that made even strangers stop and stare, an' then
applaud. The Scotia's heroes he gi'e fame gif in
the act himself became a kind o' God?

Or Campbell huggin' his guitar, elbow leanin' on the
bar, speers John the Host—Iain just back frae Germanie,
causin' new perplexity 'twixt truth an' boast?

Or where is Grimes' dark, rollin' eye, could raise
the subject to the sky, still be mundane?
Where are they now? Stockwell Street no langer
echoes wi' their feet—I search in vain.

Ah, gone those names we used recite in early days
with ardour bright as though tae light the gloom
o' night wi' saints an' sages.

But frae the shadows o' the mist, tho powers o'
dree my plan resist, I'll dip my pen an' mak a
list, my Book o' Ages.

Where is that young minstrel pair, Harvey Tam an'
Connolly there? What feasts o' music we wad
share—twa Humblebums? Your party try in vain
tae guard, you'd find them in your ain back-yaird come
doon the lum!
Or Al an' Stewart, brothers twain, who might be
found in Skerries' Lane, or drinkin' Guinness in
Dunblane wi' Johnstone Billy, or wi' yon hermit o'
Glencoe, tastin' strange old vines that grow by
Ossian's Cave an' Glendaroe would knock you silly,

Here patient Joe with brush an' shovel groped smithereens
amidst the hovel, an' sends some drunk's unsteady
feet tae stagger on the totterin' street; the night
wears on. Ah, friends an' cronies o' my day, where are
ye gone?

Here wi' his own merry band, the jovial Imlach used tae
staun, protected like some heirloom locket—he had a
bottle in his pocket, some fiery stuff wad roose the
devil an' sudden wars 'twixt Good an' Evil.

Mandolin and concertina, Grimes' rollin' eye transfixed
on Gina, the llltin' voices o' the throng rise with
an old sea-shanty song. Bush-bearded Vinnie holds the
wand—there's yin or twa can barely staun.

Wee Peter Feeney a glass the worse looks for pills
tae 'feed the horse'—man's friend now sunk so low
you'll see its shoes alone he'll guarantee. He damns
the polis, tho quite aware tae every word they're
listenin' there.

A wee bit rhymer tells his lays o' Croppy Boys an'
rebel days, an' hopes through clouds o' smoke an'
beers than Mankind's sense o' truth appears.

Outside, cold stars shine on the city. Inside a
world o' warmth an' pity—generous hands for a'
their sins wad fill the old age pensioners tins—
o' such, Old Scotia had her share, aye, aiblins mair
than onywhere.

And cam here upstarts o' the Clyde, we douced their
zeal an' damped their pride, spared not conceit nor
foolish fancies, but in the wake o' Poosie Nancy's,
the 'King or Country' raised nae cheer, we a' were
jolly beggars here.

The night must pass. Big Rab quick reaches for his
glass. The Clutha seek the 'rocky road', tae totter
hame tae their abode, while Willie Allan looks
aghast tae think the hours ha'e flown past. The
crowd now spates out on the street an' soon
the silence is complete.

Many years have long passed on, since Scotia
and its folk hae gone.' And here the old man
drew his breath. 'Many, many sunk in death.
Lads an' lassies o' the Clyde, ebbin' lives

jist like the tide! Some an earthly fame
acquired—some no higher rank aspired, children
of a toilin' race, who can ever tak your place—
the night wears on—friends an' cronies o'
my day, where are ye gone?'

PIONEERVILLE, HA! HA!

We used to be plain old Garthamlock,
But we had a fate to fulfill,
When Rosemary Lang made a visit
And named us the 'Pioneerville'

Immediately grass grew much greener,
Storms ceased and the air became still,
The bugs and the fleas put top hats on,
proud to be Pioneerville.

Indeed we have pioneers plenty,
You'll find there's a way and a will,
When it comes to screwing your meter
Or your car in sweet Pioneerville.

The hawks that hover our meadows,
Can teach us but little or nil,
We've past masters in every profession
Inhabiting Pioneerville.

They say that the toffs out in Bearsden,
Are queuing and anxious to full
The first vacant house in Dudhope Street
That haven in Pioneerville.

They say that our vandals are fewer,
Take that with some salt or the pill!
They're just waiting discharge from Barlinnie
To get into Pioneerville.

After midnight the streets seemed deserted,
You may count that a blessing until
The Hulk jumps out of the shadows,
And chibs you in Pioneerville.

In Pioneerville we've a barracks,
But not where braw soldiers can drill;
It hosts the old folk deserted
And lonely in Pioneerville.

In Pioneerville we've a Stab Inn,

Where the poor are you a powerful gill,
Oh, never dismount from your horse, man,
When you ride into Pioneerville.

We'd make C Muir mayor of our 'village',
But who would be left with the bill,
For they've stolen the gold chain of office
And pawned it in Pioneerville.

In Pioneerville, it is certain,
You will never be shifted until
The Housing agrees with Saint Gabriel
To transfer you from Pioneerville.

Freddy is known as the bard here,
Like others he's come through the mill;
That's why he writes truth and not rubbish
Of that oasis called Pioneerville.

So off with those rose-tinted glasses,
We'll never get over the hill,
Til tenants united demand it,
And make a real Pioneerville.

RAB'S IMPRESSION OF THE FIRST SUNDAY OPENING (OF THE VICTORIA BAR)

(In the Victoria, Moffat's bar, at Glasgow Brig, souvenir of an historic occasion, 23rd of October 1977)

I thocht the law wad ne'er be passed,
but help me, God, it's come at last,
an' take perdition we gang fast,
a skelping rate—
we'll save the unco-guid declare
wi' prattlin' prate.

Puir Holy Willie staunin' by,
wi' blasted wunner in his eye,
an' whether he should laugh or cry
he's fair perplexed,
but by the way he bites yon lip,
I'd say he's vexed.

John Knox and Calvin fume an' glower,
oh, wad tae God they had the power
tae be amang ye at this hour,
alas, alas.
Oh, why can't Paisley raise the stour
or Pastor Glass?

Noo by the Briggait I maun stroll
an' tak a Sabbath muster roll
tae see what Christians have tae thole
this dreadful day.
Tae think some drink an' damn their soul,
while they maun pray.

In Moffat's shop I see ye gather
this Sabbath for a hamely blether,
there's Stevie lad an' his auld faither,
tae rin the place,
an' wha wad dare take leave her oot,
we maun hae Grace.

I called tae look at Pat's next door,
an' fecht, there's boozin' there galore,

on that lane I set ma store—
it's no God's plan
tae set the gifts o' heaven before
that wee Wee Mann's.

An' Lynch's bar across the street,
They tell me is the angels' beat.
Och, ma surprise is maist complete
on sic a find.
I ne'er in ma twa hunner years did meet
ain o' their kind.

But here see Adam wi' his dram,
an' Laurie wi' his croney Sam,
an' fiddler Beaton cares a damn
for Sunday laws,
as lang as he's a pint tae cram
atween his jaws.

An' Freddy Graham, an' Bill an' Jean,
I ken noo whit devotion means,
the mair I gaze upon the scene,
nane can disprove.
The Sabbath day near Glesga Green
the spirits move.

Aye sae I hope it aye shall be,
untrammelled in oor customs, free
frae cant an' auld hypocrisy
in peace tae dwell.
An' free frae only company
makes life a hell.

SONG OF THE VICKY BAR

Ye may brag o' your Ritz an' your Waldorf Hotel,
bell-hops and plush carpets for the snob an' the swell,
but for down-to-earth patter and a friend to regale,
Ye can't whack the Vicky an' a pint o' real ale.

There's a wee pub in Glesga where the Briggait is nigh;
jist tag on Cy Laurie when he passes you by,
or that bloke with the fiddle, oor Willie's his name—
Then follow your nose an' ye'll soon be at hame.

Wi' Friends of the Earth ye can talk aboot whales,
or the Carrick beyont that nae langer has sails,
poetry and art an' the Scottish folk scene—
or join our great team for a game on the Green.

We left the Auld Scotia when that pub it went plastic,
for desperate diseases need remedies drastic,
we saddled oor horses and hoisted oor load
for the great expedition—jist over the road.

We have oor ain paper, an I don't want to brag
but the Record's just trash to the fine Vicky Rag;
now a wee Irish lad had us clients struck dumb,
When he says in his cups, 'it's to heaven I've come'.

But we nodded agreement, for the toon ye can snoop,
find service name better or a sandwich and soup,
and there's aye Paddy's Mercat if you're jaiket's for sale,
an' back tae the Vicky for a pint of real ale

THE BACK-STREETS OF GLASGOW

I saw in the back-streets of Glasgow
a child with a beauty her own,
akin to a lonely wild flower
'mong clefts in the rocks they're had grown.
And I blessed the odd whim of old Fortune
for planting that little child there
where folk unfavoured by riches
would find gold in the gleam of her hair.
And those gentle bright eyes would be treasures
amid sorrow and want and ill-health,
where the voice of that little one singing
would bring pleasures untarnished by wealth.

Years passed, I returned to that back-street—
the child in her beauty was gone,
and there stood a poor haggard creature
in a place where no sun ever shone.

THE NEW JAIL IN CARLTON PLACE, GLASGOW

Believe me this Glasgow's a wonderful town
with all the 'improvements' that's going around,
there's cafes and pubs that are open all day
but, my God, they don't half make a hole in your pay;
Glasgow's Miles Better, the smart guys declare!
Tell that to the poor on a bench in the Square!
But take caution, my friend, or you'll end up inside
the new polis jail on the banks of the Clyde.

There's thousands o' workless just roamin' the street,
and sickness and want you'll everywhere meet;
they're closing down schools and hospital wards
and with Fowler's cuts coming, there's more on the cards.
The big shots in London pretend they're too poor
but for their own ends, there's millions for sure,
bombs and destruction and great follies beside
like the new polis jail on the banks of the Clyde.

It's ugly, it's squat, just a horrid eye-sore,
a squalid grim fort and a blot on the shore.
They tell me they built it to scare folk from crime,
but yarns of that sort—sure they spread all the time;
but my hunch is a bunker for men of the Bar,
for judges and lawyers a shelter from war!
May fate on that day damn their pomp and their pride,
and blast the new jail on the banks of the Clyde!

One day for certain the truth will come out
and tell us for certain how that jail came about—
when they try to burst the unions, jail strikers and picket
all those who won't play their nice game of cricket.
Peace-marchers, protestors and folk of back-bone
who against tanks might dare raise a stone;
that day when the people at last will preside
despite your new jail on the banks of the Clyde .

WHERE IS THE GLASGOW THAT I USED TO KNOW

Where is the Glasgow that I used to know in the days of our youth
  so long long ago
When you sailed down the Clyde for a week, even more, with no thought
  in your mind of locking the door.
Where a man was a man and the women all friends, not each for themselves
  and serving their ends,
But proud of our city and the land of our birth
When the good folk of the Clyde were the salt of the earth.
Where is the Glasgow when we marched tae the green on May Days of old
  when great thousands were seen,
With red banners waving in a colourful stream
And each heart in the crowd cherished a dream.
Where are the shipyards? Where our great mills?
They've left us damn all but the booze and the pills!
They have drained the toon dry and left a dead letter,
where only Pat Lally smiles better and better.

Where is the Glasgow wi' jobs to be had, not poor, idle youngsters
  neglected and sad,
Stuck out in the wastelands of huge housing schemes wi' little hope left
  and bereft of their dreams.
Where is the Glasgow for which our forefathers strove, of kindness,
  compassion and brotherly love?
It is gone on the roadways and plush limousines, and they couldn't care less
  what our poverty means.

For the ills of the city, it's past time to mourn, and I hope that it's faults
  never return;
We have no tears to shed over poor 'no mean city', we've no time for
  do-gooders and slobbering pity.
We want homes for the homeless and real jobs for our youth, above all a city
  that welcomes the truth,
Where political gangsters no longer abide and honour's restored to the
  banks of the Clyde.

YA BASS

I am the giant of the tournament and slum,
created in your image, and quite numb
to finer human feeling.
I kill what time is healing,
like you I'm just a mean, a vicious crumb.
My razor is my little atom bomb,
Nor care I where the enemy is from.
Why create a fuss,
When he isn't one of us?
The Tongs relive the battle of the Somme.
I'm the leader of the Fleet, ya bass, pay heed!
My services perhaps you'll shortly need,
as in Sillitoe's employ
ranged the Brigton Billy Boy
and the Fuhrer found our kind a fruitful seed.
See that poor old wretch beneath the alley lamp,
Every wrinkle in his face bears your stamp.
Viciously we carve
What pitiless you starve.
To both of us he's but a common tramp.
yes, I'm nasty and I mean, but not a hypocrite.
'Neath a holy umbrella, I do not sit:
I've no army or police
To murder or to fleece,
And if I'm caught, I pay a price for it.
I haven't got a great big yellow press
Like you to hide my bloody wickedness.
I can't compete at all—
Just daft slogans on the wall.
Now, who's the bigger bastard?
Have a guess!

POLITICAL VERSE

A LETTER FROM AN AMERICAN CONVICT
TO PRESIDENT REAGAN

Dear Mister President,
I'm in here for a bit of a spell,
and, well, it's given me time to think things over—
Lord knows I ain't exactly sitting in clover—
but I've got a conscience and when I heard your speech,
it sure did reach me, like I was most overcome,
it moved me some, that bit about freedom
our willingness to die, just summed it all up—
I had a wet eye all the time listening.

I said, 'This guy knows what he's ranting about',
and then I smiled, 'Who knows but he's been up
the river himself for a while? He understands
what it means to get landed in trouble.'

Well, Mr President, I want you to know
We're with you, me and the boys,
and I ain't no small noise here. I count some.
Keep America free! That's what we say.
We'll fight for our right to be free any damn day.
We'll even die for it—yeah, here and now,
(Al and Pete are going to the gas-block anyhow,
so they're not chicken!) The sooner you quicken
the War the better—let the red bastards see
that we'd rather be dead than lose our liberty.
I'm in here for rape and assault, a few things beside,
but I swear, Mr President, I still can carry my pride,
I'm a true, full-blooded American, I'll fight to the ditch
'gainst any god-damn-Communist-son-of-a-bitch,
doesn't know what it means to be free,
out of chains, enjoying sweet liberty,
each one for himself, against everyone else,
a true son of a...
     ah, Jeesus, I wish I had a gun!

GEORGY PORGY

In the Labour hierarchy,
A vacuum seller he should have been
Two big ears and a gap between.

Georgy Porgy told great whoppers,
When canvassing among the shoppers;
He peddled poppycock and bunk,
But told the truth when he was drunk.

Georgy served the bosses well,
And serving them he served himsel'—
Thus he rose from the common horde,
And Georgy Porgy's now a Lord.

I say, old chap,
This Government
May be a trifle nuts,
But the way they fleece the workers
Shows they have guts!
I quite agree, old chum,
I quite agree,
A gut is quite essential
For a good MP,
Banquets and booze for them,
For them no cuts;
You tell the truth my friend,
They sure have guts.

HAWKS AND DOVES

To George (Jammy Dodger) Robertson and Brian (Corkscrew) Wilson.
Dedicated to their 'immoral memory'.

In a Scottish toon that's called Dunoon,
these twisters crooned the songs of peace,
Freedom praising—not Atom Bases—
Our hopes to raise for nuclear freeze.

Chorus:
This slimy pair of creatures rare
One feature share that the devil loves—
For wealth and fame—(to hell with shame!)
They're in the game of hawks and doves.

Now in power—this evil hour
When wars still glower, they turn their coats,
With voices strident, they back-up Trident
And sidle up to the Tory goats.

The dove forsaking, fat bribes they're taking,
Fortunes making, world peace they sell.
I only pray I'll see the day,
When the scoundrels pay in the depths of hell.

HOW DARE YOU, ALEX KITSON!

How dare you Alex Kitson,
Decry our land so dear!
Did you not tell the Russians
Of the freedom we have here?

Of this lovely land called Britain,
And our good old stocks and shares,
Where we're all so bloody happy
And none of us have cares?

Did you tell them of our blue blood?
Our titled and our snobs,
Our lovely class society,
And our vandalising mobs?

Did you tell them how our miners
Also happy with their lot,
And the sweet contented polismen
And fireman we've got?

Did you tell them, Alex Kitson,
In language clear and blunt,
How our freedom gives protection
To the Nazi National Front?

Did you tell them how our old folk
Have bunkers heaped with coal,
And our youngsters happy faces
As they queue up on the dole?

Did you speak of rising prices
And our social welfare cuts?
Or the Christian folk of Ulster
Where they hate each other's guts?

Did you mention Limey comics
And their endless Paddy joke?
Did you tell how much we Scotsmen
Enjoy the English yolk?

Did you speak about Polaris
And the hairies of Dunoon,

Of how we regard the arms race
As a blessing and a boon?

Did you mention Grundwick strikers
And the freedom for the scab
Or the loot that's here in Britain
For the wealthy sharks to grab?

Did you speak of true blue Tories,
And the Labour big sell-out,
How they sing The Red Flag anthem?
Aye, with marbles in their mouth.

Did you mention all such freedoms,
Like the freedom of the Press,
Where great liars have the freedom
To promote their wickedness?

Did you speak of Lords and Commons,
For well, it might be said,
We send no crooks to jail here
But to Parliament instead?

Did you tell the Russian people
To spare themselves the pains
Of trying to brainwash us,
For we haven't any brains.

MAGGIE MEETS HER MATCH

Maggie Thatcher died one day
and with her neck of brass
she thought that through those pearly gates
that she was bound to pass.

St Peter slammed the gates tight shut,
and stopped her with a grin.
'Naw if I open up for you, .
the devil I let in.'

And heaven is the home for souls,
good deeds end kindly things,
and Maggie, you have never earned
a harp or angel's wings.

Look how you stopped the children's milk,
but don't you seem well-fed—
a fitter corpse I never saw
for one who should be dead.'

St Peter read the Doomsday Book,
he read the pages through,
'Oh Maggie, I see Tory tykes,
but none as bad as you.'

You helped the rich get richer,
you trod upon the poor,
so heaven has no room for you,
not even at the door.

You raised the prices in the shops,
the unions you'd destroy,
and heaven is a friendly place,
of peace and love and joy.'

St Peter had another look,
'My God, you're quite a witch,'
'Your hair it may be blonde,' he said,
'You're deeds are black as pitch.

'You tried to ban Olympic Games,

you'd spoil the world of sport,
and Maggie, we've no halo here
for any of your sort.

'But if it's war and hate you want,
a place to suit you well
is hotter regions down below
where you can kick up hell.'

Poor Maggie took her bags and climbed,
climbed down the golden stair,
but Old Nick stood with his pitch-fork
and stopped her coming there.

'Oh, Maggie, we have heard of you
from every kind of source,
and though our hell's a wicked place,
you'd make it ten times worse,'

So Maggie wanders round the world,
still burdened down with sin—
for Pete or Nick are not the fools
who voted Maggie in.

PAT LALLY'S GOLDEN CHAIN (THE MELTING OF IT)

Deprived of the glory he basked in,
Like a Royal that's losing his crown,
Pat Lally is fuming with anger,
And he looks on his chain with a frown.

No longer seems Glasgow 'miles better',
The provost snorts hate for 'his town',
Mr Happy grabs hold of that gold chain,
And starts melting the bloody thing down.

Know how to dispose of the pieces
(He hides a big chunk for himself)
And thinks of old 'comrades' in office,
And some he won't leave on the shelf.

Robin Cook is the first of the favoured,
To help take his dolly abroad,
And then Tony Blair is rewarded
In his New Labour role as a god.

George Robertson, pudding-faced chancer,
Is next on Lally's prize list,
For no-one will share in Pat's bounty,
Unless he is able to twist.

No chauvinist pig is our Provost,
There are women MPs in the game—
Helen Liddell, the crook Maxwells crony,
And Harman, the private school dame.

There's a chunk for Clare Short and ham Glenda,
So back once again to the men,
Brian Wilson, ex-Polaris protester,
Who is itching to get into Number 10.

There's a lump for the MP in Govan,
The fraud they are trying to ban,
And 'sugar dad' Wray will get 'compen',
For his rent-bung to Stevie McCann.

And the Provost remembers his sidekicks,
Who fiddled the books nearer home,

The first of the batch, Tommy Monaghan,
With the skill of an old Zurich gnome.

Yet before he had shared all the booty,
Among such a fine, noble tribe,
Pat, lest he land in Barlinnie,
Kept enough for his jailers to bribe.

As Lazarus once rose from his coffin
And started with joy among men,
Lally hopes to repeat the performance,
And fiddle all over again.

MORAL:
If the people of Glasgow vote scoundrels,
And whatever the party they serve,
Our city will sink in the gutter,
A fate that our follies deserve.

SQUIBS, SKITS AND EPITAPHS

On A Nitwit Called Lally
Ancient times God sent the plague
Into our sinful valley,
In modern times for Glasgow's crimes,
He just sent Patrick Lally!

The Mean Sod
Old mother Hubbard went to the cupboard
To fetch a wee dram to restore her,
When she got there, the cupboard was bare—
Pat Lally had got there before her!

Pat's Prayer
'I've only one complaint, dear Lord
Only one complaint—
Get Tony Blair to knight me, Lord
Before I'm made a saint'.

On The Traitor, Jimmy Reid
A little bit of dirty muck
Fell from the sky one day,
And it collected poisonous gems
As it's sped on its way
It landed here in Clydeside
To germinate it's seed,
And that in brief's the origin
Of the creep called Jimmy Reed!

Kier Hardy's Cloth Cap
The cloth cap image of old Kier is gone
As the yuppies of Labour move up and move on!
They now blush in shame at such 'socialist' follies
As the join the brigade of bowlers and brollies.

On A Not So Poor Clare
Clare Short has got the perfect name
To suit New Labour planners:
She is very short on principles
And shorter still in manners.
Auditioned once for Hollywood,
Success seemed in her claws,

For all agreed she was typecast
For the leading role in 'Jaws'.

Janey Buchan, Labour MEP
Gentle, gracious and good-looking
That's no me I'm Janey Buchan!
Twenty years of Labour lolly
Has made me not a whit more jolly.
Starting off I was no toff,
But finally succeeded;
To clear the deck, a hard brass neck
Was all I really needed.

Epitaph On Donald Dewar
Here lies the bones of bampot Dewar,
A blethering gasbag that's for sure;
An oxygen supply will come about,
When Donald finally shuts his mouth.
Labour lawyer was his game.
Lawyer? Liar? Both the same!

On Hugh Gaitskill MP
Gaitskill came to Glasgow,
On nuclear bombs to blether;
Halfway through, he lost the cue
And talked about the weather.

On Tony Blair
Shakespeare said: 'a man can smile and smile and still be a villain.'
Blair grins and grins and grins
So much so that
He quite resembles the Cheshire Cat.
Q. Would you purchase a second-hand car from him?
A. No not even a second hand tail lamp.
Blair is an apt name for a politician.
It reminds one of a foghorn and a loud-mouth.

New Labour's Rose Emblem
No more for us the strong clenched fist
Or the scarlet banner;
We've jettisoned true principles
In a most spineless manner;
We've wrecked the sturdy socialist ship

Upon the treacherous rocks
And now we gull the public with
The rose off a chocolate box.

On Lord Alex Hume
The life story
Of this high Tory
Is certainly no mystery,
Or history of any consequence.
He helped Chamberlain
On that wretched paperchase
To Munich,
And thought Hitler a man of his word.
In his tomb
Lies coffin-faced Hume.
And what's more,
His most famous ancestor
Was a royal whore.

On The House Of Lords
Were even an atom bomb to fall,
These bastards wouldn't wake at all,
And should it fall, 'twould bounce and flick
off their skulls so dense and thick.

On Neil Kinnock (The Welsh Rabbit)
Neil Kinnock is not dead they say
(So I am over-ruled)—
If I am wrong and Neil's alive,
He certainly had me fooled.

On Pat Lally
In ancient days,
God sent to plague
Into our sinful valley.
In modern times,
For Glasgow's crimes,
He sent us Patrick Lally.

On Robert Maxwell
He examined his employees
To find if they were red,
And then one day he ran away,

And dived into the med.
Before he dived (I almost forgot to mention)
He stole the workers' pension.

Political Twins
Tory and Labour walk hand in hand,
They both are London bred,
What is a shade of royal blue,
And the other a royal red.
The Union Jack is their banner proud—
You can't tell them apart—
John Bull's rich blood runs in their veins
And links them heart to heart.
They shadow-box in Parliament—
That's sheer hypocrisy,
For one's an old friend, Tweedledum,
And the other, Tweedledee.

Farewell To Old Labour
Farewell to Old labour from Shetland to Dover,
The lawyers and con-men have taken it over.
No longer the worker has a say in its plan,
For careerists and sharpers are there to a man.
It's ranks now include the scab and turncoat,
For they use the word 'Labour' to wheedle a vote.
What a sell-out in principle! What a perilous state,
When a party-tagged clown is your next candidate.

On Lord Georgy Porgy Brown
George Brown was sozzled in parliament,
As drunk as drunk can be,
But his ambition was to make
His mark in history.
'For your service to Labour, what can I grant?'
Asked the grateful prime minister when
On retiring George was aspiring
To be the most honoured of men.
'Could you make me a peer?' said George with a leer,
'Please grant me that noble accord,
So that I can boast that among many toasts,
I often was drunk as a Lord.'

On 'Jammie Dodger' Robertson MP
Jammie Dodger Robertson whose face is well kenned

As Blair's message boy to Scotland for many a devious end,
Crows frantic with his promises (and you'd be daft to heed him),
You offer you the moon and stars, everything but freedom!

On Labour Tax Collectors
If labour so obediently
Collect the taxes
The Tory tykes inflict,
One can safely predict,
They'll jump to their toes
To collect the taxes they themselves impose,
And in fear of lost votes and shame,
Circulate stories to blame the Tories,
Who in turn will blame them;
That trick will never fail—
The old dog bites it's tail.

On John Smith
In Iona holy Isle John Smith now lies in clover,
When Labour claims its honours, since and kings move over!
Hymns of praise and accolades keep piling on and on
That even paradise itself seems small reward for John.
Incredible such tributes were earned by mortal man,
A politician too at that—what a strange phenomenon!

When Labour Wins
When Labour wins in '97,
And you dream you're on the verge of heaven.
When life remains the same and worse
And Tony Blair is proved a curse.
Will you regret
The chance for Independence lost,
And England gains at Scotland's cost;
Will you regret your wasted vote
And squirm to see the tourist gloat
At your dismay.
Electing a turncoat party which
Throws principle in the ditch
And hopes betray?

On The Gang Of Four
Long years in the Labour Party
Pretending they were Socialist

What a strange ironic twist
That the Labour Party leaders
(The bleeders!)
Are most vigilant with Militant,
Whilst the right-wing Gang of Four
Bored to the very core
And only resigned when it undermined
And could do no more damage.

My True Advice
Scots wha hae wi' Wallace bled,
Scots war Bruce has aft-times led,
Seize this chance to forge ahead
And vote for liberty!
Ignore fake Labour and bluff Tory,
Lib-Dem lies sae false and hoary,
Chase them frae Wick an' Tobermory,
An' set auld Scotland free!

On John Major
He is anything but major
Except in name.
He will acquire riches and fame
(More like infamy in reality)
But in every worthy quality,
Such as life, verve and vigour,
Major will be a very minor figure

The CPGB
This high-sounding title
Two whopping lies narrates—
The CP is not communist,
And Britain's far from great.

They Claim John Smith Was Honest
They claim John Smith was honest,
He loved the poor and meek,
But he also loved his MP's job
And two thousand quid a week!

On Churchill
The English worshipped Churchill
And did him so applaud,

No wonder Winnie thought himself
On equal terms with God.

*What Jonathan Swift Thought What Of Churchill's
Ancestor—The Duke Of Marlborough*
True to his profit
And his pride,
He made folk weep
Before he died.
(So why weep afterwards?)

On Thatcher
Hard heart,
Hard face,
A sickly disgrace
Not just to England
But the human race.

On Jimmy Reid
God found a bit of dung one day
Where crawly maggots breed
He gave it a kind of human shape
And called it Jimmy Reid.

On Norman Buchan MP
He was a folk collector,
A long, long time ago,
And he wrote a jolly jingle
'Oh, let Ramensky go!'
But as Minister of Prisons,
He changed his mind you see—
He put another lock on John
And threw away the key.
Norrie was a teacher
And in a sorry fix,
So he climbed the social ladder
By the art of politics.
Back in the streets of Glasgow
His lonely wife did dwell,
So not to pine in sorrow
She joined the game as well.
I hope you are not weeping
(Don't want to make you cry)

But on two hefty pay-pokes,
They managed to get by.
They still believed in equal rights
As Labour leaders must,
And no beggar at their door
Was ever refused—a crust!

On The Tory Sex Scandals
One would scarcely credit
They were sexually sinister,
When you see them on the telly
Debate at Westminster.
Bawling out 'Madam Speaker'
Or 'a point of order, please!'
Jumping up and down
Like circus performing fleas,
Antics that make you laugh
Though quite unfunny—
What could any women see in them?
Brains? Or looks? No—money!

Practice Makes Perfect
'What a tangled web we weave
When first we practice to deceive'.
But keep it up with firm intent
And you find a seat in parliament.

On Lord Porgy Georgy Brown (Gaitskill's Sidekick)
To seat George in the Upper House
May seem a bit absurd,
But think again—George often was
As drunk as any Lord!

On A Famous Warmonger
'Your country calls you',
Kitchener shouts,
'So join up and be brave!'
We asked him where our country was
And he pointed to the grave.

On Janey Buchan
To listen to Jane Buchan
Is not my brand of fun:

Her library stocks a thousand books—
I doubt if she read one.
It's better far to talk with her
Than cross the river Jordan,
Unless the Lord gives her lockjaw
You'll never get a word in.

Red Flag—Pink Rose!
They've turned the red flag to pale pink,
And sold the people down the drink,
And serving rich folk till they die,
They'll keep the cost of living high.
What marked difference can you see
Twixt Tweedledum and Tweedledee!
One bends the rules, the other twists them,
And they both serve the rotten system.

Another Smarty in the Party
(Some socialist this guy!)
'I oppose the Tories',
Said the labour hack,
And then in the office,
As soon as he got back,
He phoned the Sheriff
To provide facts
For the Tory poll tax,
And sent out mail
For another warrant sale.

After Almost Two Years Of Labour Cuts And Lies
From John o' Groats to Dover,
The rich have taken over,
For Labour, Lib or Tory,
It's just the same old story.
The wealthy pile up billions,
While it's poverty for millions.
Crock MPs propel the gravy chain,
Tony and all his cronies
Are a set of bloody phonies,
If you vote for them,
You've water on the brain!

THE HERO OF HOSPITALITY INN

I'll sing you a song
Of Hospitality Inn
That's the name of the place
And the source of the din.
The fat Labour frauds
Sat down there to dine,
To guzzle their grub
And swig back their wine.
A hundred quid each
Would pay for the stew,
And, of course, party funds
Would benefit too.
Then they'd sit and applaud
And with marbles in mouth
They'd sing 'The Red Flag'
And put Tories to rout.
On lashings of booze
And sparkling champagne
They'd double the seats
That Labour would gain.
Pretending to stand
For the Brit working class
Well in fact they are kissing
The fat Tories' arse.
But a Baillieston comrade,
Courageous and bold,
And who, unlike them,
The great cause has not sold;
He gatecrashed their banquet,
Which he cried a disgrace,
And then to their horror
Flung the truth in their face.
Janey Buchan collapsed
And she caused quite a scare,
They couldn't restore her,
There was only hot air.
John Smith he turned livid,
Not only from drink,
His fat jowls kept changing,
To all shades of pink,
And pudding-faced Lally

Was kneeling in fear,
And praying to God
That pal Winning was near.
The jittery Dewar then took the frights
And ran to the lavvie with some other shites.
He was stopped at the door and cried aghast, 'crumbs,
This place is full up with dozens of bums'.
Pandemonium broke loose all over the place
And Labour behaved up to form—a disgrace.
Cowardly, spineless—a self-serving crew,
The banner as ever—the red, white and blue.
But here's to our hero—the bold Jimmy Friel,
Who to his credit said what we feel.
The only sound man that emerged from the din,
And truly the Hero of Hospitality Inn.

THE KNIGHTING OF HAROLD WILSON

'Darkness shall descend upon the land and the evil be signified by whelps guised in red apparel, chaunting songs of labour outside their ken, and receiving pay-noney for their mean an devious services in the form of knighthoods and lordships among the highest in the land, when duke and dastard shall dine together'—Merlin's Prophecies

>Queen Liz has taken a shining sword
>above the podgy little man,
>'Methinks thou art the oddest knight
>since chivalry began!'
>
>'Oh, did thou ride to the joust, Sir Harold,
>or did thou tilt on the green?
>I swear to God at my tournaments
>thy face I ne'er have seen.'
>
>'Oh, I never rode to the joust, ladye,
>and I never rode to the joust,
>but I rode right high on the workers' backs
>and gave the rich a boost.'
>
>'And Harold, where is thy shining lance?
>and what is it all about.
>I see no weaponry at all
>but a dead pipe in your mouth!'
>
>'Oh, ladye fair, I bear no lance,
>and I never rode at the rings,
>but no lance nor sword did your servant need
>to make a prick of things.'
>
>Sir Harold rose a belted knight,
>as smugly as they come,
>for this great honour from the Queen,
>he almost kissed her bum.
>
>But lightning struck from darkening clouds,
>and a black storm hove in sight,
>and a voice arose from the throngs around,
>'Oh, lord, what a dirty knight!'

THE LABOUR CROCODILES

When Major was robbing the public
we voted for Labour to win
and then these traitors turned Tory
as soon as the bastards got in!

'Conservative Sleaze' was their war-cry
as they shed sham crocodile tears,
for now these two-faced careerists,
are themselves in sleaze shit to their ears.

They used to condemn nuclear weapons
with slogans quite bitter and strident,
but now like the old Tory warmongers
they're still spending billions on Trident.

Glenda Jackson, the hard hearted actress
insults the fisherman's wife,
but Jackson's pretence to be Labour,
is the greatest fake act in her life.

And Harman the private school lover,
a most Christian-Socialist soul,
is using sweet smiler Blairs hatchet,
for chopping the lone parents dole.

If in their very first year holding office,
they show such a vile wicked trend,
I shudder to think of the future,
and how low these ass-holes will descend.

THE MEAN DEVIL—MAGGIE!

I know it's hard to credit,
but truth to you I tell,
Maggie was an angel
before she went to hell.

For heaven is God's Kingdom
way up in outer space,
but Maggie thought she'd oust Him
and try to take his place.

She had a row with Jesus,
the words were very sharp,
for she clipped the wings of cherubs
and stole the angels' harps.

Now Jesus he was angry
and he did bawl and yell,
'Because you have been mean up here,
I'm sending you to hell.'

So Maggie got her pitchfork,
went down the golden stair,
and planned within her Tory mind
to cause some trouble there.

She raised the cost of fuel bills,
and raised the price of coal,
she sacked wee devils out of spite,
and put them on the dole.

The devil's then in anger cried,
'This women we don't like!'
they threw their pitchforks on the floor,
and they came out on strike.

Old Satan he grew furious,
like Jesus he did yell,
he caught mean Maggie by the legs
and threw her out of hell.

She spun and spun and outer space,

without a place to go,
and that is how she came to end
on our poor earth below.

And now she's got herself entrenched,
the saddest truth I'll tell,
here she's caused more trouble than
in heaven or in hell.

So now we've learned our lesson
and know what it's about,
let's join the imps and angels
and kick old Maggie out.

THE OLD LAG'S AMBITION

(Sung to the air 'it will never come out in the washing')

I am an old lag from Barlinnie,
And I'd rob a blind man of his tinnie,
But guided by fate,
I am now going straight,
For the sake of a foozie called Minnie.

To be Provost of Glasgow
My credentials are sound,
I have three murder raps,
And I have crippled two chaps—
So I hail from the perfect background!

Your Dollans and Lally's were Paddies,
A pair of contemptible haddies.
Why not vote for me,
And I promise to be,
The pick of the best of the baddies.

Your Mosson is merely a climber,
Shoplifter and sneaky small-timer.
Why encourage such crap,
When in me you've a chap,
A stoater, a stool and a stymer.

And I'll wear Glasgow's gold chain,
And carry more guns than John Wayne.
If you dare to protest,
And I speak not in jest,
You are dead if you dare to complain!

THE REAL TERRORIST

Mr. Reagan screws up his ugly ham-actor's face.
He says the Russians are a disgrace
To the civilisation that he knows,
And mock sincere the liar blows
A trumpet for the USA
A bloated nation in decay,
Murders, muggings, dope and rape!
Astounded, Frankenstein would gape
At such a vile, a wicked creature
The brute is writ in every feature.
In the mirror Reagan will find
One source of terror to Mankind.

THE RED FLAG

(A special version for the tour is masquerading as Labour leaders.
With apologies to Jim Connell, author of the magnificent original.)

The people's flag is deepest red,
The colour that we 'Labour' dread—
We have usurped that standard proud
Do make of it a burial shroud.

We've dug a grave for Labour's dream—
The glint of gold is now our gleam;
Forgotten now is Labour's source,
And we don't care one tinker's curse.

And did you think we'd let you grow,
The end of Capital to sow;
We joined your ranks; our poison spread
Until your movement's nearly dead.

Oh yes! We'll raise the banner high,
But first its folds we'll stain and dye;
We'll stain it to a dirty hue
Of Mother England's royal blue.

Good principles aside we pitch;
We rob the poor to feed the rich—
And as the pinch of hunger's felt,
The poor must tighten in their belt.

But Labour Lords and Knights? God! No!
The rules are made for those below;
We don't include in our 'fair' scheme
Those bellies bursting at the seam.

You often praise your matyred dead;
Our field of battle is the bed,
Our generous gift to all Mankind
Is just the stink we leave behind.

The Red Flag we may bawl and shout;
We still have marbles in our mouth

And as we stand in Labour's name,
Our faces should be read with shame.

PS
Trade union bosses off your knees!
Don't serve this lot like wretched fleas!
Scanlan, Gormley all the rest—
We no have put you to the test!
Then raise the real red banner high!
Beneath its shade we'll live or die.
Though Labour flunks and Tories sneer,
We'll keep the red flag flying here.

THE WORKER'S PRAYER

Thatcher is my shepherd,
I shall not want,
She leadeth me beside still factories,
She'd depriveth me of oil,
She guided me to the pass of unemployment for the party's sake
I fear no evil for thou art against me,
She anointest my wages with freezes,
So that my expenses runneth over my income,
Surely poverty and hard living shall follow and I
Shall dwell in a rented house forever.
Five thousand years ago Moses said:
'Park your camel, pick up your shovel, and mount your ass;
And I will lead you to the promised land'.
Five thousand years later, Roosevelt said:
'Lay down your shovel, sit on your ass and smoke your Camel,
  This is the promised land.'
Today, Thatcher will take your shovel, sell your camel, kick your ass,
  and tell you there is no promised land.
I am glad I am British, I am glad I am free,
But I wish I was a dog and Thatcher was a tree.

TWO OF A KIND

Michael Foot is Tweedledum,
And Healey Tweedledee,
And both of them would undermine
Real labour policy
The press applause them loudly,
While Benn bears all it's wrath,
For he won't let the labour cause
End up the garden path.
Oh, it's grand to be in Parliament,
And pocketing your pay,
Scuttling your principles
And eager to betray.
'Tis grand to be in Parliament,
Put there by people's trust,
And then discard your promises
And turn their dreams to dust.
How miserable such renegades
Of socialist pretence
Who sell out Labour's heritage
For Tory recompense.
Just hear the howling jackals all
Now slander Tony Benn,
For he belongs to that band
Of good and honest men.
So rally to the banner brave
And to their tricks be wise,
Labour must not tolerate
Vile Tories in disguise.
Beware of their low tactics,
Remembering, to win,
Twas Foot and Healey and their ilk
Who let the Tories in.
Labour soon can forge ahead
And this will come to pass,
When Labour serves its real support—
The British working class.

Reading the Easterhouse *Voice*

With Isobel, 1951

Cover of *At Glasgow Cross*

opposite psge:

Illustration for *The Blackberry Man*, Jim Gagahan

Illustration featuring Oiney Hoy, Fred Crayk

THE BLACKBERRY MAN

Photographed for the cover of *Oiney Hoy*

With Jim Friel and Janette McGinn

OINEY HOY

OINEY HOY

This is the story of a boy with a nickname that he did not like one wee bit until one strange day when he met a bold fellow by the name of Shaun at a Wake. Oiney Hoy was the boy's sobriquet in his native village, Creevan, in the very heart of Ireland. I was about to call it a God-forsaken wee place, but that would be a lie. Nature endowed Creevan, which is the Gaelic word for twig or little branch, with two lovely lakes surrounded by frail reeds and three small hills, one of which, with its mantle of bluebells and green ferns reflected in the still waters, is like a vision of fairyland.

No! Creevan was not forsaken by God or Nature, but by the rich landowners of Ireland, so that for centuries the poor had to leave home and search for work in foreign lands. Oiney Hoy's grandmother, however, was able to remain in Creevan, where she sold apples and oranges and bananas. She had a fruit stall in the Market Square, and woe betide you if you passed without buying some of her goods. She would hurl sharp stinging invective after your retreating figure and even lambast your poor dead ancestors. It was a tongue like hers put the curse on Cromwell that his warts would bleed venom and a restored monarch dance on his grave. On the three braes of Creevan she was known to every man, woman and child as 'The Holy Terror'.

The original Oweney Hoy, pronounced 'Oiney Hoy' in Creevan, was a poor, old amadhaun, or green fool, of the Carrick Hills to the south of the village. A tall, thin, bony man, like Don Quixote, and strange enough in his own way, he lived about a hundred years ago in a tumbledown, thatched shed on a bleak hillside. Of his many eccentric deeds, one is especially remembered for its quaintness in that remote countryside. Oiney spread the word around the Carrick Hills that, on a coming Sunday, he was going to die for Ireland. The event, he said, would take place in the Long Meadow below the chapel after second Mass. At first the wise old folk shook their heads from side to side, and said, 'How in God's name can he die for Ireland when there's not an empty gallows or a redcoat around for miles?' The antics of the poor fool, however, drew a score or two to the Long Meadow that Sunday. There they saw Oiney, stripped to the waist and standing about fifty yards to the side of a cutting filled to near the brim with black bogwater. In a few minutes he was turning his wild sky-blue eyes to the gawking spectators: 'You all forget the men o' '98 an' the bold Fenian men, for the priests don't tell you everythin', do they?' he shouted.

'What about the Famine, Oiney?' cried a smart young wag as he ran to hide behind a bank of turf. 'Do you remember that, Oiney?'

'Oiney remembers the lot! God bless Wolfe Tone an' Napper Tandy!'

Then he blessed himself three times and wearing no shoes or stockings made a mad run for the bog-hole. A mighty cheer arose from the astonished crowd when Oiney took off in a great leap. Some of them even blessed themselves. The folk of the Carrick Hills were as fervent devotees of sport as religion but they had never seen such a jump. The cheers of delight continued, but in the midst of the happy host, poor Oiney looked lost and bewildered. Then the priest came down from the chapel gates and, lifting his clothes and shoes, led the sad hero out onto the road, back to his lonely hillside shack.

A few years later Oiney died, but his leap and his strange antics became a rich memory around the turf-fires of many a home in Carrick on a cold winter's night. I remember hearing these tales when, as a boy of seven, I lay in the wooden box-bed in my aunt's kitchen watching the peat flames send the shadows flickering across the rafters high in the hills. 'Oiney's Lepp', as it was called locally, became a well-known landmark, like the priests' Mass Rock from the Penal Days. Then a peculiar thing happened., As each generation cut more peat, the famous bog-hole in the Long Meadow extended and Oiney's feat became more amazing. Wide-eyed school-children would stare in wonder at the great feat of their antecedent. Even the scholarly folklorists up at Trinity College in Dublin took a lively interest in the phenomenon when 'Oiney's Lepp' extended the whole length of the Long Meadow to become a superhuman marvel, rivalling the great, magic wonders, of Finn and Cuchulainn. Its growing importance can be illustrated by the fact that Oiney's Lepp became the subject of a three-inch footnote in Professor Seagull's great work, *An Oral History of Our Time* (Chapter 8: Legend Becomes Myth).

Oiney's strange character survived as well, and in a somewhat similar manner. With the growth of a small-scale industry in the neighbouring villages and towns, quite a number of the Carrick hill-folk descended into Creevan and became residents there. They seldom forgot their origins, however. When, for example, a trembling offspring of theirs wet the school floor on examination for First Communion or some such innocent mishap, a Creevan mother would exclaim in anger, 'Shamin' your dacint mother an' father is it? Makin' wather on the Master's clane floor! My God, but you're every bit as daft as Oiney Hoy.'

It was only with the Holy Terror's grandson, however, that the name really stuck. A tall, rather slim, gangly lad with large, innocent blue eyes, red hair and hundreds of freckles, his small mouth was ever agape in amazement at the strange world in which he found himself walking. The name clung to him like his large jutting ears and ran after him as well, playing tig with his own shadow on the summer streets of Creevan. And indeed, by a very strange metempsychosis, some of the quaint spirit of the poor, green fool of the Carnck Hills took possession of him. This quite naturally annoyed his granny who was always complaining that already there were more than enough fools in the world. It was just that he was never out of trouble.

The first time was when he was seven years old. She had bought him an emerald green jersey which was meant to serve a double purpose—his First Communion and the Hibernian Rally to the town of Cavan. The latter event was always a great day of glory for her on these occasions. She carried a magnificent green banner with a golden harp embroidered on it, joining the bands as they marched through the street playing 'The Harp That Once Through Tara's Halls' and 'Let Erin Remember'. God bless Tommy Moore, she' would say to herself. He knew the words and tunes to make the heart glow. Me harp as well he's talking about. Me harp that once through Cavan streets its soul of music shed. She did not understand deeply the politics of it all but she had a great picture of the Irish martyr-hero, Robert Emmet, over the mantelpiece in the kitchen. She had no love for Orangemen. She thought them as much Irish as the Eskimos of the frozen north or the poor aborigines of the Bush.

The boy with the emerald jersey joined three of his pals to explore one of the lakes beside Creevan. There was a secret labyrinth known only to them which ran past the swans' nest among the golden reeds. A large white upturned enamel bath had drifted in near the shore. It had probably been discarded by the local Protestant minister who wore grey spats, or by some other well-to-do; poor Catholics had only coarse zinc ones. The delighted boys hauled their find into the reeds. They filled the plughole and a smaller, rusty-edged opening with a yellow putty-like clay from the bank. From the long fresh rushes on the lakeside they wove lengths to attach to the bath through the tap-hole. Certain now that they were the owners of a seaworthy vessel, they unanimously elected Oiney to be the gallant skipper of the mighty craft on its trial run.

'Heave ho, me hearties,' they shouted. 'All aboard!' Even though, with the exception of Oiney, all of them were safely ashore.

They pushed the bath clear of the reeds into the freshwater lake under a burning sun. The snow-white swans floated gracefully beside their nest, eyeing the boy and his crazy boat suspiciously; he was aware that if aroused they could give a powerful blow with their wings. The young mariner, however, was too elated by his adventure to worry about wind, weather or waterfowl. Then, quite suddenly, dramatically, the yellow clay putty began to dissolve and shift. His short pants became soaking wet; the bath sank under him and he was left floundering and splashing in the water. His pals hauled him ashore. Soaked to the skin, he stood shivering on the hillside, not so much from the cold water but from fear of the Holy Terror: 'Oh God, she'll murdher me!' he cried. 'As soon as she lays hands on me, she'll murdher me. Oh, me good new green gansey. Would you look at it?'

'Naw, naw,' said one of the boys. 'We'll dry you out on the hill here an' she doesn't need to know a thing about it.'

He sat naked on the grass, while his friends made a close circle around him to hide him from view and keep the news of his shipwreck from the ears of his granny. Soon his clothes dried out in that hot July sky over Ireland, and all seemed to be going well. He dressed himself hurriedly, and then looking down at his clothes, groaned in dismay. 'Oh, holy God, would you look at me new gansey!'

The boys all stared in amazement. The green jersey had shrunk six inches in the drying process. 'Me arms were never that long,' cried poor Oiney. 'I can never go home to her like this.'

One of the boys had a brainwave: 'I know what,' he shouted triumphantly. 'You can tell her you just grew out of it. That's it. You had these growin' pains. Our Maisie had them. That solves it.'

An hour later the boys huddled near the door as their pal went in to face his irate granny. 'Ah, Jaysus, Mary an' Joseph,' she wailed, 'what have you done with your lovely gansey that I bought you for the big rally in Cavan on Sunday an' your Holy Communion as well, you rapscallion of a tinker's get, that brings your poor granny woe an' worry. Ah, mother o' God, would you just look at the gapin', gawkin' open mouth o' the eejit! I declare to the Almighty you're every bit as daft an' worse than Oiney Hoy, the great amadhaun of the Carrick Hills.'

The boys, chuckling with glee, crept away from the door to tell the village of the misadventure and how the Holy Terror had called her grandson all those terrible names, one name in particular that set Creevan laughing until sunset. Memories of the poor fool of the hills floated over the rooftops, hovering between the chapel spire and the three braes, and in the kitchens and snugs of the little village, where superstition and gossip often ousted common sense, a new Oiney Hoy was born in the very heart of Ireland.

THE CIRCUIT JUDGE

It was on a Sunday morning that the Gunner Reagan from Arva arrived in Creevan with his poor wife and young family. He called himself the gunner because he had served in the British Army in that capacity in World War I, and was forever boasting of his great deeds in the trenches. After installing his family in a shabby little house in the Lane where the sun seldom shone, he went into Doyle's public-house by way of the back-yard. This Doyle had a bad reputation. His brother had been shot as an informer during the Black-and-Tan War in Ireland and more recently the publican had barred an unfrocked priest.

What made Doyle really despised was that he took the priest's money and let him drink like a fish before he was unfrocked. And he had the nerve to pretend that he was only doing it for the clergyman's own good. The unfrocked priest did not take the insult lightly. Folk said that he was seen to stand outside Doyle's closed door at the dead of night with his stole around his shoulders and his right hand raised in a mighty curse. This curse ended with the terrible words, 'May the green grass grow over your doorstep for lack of customers!' People in Creevan swear to this day that for several years this came to pass, but then there are people in Creevan who will swear to anything. The poet Yeats would have reaped a richer harvest of fairy lore in Creevan than beyond in the country lanes of Sligo.

On that same Sunday that the Gunner Reagan from Arva drank his way through the last Mass, the Holy Terror was sitting on a stool at the door of her cottage. She was saying her rosary beads out loud as she gazed across the street at the pious chapelgoers on their way up the brae—she knew every mother's son of them and their cousins in America.

Oiney stood in the shadows of the small stone-flagged kitchen, wondering what he would do to pass the time. Winter in Creevan was a long weary season, little relieved by Hallowe'en and Christmas. The old woman became even more irksome during that period; she showed scarcely any festive goodwill or charity towards her neighbours or Oiney. He listened to her mumblings at the door until they became audible to him. Her voice was now raised a good deal louder as though she wanted the chapelgoers to hear her lambast them. Good God, thought the boy, what a strange prayer she was saying! If there was an Almighty up there in Heaven, He would surely strike her stone dead.

The rosary beads, polished and worn, slid through her wrinkled fingers. 'Hail Mary, full o' Grace,' she prayed, 'would you look at the bloody conceit of their sanctified faces! Full o' Grace be damned! I mind the day when the lot o' them came down from Carrick into Creevan without as much as an arse, God forgive me, to their trousers... The Lord is with Thee and blessed is the fruit o' Thy womb—Jesus!... Ah, Jesus, haven't the snotty-nosed gets risen up in the world...Minnie Downey beyond hadn't the dacint shift to her back... By the crucified Jesus look at her now an' the halo chokin' her... Holy Mary, mother o' God, pray for us sinners... Sinners an' damn blackguards if you ask me... Now and at the hour of our death. Amen.'

This prayer sounded quite a bit different from the ones he was taught in the school on the hill. The school however had its own strangeness. Oiney did not learn very much in it except the Catechism and how to write at an angle of forty-five degrees in a copybook. A few other things also. He learned that Ireland was an island set in the Atlantic, that God made the world more like an orange than a ball, flat on top, that an imaginary line ran around the middle of it called the Equator. Even more important still, he learned that he was the proud possessor of a thing called a Soul.

Now this Soul, he was taught, was invisible, odourless, and colourless, and his greatest task on Earth was to save this Soul so that it would meet other invisible, odourless and colourless Souls of its kind in an invisible world called Heaven. Oiney was taught this by the priest and the schoolteacher without as much as a wink or a wicked grin on their faces, so young Oiney accepted it as gospel truth. If by chance he did not save this precious soul of his the threat hung over him that he would cruelly burn in the snake-pits of Hell for all eternity. Faced with such a dreadful alternative, everything but the saving of his soul shrank into insignificance. Believing his elders and his teachers, for they seemed to entertain no doubts on the subject, he was prepared to believe almost anything. Illusion and reality had lost their dividing line for him; his mouth opened a little wider and he became even more gullible.

It was late that Sunday night when the Gunner Reagan emerged from Doyle's public-house and awakened Creevan with his loud bawling. 'You want to know who and what I am, do you? Well, I'll tell you. I'm the Gunner Reagan from Arva. That's what I am. I'm a Cavan Slasher an' I'll knock you all into the middle o' next week. I'll have you for me breakfast an' I'll bate the best man in the country of Ireland.' He stumbled over to the village pump at the top of the Market House brae. This cast iron fountain was moulded into the shape of a lion's head with an English constable's peaked helmet on top of it, a relic of Imperial rule.

The Gunner threw his arms around the pump. 'Hello, Sergeant,' he said in a slurred voice. 'Were you out on your own patrolling the streets of this one-horse town? Fare thee well, Enniskillen, we'll return in full bloom. You and me, Sergeant, for a square-go! Eh? What's about it? It'll warm the two of us up…'

He hit the cast iron pump a whack with his fist and then quickly recoiled with the shock. 'Aw, Jaysus,' he cried with the pain, 'but you're the hard, hard man. It's a cruel world altogether an' me a wanderer in me own land.' And then through the heavy, sodden fog created in his mind by the long day in Doyle's pub, there appeared in a sudden flicker of remembrance the faces of his wife and children and he awkwardly stumbled down the dark narrow lane where the poor folk lived. The blustering bellowing died away and Creevan, with a sigh of relief, went to sleep.

The following day, Monday, was the. eve of the Circuit Court Session, when the crusty, pompous Judge Ritchie and his servile minions presided over the trials. The old Court House lay at the foot of the Market House brae; it was a low, long, sandstone building with two Ionic columns, and a massive oak door studded with heavy iron nails. Every Court Session the door was left open, for the Judge complained, with some justification, that the place smelled like an Egyptian tomb.

In the evening of that Monday, Oiney was sent by his granny to fetch a bucket of water from the pump. He climbed the Market House brae and set his bucket down under the lion's mouth. Then he turned the serrated handle which was located where the lion's ear should have been. The clear, sparkling water flowed in abundance. It quickly filled the bucket and overflowed onto the brae. Oiney tried desperately to turn it off, but without success; the publican and the local Civic Guard had a go, but they fared no better. The gushing water spread across the street at the fountain head and poured like a stream down the brae. It was as though a mischievous leprechaun in the pump, aroused by Gunner Reagan's fierce thump, had taken over the inner workings and was determined to have revenge for its rude awakening. All evening long the water flowed, and right into the small hours of the morning. Then quite suddenly and mysteriously the flow ceased as if the imp, at last satisfied, had gone to sleep himself. There was a hard frost that morning and, later on, a light fall of snow.

Such was the idyllic picture-postcard scene of an Irish snow-clad village which greeted Judge Ritchie as he took pompous strides from the Market Square towards the Court House. What a quaint delightful scene, he thought, with the old, uneven houses, the village pump and ancient marketplace, an olde worlde scene that he hoped would endure, like his prestige, forever. And then suddenly it happened. Some say that the malevolent leprechaun in the fountain drew him towards the spot where the treacherous ice began. Others stubbornly insist that the Judge acted spontaneously, of his own volition, and should not be denied the credit of an astonishing performance.

Suffice it to say that somewhere in the vicinity of the pump the learned Judge took off, not in any legal or judicial sense, but literally took off in a physical, corporeal manner. In short, he left terra firma. If he had gone into orbit the villagers of Creevan could not have been more astonished. Wide-eyed with wonder, they gazed at an aspect of the stern law-dispenser they had never known existed. Admittedly the first sudden jerk for an instant caused some splay-footed panic in an attempt to regain his dignified stride, but by a magnificent effort of sheer willpower he drew both legs together, and with the calm composure we have come to expect from the Law, briefcase firmly clasped, bowler-hatted, brolly over left arm, he slid down the steep brae, as gracefully as any Markova.

The widow Murtagh, who lived about twenty yards down from the fountain, had this to say to reporters:

'An outstanding performance! I was doing me washin' an' lookin' over me half-door when His Worship passed. His face looked a kind of frozen stiff, but then it always does. But polite, always meticulous polite. "Goodday, your honour," I said, "A nice day for ducks." "Goodday, madam," he said, raising his bowler. Did I notice anything particular about his feet? Well, they did seem a bit glued together an' he was slidin' in a kind o' pollyglide. But I'm not versed in these modern dances.'

It was the Judge's amazing antics halfway down the brae which astonished the youth of Creevan, who foolishly imagined they were rare performers on the ice. They soon realised that, compared to the Judge, they were second-rate amateurs. First he enacted a series of hunker slides, flailing his legs from side to side like a Cossack dancer; then he performed several back-benders, arching his body like a dolphin; then a tremendous somersault, clinging unsuccessfully to his brolly and briefcase, while the boys cheered his generosity every bit as much as his prowess. Stern-faced and stony-hearted as he was generally, on this occasion he showed a generosity of spirit that was very touching.

One has only to hear poor Mrs Doyle's glowing report. 'I was standin' at me door when His Honour passed. Maybe then he was only about three feet off the ground an' doin' these crazy loop-the-loop things. I told him it wasn't right for a man of his age, to be doin' cartwheels an' the like. But he didn't answer, just threw his umbrella at me. God knows I'm grateful, most grateful for it. If I get a soakin' wet, I do get these awful pains in me joints... Ah, God bless him, His Honour was in a charitable mood that day, for Tim Ryan, the saddler, whose son got six months from His Nibs at the last Assizes, received the good leather briefcase. I suppose it was his way of atonin' for the heavy sentence... an' even the boys o' Creevan benefitted that day by his tumblin' generosity. He scattered silver an' copper coins all over the brae. They say, though, that he gave shockin' sentences after he sailed into Court through the open door that day... aye sailed... over the benches an' into his seat. And believe me, it was all the fault of that rapscallion of a boy, Oiney Hoy, who turned the pump on. For years afterwards we had many's the good laugh about it, an' we all thought for ages in Creevan that a Circuit Judge was one of them puffed up Law Lords who perform cartwheels and somersaults on the ice on their way to Court.'

IN ERIN'S GREEN VALLEYS

It was several years later. Winter was past and the bright days of spring shone on Erin's green valleys. Saint Patrick's Day was only a week away when the Holy Terror sent Oiney along the ditch to find shamrocks on the road to Cootehill, that same little flat town in the north of Cavan where some villains had murdered Nell Flaherty's drake. Near the old Boiler House at the crossroads, where the Quakers made the controversial soup in the Famine times, the young lad met Terry Doogan of the Hills, driving an ass and cart into Creevan. He was quite a tall man, with a slight stoop and a glossy brown beard; he spoke poetry and riddles with a loud deep voice. He often broke off in his conversation to recite a line or two from one of the patriotic ballads of Ireland.

'Is it true, Terry,' Oiney asked innocently, 'that you don't go to chapel?'

Terry paused for a minute. 'As true, God bless us,' he said, 'as the cross on that ass's back, and it got that cross implanted as a token of favour for carryin' Christ from the wilderness into Jerusalem on Palm Sunday. into our town-land on a night o' snow rode a man from God knows where... And that's a fact.'

'Why don't you go, Terry?' Oiney persisted.

'Ah, sure God himself only knows. Maybe it's the lingerin' smell o' him wasn't right for a man of his age, to be doin' cartwheels an' the incense or the pungent smoke o' the snuffed candles, but a great sickness comes over me when I cross the chapel door, a terrible nausea indeed, and I seem to be trapped in the temples o' the ancients. But sure "my cathedral is the glory of the skies, the heat of noon or the first sun-rise... I'm on me way, son, but good luck to you in your search!'

A little bit further up the road Oiney met a lean, dark young man in a trench coat and a hat tilted low over his brow. 'You are from Creevan?'

'I am,' said Oiney.

'Tell me something!'

'Tell you something? If I can.'

'About Doyle the publican in the Market Square. Is he dead yet?'

'No,' said Oiney, 'but he's got the Last Rites an' they've taken him to Monaghan hospital.'

The lean man chuckled.

'The Last Rites, did you say? Good.'

'Why?' asked Oiney, a little puzzled by the stranger's glee.

'Why? Ah, why? That's the question you might say. Well now… I see… Won't it be a great comfort to his crossin' the unknown boundaries o' the Great Divide?'

The man took his leave, but in days ahead Oiney had cause to remember that strange encounter.

In searching the ditch for shamrocks, to his delight, he found not only many sprigs of the famous plant but down in the deep grass a shining half-crown and a penny piece. His granny steeped the shamrocks in water and let him keep the penny. 'We'll send the half-crown to the Missions,' she said, 'an' buy a black baby. And if you're good, I'll take you on the pilgrimage to Lough Der… '

'Lough Derg, granny? What's Lough Derg?'

'It's an island.'

Oiney looked puzzled.

'An island? I thought you said it was a lough.'

'My God, didn't they learn you anything at all at that school on the hill? There's a holy island on Lough Derg, where the great Saint Patrick himself, Apostle of Ireland, prayed and fasted in a dark cave for forty days an' forty nights… '

'What did he do that for?'

She gave her grandson a look of great scorn and then mimicked his voice. 'What did he do that for? What did he do that for? Wasn't he lookin' for paper to wipe his arse with? What did he do that for! Wasn't he prayin' for the conversion of the Irish, you, you amadhuan. An' God answered his prayer except for them bloody Orange crew up north… God revealed Himself to Patrick.'

'He did what?' said the open-mouthed Oiney.

'Shut your gob or you'll be catchin' flies, gasson! God appeared to Patrick in a spinning white light. He told the saint that on a dark day ahead the lovely green valleys of Erin would slowly sink undher the waves o' the Atlantic. An' that Patrick himself would have the privilege o' sittin' in judgement on the Irish race!'

'He did not!'

'He did or else I wouldn't be tellin' you! Why else would the great pilgrimages to Lough Derg in Donegal be made for throughout the centuries? Prayin' an' fastin' an' sayin' the Stations in our bare feet. Three days an' nights with nothin' but a crust o' bread an' black tay an' the flint cuttin' your feet an' you chitterin' with the cold, with the bitther winds from the wild Atlantic crossin' the bleak, bare hills o' Donegal… '

It sounded so dreadfully forlorn and incredibly weird that Oiney, bored by the long winter in Creevan, felt a great desire to visit the strange place. So, for some weeks, he kept close to the house and ran the messages. He fetched buckets of water from the familiar old lion-headed fountain on the brae, and scoured all the little bottles which ailing neighbours sent in to his granny for a taste of the cure, when it came, from the holy island. One bottle in particular, which his granny warned him to rinse well with lashings of soap and water and elbow grease, was an empty whiskey bottle sent in by old Terry of the Hills, who she said, God forgive him, never crossed a chapel door. 'Scour it well,' she ordered the boy, 'for the evil dregs o' whiskey will polluther the holy wather somethin' awful, an' instead of a cure cause a calamity.'

One morning in June, the slow train drew the Lough Derg pilgrims westwards to Donegal… Oiney, carrying a well-rinsed and scrubbed lemonade bottle, sat beside his granny and eyed the others in the carriage. Like the old woman, many were saying their rosary beads, while others dreamed as they looked out of the windows at the grazing cattle in the lovely, patchwork of green and corn-gold fields of Ulster, in by Fermanagh where 'the Erne shall run red with redundance of blood, the earth shall rock beneath our tread… ere you shall fade, ere you shall die, my dark Rosaleen…'

Oiney, with his own innate kindness and love for his people, gazed innocently into the eyes of the other pilgrims and saw not sin nor selfishness, but instead a little bit too much humility, he thought, and the strain of overwork and worry. These were not the brash sinners that the brimstone missionaries should thunder at from the pulpits raised high above the poor. There was scarcely a soul among them knew what real sin was. These were people more sinned against than sinning, but still afraid of the loss of their invisible souls, as Oiney was afraid.

'Tickets, please!' The powerful voice of the Inspector boomed along the corridor so loudly that Oiney was amazed to discover that its possessor was in fact quite a small man in uniform, crowned by a shiny peak cap. Just then a sharp elbow dug into the boy's ribs, and he heard his granny whisper in alarm, 'Pull your trousers above your knees, gasson! Quick!'

Oiney could scarcely believe her command. 'What, granny?'

'D'you as you're bid,' she shouted frantically, 'for I only got you a half-fare ticket! For Jaysus sake, hurry!'

Oiney's face went scarlet to match his hair almost and he fumbled in embarrassment with the empty lemonade bottle, passing it from one hand to the other. Before he had time to make his mind up what to do, the ticket Inspector stood in their section of the carriage. The old woman, now the picture of piety, handed him the two tickets. He punched one of them and then looked at the other over and over again. Lifting his eyes from the ticket, he looked at Oiney, measuring him up, then back to the ticket again and finally at the empty lemonade bottle, as though it played some mysterious role in all this. 'What age are you, son?'

The old woman was ready to pounce on him. 'Is there anyone askin' you your age, is there?'

The wee man stood his full five-feet-two-inches tall, officialdom triumphant. 'I would like to inform you, madam, that I am an Inspector of the Great Northern Railway.'

'I don't give a damn if you own the Great Northern Railway. Fetch me a real Inspector that respects people's rights, an' us pious pilgrims, no less, doin' penance on the way to the holy Lough Derg!'

The other passengers had their faces turned to the windows, desperately striving to show that they had no connection whatsoever with this awful woman. But the Holy Terror had had so many sharp rebuffs in life that she shrugged off this latest one. 'What are you anyway, you impudent get,' she snapped at the official, 'that you come bursting in on top of me rosary beads? Are you a hay then heretic or worse still a bitter Orangeman that you disturb the peace of a Christian carriage? Have I asked you what religion you are or what you had for your breakfast? If you don't go this minit, I've a mind to summon you before the Stipendiary.' She had a liking for these nineteenth-century words; they sounded so important they frightened people off.

The Inspector, realising that he had an impossible case on his hands, thought it wiser to make a safe retreat, but he fired a parting salvo.

'You can be up for defraudin' the Great Northern Railway...'

She was on her feet again. 'If you don't lave me sight this instant the Great Northern Railway will be minus an Inspector before we reach the next station! We hanged a wee fella like you in Carrick during the Land War!'

For the remainder of the journey Oiney could not say that he enjoyed the ensuing peace. His granny's tongue rattled away at a great rate. The entire carriage-full of penitents seemed to be staring at his hot, blushing face, making him feel guilty of the terrible crime of belonging to the scourge of Creevan.

This was only the beginning of his penance. From the small jetty at the lough-side, they could see the lone bleak island with its basilica, guest house and other buildings. For well over a thousand years, pilgrims from Ireland, Scotland, England and the Continent had stood on these ancient shores. Soon a medium-sized ferryboat was carrying them across the waves to be welcomed on the island pier by Dean Keown. Oiney saw the Dean give his granny a very strange look, for he knew her well, and probably anticipated a rough time of it.

It was not long before the old woman and the boy began their rounds of the Stations— or beds, as they were called. There were several of these bleak, stony circles, and the barefoot route of the pilgrims lay across sharp-edged flintstone. Oiney picked his pious way very gingerly, but his granny made ample atonement for his avoidance of pain by falling on top of him at regular intervals and accompanying these falls with loud shrieks of 'Oh, Christ, me corns,' 'Oh, Jesus, me bunions'. For Oiney it was like two or three extra penances, and no one on that island was so glad to see the ferryboat arrive to take them all back to the mainland. Dean Keown saw them off and once again Oiney noticed that peculiar look in the priest's eyes as he made sure the boy's granny was safely on board. Dean Keown seemed to give vent to a great sigh of heartfelt relief.

It was a different ticket Inspector on the train home and for a considerable time nothing disturbed the peace and contentment. After the long spells of vigil on Lough Derg, most of the pilgrims fell asleep. Oiney's exhausted grandmother lay back, snoring quite loudly, while the lad counted the passing telegraph poles. Then, for no apparent reason, he suddenly became conscious of the lemonade bottle in his hand. For days he had been carrying it from place to place almost unaware of its very existence. Now he sat stunned, looking at its emptiness. In the midst of the confusion and anxiety on Lough Derg, he had forgotten to fill the bottle with holy water. Nor had his granny noticed the empty bottle either.

He sat for quite a while, really dismayed by the awful discovery. Terry of the Hills, the Widow Murtagh, Mrs Coyle, and the other poor suffering neighbours would be bitterly disappointed. Oiney had brought no holy water home to pour into the little miniature bottles. It was surely bad enough, he thought, to deprive his poor neighbours of a cure for their pains. But to have to hold up his empty bottle and to look in their sad eyes was more than he could bear.

Then suddenly, he had a flash of inspiration, a flash of genius. It was not the fault of the leprechaun of the fountain this time, but the train happened to be passing through the territory of smugglers and the like just then, and who knows but Old Nick himself had a hand in it?

Now ordinary water is the same as holy water as far as the layman is concerned anyhow. It has the same transparent colour and the same consistency. So thought Oiney, in this emergency, only in this emergency, if Terry of the Hills and the others get their miniatures filled with ordinary water, they will not be any the wiser. Of course, reasoned Oiney, ordinary water will effect no cure, but then even the best holy water from Lourdes in France will not always produce a cure. And thus the poor sufferers will not blame Oiney. It was deception, downright deception indeed, but in a worthy cause, and as the Jesuit sophists might say, the end justifying the means.

His granny, thank heavens, was still asleep, and the rest of the pilgrims resting back on clear consciences, when Oiney crept forward along the corridor. No one present, had they looked, would have dreamed in a million years that this small, freckled, pious and innocent boy had an empty bottle stuck up his jersey. He sneaked quietly into the toilet, snibbed the door behind him and filled the bottle with good clear train water from the sink tap.

Old Terry of the Hills, the Widow Murtagh and Mrs Coyle were highly delighted, as were all the others. Oiney stood, blushing with guilt, as they expressed their warm thanks. They mistook his blushes for shyness. A week later his embarrassment was even greater when they came from all parts to thank his granny for the powerful 'cure' she had brought them. 'Thanks be to God an' His holy Mother,' said Mrs Murtagh, 'for I've never felt as good in a month o' Sundays. Me spots have disappeared an' not only that, but me daughter, Peggy, is coughin' bhetther.' She patted Oiney on the head and never even noticed that his freckles had disappeared in a huge crimson blush.

'Bless his wee soul,' she added fervently, 'but who knows he's got the makin's of a holy Bishop in him yet.'

Oiney nurtured silently his terrible sin until the autumn when the missionaries roared into Creevan. Previously he had been afraid to tell his heinous sin in Confession in case the priest recognised him. There were few local lads who had ever been to Lough Derg. At least the missionaries for all their sulphur and brimstone carried your sins back to Dublin with them and well clear of the Parish. Waiting until the queue was clear, Oiney went into Confession: 'Bless me Father for I have sinned.'

'How long is it since your last Confession?'

'It must be three or four months, Father.'

'That's a long time for a lad like you. Well now, let's have your sins!'

'Well, Father, it's like this. I went to Lough Derg, but I didn't take home any holy water at all. I took train-water.' 'Drain-water,' said the priest, who was hard of hearing. 'Tell me more about this drain-water! Were you digging drains in Donegal?'

'No, Father, it wasn't drain-water; it was train-water.' 'Oh, I see. Rain-water. I see. But tell me, how did you take home rain-water from Lough Derg?'

'Father,' said Oiney, almost giving up hope, 'I filled the bottle full of water from the sink tap in the train.'

The missionary tried to get a glimpse of this strange penitent. 'And what in God's name did you do that for?'

'I pretended it was holy water, Father.'

'But sure,' said the priest, 'that kind of water wouldn't cure.'

'But it did, Father, it did,' cried Oiney almost triumphantly. 'It cured Peggy's cough, an' her Ma's spots an' Mrs Coyle...'

'Were you tempting God?' the priest asked suspiciously. 'Oh no, Father, shure I wouldn't endanger my invisible soul,' Oiney assured him.

Quaint fellow this, thought the priest, but basically harmless. 'Say the Stations of the Cross as a penance! And don't put drain-water, or train-water or whatever in holy water bottles again!'

'But Father?'

'What is it now?' said the priest impatiently.

'Father? How did the water cure them when it wasn't holy? How did it do that, Father?'

'Listen, young man, and take my word for it. Sure all the water in Ireland is holy!'

THE BELFRY

The belfry, high up in the spire of St Patrick's Church in Creevan, was a real vantage point for a grand view of the surrounding countryside. From it you could see the Carrick Hills and the twin loughs and the little historic roads winding their way down towards the ford and village. Jonjo Cooney, its sexton, was a mere mortal on the Creevan streets, but up here in the belfry, he was monarch of all he surveyed. He felt aloof and superior, looking down like a god on all the little moving dots that comprised the local residents.

He could watch, for example, 'Springheel Willie', his conceited old master, stride with that peculiar bounce on his way to the school on the hill. He could see the Civic Guard sergeant, nicknamed 'Pat Oats' after the famous porridge, loiter with intent near one or other of the public houses. On the other side of the street he could see Father Duffy, the parish priest, move to and fro among his flock, a busy beetle indeed, while Susan Cairns, that shrill soprano in the chapel choir, now seemed a mere, little ladybird insect by her garden pond.

No wonder, thought Jonjo, God feels such power and might, gazing as He does down on the world from the immense heights of the Universe. Jonjo, like Oiney, was a strange enough fellow himself who found it very difficult and sad to grow up into an ordinary dull citizen of the world. He retained a fondness for the games and hobbies of children, such as collecting cigarette cards and playing marbles. On the Castle Hill, he often flew kites. As a chapel sexton, he could no longer rob orchards, of course, but he often kept a look-out on 'Pat Oats' for Oiney and the other boys. He would always be a youngster at heart.

Peering down from the belfry window, he now saw his friend, Oiney, climb the rows of stone steps up towards the chapel door. He recognised quite easily Oiney's peculiar skip-and-jump and soon the sexton's face wore a smile as he welcomed his friend into his little kingdom on high. There were few others in Creevan had accesss to that lofty eyrie of Jonjo's. 'Good man yourself, Oiney, you're just in time.' He pointed out the Monaghan road and a far distance beyond Tullycorbet, where a small black speck could be seen moving slowly.

'That's the hearse, Oiney, takin' the publican, Doyle, back to the big shop in the Square. Tell me when he comes to Dr Nolan's house below there an' I'll start ringing the bell for the dead.'

'All right, Jonjo,' said Oiney, throwing himself down on a small bale of straw close to the window. 'I'm your man.' 'What did you learn about Lough Derg, Oiney?'

'Oh, I wouldn't go there again, Jonjo, without a fur coat. An' definitely, no granny. She's out… But d'you know what I heard the ferrymen talk about on the way back? There was a bit of a storm on Lough Derg, but they were sayin' it was nothin' to the terrible year of 1795… the fifth of July 1795 when a boat o' pilgrims sank with all hands aboard…'

'God bless us an' save us,' said Jonjo, aghast with the news, however belated, 'but wouldn't they go straight to Heaven…? A bit o' consolation indeed for their bereaved relatives. The fifth of July did you say? Maybe them Orangemen spiked the boat. You see, Oiney, that was the time Orangism was startin' up, a whole century, mind you, after King Billy… They never bothered with King Billy until a hundred years after he was dead and buried.'

'Why was that, Jonjo?'

'Well, Catholic an' Protestant was joinin' together in the United Irishmen. So the British started the Orange Order to keep Ireland divided…'

'The dirty pigs,' exclaimed Oiney. 'Me granny doesn't like them either.'

'Imagine,' exclaimed Jonjo in a sad but angry voice, 'all them poor souls lost when the Orangemen spiked the boat on Lough Derg! Oiney?'

'What is it, Jonjo?'

'Are you keepin' a good look-out on the road for the hearse?'

'I am, surely.'

'Where is it now?'

'It's just this side of Tullycorbet, Jonjo. Tell me, Jonjo, is Ireland really goin' to sink in the Atlantic five years before the end of the world?'

'Who told you that oul' codswallop, Oiney?' said the startled sexton.

'Me granny said that God told it to Saint Patrick in a cave!'

'In a cave begod,' exclaimed Jonjo with a laugh. 'No wonder He told him it in a cave, for God knows there's a hollow ring to that story, Oiney. You're a bigger cod than Doyle in his coffin, listenin' to your granny's blethers.'

'Tell me, Jonjo! What like was Doyle?'

'What like?'

'Aye. Are you sorry for him an' him dead?'

'Divil the bit. Hadn't he the good innings an' him seventy-two an' more! And he never went without a bite in his pursepround life. Him an' Keenan, the undertaker, were mortal enemies in their great bids to out-do each other.'

'In what way, Jonjo?'

'Well, I'll give you an example. When Keenan bought the paintin' of the Perpetual Supper...'

'Succour, Jonjo!'

'Aye, Succour, that's it. I get mixed up at times. When he bought this picture for the chapel Doyle had to go one better, so he bought the big statue of Saint Anthony...' 'The one that stands under the organ loft?'

'Aye, Oiney, that's the very one. You're game ball. And then what happened, Oiney? Keenan went an' bought a holy water font for baptisin' the infants. And then and behold, Doyle tops that with a set o' bright bronze altar rails... and tell me, Oiney, where is he now?'

'I suppose,' said Oiney, astonished by all their great gifts to the chapel, 'I suppose, Jonjo, he'll be reapiri' his reward in Heaven...'

'I didn't mean that at all,' exclaimed Jonjo impatiently. 'I meant where is Doyle's hearse?'

'Oh, the hearse, Jonjo. I thought you meant his soul. The hearse, Jonjo, is at Hanratty's Cross, a wee bit to come still. I suppose the bronze altar rails clinched it for Doyle then?'

'Oh, divil the bit, Oiney, divil the bit. Didn't Keenan up him with a stained-glass window over the High Altar of St Michael oustin' the filthy oul' dragon from Heaven. An' d'you know, Oiney? You'll not believe it.'

'Tell me, Jonjo!'

'D'you know there was the most uncanny resemblance to Doyle on the oul' serpent's face. There was indeed.'

'Begod, Jonjo, they must have hated each other. A stained-glass window no less!'

'They both had the wealth o' Midas an' the pride o' Lucifer in them. They were buyin' their way out o' Purgatory or Hell even, an' at the same time feedin' their conceit... They were sittin' on the camel's back an' forcin' it through the needle's eye. But as me mother used to say, pride comes before a fall. An' she was right.'

'I suppose, Jonjo, the altar rails banjaxed Doyle.'

'If you think that Oiney, you've another guess comin' to you. Indeed an' it didn't. Three months later Doyle disappeared, but when he arrived at Creevan station that August he had a great wooden crate with him... He had it brought up on a lorry to the chapel an' opened in front of the parish priest. When the boards were taken asunder, guess what was there, Oiney, guess!'

'I couldn't, Jonjo,' said the excited Oiney. 'I couldn't. You tell me!'

'A great big metal weather-cock to perch on top of the chapel spire. That's what was there Oiney. And you should have seen Doyle's face, beamin' with triumph it was. He turned to Father Duffy an' nudged him, "That gives me somethin' to crow about Father, doesn't it?" An' believe me, Oiney, Keenan was left that day grittin' his teeth.'

Oiney looked out the belfry window. 'Oh, Jonjo, you'll need to hurry with the bell. Doyle's hearse is passin'.'

The slow, ponderous chimes rang out over Creevan.

Jonjo then ran over to the straw pile and looked through the window. 'Keenan has the last laugh, Oiney.'

'How, Jonjo?'

The sexton pointed down to the undertaker's shop. 'Look at him standin' there, Oiney, with his legs akimbo as the hearse passes! There he goes raisin' his hat in respect, but I can imagine the grim oul' smirk of satisfaction on his smug face.'

THE WAKE

From Jonjo's description of the purseproud publican Mr Barney Doyle, Market Square, Creevan, Oiney had not the least desire to attend his Wake and pay respects which certainly, as far as either Jonjo or himself were concerned, did not exist. To him Doyle had always been the owner of an ancient tavern and a lonely old miser. Collecting once on behalf of the Scouts, Oiney had opened the tavern door. Immediately a cluster of bells above the door clanged out so loudly that Oiney took to his heels in fright. On the occasion now of the Wake, he would never have dreamed of attending were it not for the fact that his granny sent him to collect a little brown jug that Doyle had promised her long years ago for some favour she had rendered him.

Oiney knocked on the front door of the tavern for quite a while until at last a window was raised in a room directly over the bar. A woman informed him that if he wished to enter he would have to do so by the arched entry and lane to the back of the house. He did so, passing a small grey van parked in the yard. Opening the rear door which led to the kitchen he went in and climbed the stairs up to the parlour where the Wake was being held.

As he might have expected Mrs Coyle and the widow Murtagh were there, glasses of sherry and porter in their hands, and sharing a wooden form with an old man, Thady McNally from the Shercock Road. This veteran kept wheezing and grunting and knocking back pints of porter at a great rate. He had a claim to fame in the Guinness Book of Records for attending more funerals than any man in Ulster. A man and woman, professing to be country cousins of the deceased, sat on chairs near the head of the bed and among another small group of 'mourners' to the rear of the room Oiney recognised the bookie's clerk O'Dowd and Mrs Dignam who swept the chapel floor twice a week. After this glance at the living Oiney turned to look at the dead, and almost recoiled with the shock. Doyle was dressed in his habit all right, with his crossed pearly-white knuckles clutching a silver crucifix.

But it was the expression and particularly the position of Mr Doyle's face which so startled Oiney. The publican lay on his back but his head was turned to the wall as though he was disgusted with the present company having so much free drink at his expense. And from the little bit of his countenance that was visible, Oiney was certain that it registered the dead man's utter disapproval. Oiney could detect clearly the cold aloof scorn on Doyle's face; he wanted nothing to do, alive or dead, with this lot.

The widow Murtagh, however, was not going to allow any unkindness spoil the occasion. 'Oh my, doesn't he look grand! That month in Scotland did him the world of good. They say he collapsed with excitement at the Rangers-Celtic match in Glasgow, and never even came to to hear the final score, God bless an' save us an' keep us from harm.'

'Don't let us be morbid,' said Mrs Coyle wisely, 'for it puts a downcast spell on the best occasions an' causes indigestion. Tell you what! This honest lad Oiney with the makings of a priest in him will, if he's asked nice, do the obligations o' carryin' new refreshments up from the bar below.'

'Me cousin, me first cousin,' added the countryman, nodding towards the corpse, 'would fully approve o' them sentiments. In moderation, of course.'

Thus the unwilling Oiney was enlisted to carry fresh drinks for the merry company. And at heart he did not like to refuse. This was one of his great failings; he had this chronic anxiety to prove himself of some use in the world. So it came to pass that although he had a great repugnance towards misers, corpses and clouds of tobacco smoke, his loyalty to Mrs Coyle, who had spoken so favourably of him, made him endure all the disagreeable elements of his many sorties, upstairs and down.

The company by this time was becoming quite maudlin.

Mrs Coyle was crying. 'He was the kind man at heart, wasn't he? All that money he sent on the Foreign Missions an' the black babies an' masses for his soul. He had a conscience...'

'Conscience be damned,' exclaimed the widow Murtagh. 'Masses, the Missions, black babies an' what have you! Wasn't them his fire escape!'

'Fire escape?'

'Aye, fire escape. From the flames o' Hell... '

'Mother o' God, take care o' us!'

On one of his many sorties, Oiney was startled to notice that he was being watched carefully by two men in the shadows of the Bar. He almost dropped the tray with fright.

'Oh, don't worry about us,' said the smaller of the two men, a stout jovial fellow with a magnifcent beard. 'We'll not bother you one little bit. Just carry on your business as normal as if we didn't exist. But first tell us! Who are you?'

'They call me Oiney Hoy, though I don't like it at all, an' I came up here to fetch the wee brown jug that Mr Doyle promised me granny. Mr Doyle's friends an' relations up at the Wake asked me to fetch them some drink from the bar here.

"Do you know any o' them?' asked the stranger suspiciously.

'I only know the village folk,' said Oiney, 'not the relations, not the country cousins.'

'Country cousins me eye,' exclaimed the little fellow with a laugh of great scorn. 'They're nothin' but charlatans, moochers an' chancers come here to fleece me dead father.' Oiney's mouth opened wider with astonishment. 'Mr Doyle...your dead father? I didn't know Mr Doyle had a son... '

'Which just goes to show you that you don't know everything. Isn't that right?'

Oiney had to admit that the stranger was indeed quite right in that respect. There were some gaps in his education.

'Let me introduce ourselves,' said the jovial one smiling kindly. 'I'm Shaun Doyle, son of the lately deceased, an' this is my dear, dear friend from Shantonagh, Sheamus Tynan. All the property in this premises is mine by right, but I shall honour any agreement me father had with townsfolk like your granny. She shall have her little jug. In fact she can have all the jugs in the house…'

Oiney was so overcome by this wonderful gesture on the part of Mr Doyle's son that he shook the hands of both strangers warmly, though he had this peculiar feeling of having met the taller of the two men somewhere in Creevan or on the train to Lough Derg. He promised Shaun his undying friendship. Now he could clearly understand why Mr Doyle's face had been turned to the wall. The publican had correctly assessed on his deathbed in Monaghan hospital that his Wake in Creevan would be attended by parasites and chancers. Thus in anticipation of that disgusting conclusion to a worthless career, he had in one brave dying gesture turned his face away from such low company. Oiney indeed felt a great sense of Christian outrage at the indignity inflicted on a man who, whatever else his earthly failings, had donated such a proud gift as a lofty weather-cock to the chapel spire.

'I'll fetch no more drink,' he shouted in righteous anger, 'to that despicable crew.'

'On the contrary,' said Shaun, putting his arm on Oiney's shoulder, 'we shall turn the left cheek an' kill them with kindness. We'll double their allowance until their very wits fail them. Take the full tray up to them, but return here to report an' we'll surely be friends for life.'

Delighted with such a fine and glowing prospect, Oiney, carrying a loaded tray, staggered upstairs. The Wake had reached a new peak of elation with Mrs Murtagh collecting some 'souvenir' pictures from the wall of the parlour and the 'country cousins' doing their level best to restrain her. Oiney was only too glad to escape into the more wholesome atmosphere of the Bar below. Nor was he the least surprised to find that Shaun, the rightful heir of Mr Doyle, and his dear friend Sheamus had completely stripped the gantry of its contents and were piling the latter into cardboard boxes and bags which were lying in a heap by the back door. Oiney was only too delighted to assist in the collection of silver tankards, that Shaun, obviously trustful of his new friend's honesty, bestowed on him the special favour of emptying the contents of the till into a leather satchel which Sheamus graciously held out for him.

For the very first time in his young life Oiney was given a real sense of responsibility and trust, and he responded to this in a magnificent spirit of delight. His friends were more than pleased with him when he helped to carry the boxes and bags through the door and into the grey van parked in the yard. Shaun again put a friendly arm around Oiney. 'How shall I ever repay you?'

'Oh,' said Oiney warmly. 'I'm only too eager to help in a just cause. I was taught that in the Scouts.'

'And rightly so, and rightly so,' agreed Shaun. 'But Sheamus and I feel really obligated to you. We have had the deepest discussion imaginable on how we can repay our debt to you. And we have decided to offer you a grand tour of Ireland.'

Oiney stood wide-eyed in wonder. 'Do you really mean it? The Mountains of Mourne, the Hill of Tara, The Book of Kells, the Rose of Tralee and Danny Boy? Away from Creevan, the Holy Terror, and the boredom o' winter! Oh, wouldn't I just love it!' A tour of Ireland with these delightful newly found friends who trusted him as no one else did—with the exception of Jonjo perhaps. 'D'you really mean it? A tour of Ireland?'

'Of course we mean it,' said Shuan, and tearful lest Oiney change his mind, bundled him gently but quickly into the rear of the van.

Travelling in the back of a cramped little van over the bumpy by-lanes of north Monaghan in the dead of night is no promising start to the grand tour of Ireland. In the midst of his great excitement and confused thinking, Oiney found it quite difficult to keep up a conversation with Sheamus.

'What age are you, Oiney?'

'About seventeen, I think. I'm not sure.'

'Not sure?'

'Me mother's dead an' me father left Ireland to dig for gold in the streets o' London. Me granny says he must have dug as far as Australia be now. He never came back.'

'D'you want to be a priest, Oiney?'

'What?' The Creevan lad wondered was he hearing right.

'I thought that perhaps you had this vocation in you.'

'Vocation? What's that?'

'The vocation. The voice o' God callin' in the wind... like Saint Patrick heard when he escaped from slavery in the Slemish Mountains... You see, Oiney. I'm a failed priest meself.' .

Oiney did not know what to say. Life was full of so many surprises. 'Sure worse could've happened you.'

'Such as?'

Oiney searched wildly for an answer. 'You might,' he suggested timidly, 'you might've got ate.'

'Got what?' Shearnus turned around in the front to see if this yokel in the back was serious. Oiney's face was in deadly earnest. 'Me granny says some missionary priests were ate recently in the Amazonian rain-forests an' there was nothin' left but the stumps o' their legs. I don't like talkin' about it, God help them; if their souls were saved that's the main thing. What failed you as a priest, Shearnus?'

'It was the booze, Oiney, nothing but the booze. At first I got hooked on the altar wine, then the Benedictine, and after that anything God sent us. It nearly broke my mother's heart but I gave it up at the hinder-end. It was too late, though.'

Suddenly a great doubt flooded Oiney's mind. Here he was with two strangers travelling through the wilds of Ireland in the middle of the night, a van full of whiskey and beer, and him talking to a failed priest as well, on the eve of a grand tour of Ireland. It was more like a strange dream and too, too much to believe. 'Shaun?'

'What is it, Oiney?'

'I want you to tell me the truth, Shaun? How could you be Doyle's son when I never even saw you once in the village, and nobody ever mentioned to me that Doyle had a son? Answer me that before we go any further!'

'Honest to God,' said Shaun, 'but aren't you the oul' doubtin' Thomas? In all fairness however, you ask a very observant, pertinent question an' one that shall have an answer, no beatin' about the bush, no dodgin' it, an' no quibblin'. I think, Sheamus, we should enlighten Oiney a little more. We really hadn't much time back at the tavern, but, you see, here we are.'

Oiney immediately agreed on that point. There was no disputing it. 'Here we are.'

'Are you listenin', Oiney?'

'I'm listenin', Shaun, with both ears.'

'Good. You see it's like this. Me mother worked as a skivvy for Doyle for years in Creevan before you were born, Oiney. She slaved away, a poorly paid servant. A more pious prig of a degenerate Irishman the green fields of Erin never held than the same Doyle! Me mother was a good-lookin' girsha in them days when the dirty bowser took advantage of her in the bottlin' shed in the back-yard yonder... '

'He did not,' exclaimed the awestruck Oiney, unwilling to believe that such filthy things happened in holy Catholic Ireland, especially from a man who had donated a weathercock to the chapel.

'Oh, I know it's a terrible shock to an innocent chiseller like yerself, Oiney,' said Shaun, 'but God's me judge. An' Sheamus there that was in Holy Orders himself will vouch for it.'

'Me hand up to God, but it's the gospel-truth,' agreed Sheamus, even though the low roof of the van prevented his hand from stretching very high.

'Tell him, Shaun, about Doyle's takin' your poor mother to Dublin! Tell him that!'

'I was coming to that Oiney. When me mother was expectin' her baby, the oul' wretch smuggled her out o' Creevan to a maternity home run by the nuns in the suburbs o' Dublin, where I was born. He gave the nuns a brave few quid to look after us for a time, but on no account were we ever to set foot in Creevan again. He put on the oul' Adam act an' left me poor mother to provide for herself an' me. I grew up in the Liberties o' Dublin, an' even when I was a lot younger than yerself Oiney, I was bundlin' firewood an' sellin' scrap in the back-streets. I grew up a harum-scarum vagabond. Me mother, God bless her in them days, became a staunch rebel, Oiney. But though she hated the memory o' Cromwell, the memory o' Doyle was even worse to her. I vowed one day I'd get evens with the villain. When I began to grow up, I often stole quietly back into Creevan to take stock o' the situation. An' when Doyle began to ail, I got me dear friend from Shantonagh to wire me on the situation... '

'That's where I came in,' said Sheamus proudly. 'I gave Shaun the nod when the oul' fellow was on his deathbed in Monaghan. An' you know who I had that information from? D'you recall meetin' a stranger, Oiney, on the Cootehill road when you were out pickin' shamrocks?'

'What an amazin' world surely,' exclaimed Oiney. 'I knew I had seen you before. I simply cannot believe it. Wasn't I right?'

'You were surely,' agreed Sheamus, 'but then Shaun an' I realised your amazin' intelligence early on. The very minute we set eyes on you. That's a lad, if given a chance, could turn the destiny of Ireland and change the textbooks of history. Isn't that a fact, Shaun?'

'Without a shadow o' doubt,' said Shaun, 'you have the potential. But not to lose the thread o' me story. I went to me dyin' father's bedside in Monaghan hospital and asked him to bestow me nathural rights, but divil the budge from the stubborn oul' bugger, though the gates o' Hell were starin' him in the face. He'd rather leave his worldly gear to the chapel an' masses for the repose of his worthless soul. That's the kind of dirty oul' reprobate we've been raisin' in Ireland since they murdhered James Connolly an' the like. Doyle gave me one long mean look and turned to the wall. After that rigor mortis set in.'

'Holy Mary, mother o' God,' cried Oiney, 'but you're right. Every word of it. That's the real reason why his face was to the wall. It wasn't Mrs Coyle an' the widow Murtagh he was rebuffin'. It was you. It was you, Shaun.'

'God knows, Oiney,' said Shaun, 'you're the bright wee fella right enough. No wonder Sheamus thinks you've the makings of a priest in you. What a loss to the church an' the bench in a scholar like you. So I came to Creevan as you know to get me share before the Bishop of Clogher grabs the lot.'

Oiney sat in the back of the van, his mind completely dazed by these strange and terrible revelations. This was not the sweet little island, dear little island he had sung about at the school on the hill in Creevan.

AT THE BORDER

It was almost midnight when the van drew to a halt under a dark archway of beech trees. The three occupants were glad to descend, Oiney especially, from his cramped condition. He stood gazing at the wonderful pattern of stars visible in the heavens through some of the upper branches. His more mundane companions on the other hand stared anxiously at the lit window of a little hut perched on the side of the road about two hundred yards ahead. Oiney could not hear them clearly. Then Shaun approached him. 'Oiney?'

'Yes, Shaun?'

'What a lovely euphonious name!'

'You what,' said the Creevan lad, for his vocabulary was meagre.

'Euphonious, sweet soundin', melodious! Like the bells o' Shandon they sound so grand on the pleasant waters o' the river Lee. That's melodious an' so is Oiney. Could even be Chinese—Oi Nee Hoi! A cut above your Pat an' Mick or even Larry. Oiney Hoy! How originally refreshing! How did you ever acquire it?'

Then and there Oiney unburdened his soul, the immense granary of his youthful experiences. Under a moonlit sky and a great white cloud that came tumbling over the plain of Muirtheme and the shadowy peak of Slieve Gullion, he told Shaun the tale of the Holy Terror and the recent visit to Lough Derg and how Ireland would sink in the Atlantic five years before the end of the world.

'What an amazin' tale, Oiney, and it only goes to prove that wonders never cease in Ireland. I'm learnin' things this night I never knew existed. And that fearful bit about Ireland sinkin'. That should be brought to the attention of the Minister of Fisheries who attends to floods an' the like, and maybe to Town and Country Plannin', for they like to be informed as well. An' my God, that oul' granny o' yours, she needs a department all to herself. She doesn't deserve a lad of such knowledge as you, or even the wee brown jug you were takin' her. Wasn't it the blessin' o' God in the heavens up there that crossed our paths!'

'Friends,' exclaimed Oiney in a voice of gratitude to match the immensity of the occasion. 'How can I ever thank you enough for enterin' me life at such a vital moment when I was being sucked into the whirlpool of an inane village life—funerals, pilgrimages, wakes, prayers, publicans an' what have you? I realise now I'm only beginnin' to live. Shaun, just tell me! Tell me! What is life?' He imagined this so profound that he thought it worthwhile repeating. 'Just what is life?'

'Now you're askin',' said Shaun, who had given some thought to the subject in Crumlin Jail, and had even consulted a Jesuit at University College Dublin, without any deep satisfaction. He steered Oiney away from that debateable marshland. 'A chap I knew said that Life was the opposite of Death but not quite! But Oiney, never mind small details, we're still friends, aren't we?'

'How, how,' said Oiney with great fervour, 'can I ever repay you?'

Shaun put that warm comradely arm around Oiney once more. 'We wouldn't dream of acceptin' any payment, Oiney, but you might help us with one of those little corporeal works o' mercy which our Church is always exhortin' us to perform for the good of our souls... '

'And the souls in Purgatory,' Oiney piously reminded him.

'Them too,' said Shaun, drawing Oiney aside and pointing to the little wooden hut in the distance. 'A very, very good friend of ours lives in that hut, that small abode. Unfortunately the poor fella's mind is slightly deranged. He's the sad victim of amazin' fantasies an' casts himself in a variety of roles like a stage actor. Sometimes he is a bishop, or a deep-sea captain, or the conductor of an orchestra, an' he won't brook contradiction. He even dresses up for the part. Presently he believes he's a Customs Officer... '

'How ridiculous can you get,' said Oiney shaking his head. 'An important man like a Customs Officer in a silly little hut not fit even for a tinker. But poor fellow, it's not his fault.'

'You're right Oiney, as usual, an' I honestly blame the moon for most of our friend's troubles. If there were no full moons he'd be quite normal. Mind you, he's eccentric, an' can be a surly customer if his silly sense o' loyalty an' duty is challenged. Like Nelson an' Napoleon he carries the daft personal onus of an Empire that'll prosper or perish with or without any o' them. Our poor friend now has the strange obsession that it is his God-given duty to supervise what he foolishly imagines to be the Irish Border.'

Oiney could not resist a titter of laughter at the poor fool's expense. 'Imagine him holding such a silly, silly notion! Still, there's no accountin' for extravagant ideas, is there? There was this peasant girl in Carrick who stuck a pitch-fork in a dung-hill an' cried out that she was Joan of Arc. They took her to Monaghan asylum because she didn't know one word o' French. An' there was this other man who... '

'Quite so,' said Shaun impatiently, 'it's a cruel world but let's stick to one subject at a time, shall we? Sheamus an' I would like to present our dear friend in the hut with a little token of our great esteem. A bottle o' the best brand o' whiskey, an' this other little parcel, a clock. Convey our warmest regards but under no circumstances let him leave the hut to thank us! We'll drive quietly up the road an' you can join us later at the bridge yonder. Will you do that for us?'

'Certainly I will,' said the eager Oiney, 'for I never in me mortal life met two men with such innate goodness in them. First you give them unworthy moochers in the pub all the drink in the world. Then you offer me a grand tour of Ireland. An' now you send gifts to an unfortunate creature who values life so low that he imagines he is a Customs Officer. I'll tell you this much. You two are kindness personified.'

'Treat the poor fellow with great care, Oiney,' warned Shaun, 'an' for God's sake don't let him out on the road!'

'Just leave it in my capable hands,' said the confident Oiney.

A few second later the Creevan lad, on his mission of mercy, emerged from the archway of trees. He was whistling a merry tune that Jonjo had taught him when a tall, sour-faced individual answered his knock on the door. 'What hour o' the night d'you take this to be,' he growled. Oiney saw the strange fellow glare at him wickedly. As Shaun had predicted, the daft hermit of the hut was dressed in the rather plain uniform of a Customs Officer. He also wore a little Hitlerite moustache, which was a handsome match for his nasty temper.

'I haven't got a watch, mister,' answered Oiney, 'but be the look o' the stars it's on the far side o' midnight.'

'You're a smart little puppy,' snarled the Customs.

'Indeed, I'm not,' said Oiney modestly, 'for me marks at school were only middlin'.'

'Listen, clever lad! I've met your kind before an' I want no palaver with you, d'you hear! What have you to declare?'

'What have I to declare? What have I to declare?' cried Oiney, thoroughly aroused by this time. 'I declare to God you're the carnaptious oul' eejit, an' a sight worse than the Ticket Inspector on the train to Lough Derg. Surely I only brought this bottle o' whiskey an' a present…'

'So you're smugglin' illicit whiskey, are you?'

'It's a present for you.'

'Ah, so it's bribery as well. Smugglin' whiskey an' bribery! I wouldn't like to be in your shoes, me bucko. This is the Customs, you know.'

'This is the Customs! This is the Customs!' Oiney could not resist mimicking him. 'Well, if them are your Customs I don't like them one wee bit, for your Customs are terrible an' your grammar atrocious.'

'Listen, you fool,' shouted the angry official, 'you are at the Border, the Border I tell you. Don't you know it.

'I'm at the border all right,' said Oiney, 'the border-line of me patience.'

At that very moment the van passed the hut at great speed and the Customs Officer made a tremendous effort to rush out onto the road to sight the smugglers or at least get a glimpse of their number-plates. But Oiney hemmed him in gabbing away unmercifully at a great rate, reciting nursery rhymes and even jabberwocky to confuse and paralyse the poor man. Anything to prevent him from going out onto the road.

'You'll pay for this,' roared the irate official, several large veins protruding on his neck and forehead. 'You'll pay for this. Smuggling, bribery and now obstruction in the course o' duty.'

It was clear to Oiney now that the daft hermit was indeed obsessed with his strange notions. 'But I'm forced to conclude,' said the Creevan lad, 'that Shaun an' Sheamus are somewhat mistaken in your worth. You're not the nice harmless fella they think you are.

You haven't just got a little weakness o' mind. You're an ill-tempered baiste of a man, an' I'm just takin' the whiskey an' clock presents back to Shaun…'

'Did you say 'clock'?' shouted the Customs, turning pale.

'Aye, the whiskey an' the clock.'

Oiney now saw the Customs man go really berserk, throwing his peak-cap and overcoat over the clock. Then he grabbed Oiney by the neck and arm and dragged him into a deep ditch on the far side of the road.

'Begod, I'm holdin' on to you at least, me bucko.' Just then there was a terrific explosion and the little hut took off. The great white tumbling cloud from Slieve Gullion had drifted over by Fermanagh and Sligo, and there in the clear moonlight, Oiney saw the hut twirl and twirl in the sky until it landed in a field beside some bog-land.

'Holy mother o' God, mister,' cried the astonished Oiney in a hushed voice. 'Did you see that? Did you see that?'

'Don't come the innocent buffoon with me,' snapped the surly official. 'Don't tell me you knew nothin' about it! Don't pretend you didn't know this was the Irish border!'

'Honest to God, mister,' said poor Oiney in a voice of pathos. 'Honest to God, mister, how could I know? Sure the leafy trees are the same, beech an' lime an' oak on both sides, an' the birds the same hoppin' from tree to bush, an' the flowin' river the same north an' south an' the green grass the same on both sides. Ah, bad luck on them pair o' villains, Shaun an' Sheamus, for deceivin' me…'

The Customs Officer gave a great guffaw of sheer disbelief. 'Don't tell me that you expected the grass to turn orange or blue in the Six Counties! Tell that to the Judge an' see what he says! Smuggling, Bribery, Obstruction and now Terrorism. At least we've got you me bucko, an' we'll make you squawk. By the time you come out o' Crumlin or Armagh you'll be older than Rip Van Winkle's grandfather. You will that.'

OINEY IN JAIL

If Oiney had found it difficult to pass his time during the winter seasons in Creevan, that was surely a life of gusto and daring in contrast to the bleak walls and even bleaker faces of the warders of Armagh Jail, the prison in which he now so abjectly found himself. Coming as he did from the south of Ireland, although still within the great ancient province of Ulster, all the prison staff hated and despised him. A nasty warder nicknamed 'Shankill' particularly so. To that fine specimen of northern justice, a southern Irishman was a symbol of everything obnoxious in life—the Pope, rosary beads, the Blessed Virgin, the Celtic football team, Lourdes, the holy water, De Valera and the rocky road to Dublin. 'Shankill' knew only two songs, 'The Sash' and 'The Ould Orange Flute', one flag, The Union Jack with its Red Hand crest, and one way to deal with Catholics—down them!

He now opened the peephole in the door of Oiney's cell to have another close look at the strange creature recently hauled in from the bleak boglands of Eire. What on earth was the crazy fellow up to? He saw the frantic Oiney, a pencil stub in hand, running around the small cell from corner to corner and at the same time making peculiar gestures. What annoyed 'Shankill' in particular was that these gestures seemed to have some connection with Papish rituals and greatly resembled the sign of the Cross. The eager glow on Oiney's young face vexed the warder so much that, seizing his riot stick, he rushed into the cell.

'What the bloody hell are you up to?'

'It's just a pencil,' said the startled Oiney.

'Pencil me eye! No man rushes around the cell with a pencil stub making weird signs. Don't take me for an eejit!'

'It's a game I'm playin'.'

'Game you're playing? What game?'

'I call it "guess where",' explained Oiney.

'Guess where? Don't talk bloody riddles to me!'

'If you calm down, mister, I'll explain. Life gets a little boring if you're in this lone cell hour after hour so I made up this little game of 'guess where' to pass the time. It's really simple. D'you see that little fly that's now sittin' on the chamber pot. Well, in a second or two he'll be up an' flyin' about, so I try to guess where he's goin' to land on the wall and I mark the spot with a wee cross. It's excitin' isn't it? Wouldn't you like a shot? Have a go, mister! I know you'd like it.'

Absentmindedly, 'Shankill' accepted the pencil stub and then suddenly realising his mistake threw it on the floor and stamped on it with his studded heel.

'Would I like a shot? Would I like a shot, you priest-ridden half-wit,' he snarled. 'Guess where! Guess where I'll put this stick in a minit, you village moron. Clean up your cell this instant for the head-shrinker's comin' to see you and Christ knows he has a case on his hands! You need him surely.' The warder then, to make it easier for Oiney to tidy up, tipped the contents of the chamber pot over the floor with his heel before slamming the cell door.

It was little kind gestures like this which endeared 'Shankill' to all the prisoners. He also had a very worthy record of previous socially useful employment. Prior to his present edifying position he had been a debt collector for a rich finance company in north Belfast and before that he had been for several months a zealous and well-paid scab labourer in the shipyards. These prestigious posts had provided excellent references for his advancement to the Prison Service, but not nearly so influential in doing so as the fact that every Twelfth of July his hands were swollen and bloody from battering the big Lambeg drum to summon the Loyalist tribes to the Orange fields at Finaghy.

Shortly after his footsteps had faded in the corridor, a lean, chinless face stared at Oiney through the spy hole. Tucker Wayne, the prison psychiatrist, was a very tall thin eccentric man dressed in a white, frowsy half-length cotton coat with dark-rimmed, thick-set glasses. He had the wary habit of making copious notes at the spyhole before actual contact with the prisoner. 'Shankill' returned to open the cell for him. One of Wayne's peculiar traits was moments of extreme truth followed by sheer gibberish.

'So you are, Hoy. Don't stand up! Mind if I sit?' He planked himself on the low bed without awaiting an answer. His long legs made an angular bridge at the knees with the wall opposite. 'Not really much room here, is there? Now tell me what I can do for you—I'm your psychiatrist.'

'What would that be?' asked the puzzled Oiney, for this was the first time in his life to hear the word.

'Well now, I'll explain it as simple as I can. Let me see. I pry into the human brain box

…'

'Not mine you don't,' exclaimed the alarmed Oiney, leaping to the top of the bed. 'This is one brain box you aren't goin' to pry into an' that's for sure!'

Mr Wayne made a sharp entry in his notebook: 'Unsocial chronic anxiety neurosis verging on paranoia… extremely suspicious… ears twitching and fingers fidgety.' 'Tell me, young man, what made you blow up the hut? You can be honest with me. D'you hate Orangemen?'

'I hardly know what an Orangeman is and I doubt if he knows himself. I was taught at Creevan school that all human beings were created in the image o' God and I believe that, except mebbe for that ugly brute staring in the side of the door there…'

'Let me at him,' shouted the angry intruder who was none other than our friend 'Shankill', doing his usual eavesdropping. 'Let me at him till I knock his melt in!'

'Shut that door immediately or I'll report the matter,' the psychiatrist ordered before turning to Oiney. 'So you see, laddie, I'm really your friend. Confess everything to your dear friend and I'll see if I can have you certified. '

'Certified? What's that?'

'It's just a little valuable note written by me and signed by two other doctors which makes you hold no responsibility for the terrible crimes you committed. It will make you feel almost innocent.'

'But I am innocent,' Oiney protested. 'Honest to God up there, I did nothin'. I was only delivering a message. I can't recall a single wrong thing I did since I was enticed out of Creevan. Honest. I swear it on my granny's life I was only doin' a message.'

Despite Oiney's offer of such a high stake as his granny's valuable life, Mr Wayne looked singularly unconvinced and made another entry in his notebook: 'Prisoner admits lapsing into comatose condition… but pretends no cognition of wrong-doing… subconscious guilt transference to a dependent relative—his unfortunate grandmother…'

Then the psychiatrist stared into Oiney's bewildered blue eyes for a full minute until the poor prisoner thought he recognised what was afoot. At the old school on the hill in Creevan, when two boys quarrelled over which of them was telling the truth, they stared long and hard into each other's eyes, the first one to blink being the liar. Mr Wayne gazed in amazement at the unblinking Oiney and then averted his eyes towards his notebook.

'Caught you out,' shouted Oiney in triumph. 'Now who's tellin' the truth?'

'Strange fellow', wrote the psychiatrist, 'reflex reactions completely abnormal… optically non-existent…'

'So you see,' added Oiney still in a grand mood of triumph, 'I'm absolutely innocent.'

'Rest assured, lad. The Court won't hold your innocence against you. It might even help in getting your sentence reduced to ten or fifteen years and take into consideration the fact that it was not your fault you were born a Catholic and an Irishman with all the criminal propensities in the blood.'

Since the very inquisitive Mr Wayne, apart from having nothing better to do with his time, had formally to justify a little the fat salary he was receiving, he visited Oiney's cell quite frequently with his black notebook. On the second occasion he took Oiney's pulse and blood pressure and then made the Creevan lad lie stretched on the bed while he swung a copper ball on a piece of string above his victim's eyes. He then spoke in such a slow, sonorous drone that he almost fell asleep himself: 'Take it easy… Relax… Lie back and relax…That's better… I want you to go back in time… Go back slowly in time… Slowly… slowly… as far as your memory can…Tell me everything!'

'Blurp,' said Oiney. 'Me granny told me I had the wind often and me back was blue from her thumpin' me.' 'Carryon… Carryon… you're doin' fine… Continue from there!'

'Eeny… meanie… miny mo,' said Oiney, '…and this wee piggie cried wee, wee, wee all the way home!' 'Superb! Superb,' exclaimed Mr Wayne gleefully, certain he was on the brink of wonderful confessions.

'I'm sorry,' said Oiney, sitting up. 'I can't remember a thing. I think that's because I was born very young, too young altogether, so much so that I can't remember a thing more until I was three years old and standin' cryin' me eyes out with this big banana in me hand.'

'Crying? Is that because you were spoiled?'

'No, it just looked so nice and yellow like a big sweetie, but no one took the skin off. Those first three years of me life are a blank to me, an' after that me granny an' the master kept cloutin' me so much that any sense I may have had was knocked out o' me. So I'm not much of a guinea-pig, am I?'

Tucker Wayne was not to be put off so easily. 'Ah, this granny of yours. Tell me more about her! I'll tell you what. I'll leave a notebook and pen for you and you just jot down your early memories of her and Creevan. Will you do that and I'll see if I can help you?'

'Well, I'm sure I could do worse an' won't it help to pass the time if you keep that other quare fella out o' me cell!'

'I'll have a sharp word with him,' promised the psychiatrist before leaving.

In the weeks that followed Oiney began to fill in his notebook, first with doodle caricatures of Shaun and Sheamus, the Customs Man, Tucker Wayne and 'Shankill'; then he began his own story—best as the poor fellow could…

I was born in Creevan at the back o' beyont in the heart of Ireland. As true as God's me judge I did no man or woman any wrong except maybe that holy water in the lemonade bottle but it cured them anyway and God pitying me good intentions who knows changed it to the rale thing I was brought up a Catholic because no one said I was any different and I don't suppose they asked me. Me granny was never done callin' me a beggar's get and oiney boy that I don't remember me own name for the clouts I got from her and the masters though the lady teacher was good as gold and used to give the poorest barefoot boys a sup out of her own milk an I was told I had this invisible soul and the guardian angel perched on top of me right hand shoulder all the time though God knows I never felt the weight of a feather and it must've been dumb or in a terrible huff for it never as much as bid me the time of day. I mind tempting it and God a bit to prove they were there but the only answer I got was the empty wind sighing in the birch trees and the great walnut tree down by the edge of Dromore river. They said God made the lovely flowers and the birds and the bees but he also made the rats and the fleas to bite and wasps to sting and lightening to kill and often I felt he was as far away in Heaven as me own father wherever he is on earth. I saw a lot of poor people in Creevan and everyone so much on their knees that sometimes you'd believe that there was no job worth having on earth and they all wanted to go up above with their Amens, Amens. I often got the blame for things I never done just like this customs hut. I got this terrible picture of Hell and I'm shocking afraid of roasting there. If you don't die with a true confession on your soul and only then with a love of God you've never seen. Its an awful worry and a great puzzling thing on the big globe of the world called earth that they say spins through space at a mile a minute. Me granny the Holy Terror is as big a mystery to me as God almost but I never saw her do the things that me cousin Sheamus swore she did that night in the van the years maybe changed her 'but she did buy me the green gansey and took me to Blackrock to jump up and down in the sea and to Lough Derg with her corns and bunions and lemonade bottle when the daft ticket man had a look at me turned-up trousers the shame it brought to me red face them terrible curses too she said on Sunday at the door with God and Robert Emmet on the mantelpiece looking down on her and hearing every word she said the Almighty forgive her one day and rest her poor soul isn't she all I have with her full needle of insulin piercing her riddled arm every single day in life for the diabetes and never a rest for her mind of torment and that rogue Jemmy M'Gurk often taking a lend of her I'm sure you could save your invisible soul in Creevan as much as in the Lakes of Killarney or Galway bay where Shaun and Sheamus swore blind they were taking me .Me granny told me that Ireland is going to sink in the wild Atlantic five years before the end of the world and that ghosts run mad about the church and chapel graveyards on All Souls Night and no one should cut the lone fairy tree in Lennon's meadow for the wee folk will climb into your bed at night and jag your bare feet with the cut branches and she said that every night at the stroke of midnight the black headless horses and coach of the great Leslie family dash through the dark streets of Creevan to the family vault at the back of the Castle but I don't hear or see them with me head well under the blankets and there's a secret tunnel under the hollow sound on the brae at the haunted woods of Knockmaddy and Terry of the Hills can't cross a chapel door because one of his ancestors informed on a Mass Rock priest in the penal days and got five pounds for him being put to death and that Captain Prunty now walks with a jerky limp of his right leg he got from God for turning over the dead corpses of his poor enemies with his foot oh, you'd never guess half the great things she told me in that old kitchen of ours among the birch trees...

It was a few weeks later that Mr Wayne collected the completed manuscript with all its blots, squiggles and torn leaves. The psychiatrist seemed in such a depressed mood that he could scarcely speak. He was so downcast that Oiney, forgetting his own plight, tried to console the unfortunate gentleman: 'Look on the bright side, Mr Wayne! You haven't died a winter yet, have you? Every cloud has a silver lining an' far-off hills are green. Never put off till tomorrow what you can do today an' too many cooks spoil the broth, don't they?'

The disconsolate psychiatrist shook his head. 'Penelope is no cook. She can't even grate cheese. She's the worst cook in Christendom. But it isn't just that. It's her blustering conceit. She took this damned trumpet to Portadown on the Orange Walk and insisted on going ahead of the Bands. She nearly drowned out the big drums and made a right clown of me when I tried to intervene. She hates my literary tastes as well, my favourite writers, Zane Gray, Mickey Spillane. Wants me to read the Bible more and devote myself to writing some anti-Catholic pamphlets. She makes me feel, how shall I put it, a little inadequate. The longer I live with her the more I feel like the quack I am. What do I know about the science of medicine? The Infirmary I run here is just a sham, a halfway transit camp, nothing less, between the jail, the morgue or the asylum. If ever the notice "Abandon Hope All Ye Who Enter" should be written anywhere it is here. I'm nothing but a charlatan, lad, a quack!'

Oiney, of course, had long suspected this but his truly gentle nature made him abhor self-denigration in others. Besides, a jail is depressing enough without its inmates and staff becoming unduly morose and adding to the gloom. 'Don't lower your self-esteem,

Mr Wayne! I'm sure God has some purpose for you somewhere. You might apply for the Foreign Missions. Africa and parts of Asia they say are so short of medical people that they might even take you... It's only a suggestion...'

'I'll tell you what I'll do. I'll go straight home and put that bloody trumpet in the river or the fire. That's what I'll do.'

'Shankill' stood at the open cell door with a mean snigger on his smug countenance. After Wayne had gone down the corridor in a rage, Oiney heard the warder croak, 'Burn it or drown it, like the brave Orange Flute in Dungannon, it will still play 'Protestant Boys'.'

On a visit a week later Tucker Wayne was in an even worse state. He almost collapsed on Oiney's bed. 'There's been a calamity,' he groaned. 'I'm just the purveyor of disasters. That's what I am.'

'Has Penelope left you?' asked Oiney sympathetically.

'No such luck,' growled the visitor. 'This latest calamity occurred last Friday in Newry, a fatal day for me. My secretary and I were having a quiet confab in a private hotel, you know the sort of thing, urgent business and all that, when it dawned on me that I had left the car door open with my briefcase inside.'

'And it was stolen?'

'The worst of it was that your notebook was in that case! My God, you'll be shocked when you hear the complete story. You'll be frantic!'

'Oh, don't worry about that, mister,' said the calm Oiney. 'Them notes o' mine are better lost. Them childish ravings are best forgotten. I just wrote down the first thing came into me head.'

'Oh, it's much, much worse than that, lad. It's a calamity of the first degree. Them Nationalist folk of Newry, and the town's brimming with them, have laid their foul hands on the notebook and they've published every line you wrote in the local paper with a brief but damning preface of their own. There, you may as well go ahead and read it! Here!'

He handed Oiney the paper and the Creevan lad sat down on the edge of the bed to read it aloud; slowly his expression changed from wonder to downright consternation and anger at the contents of the preface to his own story:

JAILED INNOCENCE

The RUC and six county junta must surely be scraping the bottom of the barrel when they are holding in Armagh Gaol without charge or trial a poor harmless nonentity called Oiney Hoy, a lad from the obscure village of Creevan in the County Monaghan. We have in our possession (we will not reveal from what source it arrived with us) a personal document written by this poor clodhopper; he describes in it scores of rather pathetic incidents in his bizarre existence. We are not saying that the young man is certifiable, though the authorities may use this course, but any honest, intelligent person after reading the unique document objectively can only be alarmed at the state of the young man's mind. We merely request our readers to judge for themselves as they read on, giving the unfortunate fellow the benefit of their Christian charity, not forgetting that surely he is one of God's own.

THE EDITOR

With great indignation and disgust Oiney threw the newspaper onto the cell floor. 'How dare they call me names like 'one of God's own',' he stormed. 'I resemble that remark!'

'Resent, you mean,' said Mr Wayne helpfully.

'Whatever you like to call it,' said Oiney in a huff. 'And I'll tell them this much. I'm not a poor clodhopper and I never was. I never hopped a clod in me life. Never! Definitely not. An' what do they mane be 'nonentity'? Usin' big words to baffle me. That's them! I don't like their insinuations, not one wee bit. One o' God's own indeed! Sure, we're all one o' God's own!'

THE HOLY TERROR'S REVENGE

Meanwhile, back in Creevan, the sad demented granny was raging. Not only had the daft gasson not returned with her little brown jug, he had failed to return at all. And, since he had been in Doyle's public house the night it was cleaned out, he would certainly have some explaining to do. The Holy Terror was so angry with him that she called him all the wicked names that she knew in English, and when these ran out she summoned abusive epithets that had lingered over from her youth in the Carrick hills. Even the memory of the original Oiney from those parts returned to her in a much more favourable light than the terrible amadhaun she had raised. She could not even pass up the chapel brae either without that inquisitive sexton Jonjo asking her about his lost pal's whereabouts.

She softened a good deal, however, when the terrible news reached her that Oiney was in the hands of the Royal Ulster Constabulary and Armagh Jail; all her fury then was directed towards what she fiercely described as 'them black-coated haythens with grim visage'. Quite often in her wrath she had a glance at the large picture of Robert Emmet in the Dock and she now felt more certain than ever that like that great hero of Ireland, Oiney would almost certainly end up on the gallows tree. So she stormed up and down the braes of Creevan, determined as she was at all costs to prevent Oiney going into the history books and patriotic ballads of Ireland.

Living quite near to her home in Creevan was a crafty cobbler, Jemmy McGurk. Jemmy, for reasons of his poverty and accursed drouth, had occasionally taken harmless advantage of the old woman's paranoia. He excused himself on the grounds that he was allaying her daft anxiety, but at the same time he never refused the grateful coin she often gave him for his services. One day, for example, he had answered her loud impatient knocking on his door.

'Jemmy, Jemmy McGurk, have you such a thing as a good spade or a sharp-edged shovel in your possession?'

'The best in Ireland, Mam.'

'Well, you know that villain Mooney, that lives next to me?'

'Is it Mooney the squint-eyed spalpeen you mane?' 'None other. Well, he's tryin' to get at me undher the wall that joins our houses... '

'The bloody blackguard! Shure, nothin's sacred to him.' 'Tell you, Jemmy, I'll give you a pound note if you take your spade and dig down undher me coal-hole an' meet him halfway in his. Will you do that for me, Jemmy?'

'I will surely, Mam, an' what's more I'll knock the livin' daylights out o' his corrugated head an' his lantern jaws.' 'Good man, Jemmy, an' the pound apart I'll light a holy candle for you in the chapel.'

'Never mind the pound or the candle. Mooney's kind is the ruin of Ireland an' the plague o' civilisation. I'll settle the randy oul' rascal. Never mind the pound, Mam, or the candle. A glass o' whiskey will suffice for the day. Don't worry, I'll sort him.'

So Jemmy took his spade over his shoulder like a peat-bog mountaineer and disappeared into the depths of the dark coal-hole. He stayed there for about five minutes battering his spade against the hard stone wall and yelling as if he was in mortal conflict with Old Nick himself. Then wiping a little coal dust on his brow he emerged wearing a cute grin of triumph: 'That cooked his goose, Mam. That put the fear o' God in Mooney for good. If you hear as much as a squeak from him from now on, he's a goner. Tell him that from yours truly!'

Now it happened in the month following Oiney's arrest at the border, the Holy Terror found a big round torch battery near her doorstep, and never having seen the likes he before was certain that Mooney was up to his tricks again, this time to blow her up. She was frantic when she called on Jemmy with the suspect cylinder held at arm's length. 'Jemmy, Jemmy, what in God's name is this dangerous contraption doin' on me doorstep? Is he tryin' to murdher me? Has he no respect for life or limb?'

'Ah, bejasus Mam,' said Jemmy, 'that Mooney fella is goin' to extremes surely. But let me handle this, Mam.' He took the battery from her hand and held it gingerly. 'Have you a spare can o' wather, cold wather an' we'll soon make it defunct. That'll defeat Mooney's intent if he's thinkin' you're so aisy disposed of.' The Holy Terror gave a great sigh of relief when she saw the wicked object submerged.

'Three days an' three nights in that can and an odd Hail Mary over it will take the sting out of its tail,' Jemmy assured her. 'An' then if you like you can throw it on the dung-heap.'

That night the old woman kept brooding. Her thoughts then suddenly switched from the spalpeen Mooney next door to an even greater enemy, the Governor of Armagh Jail who was holding her gormless grandson, Oiney, in wrongful custody. After all, the latter was only a daft gasson, just a couple of years out of short trousers and still wet behind the ears. That mouth of his always open, catching flies. My God, she thought, if only I could lay hands on the amadhaun I'd knock sense into that great gap between his ears, mother o' God forgive me, him just a clumsy slip of a lad, never seen his father and his poor ma, me daughter, rushin' off to join the harp playin' holy angels. Imagine that brute of a Governor holdin' her innocent gasson. In her fury a fiendish thought struck her.

Next morning she arose early and hastened to Jemmy McGurk's door. 'It's an aisy five pounds for you, Jemmy.' 'What's that Mam?' asked the puzzled Jemmy, who never failed to be amused by her strange requests.

'You said three days and three nights in the can, didn't you?'

'I did indeed.'

'So it's still alive.'

'It is,' said Jemmy, wondering what was coming next. 'Well, Jemmy, there's a whole five pounds for you if you take that bomb out, dry it well, an' we'll post it in a package to them dirty Orange crew who are holdin' poor Oiney ransom. Do that, Jemmy, an' there's a good five pound note in your pocket!'

Jemmy hesitated a minute or two to consider the risk.

Then he decided that it was a fairly harmless adventure, and at the very worst a hoax. He agreed to take a chance, not for five pounds but that the two of them would have a drink together in Ward's pub. He dried the battery and wrapped it well in a brown package. It was the Holy Terror herself who wrote the enclosed note in her own best squiggly capitals:

TO THE GOVERNOR OF ARMAGH JAIL, SIX COUNTIES, NORTHERN IRELAND. I'M GIVING YOU TWENTY FOUR HOURS YOU ORANGE VARMINT TO LET THE DACINT BOY, OINEY, OUT OF YOUR VILE CLUTCHES. IF YOU DON'T I WILL SEND A BIGGER BOMB TO BLOW YOUS ALL TO HELL TO JOIN YOUR RELATIONS.
SIGNED 'FAITH OF OUR FATHERS'

Then she got Jonjo to address and post the parcel, telling him it was a gift for the Governor to pass on to Oiney. After a drink with Jemmy McGurk, she returned home to wait the great news that a hole had been blown in Armagh Jail wall out of which poor Oiney could climb and return home to Creevan where she would kill him herself.

A few days later, instead of good news she had a visit from the Civic Guard Sergeant Pat Oats and Spoonbait his colleague, who came to arrest her and Jemmy. There was a great commotion in the street.

'Bad cess to you, Pat Oats,' she shouted, 'take your dirty big paws off a dacint woman that kept God's commandments a sight better nor anyone else in Creevan. An' take that sourpuss sniveller spoonbait back with you to the barracks or better still to Lynch's pub where yous two are always loiterin' with intent!'

'This is a very serious matther, Mam,' said Pat Oats grandly.

'Serious me arse,' she retorted. 'If yous were doin' your duty an' caught the ones inveiglin' Oiney, yous might be worth half your pay. Instead you've nothin' betther to do with your time than hound and harass a respectable an' God-fearin' woman o' Creevan!'

'Come along with Jemmy,' Spoonbait tried to cajole her. 'Come an' we'll sort it out quietly at the Barracks!'

'Sort out the shite at the tail of your shirt, Mr Spoonbait,' she cried, 'with that hawk-nose o' yours dippin' your snot into everyone's business. If either o' yous had the guts of a sparrow yous'd be up there in the Black North causin' repercussions an' not leavin' a poor woman to sort the buggers out. I'll tell yous somethin' me buckos. Yous'll shift Creevan Market House afore yous budge me, or that I'll be seen walkin' the same pavement as turncoat civvy guards.'

And so ended the affair with Jemmy McGurk going to the Barracks to explain the harmless little hoax that had put Armagh Jail on a red alert for six hours that day. On his release with a caution, Jemmy wiped his brow and took a vow that he would exercise great care in future dealings with the Holy Terror.

THE GOOD THIEF

The Governor of the prison and Oiney did not take the least bit kindly to each other, and when 'Shankill' opened the office door to march the Creevan lad in front of this very august Mr Purdy, the latter greeted the southern Irishman with a deep growl: 'Who told you to sit? Stand in front of the desk to attention! And stop gazing around!'

Oiney was truly astonished at the contents of the office; it resembled a warehouse. Only the desk where the heavyjowled giant sat carried any appearance of clerical activities. Piled around the room was the most varied collection of garments and goods that Oiney had ever seen. There were boxes of shirts, bundles of stockings and knitwear, cartons of sweets, tins of groceries, pears, peaches and pineapples. Dozens of separate items lay scattered around on the floor and on chairs while the window ledge was heaped with a colourful assortment of gaudy ties.

'You're very popular around here,' said Mr Purdy with heavy sarcasm. 'Especially in Newry. Your published doggerel has touched the heartstrings of an easily moved populace. Gifts are pouring in. But tell me this! Why should a rascal like you be favoured more than the starving children of Africa and Asia? Answer me that!'

'I really don't know, mister, but you can have the lot for yourself if you just let me go back home to me granny in Creevan.'

The Governor gave a loud snigger that was immediately taken up by 'Shankill' who almost doubled up with great guffaws of mockery. 'Go back to your granny in Creevan? That'll be the day. That old headbanger that sent a dud battery to blow me up along with ill-wishes for me and my relations. Send you home to her? Are you joking? No fear. You just keep on writing your sob story and let the gifts pour in. But warn your friends! No more stupid gifts like files and hacksaw blades, or skeleton keys. One idiot even sent you in a rope-ladder. We only accept edible goods, clothes, books and the like. And what a bazaar and jumble sale we'll have in the local Orange Hall... '

'I do hope it's a success on behalf of the poor children of Africa and Asia,' said the generous Oiney.

'Africa and Asia my foot,' said Mr Purdy with a howl of laughter. 'Charity begins at home. On behalf of the Prison Staff's Benevolent Fund, a very important cause for warders' widows and orphans. Just you keep up the good work and we'll attend to your needs. We'll not kill the goose that lays the golden egg, shall we?'

'Are you calling me a goose, sir?' asked Oiney belligerently.

'Listen, sonny, I'm being nice to you, so just keep that effen trap of yours shut, do you hear! When you appear in Court in our own good time, we want no rag-and-bones man, so we'll have to fatten you up. We want no ugly comments from foreign observers who have recently come out of the woodwork. Constructive criticism —yes: adverse criticism—no! That's why I sent for you. It's the Prison Infirmary for you next week... '

'But I don't want to go there,' protested Oiney, remembering that 'Abandon Hope' signboard mentioned by Mr Wayne.

'You'll go where we put you,' roared the Governor standing up, 'and that's final.'

According to Mr Wayne, the head of Armagh Jail was really a moderate man politically, totally dedicated to the abolition of the death sentence and flogging except in instances where prison governors and warders or their wives and families, relations and friends were the victims. As a boy he had been a keen ornithologist, risking his neck even in climbing the highest trees in his nest hunting and egg collecting, thus relieving many of our feathered friends of the dreadful anxiety and frenzied activity of bringing up their young. Apprenticed in an abbatoir, vulgarly called a slaughterhouse, he shunned the gory scenes as much as possible and advocated animal rights, strenuously demanding quicker means of disposing with the creatures. Like the good Customs Officer, he had graduated to Government service and high position through his lifelong, loving friendship with a dear friend in Stormont.

When Oiney returned to his cell with a woebegone expression on his pale face, he was astonished to find a two-tier bunk there instead of his low bed, and standing beside it a small, lean, agile fellow with a chirpy, cheeky face. This stranger, without introduction, kept winking at him and screwing the side of his face so frequently that Oiney wondered if the poor fellow had a permanent tic. He was beginning to feel quite sorry for him and was about to enquire after his health, but his kindly solicitude was quietly circumvented when the winking newcomer drew him down to a sitting position at the rear of the cell door out of 'Shankill's gaze. 'Don't worry about me, Oiney! I know all about you. Don't worry, I'm not a grass!'

Oiney's brows furrowed. A grass what, he felt like asking; he had never heard a sentence so incomplete. A grass widow? A grass lawn? A grass cricket or a grass market? Never just a grass! The more he lived in the world the stranger it grew.

Though he now sat close to the stranger, the latter still kept winking at him. 'Don't worry about me, pal! I'm Bobby Brown from the Falls... D'you twig? I'm married to a Pape. The Falls, Pape, d'you twig? I got into your cell on pretence I'd get you to spill the beans an' then grass on you. No bloody fear. They've another guess comin'. Me name's Bobby Brown, Oiney. I'm on your side. Shake!'

Oiney's eternal glow of friendship for suffering humanity made him grasp the extended hand warmly. 'What are you in for, Bobby?' he asked with a sudden interest in the origin and statistics of the growing crime rate.

'Church an' chapel collection boxes, Oiney.'

'Oh, I see. You're a charity worker then?'

'Are you joking? I pinch them. I can't stand churches and chapels...'

'Well, if I was you Bobby,' said Oiney trying to be helpful, 'I'd just keep out o' them and avoid collection boxes.'

The stranger eyed him closely to see if he was serious. 'God knows you're the peculiar genius, Oiney, but never mind! I'm here to help spring you!'

A puzzled look came over the Creevan lad's face again: 'Spring me? What's that?'

'Help you escape, you nut. You're being transferred to the Infirmary block on Tuesday. We have a plant in the office...'

'Well,' said the confused Oiney, 'if you have a plant in the office I never seen it and I was there five minits ago. I seen ties an' shirts but not a flower-pot or plant...'

'A plant, an informer, you daft rookie. One who tells us the score. You're to be transferred on Tuesday and at ten past ten o'clock sharp that night you are to be on the flat roof of the Infirmary, via a trap-door in the ceiling of the linen room. One of the patients'll be there to guide you. Squeeze yourself through the trap-door an' close it tight behind you. Then hide behind the brick chimney an' wait the helicopter...'

'The what?' said the amazed and disbelieving Oiney.

'The helicopter. The great iron bird that's comin' to rescue you.'

'You're coddin' me now! Who'd want to rescue the likes o' me? In a helicopter as well! You're at the coddin' surely...'

'Cross me heart, Oiney! Why else would I come here an' tell you all this? You're far more important to the bhoys outside than you imagine. Especially since that article in the Newry paper. Their hearts bleed for you, Oiney. Is it all right, pal? Ten past ten sharp on Tuesday. Shake hands on it, Oiney.'

Oiney shook the stranger's hand although he still felt a bit dubious. Yet the more he thought he began to realise that almost equally strange things had happened to him in life. And that wink and twitch on Bobby's face was so completely disarming!

His excitement mounted as Tuesday drew nearer. His spirits soared at even the faint hope of getting back to Creevan. Once there if anyone pursued him he knew lots of secret haunts among the high reeds and ferns around the lough and among the trees of Knockmaddy Woods. His mind was so alert with this pleasant prospect that he found it impossible to sleep, so he took advantage of his companion's eagerness to recount tales, exciting tales of his past life, all to pass the weary waiting hours.

'Why, Bobby,' he asked one night. 'Why demean your nice character by resortin' to pinchin' out of holy places?'

'Thank you, Oiney, I've not looked on it that way before. I've a totally unchristian regard for things sacred. I mean what really have I against the good Churches? After all what have they done to deserve my relievin' them of some o' their riches? Other than Inquisitions, fanaticism, sellin' Indulgences, banner blessing for wars an' Imperial stoogery an' several other similar trivial blemishes, our Churches have a history of absolute perfection, Piety personified. Mind you, Oiney, come to think of it, my resentment may come from some strange childhood experiences. It's possible, I think, yes, just possible...'

Oiney nodded his head in agreement. 'Mr Wayne the psychiatrist says everything can be explained that way...'

'That bonehead would, wouldn't he? But since you ask, Oiney, I'll give you me story to pass the time.'

They sat together on the bottom bunk and once again Oiney got lost in the strange experiences of another mortal on our little planet.

'I was born in Carrickfergus,' said Bobby, 'of Scottish-Irish descent. Me mother Millie was Irish an' me father George a good, dacint dour Scot. He was a docker to trade, an' me mother before she married an' had me, was a mill girl in West Belfast. Although she was a Pape an' he a Proddy, they got on great an' brought me up to the age of seven without bigotry of any kind. Then, Oiney, when I was seven, a terrible accident occurred to them on holiday at Glenarm when the bus overturned, and in one night in August I lost both of them. I was taken to an orphanage outside Belfast where I stayed for three years, and I tell you honestly, Oiney, I didn't like it one wee bit. In some ways the days o' Dickens haven't changed that much.

'But there was never a lad so happy when at the age of eleven I was adopted by the

Reverend Cyril Brown and his grand missus Ethel, whose surname I still bear. They had a church mansion near Glengormley overlooking Belfast Lough an' not far from the Zoo. I spent the nicest days you could imagine in that ivy-clad house, and in the summer they took me everywhere around the glens of Antrim and up to the Giant's Causeway in the north an' the Long Man's grave an' God only knows where else. Me foster mother was a great charity worker at the Belfast docks an' there was nothin' the Reverend Brown liked to do better than read me extracts from the Good Book on the fine verandah of that house on a Sunday or quote poems from Milton an' *Paradise Lost*... I often thought since on the name *Paradise Lost*, it seemed surely to have an omen in it. They sent me to Portora boarding school down by the Border country where Oscar Wilde himself attended many years ago, but I didn't last there very long when the scandal broke out, not at the school Oiney, but at home. It was the same year as that other debacle took place when some minister ran away with the funds of the Orange Order across the water, but me foster father, thank God, wasn't involved in any thin' of that sort. He just, Oiney, had these wee sins o' the flesh, incidental wee longings an' cravings that grew insurmountable an' were looked on with great disdain in those puritan parts of Ulster.'

'I was on me summer holiday from Portora when one Sunday he took me up to his study at Glengormley—Ethel was out at the time—to teach me the rudiments of elementary sex education which every good Christian father imparts to his son or should do. I knew, of course, a little about the subject from me days at Portora, but not nearly as much as me mentor. He drew references from the Bible on the theme an' honest to God, Oiney, I never saw a man wax so eloquent... After a while of divine exhortation the sweat ran down his forehead an' cheeks, his eyes danced out of his sockets an' honest to Christ, Oiney, he just couldn't stop himself. I never in me life saw a man in such a fit of pious enthusiasm, he got worked up to the limits. Unfortunately, a maid notorious for her prattlin' tongue saw the pair of us, an' the evil word spread around the Parish. Later when the discerning public learned that the good minister, not wishin' to confine these exalted lessons to the puny precincts of his home but extend them in the spirit of Christian charity to the choirboys of Whiteabbey, a number of outraged parents banded together to pour cold water on his rampant enthusiasm. As a result, Oiney, he was lodged in confinement in a special wing of Crumlin Jail and I was taken from me lovely ivy-clad home to a Boys' Home on the Ormeau Road in Belfast, where I continued me sex education although not on such a high plane. In that Home, I learned more than mere sex. I learned some of the finer points of knavery from young bedevilled outcasts of housing-schemes and inner city slums... A sex scandal broke out there as well but not with the same lofty religious overtones. It was not long before I graduated for Borstal training. There I learned to admire the skills of deception that ensure survival, for the most popular heroes among us were assuredly not the penitents or the goodly but the wily an' fearless. Yet for all the cynicism abroad, I still retained me humanity an' certain principles learned perhaps from the Good Book in those Sunday lessons given by me foster parent in his less rampant days.

'Eventually on my release from Borstal, after a long wait, I obtained work as a cross-ferry steward on the boat that was plyin' between Larne an' Stranraer. There I was able, after pickin' up a little experience, of puttin' me generous principles into practice. The hold of that ferry at the time was often crammed with poor emigrants and equally poor farm-servants comin' an' going from their homes in Ireland. Very few o' them could afford the full price of a comfortable cabin midship, so when the boat was on its way an' most of the crew asleep, I devised the most kind, humane plan possible, Oiney. I had them transferred to these comfortable bunks at quarter the official price, an amount which I pocketed, not merely with a clear conscience but a sense of great pride. For I wasn't even diddlin' the Company. Wouldn't the cabins be otherwise empty?

'I continued in this noble and charitable enterprise for a number of years until I was shopped by an envious workmate, inspired no doubt, by the Evil One, an' thus terminated my mission o' mercy. Such is life, Oiney, so no matter how high or noble your aspirations, beware o' the snake in the grass. I was forced then in leaner times to work as an assistant stall hand in the Smithfield Market in Belfast, near Castle Junction, the city centre. It was at Smithfield with its stalls an' books an' records and a teemin' market that I decided to improve me livelihood. You see it was at this time I met me future wife Jenny, a bonny girl from the Antrim Road in Belfast, an' though we had a different background I knew she was the one for me. I didn't need to change me religion nor she hers, for we didn't make it an issue. We got a place in the Lower Falls an' funny enough, it wasn't long before I began to see their point o' view. It wasn't a religious thing, just nationality an' common sense. There were, I know, Oiney, far brighter Proddies than me came round to that decision before I was born even. Well, be that as it may, I found it hard enough to make ends meet at Smithfield so I hit on this plan o' hawkin' holy pictures around Ireland...'

'You did not!' exclaimed the astonished Oiney. 'Surely to God, a Protestant wouldn't sell Catholic pictures around holy Ireland?'

'Me hand up to God I did that very thing, an' for a long, long time made a very good livin' out of it too. I'm not boastin' Oiney, but I sold them holy pictures like hot cakes outside the chapels at Mission times and at country markets an' fairs. I'm a broadminded chap an' wasn't I servin' the masses like I did on that damn boat? I'll tell you this too, Oiney. The poor of Ireland were me best customers be far, for havin' little or nothin' on this earth aren't they lookin' for a seat o' comfort in the next. D'you twig, Oiney?' He gave one of his familiar, roguish winks.

'Tell me this, Bobby,' said Oiney. 'Did you not make enough money at the pictures to keep you clear o' dippin' in the offertory collection boxes?'

'Listen, Oiney,' explained Bobby. 'It's all a question o' Market Economy. Yes, that's what it is.'

'What's Market Economy?' asked the open-mouthed Oiney.

'It's like this. Supply and Demand, Oiney. That's how it works. Let me explain. In the average household goods there's always a quick turnover. Bread, butter, cheese an' milk are consumed nearly as quickly as they're produced. Even pots an' pans, brushes an' what have you get knocked about an' need replacin'. But holy pictures, Oiney! Now they're a different kettle o' fish. They hang up on the wall away from children's reach, an' sad to say, remain there a permanent feature. Only an earthquake, a landslide, or artillery fire can shift them. After the first sale, unfortunately they last as long, an' sometimes longer, than the house itself. They survive pestilence an' plague an' hail, rain an' snow; they hang up there despite cursin', shoutin' an' drunken revelry an' even auction sales. So you see, Oiney lad, the market's limited, and in these wretched circumstances, what can a poor man resort to but unorthodox ways o' gettin' a livin'? But think, Oiney, if you have any qualms o' conscience, think of all the gold pillaged by our good Churches from Aztecs, Incas an' the like in soul-savin' missions. They can't preach morality, can they?'

'What are these Inkas and Asticks you're talkin' about, Bobby?'

'Oh, go to sleep, Oiney, an' get ready for the high jump on Tuesday. I only wish to God I was goin' with you.'

Oiney did not sleep too well that night. He lay awake a long time thinking of the wild adventures of that strange companion lying in the bunk above him. What an incredible world surely we were all born into, with myriads of folk whose rich or sad lives are intertwined with ours yet often so far apart. Outside Armagh Jail, the wind was rising and blowing, blowing over Creevan among the rushes and sedges of the rippling lough, a peaceful, simple scene that he hoped to soon enjoy away from this tumult.

ESCAPE

A bitter cold evening it was as Oiney huddled close to the warm chimney on the roof of the jail Infirmary. No one, he felt certain, had observed his departure from the ward to the toilet and thence into the linen closet. He was clad only in pyjamas and he now scanned the darkening skies for any sign of his rescuers. He could see the lights of the ancient city of Armagh all around him, and away to the east rose the deep dark contour of part of the Mourne mountain range. To the south lay Creevan, his native village. Soon perhaps he would be walking its quiet, homely streets and telling his pal Jonjo the terrible things which can befall a man for just being decent and kind.

His granny, of course, would rant and rave at him and call him everything under the sun for not fetching home the little brown jug. She would tell him once again that he could not put a foot across the threshold without causing some awful calamity. And indeed, Oiney was beginning to believe that there was more than a grain of truth in what she said about him. With this fearful thought in mind, he left the comfort of the chimney to haul a heavy beam of wood across the roof in order to block access from the more frail trap-door.

At last, to his great relief, he heard the loud purring noise of the large helicopter as it circled to land on the roof which it lit first with a powerful beam. A door opened on its side and a muffled masked figure ran towards him. 'Quick, Oiney, quick! Get aboard!'

He recognised that voice and immediately he recoiled. There was no mistaking the rich twang of the Dublin back-streets.

'Oh no, Shaun! You're not on! You're just not on! I've had more than enough of you and that failed priest. I want nothin' to do with the pair of you. I'll even endure the antics of an eccentric psychiatrist and the greed of a grotesque Governor before I'll forgive the perfidy of a false friend.'

'Begod, Oiney, them's powerful words, powerful words indeed. But when you hear my story, you'll surely understand that we didn't betray you... '

'Tell all that to the marines,' said Oiney indignantly. 'Doyle's son, indeed! An' the deranged hermit. I suppose his hut didn't take off that night?'

'An' did you not find the Customs Officer a bit of a screwball yourself, Oiney? I'm not gain' to argue with you on top of this roof all night, but I'm tellin' you honestly, the oul' rat Doyle did desert me mother an' me… I'll explain it all to you aboard…'

The others in the waiting helicopter seemed to be becoming impatient also, for Oiney saw a young woman in a dark green suit running towards him.

'This is Aileen,' said Shaun, 'an' believe me Oiney, she admires you immensely.' And as if to prove her friend correct, Aileen threw her arms around Oiney and hugged him tightly. 'You're my best hero, Oiney, in the whole wide world.' She looked at him, those lovely hazel-brown eyes of hers glowing with worship. She had boyish, clear-cut features of firm resolve, an aspect that Oiney adored so much; she wore little silver ear-rings of a simple Celtic design, and her fair hair cut in something akin to a page-boy style had a reddish tinge. With those endearing arms around him she became to Oiney a delightful, warm vision of the heroic maiden of Erin. He did not know a single girl in Creevan or Carrick who could tread the same ground as her.

'Aileen works with props in the Abbey Theatre in Dublin,' Shaun explained, 'an' she's gain' to help us to disguise you. She belongs to the Movement.'

Oiney did not know what props or the Movement were, and to tell the truth he did not care as long as this brave girsha had her arms around him.

'Oh, I heard all about you Oiney,' she said, 'all about your Creevan adventures an' Lough Derg an' how you helped Shaun an' Sheamus over that Customs place. You'll go down into the history books for generations to come.' Oiney had completely forgotten Shaun's presence until he heard an impatient, almost gruff exclamation, 'Aren't you pair comin' on board?'

Arm in arm with Aileen, Oiney, forgetful for the moment of his feud with Shaun, was thus inveigled aboard the craft, where the smiling Sheamus and a young pilot dressed in an American uniform sat ready for take-off.

Soon they were flying south over the border. Oiney sat looking down on the little hills and lakes of Monaghan in the moonlight. His head was quite dizzy, for this was his first time in an aircraft, and he shivered with the cold.

'Give the poor fella a flask o' tay an' a sandwich Aileen,' said Shaun, adding with a smile, 'We'll have something warmer for him to wear shortly, won't we, Aileen?'

Oiney turned to his erstwhile friend. The tea admittedly was hot and very refreshing, but Shaun had still some deep explaining to do before Oiney would ever trust him or Sheamus again. He looked at the Dublin man: 'You promised, Shaun, that you would clear matters up as soon as we boarded.'

'Ah yes,' agreed Shaun, 'so I did. Now where was I?'

'Doyle had deserted your Mum an' you. During your terrible years o' deprivation in the back-streets o' Dublin your mother became a single-minded Irish rebel, which without a shadow of a doubt won your deepest admiration. Isn't that right?'

'Begod,' said Sheamus admiringly, 'your erudition and elocution grows with the hour, Oiney. I knew from the beginnin' you had it in you.'

Although Oiney did not know the meaning of the big words used by Sheamus they sounded very favourable so he let them pass.

'Yes Oiney,' agreed Shaun, 'you've summarised me statement well. Me mother in Dublin at first became a very staunch rebel, enlistin' me in the Calise as well. An' then… an' then she did the most dastardly thing imaginable…'

His voice broke and Oiney had to encourage him:

'What did she do, Shaun?'

'I never knew she could descend so low…'

'What did she do, Shaun?'

'She married a civvy guard. That's what she did.'

Aileen shook her head and made a shuddering grimace. 'Wasn't that the most disgustin' thing to do Oiney?'

'If you say so, Aileen…'

'I haven't seen me mother from that day to this,' continued Shaun. 'I left me house in a stormin' rage an' I've never been back. Oiney, we cannot keep you in the dark any longer. You've probably guessed about Sheamus an' me already. Well, you can now add Aileen. We're dedicated to the Movement an' the Border hut had to go up that night.'

'But you didn't give me time for an Act of Contrition or the last wee puff of a cigarette. I wasn't even given time to shrive me most precious possession, me invisible soul.'

'We hadn't time for such niceties,' admitted Shaun, 'but we didn't intend you to stand gabbin' with that silly Customs man for so long. We waited for you at the bridge for quite a time an' then when the thing went off, we said a prayer for the repose of your soul. We knew that as a good innocent Catholic you'd go straight to Heaven. After the explosion, we wrote you off…'

'You what?' exclaimed the astounded Oiney, wondering had he heard right.

'But we did say a prayer for the repose of your immortal soul as I have said,' continued Shaun.

'Well that was kind of you, very kind of you indeed,' agreed Oiney.

'An' besides,' said the Dublin man, 'had you gone up with the hut that night, you would have died for the Cause.' 'But supposin',' said Oiney, 'just supposin' I didn't want to die for the Cause.'

'Have you not learned yet, Oiney, that for all our plans an' weary watchfulness, we still cannot be absolutely certain of our individual destinies? Some of the greatest heroes o' Mankind are still unsung. History sometimes raises fakes to temporary grandeur, creatures like Hitler, Mussolini an' Franco, while many a real hero goes to an unmarked grave, caught in the crossfire…'

Oiney tugged fiercely at Shaun's jacket.

'Shaun, quick, we're passin' the hills o' Carrick. Aren't we goin' to land near Creevan?'

'Our plans are somewhat different, Oiney. In the manetime listen while I conclude me story. After the hut went up, Sheamus an' I continued our journey to the shores of Lough Neagh, an' an American air-base where we had a friend workin' as the canteen manageress. She disposed of the booze for us at a fair price. And betther still we made friends with some American-Irish pilots at the base. All very well until we read your story. You were like a voice from the dead. Of course, but of course, we welcomed the good news that you had survived the blast. But, my God, that notebook of yours published in the Newry newspaper… It was heartrending. Sheamus an' I used to be in tears readin' it. Aileen there'll confirm it.'

'It's true, Oiney, as I'm sittin' here lookin' at me hero. I used to see them wipin' their eyes...'

'It had a big lump in me throat,' said Sheamus, 'a lump in me throat that hurts me still.'

'But by Christ, Oiney lad,' said Shaun, 'were you blabbin'! You were spillin' every thin'. They were obviously feedin' you on dope. You were talkin' like a budgie an' next thing you'd be givin' them our identities. Remember you were the only one saw us at that Border. We had to spring you from Armagh Jail. Luckily for us, we found the right man.'

Shaun pointed to the helicopter pilot.

'Wolfe T Carey, a Brooklyn man whose father came from old Kildare. An' more genuine Irish than some o' your chancers who only concern themselves with savin' their skin in this world an' their cowardly souls in the next... Naw, Oiney, as much as we liked you, you had to be silenced. So we hit on this plan. Remember us tellin' you that Sheamus here is a failed priest. Well that's true. He went for a few years to Clunagh Monastery in Tipperary. It's a Cistercian Order an' they have this lovely vow of silence which suits our circumstances down to the ground. We intend to dhrop you there, an' you can wear this monastic garb which Aileen has kindly provided from the stage wardrobe. You can mingle, Oiney, with the good monks an' be one o' them. You can also adopt a monastic name like Sebastian, or Augustus, or Benedict... The other monks will not be able to question your presence; they'll probably think you have been transferred from Mount Melleray or England. And so for a year or two you can settle in silent piety until all this blows over. So try Oiney for size with the robe, Aileen!'

Oiney tried to make a last protest. 'But I haven't got this... this vocation thing that Sheamus was talkin' about in the van. I just haven't got it.'

'Never mind the vocation Oiney,' said Shaun, a bit gruffly. 'It's a vacation you need an' we'll see that you get it.'

Aileen attached a belt around Oiney's waist and then sat back to admire his new appearance. 'Mother o' God, don't you look lovely,' she said with unfeigned admiration, 'a shinin' saint of Heaven no less! Just a wee hair trim with the scissors an' you'd only want a halo. Aren't you the spittin' image of Saint Francis? I'll never forget you, Oiney,' she continued tearfully, 'an' I want you to remember me as well in your devotions an' prayers. An' when it all blows over, won't we meet again in far better times?'

Though the monk's habit was a great deal warmer than the pyjamas, Oiney sat somewhat mystified and shaken by the rapid turn of events. He had nothing against the Cistercians, of course, but he dreaded the vow of silence. There was nothing he loved in life better than a good chat. And those awful names Shaun had chosen. Why, Sebastian almost sounded vulgar. Benedict really smelt of the wine, while Augustus was so imperious and snobby. He had not much time, however, to browse over his fears, for the helicopter dropped lower and lower as it circled the monastery gardens. Fortunately for the intruders the church organ in the inner chapel drowned out the loud noise. The pilot signalled Shaun, who soon returned with some information.

'We cannot land, but Wolfe will dhrop you as close to the ground as makes no difference. He'll try an' find a space between the apple trees. Goodbye an', Oiney son, remember the Cause in your meditations!'

There were tears in Aileen's eyes, she hated partings so much, but Oiney had little time to study that sad face. Sheamus opened the door and a not too gentle push from Shaun had the Creevan lad falling into a new, a different life.

BROTHER EXCELSIS

The good Abbot of Clunagh Monastery, had been for many years awaiting a most important manifestation from Heaven. Ancient legend, written in the monastery scrolls and preserved in the precious library, told how one day the saintly monk Brother Excelsis would one day be rewarded for his deep devotion and good deeds. He had, while living, asked the Lord to allow him to return from Heaven to earth some future day to assure the good monks of Clunagh that their sublime faith in the hereafter was really justified. According to Excelsis, Heaven had answered his unusual request in a most favourable manner, sending none other than that very jovial messenger Gabriel with the good news. Gabriel had told him that it was such an odd request that not a single saint in the litany of saints or the whole of Christendom had ever requested this simple but important favour of assuring their relatives and dear friends of Heaven's real existence, while answering for once and for all the sceptic's eternal snigger 'that no one has ever come back from the dead to tell us about the far side'.

Indeed the long delay in Excelsis's return had in itself caused quite a degree of irritability among the monks of Clunagh itself. Why, only last week, the good Abbot Father Boniface had to admonish Ignatius for stealing a print of butter from Brother Placid's plate in the refectory. The silly deed fitted more into college rather than monastic life. Placid's reprisal on the other hand was positively outrageous; he had emptied a full basin of water over Ignatius's cell. Brother Placid had always been a source of concern to Father Boniface, who was a ruddy, jovial and tolerant friar. It was the latter who had suggested the adoption by the novice of the name Placid, to remind the monk of the state of grace for which he should strive. Brother Placid constantly relapsed into fits of ill-temper during which he jumped up and down, rolled his eyes and rattled his teeth. Boniface was forever making apologies for Placid's outbursts, for the latter was in charge of the Monastery Guest House and had driven folk away... folk who had merely sought a brief haven of peace and prayer in Clunagh.

One morning after a long night of prayer the devout Abbot was gazing dreamily at the rows of apple trees surrounding the monastery when suddenly a small brown object wriggling in a distant tree caught his attention. What on earth could it be? He crept quietly along the deserted corridor to Brother Andrew's cell; he was a young, eager monk in charge of the gardens.

'I think, Brother,' said the Abbot gently, so as not to awaken the other monks, 'I think we have an interloper.'

'Good heavens,' replied the startled Andrew, sitting up in bed and looking wildly around the cell. 'An interloper? Good Lord! Where?'

'In the orchard, on a distant tree. It's a dog or goat, perhaps. If so, it could ruin the fruit. Would you please investigate, Andrew?'

The Abbot crossed over to the window and looked out. 'Yes, it is still there, Brother.'

It was only a matter of minutes before the young monk returned to Father Boniface, all breathless and excited. 'It… it… it is no dog or goat, Father. It isn't, Father, it isn't.'

'Calm yourself, Brother! What is it then?'

'It's a monk, Father.'

'It cannot be. A monk?'

'It is one our brethren, Father, and yet not one of us'

Father Boniface on previous occasions had had to reprimand Brother Andrew for speaking like a Biblical text: I have told you before, Andrew, not to speak in riddles or divers tongues. What do you mean by "not one of us"? Summon all the lay-brethren!'

Brother Andrew knocked on the cell doors and soon all the brown-robed lay-monks were assembled in the long corridor. Brother Placid was especially grumpy at being aroused from his deep slumber, and few of the yawning brethren indeed looked jubilant. They lined up silently while the Abbot counted them. Thirty-five in all. Correct. He made a careful recount. But the total came to the same. They were all there to a man. Then where in God's name did the strange monk come from? It seemed so inexplicable.

Then suddenly the wondrous flash of divine inspiration shone through the heavy, hard stone walls of Clunagh and sent the good Father Boniface to his knees, chanting: 'Venite adoramus! Glory to the Lord on High! Our prayers have been answered. It can only be the saintly Excelsis. He has arrived at last.'

Some cynics and sceptics (atheists, no doubt) may criticise Heaven's poor marksmanship that landed the saint in an apple tree, but when we consider the incredible journey the good Excelsis had made from paradise across the star-studded universe without colliding with a star, asteroid or comet, when we consider the saint's safe landing on planet Earth even, not to mention a little island called Ireland in the vast Atlantic it is feat enough to astonish the average person. To land the good monk intact and still breathing in a targeted monastery garden, albeit in an apple tree, is so utterly beyond human comprehension that it deserves to be classified and locked away forever as one of the great mysteries of Faith. The Abbot had every cause indeed for great jubilation, and Heaven equally so for its almost perfect aim.

The monks, now guided by Boniface and augmented by the white-robed priests, all gathered around the apple tree in which poor Oiney, facing downward, was lodged. The entire monastery community was present. The brown, the snowwhite habits, the rosy ripe apples, the green leaves, the man cleft in the branches, all contrived to make a quaint scene reminiscent of some out-of-the-way mediaeval canvas. The good Abbot went on his knees under the tree and extended his arms: 'Welcome, Brother Excelsis! A hundred thousand welcomes on your return to Clunagh Monastery!'

And just in case the Gaelic language was more likely than not spoken in Clunagh hundreds of years ago, Boniface made it his business to convey his message in that language also, a custom which has been kindly extended ever since to foreign visitors.

The open, honest, bewildered and extremely innocent face of Oiney, and his prison pallor, added to by the chill of the early morning air, gave him such an unearthly glow that no one in his senses could possibly doubt his heavenly origin. Two agile monks climbed up the tree and by releasing the saint brought the divine mission to a perfect conclusion. Oiney now stood on his feet in the garden where Boniface embrace him warmly: 'Now that you have finally arrived, good Excelsis, I pray you, favour us with your heavenly blessing.'

Oiney had no trouble whatsoever in giving this small service. After the misery of that jail in Armagh and the inhuman treatment of vile screws like Shankill and the Governor, the warmth of welcome in this monastery garden sent a rich glow of gratitude through his body and he could truthfully exclaim, with tears in his eyes, 'I bless the hour God sent me among you, for Heaven knows it's great to be away from that jail and Shaun an' Sheamus even with all their dirty conniving... God knows I really like the lot o' you already, and I think that next to Heaven this is the best possible place I could be in the wide world. I give you all me blessings surely.'

The monks received this short speech favourably though with silent applause, the latter being the only kind permissible in Clunagh. At first they wondered at the strange references to Shaun and Sheamus by Excelsis, but concluded that the saint's collision with the apple tree had caused slight concussion, a better excuse than most for rambling.

'I will bring you to my cell,' said the Abbot, 'for surely, Excelsis, you must be tired and hungry after such a long journey.'

As they walked towards the monastery, Oiney could not help thinking that Shaun and Sheamus had really picked the perfect haven for him. For all his mishaps, what incredible good luck followed his path occasionally. He could not, of course, for the life of him understand the almost slavish adulation of these good monks, but Heaven knows, it was a welcome relief to a poor Creevan nonentity who had only known in the main snobbery, poverty and abuse. Even the name they had chosen for him, Excelsis, carried a sweet, unusual poetry in its very sound.

The Abbot, to be quite fair and honest, had another more prosaic reason for inviting Oiney to a repast in the quiet of his cell. He had this consuming desire to know all about Heaven. Even a desire quite stronger than that. To know all about Heaven before anyone else in the world. Just this one small failing marred the perfection that was Father Boniface. Knowing too the old maxim that no man but a liar likes to talk on an empty stomach, the Abbot had several courses of fish and vegetables placed before Excelsis. He was not prepared, however, to witness the speed with which the holy saint demolished each plateful: 'Holy Moses,' gasped Boniface. 'Don't they feed you up there? Didn't you have somethin' to ate before you came down? Nectar or ambrosia, perhaps?'

Oiney screwed up his nose. 'Nectar, ambrosia me eye! Feed you, did you say? Sure, I only had a flask o' tay an' a few sandwiches in all the time I was up there. I was starvin'...'

'Excelsis, I beg you. Tell me what it is really like up there?'

'I'll tell you this, Father. It's shockin' cold up there. If you ever think o' goin' up there, Father, you betther wear flannel drawers an' a fur coat.'

'My God,' gasped the Abbot, rapidly becoming disillusioned and desperately grasping for any little measure of merit left. 'But surely, surely, Excelsis, you were happy up there in the company o' the saints?'

Oiney gazed at Boniface, wondering if he was in his right mind. 'Happy up there in the company o' saints? Are you jokin', Father? Saints did you call them? Smugglers, Father, conspirators, Father, revolutionaries an' reds, Father! That's what they are.'

The good Abbot sank on his knees. 'Oh, my God! My God! Have they taken over up there as well?'

THE GUEST

During the first weeks which followed Oiney's miraculous and sudden descent from the clouds, the Abbot of Clunagh was forced to conclude that Oiney had never been to Heaven at all but instead to some draughty, cold region up there populated by radicals and fiery dissidents. The low temperature and location ruled out Hell. It now seemed certain to Boniface that Excelsis the mediaeval monk had been confined, for reasons best known to the Creator, to a draughty corridor somewhere near Purgatory. In all probability he had fallen through a hole, causing the draught. The recent scientific speculation about black empty pockets in the universe gave the Abbot's theory a certain plausability. The good man was also deeply concerned with some of the 'saint's' most outrageous statements about Heaven and, afraid that these might filter through to monks of lesser conviction, thought it in the interests of everyone to have the newcomer transferred to the Monastery Guest House, where he could labour under the watchful eye of the ill-tempered Brother Placid.

This Guest House was a whitish-grey turreted building just outside the monastery proper. It had the appearance more of a grandiose stage-set than a real edifice, but it had for decades been the comfortable living-quarters of people visiting Clunagh on Retreat. Others came on short periods of 'cure' for the excessive imbibing of wine or spirits. The third main category of Guest House residents were past pupils of the adjacent College returning either on nostalgic trips to scenes of boyhood glory or to participate in the annual rugby match against the current Seniors. It was, of course, considered a great honour to be invited to play against the Alma Mater.

Brother Placid saw in Excelsis a certain unworldliness of which even the most pious would be inclined to take advantage. Oiney on the other hand saw in Placid's eyes a nervous, jittery glint that predicted sudden sharp explosions. Here was a holy man one had to treat with caution.

'Your duties here will be quite simple,' said Placid in a sing-song voice he had acquired in years of chanting during the canonical hours of Matins, Nocturne and the others. His post as Guest House supervisor had given him the freedom of normal speech for only the second time in years, but as he had quite forgotten the ordinary cadences of speech he sang his phrases instead. All this bewildered Oiney at first; then it amused him, so much so that when left on his own, which was quite often, he would mimic Placid's chanting voice.

'Don't forget omnia vincit labor... dearest Brother... put some coal on the fire... Amen.'

That first day at the Guest House his voice had intoned a long list of Oiney's new duties: 'You will make the beds... lay the fires... sweep the rooms... prepare the breakfasts... lay the tables... serve the tables... wash the dishes... clean the brasses... carry the luggage...'

'And in me spare time in between?' asked Oiney reeling under the never-ending litany.

Apart from patience, however, the other great ingredient missing from Placid's character was a sense of humour.

He merely gave Oiney a sharp look: 'You will mow the lawn…and clip the hedges.'

Oiney considered asking him were there no plumbing or painting jobs but he wisely considered it safer to maintain his vow of silence in this strange fellow's company.

Placid's contribution to running the Guest House, during Oiney's term of office at least, was to sit on a broad stool in a small souvenir kiosk at the base of one of the towers facing the route to and from the main public church. Even in his very first week the Creevan lad caught a glimpse of his superior's nasty temper when the monastery cat, Batty, knocked the milk jug over a bundle of holy tracts. The irate monk swore at it in Latin, at least that is what Oiney thought; then Placid took off his sandals and slung them after the frightened, fleeing animal. The next instant he was on his knees imploring Heaven's forgiveness.

Oiney helped the penitent to his feet and began to advise him how to look on the bright side, and keep right on to the end of the road, in fact, the very same lecture he had recently read to the strange psychiatrist in Armagh. Suddenly to his deep dismay a large bible flung by Placid glanced off the side of his head. The monk had again risen from his stool, and was shouting angrily: 'You gibberin' gabbin chatterbox, d'you ever keep that gob o' yours shut? Whatever made you join an Order of silent monks, for you're the least suited to monastic life, of all the people I ever met! You should have found yourself a job in the subway or the tower o' Babel, where the masses congregate…'

Oiney nursed the bump on his head and his grievance for a few days and then forgot about both of them. It was not in his nature to harbour ill-will against the likes of Placid, who was obviously the tragic victim of some youthful mishap. The Guest House duties absorbed his own complete attention. He found the cooking to be the most strenuous, for he knew absolutely nothing about it. He had never even boiled an egg in his lifetime. For this reason the food he served sent many of the guests packing and others into hospital with dysentry and diarrhoea which, of course, eased his task considerably.

In his very occasional spare time he explored first of all the Guest House itself and then the spacious grounds of the large lay college belonging to the monastery. In the lost property room of the Guest House he saw an amazing collection of discarded or forgotten articles; among these were twelve umbrellas, a bird-cage, a Gladstone bag, a leather-bound whiskey flask, a sword, a small cannon, a suit of clothes, a pack of cards, a racing gambler's calendar, a miniature china copy of the Taj Mahal, an elephant's tusk and a teapot.

His visits through the College grounds brought even greater surprises. For an academy with a mere two or three hundred boarders and no day-boys the sports facilities were quite astonishing. There were six football pitches, three tennis courts with additional ones made up in the summer, two handball alleys, a miniature golf course and a grand pavilion. Back in Creevan he and pals had to put up with a small patch of ground and Oiney had seen the adult team play on a partially waterlogged meadow. None of the college boys ever ran these roads and lanes barefoot. Instead they were all dressed like young gentlemen of Eton and Harrow and strode through Clunagh grounds with a lofty hauteur. They passed

Oiney on the pathway without as much as a quick glance of curiosity. This was an Ireland unknown to him, and every bit as strange to him as the paradise of Boniface.

Although most visitors to Clunagh Guest House paid little or no attention to Oiney, one day there arrived a gentleman who took exceptional and somewhat unwelcome interest in his activities. Shortly after the arrival of this inquisitive guest, Brother Placid, panting and puffing, called Oiney into the souvenir shop.

'Oh, dear me, Excelsis, I see the great man himself has arrived...'

'Great man? Now who would he be, Brother?'

'P P O'Reilly.'

'I'm sorry, Brother, but I never heard of him.'

'Oh, my dear Excelsis, your education has been sadly neglected then. Treat the man graciously, for P P. O'Reilly almost died for Ireland durin' the Troubles...'

'Almost died for Ireland...'

'Yes, the Flying Column car he was in drove over the jetty in Cork harbour. The other three were drowned but P P was hauled ashore. Run immediately, Excelsis, an' tell the College superior that P P is here to see his son Luke! Take the boy back with you to the Guest House! Do hurry, Excelsis!'

Luke O'Reilly was a tall, rather frail-looking aesthete of fifteen or sixteen years. He wore gold-rimmed spectacles and had already acquired the habit from Father Francis of peering over the top of them. He was a great reader and Oiney saw a book jutting out of his blazer pocket. 'Is that a class-book?' he asked.

'Indeed no,' Luke replied, drawing the book from his pocket. 'I only wish it was. *My Fight for Irish Freedom* by Dan Breen a class-book? That'll be the day, Brother! Some of the teachers here would burn Dan Breen at the stake.

'They were in O'Duffy's Blueshirts...'

'Don't you like the College, Luke?'

'One or two of the teachers are all right. The rest are a rummy crew. Most o' the boys are snooty-nosed brats... The scholarship lads who won their way here are fine. One is my best pal. The rest of the pupils are the spoilt sons of big farmers and publicans...No, I don't like Clunagh College and I never will. Has my father been here long?'

'No, he is only just arrived. Brother Placid says he's a great man.'

'Duck's Belly would say that, wouldn't he?'

'Duck's Belly?' said the puzzled Oiney.

'Yes. that's what we used to call Placid when he taught Latin. And what a wicked-tempered brute he was if we forgot our declensions! He used to murder us. We used to ask him to translate silly phrases like "The leader of the war knows already". Dux belli scit jam. Duck's belly shit jam. See!' Luke O'Reilly burst into hilarious schoolboyish laughter that was such a contrast to his usual fairly morose self.

'My father is anything but a great man. He merely thinks he is. Most of the great men were shot, imprisoned or hounded out of Ireland.

'I hate it when my Da comes down to Clunagh. I just hate it. He brags and boasts about what he did for Ireland, and admiring clowns like Placid lead him on and encourage him. I haven't seen you before. What's your name?'

'Brother Excelsis. I haven't been here long.'

Luke gave him a quick, yet amused look.

'Say, aren't you the chap that's supposed to have arrived recently from Heaven? One of the teaching monks let it out and now the whole college is talking about it. You see there was this legend... ' Luke O'Reilly went on to explain and for the first time, the whole affair became crystal clear to Oiney. Imagine mistaking him for a saint! For an instant he considered going to the Abbot and confessing that he had been dropped from an helicopter, but the very serious consequences which would arise from such an admission horrified him. He was wearing his monk's habit and masquerading as a Cistercian lay-brother. And, even if he told the absolute truth, who would give any credence to such an unlikely story? Dropped from a helicopter and dressed up like a monk? What utter nonsense! Oiney assured the smiling Luke that he was by no means a saint and wisely left it at that.

The man who almost died for Ireland stayed at the Guest House for three days, and whenever Oiney swept the great man's rooms he was certain that he detected quite a pungent aroma reminiscent of Doyle's parlour on the night of the Wake. Then in the dining-room, he began to notice that O'Reilly was observing him very closely. Even as Oiney polished the wall mirror there was always the horrible reflection of this heavy-jowled creature staring at him with a bemused look on his flushed and ugly countenance.

On the morning of his departure, O'Reilly called Oiney over to his table. He pointed to an empty chair opposite him. 'Sit down!'

Oiney sat down.

'Brother Excelsis?'

'Yes?'

P P O'Reilly gave a great guffaw of disbelief: 'Don't make me laugh! Saint Excelsis! The monks here think you're a bloody saint.' He caught hold of Oiney's robe and twisted part of it in his large fist. 'Well I know you're no saint. Why? Because in the first instance you haven't got a halo! Every saint worth his salt has got a halo. Tell me, just you tell me! Have you ever in your life seen a picture of a saint without a halo? Have you?'

Oiney had to admit that what Mr P P O'Reilly said was gospel truth.

'There you are,' said the great man. 'And another thing. What bloody saint looks at himself in the mirror all day?'

'Tell me that!'

Oiney did not wish to inform his questioner that he was merely keeping an eye on P P himself.

'A saint doesn't puff himself up with pride and vanity,' continued O'Reilly, a great authority on the behaviour of saints. 'A saint has humility and self-negation. A saint walks with his halo on his lonely road with a simple dignity that marks him out to be a... a... '

'Saint,' suggested Oiney helpfully.

The man who almost died for Ireland looked Oiney straight in the eyes and the Creevan lad knew for certain the game was up. O'Reilly's gaze was a cold, hard one. 'I don't even believe you're a real monk. Listen lad! I haven't been a Superintendent of the Irish Civic Guards for thirty years for nothing. I've a photographic memory. You have heard of James Joyce, haven't you? Well, I can recite *Finnegans Wake* from "riverrun past Eve's and Adam's" till its last unfinished circular sentence! And I've summed you up. Not long ago, there was this country yokel from Creevan by the name of Oiney Hoy who made an incredible escape by helicopter from the roof of Armagh jail... The earth seemed to have opened and swallowed you up. But you were here all the time posin' as a saint... What a disguise!'

'I never said I was a saint,' Oiney protested feebly. 'And what are you goin' to do? Have me arrested again?'

'Not a bit of it,' said O'Reilly, ' so don't panic! Everything will be all right if you agree to my plan. I've watched you for days. An' when you're not lookin' in the bloody mirror you can graft. I must admit, you can certainly graft. Not a word to Placid or anyone else if you do as I say. I own a small, select place near Killiney, south of Dublin... a kind of unusual hotel... We cater for folk from the great Art world... Art and Literature... Now I need a new general factotum. And apart from your cooking, which God knows is abominable, you'd suit me fine. In return I'll keep your secret and pay you a few bob a week and your keep. How's that? Killiney's a fine place by the sea and you can always say you walked in the footsteps of James Joyce.'

Oiney saw that there was little chance of escape from the cunning net which O'Reilly had cast. On this occasion he would play for time: he did not relish being under the great man's roof. 'You'll have to bring me some suitable clothes, Mr O'Reilly. I can hardly do hotel work in this outfit.'

The hotel owner gave him a little card and some money. 'So it's agreed, then. I'll be down on Saturday morning with some clothes. Mind you, I'm keeping you to your word and woe betide you if... '

The situation was desperate. Oiney could only pray that some miracle would save him. He tried to be more pleasant to Brother Placid should the worst happen and O'Reilly reveal the truth. 'I understand, Brother Placid,' he said next morning, 'that you are a very holy man in spite of little minor lapses of temper.'

'Good heavens, no,' exclaimed Placid. 'If you want real holiness you would need to visit my cousin, Pat McNulty, in the village of Roshinne. Now there's a pious fellow for you. Pat's the boy for you. I hear rumours even of his miraculous powers. Ah, that's what I'd call sanctity galore.'

Later that day while Oiney was cleaning P P O'Reilly's vacated room, he discovered a discarded whiskey bottle in a drawer of the press. He was about to dispose of it in the open rubbish bin when he heard the low sing-song voice of Placid coming from the corridor.

'Rinse it in the sink... Remove the label... Wrap the object in an old newspaper. Everyone of us has our little failings... Even the great. *Humanum est errare*... To err is human.'

Oiney was so taken aback by the rapid succession of strange events that he decided to take a quiet stroll that evening by the pleasant banks of a little stream which flowed down the green fields at the rear of the Guest House. He had walked about a quarter-mile when he encountered a poor traveller of the roads playing a tin-whistle by the riverside. He was a small bearded man of sixty years or so with a merry twinkle in his eyes and a battered tweed hat pulled down about his ears. He reminded Oiney a little of old Terry of the Hills, and he stopped in his tracks.

'Good evenin', Father,' said the stranger.

'Oh, I'm not a priest. Yourself now, you seem to have the right Northern accent?'

'I'm from Donegal.'

'That's not far from Monaghan, is it?'

'Less than fifty miles I'd say as the crow flies. But who would want to be a crow except maybe to escape from prison bars!'

Oiney, being a Creevan lad, soon was sitting in the rushes beside the old Donegal traveller, talking about the town-lands and parishes of Monaghan and Donegal until the very stars of Heaven came out to listen. It was only the loud tolling of the monastery bell brought Oiney back to a different, sadder reality. 'Good Lord,' he exclaimed regretfully. 'I'll have to leave. But tell me, friend, where are you stayin' the night?'

The old fellow slapped a side-pocket triumphantly. 'I've me night-cap here. and it'll not be the first or the last time I've slept undher the canopy o' Heaven.'

'You'll do no such thing,' Oiney insisted, 'for I'll bring you into the Guest House where I'm in charge, well a kind of. But we'll need to tread cautiously, not to arouse Brother Placid.'

'Surely to God,' said the Donegal man, 'you couldn't arouse a man with a name like Placid?'

'You'd be surprised,' Oiney replied. 'In fact you'd have the quare oul' shock comin' to you.'

It was early on the following day that the reckoning was to come. Brother Placid had scarcely taken up his usual place on the broad stool in the souvenir shop when to his horror he saw this tramp stagger out of the Guest House and disappear into the nearby woods. He rushed up to Oiney, who had just failed to prevent his guest going out the main door

'Who was that?' shouted Placid angrily.

Oiney kept a calm exterior. 'Ask and you shall receive,' he answered Placid. 'Knock and you shall enter! He was one of God's children. That's who he was.'

'God's children indeed,' snapped Placid. 'The Guest House is not for tramps and drunks. There's a green door in the monastery wall where they can beg for alms. You're far too soft-hearted, Brother Excelsis.'

Just then Oiney remembered an old tattered book at home called *The Lives of the Saints* written by a man called Butler. In a gloomy day of boredom he had read several chapters. 'Is it not true, Brother Placid, that Saint Martin, Bishop o' Tours, shared his cloak with a poor naked beggar he met on the road? Is it not a fact that Saint Damien, moved by their sufferings, went to live among the lepers? And here in Clunagh we can only have a remote green door. A day will surely dawn soon when we have a robot tuned to serve the poor and record their gratitude on tape.'

Placid was uncertain how to respond and suddenly Oiney, in his desperate urge to get away from not only Clunagh but O'Reilly as well, remembered something else. He rushed upstairs and quickly changed into the suit which had lain for long in the Lost Property room. It was not an exact fit but it would serve its purpose. He folded the robe over his arm and in that state appeared before the astonished Placid.

'Oh, think twice, Brother, think twice! Whatever shall I tell the good Boniface?'

'Tell him,' said Oiney, 'that Excelsis had a call from on High cancelling an' supersedin' all previous orders. Tell him I've been ordered by the Lord to broaden me mission, to go out into the great wide world an' convert the awful sinners that abound in it. In return for the suit, I'll donate me robe to the monastery. Goodbye, dear Brother Placid, goodbye an' pray for me!'

THE MIRACLE MAN

Oiney got lost in the woodlands around Clunagh and although it was his intention to catch up with the Donegal man and travel part of the road with him at the very least, this was not fated to be. It was by the sound of a passing train that he managed to guide himself onto a road he hoped might lead to Dublin. He only had the little money that the 'great man' O'Reilly had provided him with, but his new sense of freedom created a sweet buoyancy in his heart. Towards noon however his legs grew weary of the walking and added to this came a heavy downpour of rain which made him run for shelter in a hay-loft off the main road.

He lay down in the comfort of the hay, listening to the heavy raindrops lash the corrugated iron roof of the loft. He tried to make plans for his future. He would avoid the Killiney hotel owner like the plague. If there was anyone in Dublin who would help it would surely be Aileen, Shaun's friend, who worked at the Abbey Theatre. She might be disappointed at his desertion of monastic life, but then he had warned them all on the helicopter that he was quite certain he had no vocation. He would tell her how much delight it gave him to be her hero, but that he could not endure life with the silent Cistercians even for her sake. He would also explain to her the homicidal tendencies of a monk called Placid, and surely then she would understand his very good reasons for fleeing this dangerous monastery.

In a few months he could make his way back to Creevan, though he was still very much afraid of his granny. She had often threatened him as a boy that she would 'murdher' him; this time he was quite certain he had given her every good reason to fulfil that promise. He also remembered Jonjo in his high belfry above the village. The sexton would scarcely believe the strange adventures which had befallen him. After a while the rain ceased, and he resumed his journey again.

It was a strange world indeed to be born into, he thought, where a decent body had little or no say in the terrible things that can happen. If he had not gone to the Wake that fatal night, he might this very minute be flying kites with Jonjo on the Castle Hill. If he had refused to go to the prison Infirmary or on to its roof he might still be rotting in Armagh Jail. If he had not written those stupid notes for the daft psychiatrist, the greedy Governor would not be collecting his presents. Reality was so complex that it wearied poor Oiney's brain to even think about it, so he gave up fruitless speculation and merely sauntered aimlessly almost along the lovely green countryside.

It was early in the afternoon when, hungry and exhausted, he sat down on the slope of a ditch, staring idly at a sign-post on the other side of the road. One of the places named on it struck him as familiar. 'Roshinne—2 miles'. He recalled it as the home of the pious cousin of Brother Placid, the man called Pat McNulty. Hoping and praying that Pat was a wiser and calmer person than his relative, Oiney took the gamble and the side road into Roshinne. The gnawing hunger pains played an important role in his decision but neither was he averse to meeting a man of unusual piety in a world where, the good Church constantly reminded us, gross materialism was making gigantic strides, even in little Catholic Ireland.

In the picturesque old village he had little trouble in locating Pat's abode. Everyone knew Pat and had the kind word to say for him. So it was with confidence Oiney knocked on his door. A tall man with a kindly face and a perpetual smile in his warm, brown eyes came to the door. Although Pat had not yet the faintest idea who his visitor was, the boredom of this small village was such that it relished even thunder and lightning to relieve the monotony. 'I come from Clunagh monastery where Brother Placid spoke of you kindly,' said Oiney by way of introduction.

'Ah, come in! Come in! Dear old Duck's Belly! Tell me, does he still jump up an' down an' rattle his teeth?'

'Unfortunately, yes, but otherwise he's quite normal.

But he does hold you in the highest esteem for your great piety.'

Pat's cheeks wrinkled into a modest smile of pleasure. 'Of course, he's exaggeratin',' said he, genuflecting as he led Oiney past the red lamp burning under a huge picture of the Sacred Heart on the mantelpiece. 'The humdrum duties of ordinary life leave little time for real sanctity. Shall we say a decade of the rosary or maybe you'd prefer a cup o' tay first?'

'God forgive me but I'll go the tay. I've this terrible drouth. It will help clear me throat for the prayers.'

Though the tea was only what they call in Ireland shamrock tea (three leaves to a cup), Oiney found it hot, if not invigorating. The kindly Pat then extended a plate with a soda farl on it which Oiney grabbed rather greedily. When he had devoured the last crumbs, as though in penance and to please his host, he went on his knees under a picture of Saint Theresa and waited on Pat to join him.

'Oh no, it was her turn last Saturday,' said the holy man.

There were seven or eight pictures of saints and Oiney was perplexed. 'What about Saint Sebastian then?' he asked, pointing to a painting of the almost naked martyr pierced with several arrows.

'Oh, no, no, no,' said Pat, covering his eyes. 'I can scarcely endure the poor man's agony.'

'Saint Monica, the mother of the great Augustine then,' suggested Oiney.

'Not her either. Monica is for Tuesdays and this is Friday,' Pat replied. Then he shook his head. 'How could I ever forget? This is Friday, I'm sure. Then it's the turn of the little wooden crucifix on the wall beside the room door. Let's kneel there!'

Pat began the prayers and Oiney intoned the responses as they both knelt on a rough bit of carpet under the crucifix. Oiney noticed in a quick sidelong glance that Pat's face had such a pious, bland expression that only a halo was missing to bring it into perfect harmony with any saint's effigy on the walls.

Oiney's thoughts wandered as the prayers reached their conclusion. He was staring at the wooden cross when suddenly a flicker of movement on that holy object drew his startled attention. 'Pat, Pat?'

'What is it?'

'Pat, look! The crucifix is drippin' blood... Look!'

'Blood? Nonsense!' Pat arose to take a closer look.

'Begod, you're right. Your nose isn't bleedin' by any chance?'

Oiney felt one nostril and then the other and shook his head.

Pat looked up at the ceiling and stroked his chin thoughtfully. 'Perhaps it's a mouse the cat's killed in the attic?' Yet there was no stain on the whitewashed ceiling.

Oiney went over to the crucifix and had a closer look. 'Pat, look, it's the wounds that are bleedin', where the nails went.'

'Ah hold on, sir,' said Mr McNulty, 'one has to be most careful in scrutinisin' before comin' to conclusions. Let me see! Begod, you're right. Now, who would believe that? What day did you say it was? Ah, Friday. Isn't that a coincidence? Good Friday was the very day of the Crucifixion and the good woman in Germany had the stigmata on a Friday too. My God, but that's the shockin' coincidence!'

'What's stigmata, Mr McNulty?'

'Stigmata? Them's the jagged wounds on the palms o' her hands, miraculously induced, I'd say. But look at the crucifix yonder. Begod, that fella's goin' great steam, isn't he?'

Just then a knock sounded on the front door and Pat opened it to allow in a poor thin woman who had the season of Lent written permanently on her features.

'Have a seat, Annie Bryson,' said Pat, 'an' houl your tongue for a minit. I've a great secret to confide in you, a deeper an' more important secret, Annie, than the ears o' the ass o' King Laoghaire.'

'What is it, Pat, what is it?'

'You'll hardly believe it, Annie, but me friend an' I think that a miracle o' God has come to Roshinne.'

'Aye, Mrs Bryson,' said Oiney, trying to be helpful as usual. 'I'll vouch for it meself.'

Annie was almost overcome with emotion and dropped on her knees to the floor. 'Oh, glory be to Him in the highest. I always knew the good Lord above would never forget the good folk of Roshinne... I always knew He'd favour us with a miraculous creation like He did Knock Shrine in Mayo, an' Brigid's Well in Faughert an' Saint Patrick's Purgatory in Lough Derg and God bless us an' save us, the preserved head o' Blessed Oliver Plunkett in Drogheda. Shure, God knows our wee land is brimmin' with miraculous shrines an' wells an' statues an' why should Roshinne be left behind...'

'Now you're talkin', Annie, now you're talkin',' cried Pat with growing enthusiasm. 'Why should our poor forsaken wee village not have the coach-loads o' pilgrims to restore our lost trade an' the faith o' poor sinners. Annie, get up on your feet an' take a good peep at the Man on the Cross, the Crucifix... on the wall!'

Annie did so and almost fainted at what she saw. She drew back in fright and made the sign of the Cross. 'Holy mother o' God, Pat! Would you give me a chair before I drop stone dead! Oh, my God, I'll never get it out o' me mind... the...the Bleeding Crucifix o' Roshinne.'

'An' keep a quiet tongue in your head about it Annie,' cautioned Pat, winking at Oiney, 'for I don't want me good lino worn to shreds too soon.' He knew for certain this was the one effective way of getting Annie to spread the news.

Soon the whole village had heard about the great wonder of the bleeding crucifix, and, while the wise old men shook their heads, the McNulty house and the strange happenings there became the subject of many a stormy argument. Memories were recalled of Pat's pious Aunt Mary, who had lived in that very house twenty years previously and who was widely regarded by everyone as a living saint, attending for twenty-five consecutive years every Mass, funeral, marriage, baptism, Benediction plus all the minor services ever held in Saint Claire's. As she had no family all her wordly possessions went to her nephew Pat, who was very fond of her. She had died of a brain tumour long before she had reached middle age. The village folk, therefore, had good cause to believe that poor Mary had some connection with the recent miracle. There was a saying in Roshinne that if anyone in the village ever earned the right to be in the arms of Jesus, it was Mary.

It was in Annie Bryson's house on the hill that many folk gathered to hear her account of the strange event. 'Oh, it wasn't just a dhrop,' she said, exaggerating somewhat, 'it came in torrents an' every bit as fresh as that day on Calvary hill two thousand years ago. An' if you ask me, I think the Lord is makin' up to Mary for the miracles denied her in her lifetime. I was with poor Mary the night o' her passin'. I mind it well, it was All Souls' Night, when the oul' graveyard beyont does be haunted. I heard Mary's last words. "I'll never forget Roshinne," she said with a wan smile on her lips, "I'll put in a good word for you all with the Almighty." An' them were her very last words.'

'Ah, shure, may God bless the dacint wee soul,' was the fervent prayer of all present.

'But I remember years before,' continued Annie, 'when Mary had her keen disappointments an' severe tests to her Faith. God only knows how she survived. I did some sewin' an' washin' for Mary as you all know. Well, one morning I seen this expression on her face of heavenly joy. She had said a prayer the night before that God would let her know the number of her days so that she could do as many works of mercy as she could before she died. And she imagined that God had given her a date. But the day passed and a year and another year but Mary was still walkin' the ways o' the world. I think her failed prayers nearly broke her heart. She never got over that. That's why I think that now she has God's ear in Heaven she's gettin' a betther response.

If millions an' millions o' people on earth are all seekin' favours at the same time, wouldn't God be hard put to give answers straightaway? I know I would.'

'My God Annie,' said Blind Packy, who was sitting by the stove. 'Haven't you the convolutin' tongue an' an imagination that stretches further than a voyage o' Brendan's! You should take up writin' them Kitty the Hare an' banshee stories for Ireland's Own. When the Lord gave poor Mary the date o' her demise maybe it was the Old Calendar He was goin' by. Someone should check up on that... He! He! Haw! Haw!'

'Someone should check up on you,' Annie retorted sharply. 'Blind is he, the disbelievin' oul' fox? Every time the Judge sits, Packy's undher his nose ferretin' out the secret sins o' the parish. Blind is it? Packy can hear the very grass grow an' he doesn't fool Annie Bryson one wee bit.'

There was a man in Roshinne, however, who took a very serious view of the Bleeding Crucifix, for he had the sorry experience of a similar 'miracle' in a remote corner of County Kerry. This was Sergeant Mannion of the local Civic Guards, or Garda as this body of the Law is known in the Gaelic. As a young constable he had allowed these rumours to spread until the Kerry village was swamped with hordes of frantic, eager pilgrims and scarcely any amenities to meet their daily needs. Pandemonium had been created and it had taken another miracle almost to disperse the crowds and get them back to the four corners of Ireland. Sergeant Mannion had learned his lesson.

This then was the stern officer who stormed into the McNulty home when he learned the news.

'What's this bloody nonsense all about Pat?'

'Nonsense? What nonsense?'

Like all good Irishmen, Pat had a sound distrust of law-enforcing agents.

'Come off it! This bleedin' crucifix all Roshinne's talkin' about!'

'Oh, the Crucifix! Oh that! I see what you mane. It was bleedin', but you can see it's stopped.'

This news had the Sergeant puzzled. 'But it was bleeding?'

'Aye, a while ago. Me friend from Clunagh Monastery saw it an' Annie Bryson saw it.'

'You'll be tellin' me next that Blind Packy saw it,' snapped the Sergeant with heavy sarcasm. 'You'll be tellin' me great lies like that.'

Then he turned to Oiney and the Creevan lad saw the Civic Guard with the hawk's eye looking at him wickedly from head to foot like he was measuring him for a coffin. 'Tell me then, where do you fit in?'

Oh here we go again, thought the frightened Oiney. It was bad enough getting involved with Shaun and the Cistercians and P P O'Reilly without getting mixed up in miracles. Was there no peace for a man in Ireland at all? 'Oh, it's quite all right, Sergeant, I just came here because I knew Placid in Clunagh. I saw the Crucifix bleed. I'll swear to that.'

'The only swearing you'll do is in Court, young man. I've been in Roshinne for ten years and there's been no trouble until you landed here. Can you explain that?'

Oiney stared at the ground and wished it would open up and swallow him. How could he tell the Civic Guard that trouble hounded him all around the four provinces of Ireland, that it was his constant companion and bed-fellow? Could he explain that? If he could, he could explain the mysteries of religion, including the miracle of Roshinne. The Sergeant was about to go for his notebook and pen when the door opened and Father Rice the Parish Priest arrived in a great flurry. He took the Sergeant aside but Oiney could hear him quite clear.

'Sergeant Mannion, we don't want any undue commotion or arrests. We want this to pether out slowly. Otherwise we'll be the laughin' stock of Ireland and the Outer Hebrides. No great damage has been done yet that can't be righted, but don't let's get excited! For we'd rue that day. It would do you no great favour either with the Chief o' the Garda in Dublin or the TDs an' Senators. Let me attend to this in me own way, for I think I know what's goin' on...'

'Very well Father, and I hope to God it's settled soon.' the Sergeant turned to Oiney and glowered menacingly. 'If you're not out of Roshinne prompt, I've got lodgings for you.'

'Who is this?' said the priest pointing at Oiney when the Civic Guard had left.

'Oh, just a young fella, Father, who knows me cousin Placid in Clunagh.'

'Well, I'd rather he wasn't here.'

Pat opened the room door. 'Go in there lad, till Father Rice an' I have a wee talk!'

The room door however proved small obstacle to Oiney's powerful curiosity. He listened eagerly, his ear against the keyhole.

'Now Pat,' he heard the priest say angrily, 'all this miracle nonsense'll have to stop. You can't be arousin' the emotions an' expectations of these poor people. I have only been in Roshinne a couple o' years, but I knew the last Parish Priest well. We spent three days' Retreat at Clunagh Guest House and he let me know Roshinne inside out. He told me, Pat, you were good with your hands, that you had mended his watch in no time and the church organ in a couple o' days. Oh, he told me all about you, Pat. The rollin' eyes in the picture o' Saint Francis, Pat... two drops o' mercury cunningly placed and the fallin' petals o' Saint Theresa, the Little Flower strung, Pat, with almost invisible thread... and the nails of the True Cross that probably came from a stable door an' manufactured in Birmingham. Pat, tell the truth! You just can't resist a miracle can you?'

Oiney's ears were glued even tighter to the door. 'You know how it is, Father. Shure it's only a bit of a joke, Father, to stir up life a bit in this god-forsaken oul' village. All the excitement it does create an' the wonder in folk's eyes. How the people must have cheered when Jesus walked on the waters! I'd have loved to have been there at yon great carry-on of the loaves an' fishes. I wonder was there any brown bread among the lot or a soda farl? Father, I'll tell you the truth which I never did to the oul' priest before you.

'I saw me poor Aunt Mary pray for miracles all her days an' what happened? She lost her father an' mother when she was still young, an' she went into bad health herself. For all her chapel goin' an' prayin' night an' mornin' she had twelve years o' epilepsy an' screamin' headaches. Instead o' proper attention in a Dublin hospital, she was goin' to Knock Shrine an' Lourdes an' Faughert till eventually she died of the terrible tumour that was on her brain, an' cause of half or maybe three-quarters of her visions. Miracles be damned Father! I rigged me own up. I bored tiny holes in the figure on the Cross, Father, and I ran these narrow, narrow tubes up by the back wall, an' comin out undher the floorboards. Undher the lino, Father, an' the bit o' carpet, I have a small rubber pump with this heavy red dye in it. Will I give you an exhibition, Father?' said Pat excitedly, proud of his workmanship. 'A few squeezes on the pump, Father, and you're made!'

'You'll do no such thing,' exclaimed the alarmed priest. 'And just you get your darn contraption dismantled till I exorcise this place of the evil spirits that occupy it includin' that fellow in the room there! I'm not sure at all he hadn't a hand in this. He's an innocent enough lookin' gawk, but them's the ones to look out for. Get that contraption down this minit, Pat McNulty, and that fellow out of Roshinne before we have brimstone an' gnashin' of teeth!'

'I believe, Father, I could manufacture them too, if I was hard put to it,' said Pat with a sigh.

KILLINEY

Oiney, glad to leave Roshinne and Pat McNulty behind him, reached Dublin that same night. The size of the city together with its many fine buildings amazed him. He walked about the streets in a daze passing Trinity College, Nassau and Kildare Streets up into that lovely little square, St Stephen's Green, where he admired the bust statue of the poet Mangan and shared some of his biscuits with the ducks at the side of a little pond. Then he retraced his steps down to O'Connell Street and along to the Parnell Monument beside the Rotunda and Findlater's Church. He was sad about the numbers of poor travelling women who sat on the pavement in Talbot Street begging alms from the public on its way to and from the northern railway. This was the sad contrast to all the fine buildings and shop windows packed with grandiose wares.

On the railway platform he talked to a porter who advised him to get lodgings at Iveagh House, which was not only clean but inexpensive. The warden of that hostel spoke to him next day in the foyer.

'I see you there hanging about, unsure o' whether to go this way or that. Well, take me advice, son, an' make your way to Saint Michin's! You haven't been to Dublin, son, unless you first shake hands with the Crusader in the vaults of Saint Michin's. It brings luck, you see!'

So Oiney, in need of a bit of luck, set out for the old church in the very heart of Dublin.

Climbing down through a doorway, or access, low in the wall of the church which also housed the organ used in the first production of Handel's *Messiah*, he followed the small queue of sightseers past the coffins and the severed preserved heads of those patriot-barristers the Sheares brothers. The Crusader, with legs broken and crossed as was the ancient custom with Knights Templar, lay on a wooden, rectangular plinth. He was quite gaunt and leathery and, in Oiney's opinion, somewhat gruesome. Urged by the attendant to shake hands with the dead man for good luck, Oiney, with a shudder and somewhat unwillingly, did so. This eerie feeling crept over him and he thought he felt one of his fingers go numb.

He was glad to crawl through the opening in the vault wall into the clear sky again. Perhaps it was merely his imagination but he had this strange feeling that he was being followed. Then quite suddenly, before he could leave by the gateway, a cold, clammy hand brushed his cheek and came down on his shoulder with a steadfast grip. Oiney gave a start and almost dropped with fright. He turned slightly, as much as he could in that grip, and saw the grinning heavy-jowled chin of the man he was trying to avoid—P P O'Reilly.

'How... how did you know I was here?' gasped the bewildered and unhappy Oiney.

'Quite simple for a Dublin man,' said the smug hotelier. 'Every new visitor to the city presents himself sooner or later to the Crusader in Saint Michin's. It was only a matter of patience, an' Patrick Paul O'Reilly has plenty o' that. Though you are tryin' that patience sorely, me boy. I went down to Clunagh with clothes on Saturday, but you had broken our gentleman's agreement, hadn't you?'

Oiney squirmed with the pain as the grip tightened. 'You left Clunagh on Friday, didn't you? And got involved with that miracle-man in Roshinne. Sergeant Mannion, an old friend, gave me all the seedy particulars. You hitched a lift on a peat-lorry to Dublin that day. When are you goin' to settle down? Just tell me that!'

The hotel owner did not relax his hold on Oiney until they were both safely seated in the rear of a chauffeur-driven limousine. It was only later that Oiney discovered the reason why the driver kept glowering over his shoulder on every convenient occasion. Three hotel hands had already been sacked and the chauffeur was uncertain about the security of his own position. A few driving lessons, a licence, and there was this bumpkin behind the steering wheel.

The Bloomsbury Hotel was the strangest place that Oiney ever saw and that included the jail and monastery. It faced towards the sea a little to the west of Killiney village. Though the view from it of the famous Martello Tower, where Stephen Daedalus the hero of Ulysses lived in the opening chapter of that book, was slight, P P O'Reilly did not hesitate to call it in his advertising brochure 'a fine, frontal view of the literary landmark'. 'The Bloomsbury' was a large Georgian house with extensions at the front and rear to make it a suitable and convenient residence for all the disciples and admirers of James Joyce who flocked to Dublin annually for Bloomsday, the celebration of the great day in June 1904 when Leopold Bloom, the Jew from Eccles Street, found immortality.

Given a small cubicle at the top of the hotel Oiney changed into the waiter's uniform that O'Reilly had provided and presented himself in the foyer of the hotel to be introduced by his boss to a genteel, bright little lady who sat in an armchair by the reception desk.

'This is my wife Kathleen,' said the hotelier. 'Kathleen, this is the lad I was telling you about. A proper rapscallion. I had to corner him in St Michin's. He'll be our general factotum and what have you...'

'I hope,' said Kathleen almost under her breath, 'that he lasts longer than the others.' She gave Oiney a kindly glance of sympathy which immediately kindled a great liking in Oiney towards the lady. She was so different to the large overpowering O'Reilly that it puzzled the Creevan lad how the pair had ever come together. Kathleen arose from her seat and accompanied the new waiter around the foyer in a sort of conducted tour. She brought him to examine several brightly illuminated show-cases standing close to the walls of the carpeted hall.

Oiney stared bewildered at the first show-case, for inside the glass frontage was a black porter bottle stuck in a little heap of grey sand and dark green seaweed.

'What in the name o' Jesus is that bottle an' dirty sand doin' in there?' he exclaimed. 'Will I get a brush an' shovel to clean up the mess, Missus?'

'Over my dead body,' roared a voice behind him. 'That's precious Joyceana, you nitwit.'

'Oh, I'm sorry, Mr O'Reilly. Sure I've seen dozens of oul' bottles like that on the dung-hill in Creevan.'

'Not that bottle,' hissed O'Reilly. 'That bottle is the identical one that was stogged to its waist in the cakey and dough of the third chapter of Ulysses!'

'Cakey and dough,' said the bewildered Oiney.

'The stuff around it, you fool. The seaweed, sand and slime, scooped up from the "snot-green sea" at Ringsend.' 'Grr,' said Oiney moving to the next case. 'Clay tobacco pipes? You could buy them one time back home for a penny a piece. I used to blow bubbles with them.'

'Not them pipes you didn't,' sniggered the hotelier proudly. 'Them pipes were the proud possession of old Barnacle... Nora Barnacle's father. Molly Bloom... Joyce's wife, Nora.'

The trio moved on to another case, a small gold coin on a purple cushion.

'What would that be then?' asked Oincy.

'That's one of our rarer exhibits,' said O'Reilly. 'That's the very half-sovereign the poor, dull skivvy gave to that chancer Corley in the story 'The Two Gallants' in *Dubliners*.'

'How do you know, Mr O'Reilly?' Oiney was about to ask when he was distracted by a loud guffaw in the company who were assembled near the bar in the corner.

If the objects in the glass cases caused him some amazemerit, the various self-proclaimed disciples of the famous Dublin author were even more astonishing. They were a motley crew of Irish, American and English high-browed rich poseurs. He had never been in such company before. They spoke the same language as him but they gave it such a high, nasal, whining twang that he could scarcely make out a word they said. And so many of their words were what was called in Creevan 'jaw-breakers'. These were enormous jaw-breakers like 'unphiloprogenitive onanist' and 'idiosyncratic psychosis'.

There were two Yale professors with strident voices arguing with an Oxford don about the precise time that Leopold Bloom broke wind on the 10th June 1904. Up and down the foyer strode the tall, lean aesthete Wingham Pratt, who had been hissed off the stage at a recent Edinburgh Festival show for masturbating publicly in Nausicaa, a stage version of one of the scenes in Ulysses. Critics, too, had hurt his sensitivity by saying that he was carrying his 'contemporary realism' a little too far.

Oiney left the main literary 'stream of consciousness' to proceed to a corner near the door where an artist with a yellow beard and a black beret was painting the scene outside of buildings and sky. Ah, thought Oiney, this is more in my line. I will understand this simple down-to-earth setting. He took a glance and then backed away in astonishment. It had nothing, absolutely nothing in common with the scene outside! Well, both did contain a sky. Oiney saw a calm, sunny day with a few clouds, but the artist painted a great mad whirling tornado full of teacups and vases while below lay a crudely sketched cromlech on which lay a tormented fish with one huge staring eye. Oiney scratched his puzzled head and asked a bystander, 'What in the name o' God is that?'

'Well, your guess is as good as mine.' The speaker had a broad Dublin accent which well suited his caustic maner. 'That's Philip Hadden Anker, the doyen of Greenwich Village who turns up in Ireland every Bloomsday, the day that equalled in the oul' country the Year of the Short Corn and the Year of the High Wind. Did his nibs O'Reilly not educate you in this?'

'Please; excuse me ignorance, sir,' said Oiney.

'Oh, don't let that worry you. We're all just learnin'. O'Reilly thinks he knows every thin', the big clown of a man. He can, I know, recite *Finnegans Wake* backwards, but honest to God, it sounds the same both ways to me… I come here more to watch the antics o' these eejits, exhibitionists and careerists every man jack o' them… Them two Yale professors and the Oxford don yonder have made a small fortune lecturin' on *Finnegans Wake*. Mind you Joyce is a unique artist and innovator, but these phoney idolators give me the pip. It's just self-adulation of the bourgeoisie…'

'The what?' said Oiney.

'The middle classes. The butcher, the baker, the candlestick-maker and the vicar of Bray… The dullest, deadliest class in history .. .'

'Serve the wines,' ordered O'Reilly, drawing Oiney to the side and pointing to a wine tray on the bar counter. 'And stop talkin' to that cynic Costello. Some of these days I'll run him head-first off the premises, with the bitther oul' tongue o' his.'

In the process of serving the wines disaster struck. Oiney had served Wingham Pratt and had just moved back from the smell of his nauseating perfume when he collided with the easel and canvas and scattered the painting face-downward on the floor where grit and sand had been blown in. 'Oh, sorry, sorry,' exclaimed the shocked waiter, lifting the canvas and starting to clean away the grit.

O'Reilly descended on Oiney with his arm raised.

'You stupid, stupid clodhopper...'

'Don't... don't... don't touch it!' exclaimed the painter in horror. 'Leave the grit! Leave the pebbles! It's superb! Supreme. The final effect I was searchin' for. A complete manifestation of haphazard existentialist creation. You have made my day. Let me shake your hand!'

'Oh it was nothin' nothin' at all,' said Oiney. He extended his hand for Philip Anker to shake, but when that exotic artist started to exclaim 'Let me embrace you,' Oiney, dreading the perfume as much as the embrace, fled to the bar and the protection of Mrs O'Reilly.

'Oiney,' said Kathleen, 'don't let it upset you! You don't belong to this set, and believe me, you're not the only one.' She gave a long sigh accompanied by a look of utter weariness. This surprised him, for he had long imagined that opulence and contentment went hand in hand.

'Listen, Oiney,' Kathleen said, as though by way of consolation. 'When they retire to the Martello this evening you and I can go on a literary tour o' Dublin in our own time. Now wouldn't you like that?'

Oiney had not the faintest idea of what a literary tour of Dublin meant, but if it took him away from the hotel and O'Reilly, even for an hour or two, he was all in favour of it.

O'Reilly and his entourage departed for the Martello. Kathleen returned in the chauffeur-driven limousine after seeing a friend off to Killiney railway station. With a dark scowl the chauffeur opened the door to let Oiney take a seat beside her.

'I've something very important to tell you after we jettison his nibs,' she whispered, nodding towards the driver. The car went speeding into the heart of Dublin as darkness descended.

'Pick me up at eleven at the Four Courts, Frank,' Kathleen ordered the driver, and Oiney and she stood on the curbstone until the car was out of sight.

There was a large public house just off the main road. 'Let's go into The Brazen Head for a drink, Oiney. I feel done in.' She ordered up the drinks from a seat in the corner. 'This is a very, very old pub,' said Kathleen. 'Wolfe Tone used to have a refreshment here when he was studying at Trinity.'

'You mean to say,' exclaimed Oiney, his eyes lighting up, 'that Wolfe Tone, the great Irish hero, had a drink here one time? Wolfe Tone that's buried in Bodenstown... In Bodenstown churchyard, there is a green grave...'

'The same man. And if Tone was here, then the Emmets an' Miles Byrne, an' Russell an' Napper Tandy an' God knows who else was here.'

'An' we're here too, Mrs O'Reilly', said Oiney with a strange pride. Outside, in the little yard that ran beside you open window, a folk singer with the guitar was playing 'Patrick

Sheehan', an old ballad of the last century. It was the first time since they met that Oiney had seen contentment on Kathleen's face.

'This is one of the few escapes I have, Oiney,' she confided in him. 'To come here of a Saturday maybe, or a Sunday, to hear some of the old songs of Ireland, none o' your arty stuff, or cowboy nonsense sung by some young chiseler from Inchicore. After this we'll go up to McDaid's off Grafton Street, where Peadar Kearney who wrote *The Soldier's Song* drank. I knew him well meself.'

They had a drink in McDaid's and then they went into a quiet wee pub near Talbot Street.

'This is where, they say, James Clarence Mangan wrote that powerful poem "Roll forth my song to the mighty river",' Kathleen whispered with awe. 'And they say too that Yeats and Synge used to come here for a gill. When it came near closing time W B Yeats used to stand up and recite, *I will arise and go now*. So they say. Listen, Oiney!' Kathleen suddenly became very serious. 'I'm booking you into Moran's Hotel for a day or two here in Talbot Street. You can't possibly come back to Killiney after what I've seen. O'Reilly has built a real hate campaign against you Oiney, I saw it at the railway station.'

'What did you see Kathleen?'

'You know the platform notice where it used to read the word in big letters 'KILLINEY'?'

'Well, me husband P P has got them all worked up against you so much that they're all out to murdher you, Oiney. And in their burnin' anger they have added an 'O' to the platform sign so that it now reads 'KILLOINEY'!'

Oh, I've not the least doubt that if you go back, some of these dark nights they'll do you in. I'm all for bookin' you in Moran's quietly an' I'll see you safe out o' Dublin.'

Booked into Moran's Hotel, Kathleen decided they would have a last drink before parting for the night. She chose a little, quiet public-house near Fairview Park; she was an old friend of the owner Tom. 'A shandy an' a sherry, Tom, a glass of sherry. Listen Oiney. This is where Brian Boru had a drink before the Battle of Clontarf in 1014 AD.'

Oiney looked around the sturdy walls in amazement. 'More than nine hundred years,' he gasped, 'and it's here still?' 'Oh it wasn't like this then,' explained Kathleen, 'it was probably a little shebeen o' clay and wattle made. Tom!'

'Yes, Kathleen my dear?'

'Didn't Brian Boru come in here for a pie an' a pint before the Battle o' Clontarf, Tom?'

'He did indeed Kathleen,' said Tom turning to Oiney. 'He sat on that very chair you're sittin' on this minit. There's not a man in the city o' Dublin can contradict that...'

An irate little man, red-faced and wearing a deerstalker hat, arose from his seat near the fireplace. 'I'm the boy who'll disprove your statement, for it's a downright libel on the oul' Catholic heroes of Ireland. How could Brian Boru ate a pie when the battle took place on a Friday, a Good Friday at that, an' him with no dispensation from the Pope to ate meat?'

'Sit down Boylan,' shouted Tom, 'or I'll put you out again!'

'An' sure, maybe it was an apple-pie,' Kathleen suggested helpfully. 'But irrespective o' the pie, them's Brian's swords an' shield on the wall. Isn't that so Tom?'

'I thought so meself Kathleen, until I turned the shield round an' found "Made in Hong Kong" on the back. The swords maybe but...'

'Oiney?'

'What is it Kathleen?'

'I like you Oiney, an' I want no harm to come to you. That P P O'Reilly's a brute. I don't know why I ever married him…'

'Why did you Kathleen? You're two different kinds o' people entirely.'

She sat in silence for a moment or two, trying to recollect her memories. 'He was different when I met him, Oiney. He professed to be a rebel like meself. He was a friend o' Michael Collins long before the Treaty… he was a member of the RIC, the Royal Irish Constabulary, that was then the British Police Force in Ireland. O'Reilly was a sergeant attached to Dublin Castle. He brought Collins news of every move o' the enemy. I was left in the back streets o' Dublin with a son of another man. I had to fend for meself an' the boy, but he grew up to be a good lad, if a bit wild at times.

'My son knew I was goin' to marry O'Reilly but he only saw him as a policeman, a British one at that. The work was too important to Irish Freedom to risk it seepin' out. Even Collins forbade it. I didn't know that Collins would've signed that damned Treaty… James Connolly would not have signed it… But he signed it an' got himself executed at Beal Nam Blath. I didn't know, Oiney, that O'Reilly would rise to be a Superintendent of the Irish Civic Guards undher that horrible blue-shirt General O'Duffy…I didn't know these things at the time. Honest to God I didn't. Never even guessed…'

Kathleen sat back on the chair, almost exhausted, while Tom laid another drink in front of her.

'It's alright Kathleen, it's on me.'

'I may as well finish me story Oiney. Once the twentysix counties of Ireland were created an' that ugly Border established, Cosgrove, O'Duffy, Blythe, Mulcahy, the lot o' them didn't care a damn. The church neither. Irish Freedom was jettisoned by that crew. They carved out careers for themselves in politics, businesses and the Army. Before O'Reilly retired on his big pension he didn't give a frig about James Joyce or anyone else in literature or art. I heard him with me own two ears back in the twenties swear he would willingly shoot Joyce for corruption of literature and using filthy words. But now they've made a business out of Joyce an' poor Paddy Kavanagh up north… But I'll never see me son Shaun again, for he walked out of the house the day I said I was marryin' the RIC. man O'Reilly. I'll never see Shaun, an' me other son's stuck in that snooty college in Tipperary…'

Oiney could scarcely believe what he had just heard.

He took Kathleen's hand in his own and held it gently. 'Kathleen, did O'Reilly not tell you that I come from Creevan?'

Kathleen wore a startled expression. 'Creevan? You don't!'

'I do Kathleen, an' what's more I've met your son Shaun.'

'Met Shaun?' she stared straight ahead of her as though she could not absorb this almost incredible news.

'Yes Kathleen, and I can find him for you. I know who will bring him to you. Aileen at The Abbey. She's great, Kathleen, she'll bring you and Shaun together.'

Mrs O'Reilly was naturally in tears of joy at this heartening news. Her spirit soared with delight as she listened keenly to Oiney narrating his tale of the Wake and the mad Customs Officer and all the strange, strange folk that walk the green fields of Erin. She called for a taxi and left Oiney off at Moran's Hotel. He gave her a little farewell kiss and promised he would go in search of Aileen that very next day.

BARROW BOY

During his stay in Clunagh Monastery and guest house he had thought about Aileen, remembering their first meeting that cold night on the roof of Armagh Jail. His heart gave a great surge of delight as he saw her now approaching on the roadside close to the kerb. Her pretty face was slightly flushed as she pushed a kind of trolley-barrow towards the stagedoor of the Abbey Theatre. She was wearing a deep orange-coloured headsquare but the same dark green suit as before. She did not recognise Oiney at first but when she did she drew the barrow to a halt. She stared at him in amazement.

'Oiney,' she exclaimed, 'where's your robe? I just don't believe it! Let me feel you! Are you real? I just don't believe it.'

'You an' Shaun an' Sheamus had no right whatever in incarceratin' me in that monastery,' said Oiney quite angrily, 'an' if more important matters hadn't arisen, I don't think I would ever speak to you again.' He then went on to describe how he had met Kathleen, Shaun's sad mother, who was married to that dreadful creature O'Reilly, and how she realised the terrible mistake she had made.

'My heart breaks,' Aileen replied with sadness in her eyes, 'for the unfortunate women of Ireland. Shackled in slavery. And I'll bet you she doesn't even believe in the Pill, does she?'

'Does she what?' asked the puzzled Oiney.

'Believe in the Pill? Don't tell me you don't know what the Pill is?' Poor Aileen looked so exasperated that Oiney wished they had taught him more than religion at that school on the hill.

'Never mind Oiney, about the Pill meantime! We must do something about Kathleen right away. Shaun's presently in Belfast. But wait! If I could find one of the women to take my place with the barrow tomorrow, I could go up north then and fetch Shaun down. I'm working at the theatre this evening. Tell you what Oiney,' she continued, 'I'm takin' this yoke here up to my place on the North Circular Road and if you wait I'll be back within the hour.'

It was only after she left him that Oiney wondered why she was pushing a barrow along the streets of Dublin. He had not seen much on the barrow, only a few bundles of pamphlets on the shelves with some cardboard boxes, while three or four queer-looking balloons tied to the shafts floated over the lot.

It was early afternoon when they met again and Aileen suggested that they take the bus out to the Dublin Hills beyond the Hell Fire Club. On the journey Oiney learned a great deal about his youthful companion. She had been born and bred on the Antrim Road, Belfast, under the shadow of the famous Cave Hill mountain where the brave United Irishmen had planned the 1798 Rising. Her father, a Catholic shipyard worker, had been murdered in an Orange pogrom in the Musgrave Channel, part of the Harland and Wolff complex.

Struggling for his life in the water where he had dived to save himself, they had hit him on the head with iron bolts. Although a Catholic herself, she regarded her Church as wrong in some respects about politics and women's free rights in Ireland. In this respect she regarded it as mediaeval. She had no bias against Protestants. Her sister, Jenny in fact had married one of that faith, but Orangism she detested, regarding it the same kind of reactionary disease as the Ku Klux Klan and Fascism.

Oiney and Aileen sat together in the moss and bracken of the hills above Dublin Bay. It was a lovely summer's day when Ireland looked her grandest. He would retain a nostalgic memory of this day forever.

'I tried to find someone,' said Aileen 'to do my rounds with the barrow tomorrow, but up to date I've had no luck. No one seems to be free.'

'I'll watch it for you then,' Oiney volunteered, only too eager to get Shaun down from Belfast.

'If you do that'll be fine. I'll show you the streets. The Durex packets cost two shillings; the pamphlets, well I'll explain about them later.'

'The Durex,' said Oiney with a puzzled look. 'What sort of a thing is them?'

'The Durex... the contraceptives!'

'The contra what?'

'The contraceptives. Oh don't tell me you don't know about them at your age!'

'Oh yes of course,' said Oiney quickly, not wanting to appear ignorant in Aileen's lovely eyes. 'Yes, indeed. The contraceptions!'

'You see Oiney, we're pro-abortionists. You understand?'

Oiney nodded eagerly. If Aileen was a pro-abortionist that was good enough for him.

'The pamphlets on the barrow are to be handed out free of charge. We don't want any more of those backstreet abortions, do we?'

'Indeed an' we don't,' exclaimed Oiney, wondering what they were. 'We don't want any more backstreet abortives, not if you say so Aileen. An' how much do the balloons cost?'

She gave him a sharp inquisitive look. 'Now Oiney, stop your fooling. Peter Flynn blew up a couple of Durex for advertising and a bit of a laugh.'

Her hazel-brown eyes had a bright sparkle, and Oiney felt a great longing to kiss those rosy lips. 'Aileen, I love you.'

'I bet you tell that to all the girls in Creevan.'

'There's ne'er a girl in all Creevan or Carrick like Aileen,' he said quietly, and meaning every word of it.

The next morning, before she left for Belfast, he collected the barrow from Aileen. She told him to be careful and not to make himself the target of any fool's abuse. Oiney assured her that he would be on his best look-out, meaning that he would not let any thief steal his wares. For this reason when he entered into the old backstreets of the Liberties in Dublin he parked his barrow on the roadside between a Catholic church and a convent. It gave him such a warm feeling of security to be near such havens of sanctity. Then he began to declare his wares.

'Dulux an' contraceptions,' he shouted. 'We don't want backstreet abortives, do we? Dulux an' contraceptions, all for next to nothin'!'

A tall lean man with his hat at a jaunty tilt sidled over to him. 'Could I buy one o' your balloons,' he said, winking at Oiney.

'No sir, definitely not. Them balloons are not for sale.' 'Stop your nonsense,' said the customer, offering Oiney two shillings, 'an' give me one of your French Letters!'

'French Letters, French Letters,' said the puzzled Oiney. 'I am afraid, sir, you've come to the wrong shop. There's a bookshop in Nassau Street, or maybe you could ask for them in your local library.'

'Give me a Durex,' said the man irritably. 'You… you… you coillte… '

'Oh a Dulux! Certainly, sir. An' you can call me all the names you like, for I'm used to them.'

His trade at the barrow was not too bad at all, but some folk passed him by with an angry glare or turned their holy heads away. Oiney never in his life dreamt there were so many surly people in Ireland; they were not like the Creevan folk at all. Then he saw the nuns gathering in their black robes at the convent door shaking their fists at him, and in a short while the Parish Priest came out to the chapel door and began to splash quite a sprinkling of holy water in his direction. He was completely amazed by the strange antics all around him.

Just then a little pot-bellied man with a red nose, very poorly dressed, brushed past the barrow and tried to overturn it. When he failed he began to shout at the top of his voice, his cheeks and neck reddening to match the colour of his nose. 'We want none of your filth in holy Catholic Ireland. Christ didn't die on the Cross at Calvary for you vermin.'

For the life of him Oiney could see no connection between his barrow and the Crucifixion, although he was soon destined to resolve that enigma. He was drawing the sad conclusion that quite a number of Dublin folk were utterly irrational when suddenly, and as though to verify it, he heard a loud shout, and a great mob descended on him. Led by the Parish Priest and the nuns, a larger crowd than had turned out for the Fenian Rising of 1865 descended on him. From the rear of the mob the little pot-bellied hero was shouting 'Let me at him! Throw the dirty sod in the river! Let me at him!'

And no doubt they would have done just that had Oiney not immediately grasped both shafts and pulled the barrow after him. He would not dream of returning to Aileen without a barrow. The angry mob still came in hot pursuit. An astonished Civic Guard at a crossroads made the way clear for them and then joined in the melee. Oiney puffed and panted up hill and down until he was utterly exhausted. He could go no further. He said a powerful last Act of Contrition that would surely help his invisible soul meet other invisible souls in an invisible world called Heaven. He finished it off with a wee prayer that his granny would forgive him for not bringing home the brown jug from Doyle's Wake. The rest was darkness. He collapsed under the barrow and the crowd, unaware of his presence even as they followed their leaders, pressed him deeper and deeper into the hot tarmac until he was almost invisible.

When he came to several hours later he thought for a moment or two that he was in Purgatory. He was lying on his back staring at a whitewashed ceiling. His pain-wracked body was dressed in a brown habit Not unlike a monk's robe. His arms were folded across his chest and his fingers clasped the crucifix of a pair of rosary beads. A holy candle burned in a dirty saucer at his feet. The only really incongruous object in this scene of piety was a bottle of cheap wine, half empty, which sparkled in the candlelight. Then Oiney heard a gruff voice ascend in the shadows. 'Give us another swig o' that, Barney!'

A weathered sinewy hand came out of the darkness, lifted the bottle and drew it quietly into the shadows.

Oiney lay there still and silent, his head in a great turmoil. The only man he had ever seen dressed like this was at the Wake in Doyle's parlour. The Creevan lad was tongue-tied with astonishment and horror. Surely someone was making a terrible mistake, thinking that his soul had parted from his bruised body? And then he heard another voice that was somehow vaguely familiar.

'This young fella,' said the voice, 'has led the quare oul' life. The last time I met him he was nothin' less than a monk in charge of a Guest House in a monastery in Tipperary.'

'A monk begod,' exclaimed the other with awe in his voice. 'A long journey that, to the mud o' Dublin. Still, he's some poor woman's son, God help her.'

'Oh, he was decent enough to me,' said Barney. 'That's why I took special pity on the poor fella an' him dead...'

Oiney could scarcely believe his ears. It was none other than the Donegal travelling man. Even if he had wanted to, the Creevan lad would have found it very difficult to jump up, no matter his delight to be alive. Instead he lay there still and silent and even beginning to enjoy his Wake. The conversation, however, as it continued, became less complimentary.

'I think,' said Barney, 'this fella had somethin' wrong with his brain-box.'

'How is that, Barney?'

'Well, for one thing, he puts me between clane white sheets an' me with no bath for weeks. He probably got his books from Clunagh, 'cause they're awful fussy about good honest dirt down there. An' next thing, the daft fella's sellin' French Letters in the backstreets o' Dublin. Did you ever hear of a Cistercian monk sellin' Durex?'

The two old hoboes were doubled over with laughter and sharing the bottle between them. They were even daring to tackle Church Law. 'What makes the Catholic Higher Archy down on abortion so much Barney?'

'Hierarchy, you mane?'

'Aye, that's what I said. Higher Archy. The top brass!'

'The Pope, the Bishops, the lot I suppose,' said Barney, taking a last swig at the bottle, 'I suppose it's all a question of population. The more abortions the less Catholics. There was a woman not long ago in the County Fermanagh died, leaving twenty-two children, one for every year of her married life. What a poor, terrible existence! I don't think that God bothers His head one wee bit about abortions. D'you know, Danny, that God kills off about a hundred and ninety-nine million spermajigs an' just lets one reach the stage o' conception... Did you know that Danny?'

'Bejasus I didn't. An' isn't it the shockin' waste? Shure, if He was God couldn't he have just created one or two in the first instance an' not waste His valuable energy an' material?'

'If you ask me Barney, God would be a lot more concerned with the numbers of wee children murdhered in their millions in war and unnecessary famine. There's no dispute there about whether they're six or eight weeks in the womb. They're six and eight years old when their lives are aborted. That's the rale mass murdher, Danny. That's what your Church should be declaiming, an' lave the poor mothers alone!'

'An' yet Barney, you say this fella was a bit quare to risk his neck?'

Oiney squirmed uncomfortably.

'Bejasus Barney,' said Danny startled, 'Did you see that?'

'Did I see what?'

'The corpse twitched, Barney, the corpse twitched. I seen it with me own two eyes. If you'd ask my opinion, I'd say this corpse is only half-dead! There it goes again!'

'Half-dead me arse,' said Barney. 'This corpse is as dead as the Dail in Dublin. It's just the last twangin' o' the nerve cells ere rigor mortis sets in. Though there was the instance of a man up the street, Tim Finnegan by name, who got up from his own wake, drank all the porter, lit a pipe an' then lay down again an' died dacintly.'

'Rigor mortis be damned,' cried Danny, taking to his heels, hotly pursued by Barney, as the corpse sat up.

'Come back! Come back!' pleaded Oiney. 'I want to thank you both for rescuing me. That's better. Barney, Barney, there was never a man I was so glad to see. But what did you do with me clothes!'

'Tell him, Danny,' said Barney sadly.

Danny searched his pockets and produced a crumpled pawn ticket. 'We got the woman next door to clane an' iron your waiter's suit an' then we had to pawn it, hadn't we, for the shroud an' the candle...'

'An' the wine,' said Oiney.

'Shure, when we dug you out of that tarmac you were—as flat as a pancake.'

'Well,' said Oiney, 'I'll need to get me clothes back.'

The two men, shrugging their shoulders and obviously unable to raise any money to redeem the pledged suit, backed quietly out of the room, leaving the unfortunate Oiney to resolve his problem as best he could. He would not dare send a message to Aileen, for apart from losing her barrow, she would howl with laughter if she saw him dressed like this. And Kathleen, for all her personal sadness, might just do the same.

He had now no option but to walk boldly through the streets of Dublin. It was midday and the city was at its busiest, which perhaps was as well, for with the dense crowds on the pavements very few pedestrians got a full-length view of him. Some children however did, and immediately burst out giggling thinking he was going to a fancy dress party. Several old women saluted him, mistaking him for a Franciscan priest. Most folk merely passed a sidelong glance and took him for some foreign ambassador.

The pawnbroker's hair stood on end when Oiney, the pallor of his face contrasting with the brown shroud, handed his pawn ticket over the counter. The frightened man made the sign of the Cross and said his Jesus Mary and Joseph. Some of his customers undoubtedly made very long journeys to redeem their pledges but this, surely, was the first ever to return from the other side.

The sad tone in Oiney's voice moved even the pawnbroker. Besides, he worried about the apparition being bad for his business. And so, Oiney, restored to life and having changed into his suit in the cubicle, walked joyfully into the glorious sunlight of Dublin city.

THE TRICK CYCLIST

As things turned out it was a rather crestfallen Oiney who had eventually to report the loss of the barrow to that ardent activist Aileen. The fact that she was so busy striving to unite Kathleen and Shaun might serve to distract her a little and soften the blow. Yet Oiney felt that he must somehow find a job and raise the funds for another barrow.

A note from Kathleen left in Moran's hotel requested his presence at six o'clock that evening under the arched entrance to Trinity College at the foot of Grafton Street. Although Oiney had suffered many alarming experiences and was becoming slightly inured to them, the thought of meeting Shaun, Kathleen and Aileen at the one time set his nerves jangling. Near six o'clock he walked over O'Connell Bridge on his way towards the historic venue. Swift, Tone, Emmet, Goldsmith, Davis, Sheridan and many other prominent people had passed under this proud archway.

The others were awaiting his arrival. There were tears of joy in Kathleen's eyes and even Shaun seemed to have lost some of his aggressiveness as, arms linked, the four friends began their walk of the cobbled quadrangle. First there was some eventful news to narrate. Kathleen told how in a fit of rage at the idea of Shaun's return P P O'Reilly had rushed out of the Bloomsbury Hotel, swearing loudly that Oiney was the source of all his bad luck and that misfortune had trudged him since ever he had set eyes on that pious fraud in Clunagh Guest House. He vowed as well that Oiney's neck would be more twisted than a corkscrew if ever he should lay hands on him.

'An' where did you leave me barra?' Aileen asked anxiously. Oiney then stammered out the sad tale of his misadventure.

'My God,' exclaimed Kathleen, 'd'you mean to say you hadn't a cup o' tay in all that time or since?'

'Divil the cup or morsel has passed me lips,' said Oiney. 'Well, we'll soon make up for that in Grogan's Bar,' Kathleen assured the company, 'for we've real cause to celebrate at me meetin' me son Shaun again.'

In the privacy of Grogan's lounge Aileen also had a word of comfort for Oiney. 'Don't worry about the barra, Oiney, just don't! There's a lot a spare wood lyin' around the theatre backstage an' we'll knock somethin' together. I'm not goin' to let the holy brigade put me off me mission. I'm not indeed.'

But Shaun was more annoyed: 'I don't know what it is, Oiney, but you have the unfortunate habit of muckin' things up. If you had stayed in the monastery where you were put none of this would have ever happened.'

'And no one would have ever brought us together,' said Kathleen, 'would they? Leave the poor fella alone! Remember he's just a young country-boy from the backwoods o' Creevan, as innocent as meself one day. But Oiney, keep clear of the south o' Dublin. O'Reilly an' me are partin', an' he's vowed revenge. The Bloomsbury's in my name an' we're turnin' it into a hostel where the wives of political prisoners can meet, and girls who have gone through the despicable ordeal of strip-searching. There'll be a room downstairs where qualified staff under the aegis of Aileen an' her group can give sound advice on abortion. We're callin' it The Sanctuary. Another thing. I'm takin' me son Luke out o' that snooty-nosed college in Tipperary. He can come home and study for Trinity or UCD or whatever he likes, in one of the day-schools.'

Aileen had a suggestion too for Oiney: 'You could do a lot worse,' she said, 'than get yourself any wee job in the north side o' the city. You could learn a bit about city life, for God knows, some country places in Ireland are still a hundred years behind the times. You could go into cheaper lodgings. I saw some jobs advertised only this mornin' in a shop window at the corner of Gardener Street.

Thus it was that Oiney came to be interviewed by the Manager of. Fairview Toy Factory, not far from the pub in Clontarf where Kathleen and him had been recently. The bald and very important looking manager was not entirely convinced that this country chap had all the necessary qualifications for this important job. But he was willing to give him a fair trial.

'This task,' he assured him, 'will require your maximum concentration. It's what we call a precision job. A wrong move to the left or the right would be a calamity. You will require a training period, perhaps, at a reduced salary, of course.'

Oiney was on edge with excitement at the prospect of his first real job. He told Aileen the great news.

'What exactly do you do?' she asked.

'I don't know what it is, but it sounds real important. 'Precision is the key word. I just can't wait. Isn't it exciting?'

The following day the manager showed him around the toy factory and then into an annexe where seven girls were assembling hobby-horses on a conveyor-belt system. His guide brought him to the end of the belt where there was a large pile of batches of black hair. The manager without any ado lifted a single batch, dipped one end of it in a large pot of hot glue and then stuck it with unerring accuracy plumb on to the bald hindquarters of a recently painted hobby-horse. Another and then another. 'You'll understand now what I meant yesterday by precision,' he said.

The amazed Oiney looked at him hard to see if he was serious, but there was not even the hint of a smile on that grim countenance.

'D'you think you can cope?' he asked Oiney.

How could he possibly fail, Oiney wondered, unless by chance he lost his eyesight or the use of his hands. He merely replied however that he would try to be accurate and, giving the manager an assuring exhibition of his ability in sticking tails to the hobby-horses' behinds, he was left to continue on his own this most edifying and noble task.

Oiney for the life of him could not imagine a more monotonous and soul-destroying job. Admittedly the horses were painted in a variety of colours: black, brown, white, grey and piebald, but the tails were uniformly, without exception, jet black, all of equal girth and each exactly eighteen inches long. Occasionally as the day dragged on one or other of the girls would smile over at him in sympathy. He, however, for a good part of the time kept watching the clock for the happy hour of his release, and when eventually it came, no one could run faster to the gates. He had not enough humour in him to tell Aileen or anyone else the exact nature of his job. They might, on being told, tell him of the great happiness he was giving children, but then they would turn their faces away to hide their laughter.

On the way home past the wide curve of the open road he often stood to watch the amazing performances of passing cyclists who, coming from their various places of work also, had to pass a Catholic church at this rather dangerous corner. The dexterity of these cyclists really astonished him and it became almost a ballet of extreme beauty as they raised their right hands from their bicycles and made the sign of the Cross. It all recalled to his memory that fantastic day long ago in Creevan when the Circuit Judge had entertained the village on the icy brae. Oiney vowed that he would keep sticking tails until he had at least enough money to buy a bicycle.

Eventually that happy day dawned. Before riding it to work, however, Oiney practised each morning and evening in a quiet corner of Fairview Park. When he had learned to ride he still had the task of holding the handlebars steady with one hand while he blessed himself with the other. The bike wobbled unsteadily on his first few attempts but after a time he mastered the feat and was at long last fit to take his worthy place on the thronged roadway.

He felt a great pride and delight as he joined his fellow cyclists on the sweeping curve past the church. Then, in harmony with them, in a wonderful declaration of Faith, he raised his right hand from the handlebars: 'In the name of the Father, and of the Son, and of the Holy Ghost, Amen.' His face beamed in holy delight, and then…

He can never explain it to this day what tempted him to take his other hand off the handlebars to complete the perfect blessing. Perhaps it was an absolute trust in the Almighty to guide us through shadow and storm.

Whatever or whoever it was that tempted him, he was crazy enough to succumb. He sat back on his saddle, his face flushed with triumph at this superb miracle of Faith and looking around to see if any of the others were admiring his marvellous skill when the disaster struck. He did not notice the great puddle of water that soaked his tyres and caused him to take a long low slide at a rapidly diminishing angle which brought him into collision with more and more bicycles.

Dozens of bicycles and their riders piled up on the stretch of roadway and the pious ejaculations of a moment or two previous were now replaced by some of the loudest oaths he had ever heard in Christendom. Oiney lay at the very base of this squirming wriggling mass, but fearing for his life, he hauled himself and his bike to the far pavement and down a side road. Needless to say, after that dreadful experience, he never attempted even to raise his right hand from the handlebars but merely gave the church a courteous nod, knowing that if there was anyone up there, He (or She) would understand.

ONE BISHOP HAS A BASH

Long, long ago when he was just a boy of ten years or so, Oiney's granny had him enlisted in the local Boy Scouts. One fine summer, Oiney remembered it well, the troop had gone on a camping expedition to Termanfeckan where there was stretches of fine sand. From this spot, it was no great journey by the seaside to march into Drogheda on the river Boyne, where in 1690 King James had lost the battle but won the race into Dublin.

The young Scouts were taken to see the preserved head of Oliver Plunkett (now canonised) in a side tabernacle at Drogheda cathedral. The shuddering memory of that visit remained vividly in Oiney's young mind for the simple reason that, like the Crusader whom he had recently seen in Saint Michin's, the head of Blessed Oliver did not look the least preserved. The face was awful grey-like, thought the boy as he stared at the glass door in the tabernacle. If God had really wished to preserve the saint's head, surely thought Oiney, could He not have done it decently and given him a nice, fresh, smiling face to show that he was happy above. That kind of display would be certain to convert everyone, except Orangemen of course.

Oiney had discussed his grave doubts with Jonjo the day after his return from camping. 'I'm sorry, Oiney,' said the sexton, after thinking the matter over. 'Now put yourself in his shoes. I don't think you would be in a happy smilin' mood, if your head was being chopped off be an English axe-man. Another thing. Maybe you saw him in a black mood—on one of his off-days. Maybe he was feeling a bit morose. Saints I suppose do have their ups and downs like the rest of us.'

Oiney thought this was a rather threadbare explanation, so now that he had his bike and a free Sunday, he decided to cycle up to Drogheda and have another glance at the tabernacle. He rode through Kerries and the other pleasant little villages by the north of Dublin and then cut in by the ancient plains of Meath to the large cathedral town. He left his bicycle behind the gate wall and made towards the side aisle where the tabernacle was situated. Something strode towards him out of the shadows and Oiney gave a sudden look of recognition: 'In God's name, Pat McNulty, what are you doin' in Drogheda!' exclaimed Oiney. The words were scarcely out of his mouth when he realised his mistake. The man was wearing a clerical collar.

'I'm Father Twomey,' said the priest. 'I'm sorry, I'm not you Mr McNulty. I'm the sacristan. Would you like to see Blessed Oliver?'

He was a nice, gentle-faced man and spoke so warmly about the saint that one felt that Oliver was alive and well. The priest led the way up the aisle to where the candles burned in a shining brass tray and lit up a small, veneered oak stall where a collection of slim pamphlets lay with the rather rhetorical title of 'Do Miracles Happen in Ireland?' Oiney was about to express the severe testing that his Faith was undergoing, when suddenly he had a glimpse of the tabernacle: the cheeks of the saint had a somewhat ruddy glow, and his entire appearance seemed so different from what Oiney had seen on his last visit. 'Father Twomey,' gasped Oiney, 'I just can't believe it. Oliver seems to grow younger an' better-lookin' with the years. Do you do him up?'

'Nonsense, young man,' said the priest. 'Miracles are divine manifestations. Surely you don't imagine...'

'Oh, it's nothing, Father. It's just I'm amazed to see him lookin' so fit an' well. A great change for the better.'

Oiney made a quiet retreat down the darkened aisle.

He was about to leave the cathedral when he halted in his tracks. Above a confessional box at the rear of the aisle, he detected a slight movement. He stood for a moment gazing in wonder. There: it moved again. A large painting of Judas hanging himself in the garden was moving up and down.

My God, thought Oiney, this place is surely brimming with miracles! He was about to call Father Twomey's attention to this strange phenomenon when the priest disappeared into the sacristy.

He looked up again to see the picture come off the wall completely, and standing on top of the confessional was a tubby little man who shouted, 'Hey, you there! Give me a hand down with this! It's for cleanin' an' restoration!'

Being a kindly fellow, as we all know by this time, Oiney gave the industrious man a helping hand, and even put his shoulder to the picture to assist in carrying it down to a van which lay parked a little down from the main gates of the cathedral. It was only now that he was able to see the man's face clearly for the first time, and when he did so he was truly astonished. For this was the very man who had been roughly thrown into his cell in Armagh Jail the week before his escape! None other than Bobby Brown the Belfast Protestant! 'Well, of all the wondhers o' the small world,' said Oiney, shaking hands with Bobby warmly, so delighted was he to see him, 'an' what in God's name are you doin' in Drogheda, Bobby? Have you the good job at the resthorin'?'

'Well, to tell you the truth, I haven't restored anything yet. I've taken but not restored if you know what I mean. An' the job, like many another has its ups and down. I was up when you seen me, up on top o' the confession box…'

'You mean to say you… you are stealin' this holy picture an' I'm helpin' you… I'm helpin' you?'

Bobby nodded his head. 'I'm sorry, Oiney, but what you say is only too true. But I did take your advice… the advice you gave me when we first met. I haven't touched an offering-box in a church or chapel ever since. I only do cathedrals now, an' believe me, Oiney, yours was sound advice. There's far better pickings.'

Oiney felt a wave of disgust flow over him. 'Bobby Brown, we're puttin' that picture back. I've made up me mind, an' I don't want to have to tell that sin in confession… and I'm not lettin' you steal church property. I'm definitely not goin' to be part or parcel of this.'

'Oh, just this once, Oiney,' pleaded the icon-stealer. 'It's only for Jenny an' the four children. You wouldn't have them starve, Oiney. You wouldn't have them cryin' out for fish suppers last thing at night, would you? All for one oul' paintin'? Remember I helped you out of jail? Just this once, Oiney.'

'Well, just this once,' said Oiney softening, thinking that one picture would be no great loss to a church that has riches beyond measure and countless art treasures. Oiney then said farewell, but when he returned to where he had left his bicycle it was gone. Frantic, he searched rapidly around the buttresses of the cathedral, but there was no sign of it at all. He then hurried back to the van and told Bobby the sad news.

'God above,' said the Belfast man. 'Some folk have no piety about them at all. They'd even steal from sanctified ground. Tell you what, Oiney. We'll run this painting into a store I have in Dundalk, and then I'll give you a lift back to Dublin.'

On their way into the grand old town of Dundalk, Oiney thrust his concern about his lost bicycle out of mind for the time being, and began a conversation with the driver. 'Tell me, Bobby, how did you know a helicopter was comin' to lift me off the Infirmary roof?'

'Ah, that'd be tellin' you the secrets o' the game, Oiney. But I'll give a wee clue. Does the letter 'A' ring a bell?'

'Aileen?'

'Aye. I'm married to her sister Jenny, so there's the tie-up for you. She's a great girl, Aileen, an' not an ounce of bigotry in her. I'm a Protestant an' honest to God she couldn't care less, whether I was a Hindoo or a Hottentot.'

Oiney, tired from his cycling and his work in the toy factory, fell asleep, but not for long. On the edge of Dundalk six rather vicious Civic Guards surrounded the van, and finding the stolen painting, arrested the icon-stealer and Oiney. Soon they were lodged in the local prison and charged with pilfering Judas Iscariot and desecrating sacred ground.

'No wonder Christ wept in the garden,' shouted Bobby kicking the cell door and demanding a lawyer. He gave Oiney the few pounds he had on him and asked him as a favour to approach the local Bishop on his behalf and plead for clemency. To be fair to Robert Brown, he exonerated Oiney completely and took all the blame on his own shoulders, saying that he had merely given his co-accused a hitch on the road to Dundalk.

On a bright summer's day, the Bishop of Meath sat in his study basking in the delight of the lovely countryside. He was a stout, ruddy, jovial man with three or four chins all of which rippled with laughter, especially at good clean harmless jokes of religious origin, jokes, he believed, that even God Himself would enjoy. As he sat back in his plush armchair, he often thought to himself: why should atheists and the like have all the fun? He felt he had earned his comfortable bishopric after many years of service in the Missions abroad. The study was large and luxurious with a great sideboard displaying ivy and jade ornaments, trophies and gifts acquired during his more hectic years in Africa, India and China. At the far end of the study there was a wide, magnificent bay window leading on to a verandah overlooking a well-kept lawn which was occasionally used as a tennis court. His grounds were surrounded by rhododendron bushes and presently the soft breeze bore their pleasant perfume through the open window.

He was sitting back in his beloved armchair reading anecdotes of the great Dean Swift. One of them in particular had his several chins sagging and wagging. It was the letter the Dean had written to his superiors in London who, after exiling the great man to the fairly obscure post of the deanery in Dublin and giving in his stead high bishoprics to inferior and sometimes worthless clergymen, had the effrontery to enquire from Swift if the recently appointed new bishops had arrived in Dublin. Would the Dean please inform them? The great man was furious as he reached for his quill: Gentlemen, wrote Swift, it seems as if the three bishops who were appointed in London were proceeding to Hollyhead, when they were waylaid by three highwaymen in the woods in Wales who stripped them of their clothes and worldly possessions, and disguised as bishops, these three gentlemen have landed in Ireland at Kingston.

As the Bishop of Meath rocked with laughter, his faithful servant Christine entered the study. 'Sorry, my lord, but your visitor has arrived.'

'What visitor is that, Christine?'

The servant was accustomed to his absent-mindedness. 'The lad who wrote you the letter, a Mr Oiney Hoy.'

'Oh, oh yes. The one who penned that strange epistle, utterly outside my comprehension. Do show him in!'

Oiney, gaping at the magnificent splendour of this heavenly representative, was ushered into the study. 'Sit down, young man! And tell me now, what can I do for you?'

The nervous Oiney sat down in front of the Bishop, and poured out his heart in a fervent plea for his imprisoned friend. He told the good Bishop the man's sad story, how he had lost his parents when he was but of a tender age, how he had been slightly corrupted by a well-meaning but weak clergyman, the lone years he had spent in Homes and Borstals, how he had lost his best job through his generosity to poor Irish emigrants on the ship, how his broadmindedness had allowed him to marry a Catholic and how he had four equally sad little children. Oiney went on to narrate a few of Bobby Brown's minor faults, how he was given to dipping in church collection-boxes, which, of course, was wrong as these boxes were for the poor. Yet wasn't it only a time difference if one looked at it sensibly? Wasn't Bobby himself poor and only taking in advance what was his by right? His sin, therefore, was surely only of impatience. His biggest mistake, Your Worship would agree, was that of stealing the oil painting out of Drogheda Cathedral. But surely the great wealthy Church could easily afford one painting if the value of its sale might bring several years of food, shelter and comfort to six poor lambs of God? And all said and done, Oiney concluded his passionate plea, the picture was returned intact without as much as a scratch on it. Surely all this deserved clemency?

During the latter part of his speech, Oiney wondered why the Bishop kept shaking his head and blowing air through his pursed lips. Finally the great man arose and paced up and down the richly carpeted floor. 'What a great, great pity,' he said sadly.

Oiney's eyes lit up with hope. 'So you are sorry for me friend, your Worship?'

'Not so much that, I'm afraid. The painting I'm talking about: it should never have been returned. Only one painting you say: what a pity!'

'So you are not angry, your Worship?'

'Angry? Good heavens, no! I'd be delighted if all the pictures and paintings in churches were to disappear from the face of the earth!'

'You would!' gasped the astonished Oiney.

'Yes, and all the statues and Stations of the Cross as well.' Oiney's gaping mouth opened wider and his eyes wore a startled look as the Bishop continued.

'I wouldn't bat an eyelid if they all were bundled over the Cliffs of Moher into the waves of the Atlantic or a huge bonfire made of them on the Hills of Slane.'

'Even... even the Blessed Virgin?' whispered Oiney in shuddering anticipation.

'The Blessed Virgin especially,' roared the Bishop now fully in flight with one of his pet themes. 'Ireland is thoroughly saturated with statue worship and mariolatry. I would like to sweep the lot into oblivion. Only that I cannot associate with criminals, I would like to shake your friend's hand.'

It was Oiney's turn to explode. 'You're not shakin' nobody's hand! Talkin' about the Blessed Virgin like she was Guy Fawkes!' Oiney made the sign of the Cross and thought hard and wildly. 'I'm writin' to the Pope,' he said threateningly. 'That's what I'm doin'—I'm writin' to the Pope.'

The Bishop of Meath stared intently at the young fellow shaking with anger in his seat. Then the truth dawning on him, he threw back his head and roared with hilarious laughter. 'Write to the Pope! Oh my God, it's rich, it's rich. Listen, sonny, I see, I see. You thought

I was the Catholic Bishop of Meath. Oh, Lord above, how funny, how funny. You see, Mr what's-this-they-call-you... oh yes... Mr... Hoy, I'm the Protestant Bishop of Meath. How's that for a little faux-pas?' And again he burst into rollicking laughter. 'But we all make mistakes, laddie, even bishops. We will have tea together, shan't we? Christine,' he shouted going towards the door - but as soon as his back was turned, Oiney took a flying leap out through the bay window over the verandah and a mighty descent onto the lawn, a leap that easily matched the great feat of his spiritual ancestor in the Carrick Hills. He ran down the avenue from the Bishop's residence as though he was escaping from Hell itself, and ran breathlessly, pursued by two yapping poodles nipping his heels.

After this most embarrassing experience Oiney made full certain that he would present himself at the proper Bishop of Meath's house—well, the one that he thought proper. The Catholic Bishop was the antithesis of his jovial counterpart. He was tall, lean, sallow and ascetic. He seldom smiled and had deep, dark eyes which seemed to bore into Oiney's conscience, making him feel uncomfortable. After listening to his visitor's long, rambling, sad story, the Bishop raised his eyebrows and said, 'Oh, we shan't hang him. But tell me, young man, what do you think I can do?'

'Well, your Eminence, if you could say something favourable for Bobby it might help. I'm sure it would.'

'I never liked that particular painting,' said the Bishop.

'You didn't?'

'No, it was never my cup of tea, aesthetically I mean... '

'Aist what?' said Oiney

'Artistically. It was so sordid and sombre that I had it hidden above the Confessional. The obscure artist who painted it was a professional idiot. The rope around poor Judas's scrawny neck is not even taut and that thin branch to which it is tied could not even support a small sack of spuds.'

'That's right, your Holiness,' Oiney agreed, even though he had scarcely glanced at the painting. 'So you'll plead for clemency for poor Bobby, your Worship?'

'I will, surely. I will make such a speech that will put the great Demosthenes himself in the shade. Besides, we cannot allow three, or four is it, children of his to be crying out last thing at night for their fish suppers, can we?' The Bishop gave Oiney a very wan but knowing smile.

'Four of them, your Holiness,' said the astonished Oiney. 'But them's Bobby's exact words. How did you know?'

'Oh, Bobby Brown and I have had our dealings before.

I'm afraid his interest in ecclesiastics is rather intense.'

The trial took place in Dundalk Court. Oiney's hopes were high until he saw the grim face of the notorious old Circuit Judge Ritchie on the bench. The arrival of the tall Bishop raised his spirits a little, even though that good man had to be helped into Court by two able assistants. After a disappointingly weak defence case, the prisoner threw himself at the mercy of the Court and admitted his guilt, giving Oiney at the same time one of those cute, twitching winks of his. The Bishop then rose to plead mitigation of sentence. He gave a heartrending description of the sorrow and onus which descends on the shoulders of the custodian of Church goods when something in his care is abused or stolen. Yet in the spirit of the good Jesus himself, he had left his sick bed to travel a fair distance to plead leniency for this seasoned sinner.

The Bishop continued in this poignant, plaintive manner and Oiney shuddered as he noticed several women and even some hardened businessmen on the jury take out their handkerchiefs and weep openly and profusely—not for the lost sheep, unfortunately, but the poor shepherd himself. The stony-faced Ritchie summed up everyone's sentiments. 'We must save our good Bishop from his own kindness. He has left his sick bed in his frail old age to come here and plead for a miserable hardened sinner and a cloister thief from Belfast. Are you not ashamed of yourself, Mr Brown, to not only witness but be the root cause of this man's sufferings? We must teach you a lesson, indeed.'

It was thus Bobby Brown got a much stiffer sentence on account of Oiney's effort. And now he earnestly wished that the good Bishop had stayed in his bed and died peacefully.

GHOST STORY

A dispirited Oiney walked the streets of Dundalk that afternoon. His mission of mercy had failed miserably, his pockets were empty and he had nowhere to shelter for the night. He would have to find some stable or outhouse up one of the entries off these busy little streets. He loitered at the railway station for a while watching the train to Clones and Creevan draw out, but still fearful of his granny's wrath, he turned away from the platform and dandered slowly down past the old churchyard and the monument over the grave of the sister of the great poet, Robert Burns. He passed the large hotel at the foot of the street to .arrive at the Maid of Erin statue. This is the rich legendary country of Cuchulainn, Ireland's greatest folk hero; Oiney had read all about him in that enchanting book Celtic Romance. From here up to Carlingford and beyond to the slopes of the Mourne mountains and the southern boundaries of Down and Armagh lay the ancient plain of Muirtherne, the Gap of the North, renowned in the colourful sagas of the Red Branch knights and the warriors of Finn MacCool, the Irish giant. Hungry though he was, Oiney felt elated by their memory even, breathing as it were the same air and walking in their footsteps.

It was on a public bench near the Maid of Erin statue that he encountered the Creevan man Bert Corrigan. At first Oiney hesitated, afraid that news of his whereabouts might seep back to his irate granny, but his hunger and his curiosity got the better of him and he approached the man.

'Is that yourself, Bert?'

Bert stared in amazement. 'Well, if it isn't Oiney!

Where in God's name have you been, Oiney? All Creevan's talkin' about you an' mystified by your sudden disappearance. Some say that the Wee Folk snatched you for cutting down the Lone Tree; others tell the quarest stories about you hitch-hikin' to America in a Flyin' Fortress, but the strongest rumours are that you have a job dealin' with horses in the north of Dublin and have applied to join a Trappist monastery in north Tipperary.'

Oiney could not resist a good laugh. 'Just leave it to the Creevan folk, Bert, to get it all mixed up. How is me granny doin', Bert?'

'Fair to middlin', Oiney, but she's still rampagin'. She says she won't send you on a message again in a hurry. An' there was this big hulkin' brute from Dublin came pesterin' her about your whereabouts an' runnin' you down to the lowest. In the hinderend she paid Jemmy McGurk, Jonjo and another lad to pitch him into the deep end of Creevan lough.'

Oiney clapped his hands and gave a great hop of delight. 'Oh, good for her, Bert, good for her. O'Reilly himself would be no match for the Holy Terror.'

'You should watch the company you keep, Oiney. That big fella slunk out of Creevan with his tail between his legs, but he was swearin' revenge. He said he would get you if he had to search the sewers of Hell. If I was you, Oiney, I'd steer clear of yon fella.'

'What are you doin' in Dundalk, Bert?'

'I'm waitin' here on the single-decker bus to Blackrock.

You'll hardly believe it, Oiney, but I bought a neat wee pub on this bit of headland at the near end of the village. It's called Uncle Tom's Cabin. I read the book but the title's the best part of it. I was in Court this mornin', a smugglin' case. That Ritchie one, the judge, would hang a dog for trespassin'. Remember him on Creevan brae? I never laughed so much to see oul' frosty face with his bowler on an' biddin' the time o' day to the women…'

'Bert?'

'What is it, Oiney?'

'I don't want to go back to Creevan just yet.'

'Don't worry, Oiney! There's a spare room in my place if you want it. You're welcome, Oiney. Sure I knew your mother afore you were born. It was me that helped her, God rest her, with her Da's coffin to Castleblayney poorhouse. I watched you grow up with the Holy Terror an' Heaven knows she's not the aisiest woman in the world to live with. Everyone in Creevan knows that, but sure it takes all kinds… Here's the bus comin', Oiney. Let's be off!' He put a friendly arm around Oiney's shoulder and led him to the bus stop.

At Blackrock the bus drew to a halt about fifty yards to the north of the Post Office and there on a grassy headland looking out both on sea and shore stood the cosy little tavern called Uncle Tom's Cabin. It was a popular inn for both locals and visitors. Blackrock was a lively village with a long promenade and a colourful row of shops and hotels. Outside the shop doors there hung bright little sand buckets and spades, balloons and stick windmills. From a skating rink not far from the 'Cabin' a loudspeaker blared out popular tunes. Happy, smiling holidaymakers thronged the street and walked along the promenade with their children; some wore sunshades or dark glasses. Far away to the south one could see the faint cliff of Annagasson Point on the horizon, a mysterious beckoning wonder to a child, like the edge of the world. The long gentle ripple of the sands leading out of Dundalk Bay to meet the sea seemed endless, as though the waves were weary or else reluctant to reach the land.

Oiney had a room to himself at the inn; he helped to repay Bert's kindness by lifting tumblers, drying dishes and sweeping the floor. He would have felt perfect contentment in Blackrock, except for two nagging worries: his granny and that irate parasite, O'Reilly. Oiney was so proud of his granny's stand against the creature. She was an indomitable woman surely, and many a time walking along the quiet sands away from the crowded beach, he would think of long summers past, when she had held his hands and jumped up and down with him in these waves. Nothing pleased him better now than to sit in a quiet niche among the rounded rocks and gaze out at the wide immensity of the sea. There he would reflect on his terrible year of adventure in the wicked world. His sins he hoped were merely venial not mortal, but even they merited him a few thousand years in Purgatory, an uncomfortable region, he imagined, halfway between Hell and Heaven, where one lived on simple fare like bread and water and in perpetual twilight like his granny's coal-hole. He shuddered at the thought of it. The sooner he made his terrible confession the better. It brought him some solace to know that the Blackrock priest would be a complete stranger to him.

The chapel lay on the slight crest of a hill a little up from 'Uncle Tom's Cabin' and overlooking the bay. Oiney climbed the steps hoping to find the priest on call. A dark figure crossed the path at the top of the hill and went in through the main doorway, the priest or the sexton. Oiney was glad to find the chapel almost empty; an old woman was just finishing the Stations of the Cross and about to leave. In a side aisle, the curtain of the middle compartment of the Confession Box rustled and the anxious sinner gave a sigh of relief. The priest was on duty and soon the worst would be over; he would then enjoy that wonderful exaltation of a clear conscience and a cleansed soul. He went into the shadows of the box and waited until the small grille door was drawn aside.

'Father, forgive me for I have sinned.'

'How long, young man, since your last confession?'

'A year, Father.'

'A what?'

He heard the priest growl ominously. 'A year, Father.' 'Disgraceful. Carry on! Let us have them!'

'Father, you won't like this but I was involved in blowing up the Border.'

There was a dreadful hushed silence as though the good priest had dropped dead. 'Good God,' said the confessor, 'but carry on!'

'I masqueraded as a Cistercian monk, Father, an' I sold French Letters in the streets o' Dublin.'

'Merciful Jesus,' cried the priest, 'is there no end to your depravity?'

Oiney felt really sorry he had come but there was no way out of it now. 'I thought they were balloons, Father.'

'Stop adding lies to your iniquity!'

'I... I helped this Protestant steal a holy picture from Drogheda an' I didn't believe in Blessed Oliver's head.'

'Christ almighty,' roared the priest, 'aren't you the blackest, most accursed sinner ever to darken this box? Aren't you the dyed-in-the-wool scoundrel? Let me hear the rest of your behaviour!'

Oiney was glad that he had nothing else to confess. 'I've no more sins to confess, Father.'

'No more you say. Come off it you bloody little liar!' Oiney knelt, mouth wide open with astonishment at the vehemence and coarseness. He had been reprimanded in Confession before but this grilling made his own local priest, Father Duffy, seem like an angel. But he was in for a bigger shock.

A voice roared in his ears, 'Have I got to squeeze it out of you?' Then a great hairy hand shot around the corner of the box and grabbed him by the neck. 'So you've no more sins. What about the the vilest sin of all, tearin' apart the holy vows of matrimony between man an' wife an' dhrivin' me a ragin' beast through the provinces of Ireland to destroy you, you little verminous insect?' The coarse voice and the hairy hand of O'Reilly were now too obvious to Oiney; the bully was raging mad as he dragged his young enemy out into the deserted aisle which re-echoed with his insane laughter. The grip tightened on Oiney's throat but when he saw O'Reilly dressed in a black suit like a priest his own fury mounted at this desecration of holiness and now with the little breath left in him he managed to gasp, 'Are you not ashamed of yourself, Mr O'Reilly, doin' the very same as that dirty Yeoman captain in the Croppy days, disguisin' yourself as a man o' the cloth in Confession to vent your anger on me? God or man'll never forgive you!'

The taunt only served to make the brute more angry. 'Who are you to talk about disguises you pious little prig,' he shouted, tightening his squeeze until the veins stood out on his victim's temples. 'You that masqueraded not only as a monk but a very saint...'

Stars flashed through poor Oiney's brain as he bravely muttered a last Act of Contrition for his invisible soul when suddenly the greatest miracle of his young life happened.

A slow, ponderous bell rang out in the chapel belfry and resounded over Blackrock. The hand suddenly relaxed its hold on Oiney's throat and joined another hairy hand in pious supplication. It was none other than the Angelus bell struck each day at noon. Ever since he was a child, O'Reilly had been taught to relinquish every other activity, no matter how important, at the very first peal of this bell. Even through critical moments in long years of service as a garda, the habit had become so engrained that it was really second nature to him. Oiney, of course, blessed himself as well, but more in gratitude than real piety. And then in a flash he took to his heels and ran out of the chapel into the sunlight and down the path to the safety of Uncle Tom's Cabin. Even as he ran, he thanked God for the staunch devotion of the Irish people.

Bert Corrigan's face wore a look of deep concern as the breathless Oiney almost collapsed into a chair in the bar. When he had recovered a little he told his friend how he had encountered his enemy in the Confessional.

'He'll come to a bad end that scoundrel,' said Bert angrily. 'But I'm afraid there's even worse news, Oiney. This telegram arrived an hour ago from Creevan for you.' Though his heart fluttered and his fingers shook, Oiney opened the envelope:

YOUR GRANDMOTHER DIED THIS MORNING STOP COME HOME FOR THE FUNERAL STOP
SIGNED FATHER DUFFY PARISH PRIEST STOP

The two men looked at each other in sad silence.

An hour later Oiney sat in the carriage of the train on the way home to Creevan. Bert had provided him with some money to cover funeral expenses, but he dearly wished that he had not to return to the wee town in such solemn reverie. He still felt a sense of guilt towards his granny. Admittedly she too had her faults, but God knows, she had her good points. She had bought him that green gansey and all his other clothes and given him holidays at the seaside as a boy. Many of her strange doings made him smile. Those dreadful prayers she used to say at the doorstep as the pious passed on the way to chapel. And her corns and bunions on Lough Derg. It was hard to believe he would see her no more. He would love to have told her the least harmful of his adventures but perhaps in the Kingdom above she was reading the unabridged edition of his every deed. That Holy Terror of a granny, wherever could he hope to find her like again?

He felt very sad as the train moved under the shadow of the familiar Slieve Gullion and into the homeland of Paddy Kavanagh the poet and the great Gaelic bard of the nineteenth century, Art McCooey, close by Glasdrummond and Culloville. This was the western edge of the plain of Muirtheme and the Gap of the North. Soon they halted for a moment at Castleblayney station with its poorhouse walls still visible from the train. There it was that the two coffins had been brought that strange night of his grandfather's funeral among these little hills. What had made his granny the fierce indomitable woman she was? Perhaps the frightening tales of the terrible Famine she had heard as a child in the Carrick Hills when the memory of them was so fresh and bitter.

The train moved slowly into Creevan and he had a great view of the Bluebell Hill in full bloom above the lovely calm lough. A thrill of excitement ran through his veins, despite his sadness, to see his native fields and surrounds again. As the train drew to a halt, he looked out on the platform. My God, he thought, what am I seeing? He could not believe his eyes. Nor was it her ghost but her wee sturdy plump self, standing with the little brown jug in one hand while with a smile on her face she shook the other gnarled fist of welcome at Oiney. On either side of her stood those grinning pair of rogues, Jemmy McGurk and Jonjo, who had joined her conspiracy to send the fake telegram to lure him back to Creevan. Who in the world but herself would connive such a plan? And Creevan itself wasn't it splendid that day, none but a fool would leave it with its loughs and rivers and lush green fields and winding blackberry lanes in the hidden hills of Monaghan! Overhead on the tapering chapel spire above Jonjo's belfry the famous weathercock still had pride of place and Oiney smiled too remembering the tale and many others of his home in these little Ulster hills, tales that will endure in a world of peace, still to be won, aye, even a million years ere Ireland dreams of sinking in the wild Atlantic.

THE END

SHORT STORIES

THE BANSHEE IN THE CORN

I met him casually at an exhibition of paintings in the McLellan Galleries, Sauchiehall Street. He was a small, bearded man with a monocle which he handled with extreme delicacy as he scrutinised the pictures. He conveyed to me an impression of great energy as he moved to and fro, measuring, it seemed, the distance between himself and each painting, like a corporation official who had forgotten his tape. All accompanied with exclamations of delight, even rhapsody, which he used abundantly and with complete indifference to the attention he was attracting.

'Splendid! Magnificent! Supreme!' I was not very familiar with the art scene, but I could not help wondering what fantastic beauty he could see in the magnification of a cat's eye set dead centre in what appeared to be a roasted potato lying on a sandy beach. I glanced around and since the galleries were fairly empty, I decided to approach him

'Sir,' I enquired, as courteously as possible, 'what qualities in this particular painting makes you regard it with such admiration?' He turned on me with the haughtiness you can often observe in a connoisseur of the arts. 'Good heavens, my dear fellow,' he exclaimed, 'I am not in the least bit interested in these paintings!'

I was about to dismiss him as an occasional eccentric of the sort one meets in the city when suddenly he lowered his monocle and continued. 'I never go to the art exhibitions of this kind to look at paintings. Good Lord, no! It's the frames I'm interested in. I'm not prejudiced. You cannot possibly blame the frames for what is happening here. Why, sometimes you see the most exquisite frame encasing a very monstrosity, a very Caliban of art. Some of these frames, if given the chance, would jump clean off the wall and run for dear life. Prince Luigiano actually tells me of a case in Florence when a magnificent frame compelled to house one of these distortions, one night, when no one could observe it, moved its four sides simultaneously towards the centre, crushing the horrible thing out of all recognition. An improvement, I would say. Unfortunately, my dear chap, such happenings are too infrequent. These frames are mostly poor prisoners. I feel sorry for them. I learned this compassion from the Prince, a wonderful chap. Have you heard of him?'

I had to admit that my intimacy with the aristocracy was very limited, that I was at the time staying in a cheap lodging-house in Anderston, using the adjacent library for a more critical study of literature. And that I was attempting to write some poetry

'How interesting!' he exclaimed. 'Say, old chap, would you care for coffee. I've seen enough of these to suffice me for the day.'

We retired to a nearby cafe and on the way I could hear him murmuring in words scarcely audible, 'A great pity!' It was not, however, until we were comfortably seated and sipping the warm coffee that the words became significant. He leaned across the table and whispered confidentially, 'A great pity indeed! If only you had known the Count Berenzosky! He was passionately fond of poetry. He simply adored it. I say, old chap, have you forgotten the sugar? I stayed at the Count's place in Lucerne and later in Bavaria. An intimate friend of Lord Vaux with whom we went yachting last summer off the Riviera! A splendid sail… Leghorn, Naples, Corfu… jolly good sports. No stuffed shirts either… They might be sitting beside you at a bar or opposite you in a cafe and you wouldn't know it. Splendid chaps! By the way, what's your name?'

I told him.

'Mine is Duddens,' he said, 'but they call me Dene. Can't guess why!'

His surname had a good plebeian, downstairs ring about it, but I was not going to allow that, or the fact that he spoke with a slight trace of Glaswegian in his polished accent, deceive me into imagining that this consort of princes and counts could be of any common origin.

'What kind of poetry do you write?' he asked.

'Mostly lyrical. And at the moment, seeing I don't know Glasgow too well, it is Irish...'

'Oh, I gathered you had your origins in the Emerald Isle of Kathleen Ni Houlihan,' said he with a flourish and peering at me through his monocle with a sparkling intimacy that made me think he was on speaking terms with the Bishop of Clogher, 'What a coincidence you coming from there. Do you know the Leslies? They're related to the Churchills... on the mother's side, of course. I was speaking to Shane Leslie, the author, just the other day in London. Care to come up to my place and let me hear your poetry?'

I looked at my shabby suit and felt I might be drastically out of place in his obviously opulent background, but then there was a sort of democratic bohemianism about him to make clothes and wealth seem relatively unimportant. His suit was a tweedy one, with several leather patches on the sleeves, expressing the aristocratic virtue of thrift, or perhaps a kind of worthy self-denial, merely temporary in character, of course, while the family estates were undergoing extensive repairs. As I placed myself under his guidance and walked along the Cowcaddens seeing no chauffeur-driven limousine awaiting us, I was hoping that his residence was not too far out in the suburbs, entailing a long walk home, as the few coppers in my possession would not amount to the bus fare. Suddenly, I found myself walking alone and I was about to move off on my own, still wondering what had happened to this friend of Princes and Peers, when I saw him emerge from a narrow little restaurant clutching two fish suppers. He generously handed me one of them. I was quite hungry but completely outclassed by him in the quick and efficient manner in which he disposed of the chips. Only a great deal of practice could have achieved such astonishing result and I was left to wonder if Lucerne or Genoa surpassed even Glasgow, so justly famous in this particular art.

'I enjoy these proletarian snacks,' Duddens explained, devouring half his fish in one mouthful. Then without warning, he turned on the pavement and went into a dark tenement close next to a pawn-broker's shop. Before climbing the stone spiral of stairs, however, he spoke to me quietly, indeed almost mysteriously.

'I want you to take no notice', he confided, 'of anything that goes on in this place. It is only temporary, of course. I'm moving off with Luigiano in the Spring. For one thing, there's no semblance of culture up here. But it is convenient for the galleries... and the library... I'm doing quite a bit of research at the moment. Anything that strikes you as odd up here, just close your eyes and talk to no-one. We artists cannot have everything to our taste in this neurotic world, can we?'

With these remarks, he gave the pathetic little laugh of unappreciated genius confronting the impossible, imparting at the same time a look of intimacy to convey, I think, that, for better or worse, we were both joined in common bonds in the same horrible struggle

Fore-warned thus, it was not without certain misgivings I followed him into the tenement flat. Immediately on entry, however, I saw no cause for alarm. On the contrary, the place presented quite a warm and pleasant atmosphere with two girls in their late teens cooking and cleaning with great industry. Duddens walked past them without exchanging the courtesy of even a greeting, and I noticed that the girls ignored his presence as well. But the older of the two looked at me with such a sharp curiosity that I could not feel other than uncomfortable.

Duddens's room I would describe as being of average labourer's comfort, but for a prince's footman even, it was incredibly poor and about the same level of furnishing as my own lodgings. Six secondhand books lay scattered on a great grotesque mantlepiece above an empty fireplace. He motioned me to a black, shiny horse-hair couch in one corner, and seating himself in an armchair, chin in hand, requested a sample of my poetry.

Its effect seemed electric, for when I had concluded, he jumped up to exclaim that it was a very moving experience indeed, and as though to prove the absolute sincerity of his remark, he began to pace up and down the room diagonally in deep profundity: a very impressive gesture, had its grace not been marred by the awkward body-swerve he had to take each time to avoid the table in the centre.

Then he clicked his fingers and stopped dead in his tracks with the air of a man who had reached a supremely confident final decision

'Yes! Yes! Splendid. The Count... Count Berenzosky must have them! Signed copies, if you don't mind! You don't mind, do you? The Count'll be positively charmed. His English , of course, isn't of the highest order.' And here Duddens gave me a look of much significance, 'But I'll translate some of the more difficult passages for him. I'm used to that sort of thing. Splendid!'

Later on that evening, for my greater enlightenment, he narrated some of his experiences with our own Scottish nobility, but never in the same favourable light as his continental heroes. The degree of intimacy, however, was so impressive that had the Duke of Buccleuch and the last of the Baskervilles entered hand in hand at that instant, I doubt very much if they would have been able to distract my attention from the absorbing reminiscences of Mr Duddens. Close on midnight, he asked me if I would accept, in lieu of his more normal hospitality, the inconvenience of a bed-chair in the living-room. I accepted, for at least it was as comfortable as my lodgings at Anderston. And I was still curious

In the morning when I was moving about, the elder girl, the one who had given me the sharp glance, entered the living-room to lay the fire. I sensed that she wished to speak to me, but was somewhat afraid of my reaction. A huge blanket of fog had come down on the city, and I chose this fact to open conversation.

'You're Irish,' she said. 'When did you meet him?' There was a strong, depreciative emphasis on the 'him' and a nod of the head towards the room.

'Just yesterday. At the McLellan Galleries. He was examining the frames.'

'Frames? What does he know about frames?'

I did not like her sense of superiority, although I had a deep common bond with many working-class people, I thought it wrong of them to be suspicious of specialists in the more unusual spheres of activity. I was a little angry.

'Oh, perhaps,' said I, 'he knows more about frames than you imagine. And some of the other arts that his friend, Prince Luigiano, appears to appreciate.'

Suddenly I saw she was staring at me with a look of great incredulity and I stopped speaking. I could see she was about to say something, but had changed her mind and turned her back on me to attend to the oven. She pretended to polish the handle although it was already sparkling. Then I heard a titter of laughter, which she tried frantically to restrain, but which grew into an uncontrollable and disconcerting hilarity as soon as I mentioned Count Berenzosky.

She ran into the side-room, obviously unable to contain herself, where she joined the other girl and, despite the fact that she closed the door behind her, I could hear the convulsions of laughter, to which the younger girl now added her own brand. In a short while, however, she returned to the living-room, wiping her eyes with a handkerchief.

'I'm sorry,' she said, 'but did he tell you all that?'

'All what?'

'About Prince-what's-his-name and the other queer fellow?'

'Well,' said I, a bit peeved, 'if you don't like him, you'll not have to put up with him very long. He's going off with Prince Luigiano in the Spring'.

'He's going off with the cuckoos in the Spring,' she retorted, 'if he's not already there. If you'd been in Glasgow for long you'd know Harry Duddens. But don't worry ! You're not the first I've warned about Harry and you won't be the last. He hasn't been out of Glasgow since the day he was born. Well no, I'm telling a lie. When Harry wis a bairn, he did go wi' the Boy Scouts to Arran an' of course he's been to the Edinburgh Tattoo… only once though. He thought it beneath him… too vulgar for his taste. Said it had as much to dae wi' Scottish culture as Harry Lauder's walking stick. Sissy an' me loved the Ghost Piper on the castle rampart but he called it a load of baloney. Said that the kilted piper should be hauled before the Judges o' Edinburgh Courts for gross impersonation o' the dead.'

In deep bewilderment, I asked the obvious. 'How long has poor Harold been this way? And why?'

She shrugged her shoulders and, hearing a slight stir in the room adjacent, whispered her reply.

'Ever since my father's death, when Ma joined the spookies… '

The girl saw my puzzled expression.

'Spookies? The Spiritualists. Table-rapping, mediums and ectoplasm. She had this Eskimo guide come doon every Christmas as regular as Santa Claus frae the frozen North. She got the spae-wife as weel to read the tea-leaves and forecast a wunnerful future for Harry. He'd be a great traveller she said. Like Marco Polo and Livingstone an' meet the Nabobs and high-heid yins o' the universe. That's when it started I think. Sssh,' she warned putting a finger to her lips. 'I think that's him.' The room door was opened very slowly and cautiously and a monocled eye gazed directly at me with certain disapproval. Harry had a sheet of paper in his hand.

'May I have a word with you, friend ?'

I joined him in the room. His arm embraced my shoulders, and he drew me into a distant corner away from any possible eavesdropping by one or other of his sisters.

'Familiarity breeds contempt,' he said with a grim hauteur, glancing malevolently back towards the door. 'I warned you about fraternising with the masses, the philistines. Don't fall into the trap, my friend, or you're finished, culture wise. Take my word for it! Next thing, they'll be asking you to the Bingo or the Dennistoun Palais. I dread to think what will happen then. Probably an invitation to join them at the berry-picking in Blairgowrie—or worse still, a fortnight at Butlins in Ayrshire, my good friend. What a descent! Your poetry will be squashed through a common clothes-wringer. And to think that your melodious Irish verses, with shades of Yeats and Joyce and Synge have been such an inspiration to me. Last night when I retired to my couch', he continued, pointing carelessly in the direction of the crumpled sheets on an iron bedstead in the corner of the room, 'I couldn't repose with the stream of consciousness that your eloquent verses aroused in my inmost soul and I strove to emulate your genius in the atmospheric mystic lingo of the Gael. Your work inspired me to write an Irish poem myself. I am sure you would love to hear it and any minor criticisms will, of course, be most acceptable.'

Good God, I thought, what have I done to deserve this?

He freed my shoulders from his arm's embrace and then as he had done the previous night, began to walk, this time on tip-toe, the diagonal of the room, swerving as usual, but more dextrously to avoid contact with the square awkward table which traversed his poetic passage. If I was amazed at the high droning pitch of his voice—in imitation of W B Yeats who in turn believed he was following the poetical traditional chant of the Druids or Gaelic bards, or perhaps even the ancient Greek chorus—I was utterly astonished at the words:

'The night I met the Banshee in the corn,
I saw her when the skies of light was shorn,
The words she had for me,
She conveyed mysteriously,
And left me feeling lonely and forlorn.
The night I met the Banshee in the corn,
The twilight merged into the misty morn,
She blew to me a kiss,
I was petrified with bliss,
For only a white sheet did she adorn.
The night I met the Banshee in the corn,
My mystic ardent spirit was reborn.
A cultural resurrection
Evolved from that connection
Soul piercing notes played on a fairy horn.
Oh I never more will meet,
In the shadows of the street,
That lovely little Banshee in the corn.'

Tears came to my eyes with each successive verse. Duddens didn't know if their source was laughter or sorrow, and in return for his hospitality in the dark dunnies of Glasgow, I hope that he gave me the benefit of the doubt. I merely told him his 'poem' carried the riddle of the Universe and that after hearing such enigmatic cadences, I myself would forsake the Muses and humbly return to carrying the hod.

The next time I saw him, years later in Paddy's Market, he was wearing a black beret and smock and peddling gilt pictures frames from a stall. I was glad to hear that he too had left the field of poetry, for the man who could write 'The Banshee in the Corn' was not a stone's throw away from the Bingo and Butlins and the Edinburgh Tattoo that he so heartily despised.

A LEGEND OF SAINT MUNGO

Once upon a time; long, long before this story was written, there dwelt on the banks of the Molendinar, which was a little burn or brook running into the great Clyde, a poor monk called Mungo. His piety, however, was not so much expressed in prayer as in industry, and for this some of the other monks would chide and even ridicule him, saying that his mind was too much on the vain and temporal things of the world when his thoughts should be more devoted on the affairs of the kingdom above. Yet Mungo could not help lamenting the carelessness of men towards the beauty around them. Looking down from the heights where the cathedral of Glasgow now stands, a woodland grove where sweet birds sang, he saw the lovely vista of the river valley, stretching towards the rich, green fields of Lanarkshire on the east of him, and westwards to Dumbarton and Renfrewshire and the wonderful blue sea that was still a mystery to men.

For all their chiding Mungo still had a great love for the poor beggars and peasants who flocked at times to the monastery gates. In the darkness of his little cell, he prayed that the rich and lovely land be cultivated for the happiness of all, and, whilst the danger remained unknownst to him, he gradually built in his innermost heart a tremendous longing to see this done in his own lifetime. It was only when he was near his death bed that the full significance of his longing struck him forcefully—all his unfulfilled dreams and desires, and a great anguish came over him that he would have to leave all this behind him.

Then in the middle of his sorrow, just when it seemed to heavy for him to bear, his dark cell was lit by a great golden light, and he heard a loud voice saying, 'What is it, Mungo, servant of God, what is it that grieves thee? Is it to exchange the glory of heaven for the toil and suffering of men? Then the Lord sends thee this message. If it be thy wish, in lieu of His Kingdom, thou mayst bide on the earth and see these things come to pass. The Clyde shall be peopled, the green meadows give way to the dwellings of men, huge ships of iron shall sail on the river, and the valley will ring loud with the hammers of industry.'

When Mungo heard of the Lond's fulfilment of his wishes, his heart rejoiced and he blessed His wisdom. 'Yet it shall not be easy, Mungo', said the Angel, 'to abide through the years until the brotherhood of man dawns. But the Lord sends thee this message of hope; that while one bead alone on the rosary remains whole, it shall at any time through thy wish be thine passport through the gates of heaven.

With these last words,, the Angel disappeared and when morning dawned on Clutha Valley, Mungo found himself in the garb of a poor peasant outside the monastery and the gates shut against him. But he still clutched his beads. None of the monks recognised him, for the Lord had endowed him with great youth, and when he begged for food, saying he was Mungo, they scoffed at him saying that Mungo had long since passed over to the Kingdom of God, that he was never a beggar but a great saint, as time would prove, long to be remembered in the annals of Glasgow. On hearing this, the poor saint was very perturbed, but try as he might to convince them, he only succeeded in making them laugh the more until the very fir trees of the grove rang with hilarity and it sounded more like the work of the devil.

The sad monk had no option but to repair to the banks of the river Clyde where he built himself a littie hut of wattles and lived on the fish he caught in the river He counted the beads daily—but being more a man of industry than prayer, he decided to serve his fellow man. Accordingly, he planted a fir tree on the river edge, from the branch of which he hung a bell to warn the curraghs from Ireland of the reefs near the Broomielaw. Apart from this good action, he took upon himself the job of protecting the banks of the river from the waves, which were already damaging it and in this humble origin began the Clyde Navigation Trust, such a byword today in the city of Glasgow.

While Mungo was engaged on this strenuous task, the bell was becoming neglected, so he caught and trained a bird, one of the many pigeons who centuries later were destined to desecrate the Municipal Buildings in George Square. He trained this bird to sit on the branch of the fir tree and peck away at the rope of the bell, whenever it saw a boat approach the reefs, particularly in the dusk or early dawn. Thus it was that Glasgow derived its coat of arms—the tree, the bird, the fish and bell, so often narrated by school-children in the rhyme:

This is the tree that never grew,
This is the bird that never flew,
This is the bell that never rang
And this is the fish that never swam.

However, the rhyme refers to the city's badge, not the friends of the mariner and Mungo. But you haven't heard half the story yet!

All of Europe and Asia was in a great hullabaloo (America had not as yet the opportunity to add to the turmoil, since it all happened before Columbus) and fancy knights roamed the scene on horseback, pillaging and slaughtering, often in the name of religion, a fact which made the good Mungo wonder greatly at the strange ways of men. And like the flow of the river, the years rolled by, the decades and the centuries with Mungo destined to stay by his own choice in the lonely field at the water edge, and small shape or sign of the city of God's promise, and the great brotherhood, about which he had spoken, not between monks but between all men. Then as the years passed, wooden shacks like his own, or cottages built from mud and with thatched roofs of straw appeared in little rows around him. Mungo welcomed his brethren, from what hillside or distant place they came, and together they eked out a living by Clutha's clear stream. The knights rode by in glittering pageantry, the wandering friars counting their beads, and ambling behind came the crippled beggars. And as slow as the latter was the passage of time. The poor in their industry and needs created boats, roughly at first and small, and Mungo himself was among them, toiling himself and spurring them on when necessary, though none knew he was a saint filled with the vision of God. A small village arose, a single long street, and after their trade they called it the Fisher's Yett, or Gate, in that very place where the busy Saltmarket now stands. Bigger boats were built and bolder hearts to man them, venturing down the river to more distant places, and the coals of the earth were dug and more clothes woven. The little village on the Clyde prospered a while; then suddenly out of the night the plague came, a mysterious affliction, and they had scarcely buried their dead, when marauders from north and south bore wildly on them, sacking their houses and decimating their numbers. They built once again and were happy a while, but like a spirit of fury the river arose in spate, flooding the houses and drowning great numbers. The saint grieved bitterly at this repeated destruction and loss, when suddenly out of his tears of despair, the Devil himself arose, and pointing to the huge and wonderful cities he conjured up before him, cities with tapering minarets and golden, glittering domes, addressed Mungo.

'Why dwellest thou in this derelict valley, Mungo of dreams, when all this and more can be thine in exchange for thy rosary?'

But Mungo turned his eyes from the demon, and looking at the sparkling waters of the Clyde and the men bending over their little boats, cried out like his Master,

'Get thou behind me, Satan!'

On the spot where the Fiend had stood, Glasgow Cathedral was built. The Clydeside was peopled; the green meads gave way to the dwellings of men. Huge iron ships sailed on the river and the valley rang loud with the hammers of industry. Everything had come to pass as promised, everything that is but the brotherhood of man. The ancient fears and greeds remained, and though Mungo moved among them preaching more by the example of his charitable deeds, many men were obdurate and slow to learn. One day the good saint was walking by the banks of the river, when he heard a sharp cry of fear, and looking down towards the waters edge, he saw a poor tramp slip from the embankment into the swirling waters. He immediately hastened to the assistance of the unfortunate one, but the drowning man was about an arm's length outside Mungo's reach. Suddenly the saint remembered his stout rosary beads, and without considering the consequence, he held them out for the other to grasp. He hauled the poor man ashore, but in the strain the chain broke, the beads one by one fell into the rushing waters and were swept out to the wide ocean.

Thus Mungo's passport to heaven, which he had refused to surrender to the Devil for all the pomp and glory of the world, was freely given to the poorest and most lowly of humankind. And the saint still walks in the city, though known only to such folk as have the real interest of the Glasgow people at heart. And another strange thing happened. The waves of the ocean scattered Mungo's beads to all corners of the globe, where in later centuries, the voice of the Scot would be heard. The beads were found by the natives of these distant lands, and they were buried in the deep earth for they thought they were charms And charms, indeed, they were. From each spot where one was buried, a tree grew, a bird tiew, a fish swam and a bell rang.

THE ROSE AND THE THORN

The frail lady with the battered portmanteau boarded the ship at New York on her return to Scotland for the first time in seventy years. Seven long and often weary decades but with intervals of interest and excitement even. She distrusted the latter intensely, for it brought back memories of youth, frivolity and—stark horror. Ninety-two years old, she was not fit for this long voyage into the past, but it had been forced upon her. A good deal of her vibrant life had been spent in avoiding photographers and now these movie cameras that ruined one's privacy.

The tall, handsome steward took hold of her portmanteau, and, bustling aside the two photographers, led her gently by the arm up the gangway to her spacious first-class cabin.

'This way, Mrs Sheehy. The captain has asked me to take particular care of you. Dunwoody's the name, madam, at your service. I trust you find the cabin to your liking, and I wish you a pleasant voyage.'

'I'll be fine, Mr Dunwoody, just fine. Do your utmost to keep those camera and newspaper folk at bay!'

She spoke clearly and very politely, in addition there was a faint but pleasant Scottish burr in her voice that even her youth at an English boarding-school had not erased.

'Don't disturb yourself, madam, on that account. I have been briefed by the skipper. Nobody on board will be allowed to intrude on your privacy, I can assure you.'

'Thank you, Mr Dunwoody. Now, where's that bag of mine? Ah, there it is. It may be old and travel-worn like myself, but I treasure it. It belonged to Mr Wardle, my first husband, a thorough gentleman, close friend of William Morris, the great poet and artist. You've heard, of course, of Morris?'

'Yes indeed, Madam. I have a book of his Arthurian legends in my library at home in Dumfries, and my good lady loves his designs. Can I be of any further service to you, madam?'

'No, thank you, Mr Dunwoody. I'll be fine, just fine.'

The chief steward reported to the captain in the latter's cabin. 'Mrs Sheehy is safely aboard, sir. I've instructed the crew to safe-guard her privacy. They were somewhat curious, sir. Mystery always provokes the inquisitive mind. I'm not immune to it myself, sir; she seems to me quite a well-bred, educated, genteel old lady.'

'She is all that, Dunwoody. Take a seat and I'll briefly explain. Remember, however, it's between you and I. Not a word to the others. Mrs Sheehy is none other than the famous Madeline Smith... '

'Good heavens, sir! The young woman who was tried for murder in Edinburgh many years ago. I read an article about it. Sordid and yet fascinating. She was found not proven. Which, of course has left lingering doubts ever since.'

'That describes it, Dunwoody. Seventy years after the trial the press and curio hunters have never really left her in peace. A new harassment has come from the sharks in the Hollywood studio set-up. They want to film the murder and engage her as a consultant for as many dollars as she cares to name. Who will blame her, Dunwoody, for rebuffing such downright audacity? The political hot-house atmosphere has intensified in America since the trial and execution of the anarchists. The film moguls have discovered that, since Madeline's flight from Scotland to London to avoid publicity, she has been associating with socialist visionaries like George Bernard Shaw and William Morris.'

'She told me as much, sir.'

'She did?'

'Aye, sir. She said that her first husband was a Mr Wardle.'

'William Morris's right-hand man. The artist in the black cloak, like Morris, a dreamer. After he died at the turn of the century, Madeline emigrated to New York and several years later married Mr Sheehy, a quiet inoffensive Irishman. She's lived here ever since…'

'I think, sir, they should leave the unfortunate old lady to her conscience and the good Lord above.'

'That would be the opinion of any fair-minded individual. But it doesn't end there, Dunwoody. Far from it. When we docked here, I had a private letter from Mrs Sheehy's lawyer requesting an interview with me. An intelligent young man who put me in the complete picture. After Mrs Sheehy's rejection of the Hollywood offers, the US Immigration authorities say they were bombarded with letters claiming that the woman involved in the sensational Scottish murder of years past should be made to prove that she has enough money to provide for herself and will never be a burden on the US tax-payer…'

'Good heavens, sir. Who would believe it?'

'It seems incredible, Dunwoody, but it's a fact. That's why her American lawyer took me into his confidence. He wants all this pressure taken off the old lady and a trip back to bonny Scotland without publicity or fuss is not such a bad idea. She has to collect documents of her property assets in the neighbourhood of Glasgow from her agent there. He will meet her when we dock at the Broomielaw and take her to a guest house in Kelvingrove. Think of it, Dunwoody. Ninety-two, and no living relatives in Glasgow. Madeline, who in 1856 was almost doomed, has outlived them all. Judge, jury and accusers as well. It is a strange world indeed.'

Mrs Sheehy kept to the privacy of her cabin during the long voyage across the Atlantic, but as soon as the liner reached the mouth of the Clyde past the huge, lone rock, Ailsa Craig, she made the occasional sortie on deck, always towards the railings on the port side, scanning the Kilpatrick Hills in the distance. Then, suddenly she had a glimpse of what she was searching for. The roof and small turret of the familiar country house designed by her father, the builder, James Smith, were just visible among the swaying foliage of beech and willow trees. Below these trees, a short distance from Helensburgh, stood the fine sturdy house and gardens, poetically called 'Rowaleyn'.

It was among these romantic surrounds of hills and trees, rhododendrons and rose bushes, that young Madeline snuggled her Jersey-born sweetheart L'Angelier, in his occasional secret trips to the village of Rhu. This charming background had so bewitched the English essayist Sitwell that he waxed lyrical on the loss of the young Victorian maid's virginity in this Arcadian rendezvous. The reality was quite the opposite, as the old woman leaning on the ship's railing sadly remembered. L'Angelier had deceived and blackmailed her. Ten years her senior and a man of the world who had spent four years in the National Guard in Paris against the 1848 Revolution, he had dominated a silly eighteen year old ex-boarding school girl who was dazzled by the novelty of this conceited popinjay and, even though the long decades had passed bringing with them a host of experiences, some sad, some happy, the old woman's eyes dimmed with tears at the memory of these early traumatic events that had blighted her young life. The liner gradually slowed as she passed the Erskine Ferry, and only the clang of the caulkers and riveters of the bustling ship-yards of the Clyde aroused the old pilgrim from her deep reverie. With a last fond look at 'Rowaleyn' she sought the peace of her cabin.

At the crowded Broomielaw Quay, the Captain invited Mrs Sheehy to have tea with him while all the other passengers scurried ashore among their welcoming families and friends.

'It's just a precaution, Mrs Sheehy.' he explained, 'When the wharf is cleared, Dunwoody will see you off at your leisure. Your Glasgow agent has arranged to meet you with a cab outside in Clyde Street and he will accompany you to your rooms in Kelvingrove. Have you had a comfortable journey, madam?'

'Very much so.' She smiled gratefully. 'Your good officer saw to my needs perfectly.'

She looked, for her great age, remarkably preserved, he thought. In the bloom of youth back in that grim Court of Judiciary in Edinburgh seventy years ago, even though she would have been pale with prison confinement and stress, she would have struck quite a vivid impression. No wonder the young beaus of the capital applauded the verdict. Age had, of course, carved its inevitable wrinkles but there was still the glow of character in Madeline's face.

'Kelvingrove,' she mused dreamily, 'a lovely poetic name. I lived near it in India Street, our first town residence. I remember there was a song about it. 'Will ye gang tae Kelvingrove, honey bonnie lassie o.' Our maid used to sing it.'

The Captain nodded and whistled a bar. 'Oh, it's still going the rounds of the old music halls,' he said, 'I've heard it in The Metropole—that used to be the Olde Scotia before the Short Family and the Logans.'

'Oh,' said the old lady with a superior smile and a tilt of her head, 'we were above all that, us Blythswood Square folk. Nothing less than High Opera. We left the music halls to the riff-raff in those pernickety times.'

The Captain grinned at her fine mimicry. No wonder, he mused, that the old leprechaun genius, George Bernard Shaw, found a liking for this Scottish lass in her exile among the Chelsea set.

When the wharf was cleared, Dunwoody, carrying the portmanteau, escorted Mrs Sheehy to the square Ford cab awaiting her at the corner of Jamaica Bridge, a short distance along Clyde Street. Her law agent welcomed her to the city of her birth. She thanked the head steward for his great kindness and left him with a strange tale to narrate in his older days at Dumfries.

The agent drove slowly along Hope Street past Central Station where in Madeline's youth that pitifully slim Glasgow worthy called 'The Tay Pot Man' stood; one of his arms curved in a semi-circle to his hip while the other made a perfect spout right out to his extended hand offering a newspaper for sale to the public. The poor man had long since disappeared into a pauper's grave in Anderston and in his stead stood a dull, characterless kiosk. Yet Madeline was soon reassured that Glasgow had not lost its local colour. As the agent drove around the corner into Sauchiehall Street shopping centre, she was somewhat taken aback by the sudden appearance of an old, tall, white-bearded man wearing a lum-hat as he strutted with dignity on the near pavement. He crossed in front of the car, signalling for it to stop, and then made his way to the other pavement. His back was now turned and the old lady read a placard on his long swallow-tailed coat.

'Kiss me under the mistletoe!'

A green sprig of the latter was pinned much lower down.

'Good heavens!' exclaimed the startled woman, 'What has happened to Mungo's holy city?'

The agent was obviously enjoying the scene.

'That's the famous old Glasgow Clincher, madam. The only man in Scotland with a certificate to prove he is sane. He writes, edits, prints and distributes his own broadsheets. 'The Clincher' he calls it. It clinches all arguments and debates, and if that's not enough, it even solves the most obscure riddles of the universe. The Clincher has been lifted dozens of times by the Glasgow police but there's no holding him down.'

'Stop the car, my good man, and purchase one of his papers for me.'

The following day was the Sabbath and she attended the church service in St Jude's on the other side of Blythswood Square; the Smith family once had their own pew there. On a Sunday long past, L'Angelier had often lurked in a seat at the rear. He had pretended to be as staunchly High Kirk as herself and for his ends had ingratiated himself into the good graces of the local minister. No-one in the church now recognised her, of course; otherwise she would not have dared to attend. The text of the sermon was the agonised cry in the garden at Gethsemene, 'Oh, Father, why hast Thou forsaken me?' How often had she felt the terror of that cry herself as the trial loomed in Edinburgh. Yet her father had not deserted her. Thousands of pounds from his hardearned money had gone to her security and comfort in Chelsea and, even now, he was protecting her in the twilight of her life.

After the service, the afternoon being sunny, she made her way slowly down to the serpentine walks in Glasgow Green where her grandfather, the famous architect, David Hamilton, had designed the Nelson Monument years before her birth. All her family had long since departed, but Hamilton's glory still lingered in a dozen edifices throughout the city. As Madeline roamed the Green, she gazed at another piece of his architecture that both the Hamiltons and the Smiths would prefer to forget; the sturdy gaol with its iron cells that lay at the foot of the Saltmarket. That wealthy, industrious designer would never have dreamed in a million years that, with the ruthless irony which sometimes history mockingly displays, his own young granddaughter would one day be lodged in one of these horrible cells before her transfer to Edinburgh. In some respects it reminded one of the nemesis that brought the ill-fated doctor under the blade of his own guillotine.

Madeline returned to Kelvingrove for her tea. Within the week the documents would be delivered to her and she would set sail for the deep shadows of Long Island. From a room nearby she heard the faint sound of a new HMV recording. It was familiar, yet as tragically poignant as all the great old ballads of Scotland, the dying lilt of the last verse floating from the Kelvin to the Clyde and out to the vast sea: 'My fause lover stole the rose and aye he left the thorn with me.'

PLAYS

KRASSIVY
(A PLAY ABOUT THE GREAT SOCIALIST, JOHN MACLEAN)

PRINCIPAL CHARACTERS
(in order of appearance)

LORD PROVOST
PSEUDO
HARD MAN
ANNE (MACPHEE MACLEAN) — John's mother
JOHN MACLEAN — As boy aged nine
TEACHER (MR HARVEY)
HEAD (MR GOURLAY) — Headmaster
JOHN (MACLEAN)
CLINCHER — Glasgow character
JIMMY (MACDOUGALL) — John's first lieutenant
GOSPELLER
AGNES WOOD MACLEAN — John's wife
RUPERT BROOKE — English Great War poet
GLASGOW SOLDIER
PADDY (IRISH SOLDIER)
MRS (MARY) BARBOUR — Activist, 1915 Rent Strike
LORD STRATHCLYDE — Trial Judge
JAMES CONNOLLY — Irish Republican
PATRICK PEARSE — Irish Republican
FLAPPER
SPECIAL CONSTABLE

ACT 1, SCENE 1

FIRST VOICE
I am a poor woman from the Highlands and I came to this city many years before John Maclean was born. Every truth I knew in my heart, John Maclean spoke.

SECOND VOICE
I am a wee lassie in the mills, and through the days of my sorrow, all that he said had the glimmer of hope.

THIRD VOICE
I am Irish and strong, even in age, and what was true in his words and his deeds for Scotland was as true for Ireland.

FOURTH VOICE
I am Glasgow, and believe you me, capable. In case you doubt it, let me describe. We made the Clyde. The historians say the Clyde made us, but think again. Every rock, every channel, every block on our way we shifted, countless generations of toil, until our river ran free to the sea.

THIRD VOICE
The river ran free, but we who scooped that mighty channel were in chains.

FOURTH VOICE
Wage slaves! In the shipyards and mines.

SECOND VOICE
In the dark satanic mills...

(MARY BROOKSBANK'S JUTE MILL SONG)
Oh dear me, the world's ill divided
Them wha' dae the maist
Are the least provided,
Weaving bobbins coarse and fine,
Oh, ye canna get a living
On your ten and nine.

Labour was cheap and life even cheaper.

FIRST VOICE (GREAT BLAST OF AN EXPLOSION)
My God, what was that?

NEWS VENDOR (RUSHING ON STAGE)
Read all about it! Great pit disaster at Blantyre. 174 men and boys still trapped at Blantyre. Read all about it!

(SONG THE BLANTYRE EXPLOSION)

FIRST VOICE
From the mines and the mills into grey, dingy, over-crowded tenements... From pit disaster to slum disaster.

NEWS VENDOR
Read all about it! Terrible tragedy in old Trongate tenement. Floor collapses in over-crowded hovel. Seven buried in the rubble.

SECOND VOICE
And this was but a stone's throw from a street once described by Daniel Defoe as one of

the finest and most picturesque in Europe.

(A FAN FARE OF TRUMPETS AS THE POMPOUS LORD PROVOST ENTERS, GOLDEN CHAIN, ETC, AND READING A SCROLL).

LORD PROVOST
Ladies and gentlemen, I solemnly pronounce this coming year to be the year of the…

HECKLER
The Year of the Child?

LORD PROVOST
My dear fellow, don't be facetious! I, Lord Provost of Glasgow, solemnly pronounce this to be the Year of Victorian Glasgow, and this year we shall have guided coach tours of the city to charm the visitors with the grandeur of that Monarch's glorious reign. First of all, we must examine the guides… Bring on the first applicant…

LACKEY
First applicant!

(ENTER SLICK SOPHISTICATED PSEUDO).

LORD PROVOST (BEAMING WITH APPROVAL) Splendid! And are you all set to show our overseas visitors the glories that once were Glasgow…

PSEUDO
But, of course, I am, my dear Provost. I will, in the course of my duties, point out to them our Cathedral and Art Galleries, our Botanic Gardens, our illustrious University…

LORD PROVOST
(ASIDE) This chappie's been well briefed. Say no more, my good man! You're capital, splendid, ideal and perfunctory…

PSEUDO
Per… what, my Lord…

LORD PROVOST
(ASIDE) A right twit this. Never mind, my dear fellow, you'll fit in perfectly. A last question then?

PSEUDO
Anything you like my Lord.

LORD PROVOST
(ASIDE) Well, for a start I'd like a knighthood, but never mind, in due course that will come. Now tell me, (PUTS HIS ARM AROUND PSEUDO'S SHOULDER) my fine obsequious fellow, have you ever heard, inadvertently or otherwise, of things not fit for the ears of tourists or sightseers…

PSEUDO
Oh no, my Lord!

LORD PROVOST (RUBBING HIS HANDS)
What a superb creep this is! And you never heard of the shady affair between the Committee Convenor and the waitress?

PSEUDO
Oh, not even a whisper, your Worship! I never heard even a whisper of that scandal… or the Mrs Cantley affair either… I can't even guess how her son got that fine house, and I never heard of the Councillor up the chimney, nor the Hutcheson Housing fiasco, nor the expenses racket, nor the dinner for the South African pro-Nazi…

LORD PROVOST
What a splendid, delightful liar this is! Say no more my good man, the job's yours, with a flat seventeen up overlooking the Blochairn gasworks, and a pension in eighty years time. Next applicant, please! (PSEUDO CRAWLS OUT).

LACKEY (SHOUTS)
Next applicant.

(ENTER THE 'HARD MAN', BONNET AND FAG-END)

LORD PROVOST
My God, where did this come from? Sorry my good man, but the Lord Provost's Fund for beggars and stray cats is shut on Tuesdays, and besides I'm…

HARD MAN
Aw come off it, mac! I'm no' a beggar. I'm no' a stray cat. Tell me mac! Do I look like a stray cat?

LORD PROVOST
(Aside) I've seen better. But tell me, my good man, what's the purpose of your visit? I'm a very busy man, you know…

HARD MAN (SINGING IN MIMICRY. SUNG IN AN UNDERTONE THAT THE PROVOST CANNOT QUITE HEAR)

Oh, our Provost is a very busy man,
You could ask it of old Liddell or Dollan,
When he isn't cutting ribbons,
He's banqueting or fibbin'
Oh the Provost is a very busy man.

Oh the Provost is a very busy guy.
He's a clever little B and just as fly,
Pass the buck or cover-up.
They should give my Lord a cup.
Oh the Provost is a very busy guy.

LORD PROVOST (BEAMING)
Oh, yes, we must always remember the dignity of office, mustn't we?

HARD MAN
Oh, the Provost no, is never off the job,
You can see he is a randy little slob.
His legs are warped and bandy
To prove his love of candy,
Oh, the Provost, no, is never off the job.

…But never mind, am I gettin' the job or am I no'?

LORD PROVOST
What job are you talking about, my good man?

HARD MAN
Ach, ye know fine.

LORD PROVOST
No, I don't.

HARD MAN
Ach, ye dae! The job o' conducting all they wealthy Yankee curio seekers around Glasgow and gi'eing them big speels outa wan o' Jack House's integrated circuits o' Glasgow, jist in case they rin into some fly-man who would sell them the Tolbooth Steeple or the Suspension Brig' for a few bottles o' El-D…

LORD PROVOST (BURSTING INTO LAUGHTER)
You… as a city guide? You… you… oh, no, please… don't make me laugh. The idea's preposterous…

HARD MAN I don't care whether it's preponderous or no', and I'm warmin' you, mac, take that silly grin off your face, or I'll make it fit to join the row o' Tontine heads on the Green! I'm warnin' you, mac.

LORD PROVOST
Of course, of course. We live in a democracy, don't we? I'll give you a trial. Now supposing I am a visitor to Glasgow and you are my guide, what would you show me and what would you say? Let us presume, my friend, that we're starting here from George Square on a tour of the city. Starting with the City Chambers, what would you say?

HARD MAN
What would I say?

LORD PROVOST
Yes.

HARD MAN
Ladies and Gentlemen

LORD PROVOST (CLAPPING HIS HANDS)
Excellent... Excellent...

HARD MAN
But I've said nothing yet. I'll take the applause and ony spare cash that's going at the end o' the tour. (HANDS IN HIS POCKET HE POINTS HIS TOE AT THE CITY CHAMBERS) Ladies and Gentlemen, that's whit's cried the Municipal Buildings, and if they're municipal, they're anything but munificent. Last winter, they shut the models and doss houses tae the poor winos and dossers, and they were left tae freeze tae death on the park benches or the crumblin' masonry o' the dank an' deserted tenements. Our city Fathers which art in heaven while the poor they art in hell. (GOES DOWN ON HIS KNEES) Hallowed be thee, thou great pile of Victorian ornament, thy mosaic tiles and ceramic walls! Give us each day thy daily banquets and deliver us not from evil! Amen! (RISES)

LORD PROVOST
Splendid! Bravo! But my dear fellow do you not think your delivery is a teeny-weeny bit forceful, a shade might I say, too dramatic.

HARD MAN
Naw, I don't.

LORD PROVOST
You don't?

HARD MAN
Naw I wis jist right.

LORD PROVOST
You were?

HARD MAN
I wus!

LORD PROVOST
Just right. I see. Well now. And what would you have to say for that statue of Queen Victoria herself?

HARD MAN
I'd get rid of it. It blocks the view of the No. 2 bus stop.

LORD PROVOST
And Gladstone there?

HARD MAN
Get rid o' him as well! There's plenty o' money in auld bronze. Melt him! In fact sir to tell you the truth I'd melt the whole bloody lot except Rabbie Burns there and James Watt. I'd save them. At least they did something for mankind.

LORD PROVOST
So you would revolutionise George Square?

HARD MAN
Aye that's exactly whit I'd dae. I'd revolutionise it. And the great pity is that it didnae happen long ago.

LORD PROVOST
(ASIDE) The man's daft. But I'd better humour him. Well, what do you propose we do for a start?

HARD MAN
Ah'm no' glaiket enough to think ye'll dae it, but d'ye see yon statue o' Walter Scott stuck on the top of that eighty foot column? I'd parcel him off tae Abbotsford or Melrose where his royal North British heart belonged, and on the vacant pedestal I'd place a fine monument of John Maclean, the greatest son of this city…

LORD PROVOST (SCRATCHING HIS HEAD)
John Maclean? Now let me see! John Maclean? The name sounds familiar, I've heard it echo down the Chamber corridor beyond…

HARD MAN
You'll hear it echo down the corridor of time…

LORD PROVOST
This strange fellow's maybe not so daft after all. This man Maclean? Tell me more about him! Now supposing I am a tourist to Glasgow…

HARD MAN
But, my good Provost, that's exactly what you are—a mere tourist to Glasgow. The man who doesn't know the heart and history of his city, is a mere sightseer. Could any Scot be forgiven for not knowing the story of Rabbie Burns, our greatest genius, in literature and song? Or William Wallace?

LORD PROVOST
My dear good fellow, where did you learn all this? You must have been the bright wee chappie at school.

HARD MAN
Don't make me laugh! The only school I learned onything at was the card-school. School was a scunner with their 'enlightened despots', and degenerate kings. Naw, naw, I got my learning in the nick.

LORD PROVOST
The what?

HARD MAN
The nick, the jile, the jug… That exclusive academy called Barlinnie…

L.PROVOST
Barlinnie?

HARD MAN
Aye. I wis in this draighty cell wan grey December and some previous inmate had stuffed the ventilator with a thick book to keep out the icy cold, and there wis I with nothin' tae read, and the other choice wis freezing tae death wi' a book in my hand, so I took the book. Wan o' Dickens's, guess the name?

LORD PROVOST
Haw… Haw. 'Hard Times' was it?

HARD MAN
No' far oot. 'Bleak House' it wis called. I sat there chittering wi' the cold, but I read it once, and then I read it twice, and then I sat once more lookin' at yon blank, bleak wall for days

on end, until wan day I noticed a faded bit of writing scratched in the top corner of the wall. 'John Maclean was in this cell, 16th October 1922'. So I asked wan o' the less bent screws about this John Maclean. A week later, he brought me a wee red book called 'John Maclean, a Fighter for Freedom', and that's where I got ma education. If I read it once, I read it over and over again. A great man if ever there wis one, and his mother a hard working woman, Anne MacPhee, was her name, a weaver tae trade and a bonny fighter… Like Burns' mother, Agnes Brown, she taught her wee son all the legends and folklore o' Scotland, and like Burns' mother, she sang like a lintie…

(End of Act 1, Scene 1)

ACT 1, SCENE 2

(ANNE MACPHEE SINGING 'THE ISLE OF MULL' TO HER SON JOHN, THEN AGED NINE)

ANNE
Aye, son, your father, came from Mull and now the poor, brave man lies in a Glasgow cemetery, far frae the hame of his childhood.

JOHN
Why did he leave Mull, mummy?

ANNE
Aye, indeed, why did he leave it? Island of sparkling fountains and high-towering mountains. Lovely in scenery and song as indeed we might speak of the Garden of Eden before it knew the snake.

JOHN
And did Mull have snakes too, mum?

ANNE
Oh, laddie, you're forgetting the Good Book. D'ye no' remember? The snake was the de'il… and the de'il came tae Mull in the form of the same mCampbells, the Dukes of Argylls, that slaughtered the poor MacDonalds o' Glencoe and now robbed the Macleans of their land. I know the Gaelic, son, and Campbell means 'twisted mouth', and believe me laddie, if the Duke o'Argyll had a twisted mouth, his heart was even more so. Forty years ago, the Famine came to Mull like it did to Ireland, and the coffin ships sailed from Scotland jist as well… Aye, laddie, you're ower young to know the hauf of it, but your poor faither was forced like mony ither braw Highlan' lads an' lassies tae find work in the cities…

JOHN
Last year, I mind my Dad telling me that some Highlanders joined the army.

ANNE
A great deal too many o' them son. And now the poor lads lie at Balaclava and Sebastapol, thousands o' miles frae the hills and glens o' Sotland.

JOHN
Why did they do it, mum?

ANNE
Some did it for a strange thing called 'Glory' though God knows what kind o' glory is to be found in bayoneting some poor mother's son in a foreign trench. And some did it for the pride of uniform... to be dressed like a peacock...
(SINGING)
Oh bad luck to the marching,
Pipe-claying an' starching
How neat one must be
To be killed by the French.
Oh, I like the 'Garryowen',
When I hear it at home,
But it's not half as nice
When you're stuck in a trench!
But mony of them that joined were forced into it by poverty an' hunger. Are ye heedin' me John?

JOHN
Yes, mum.

ANNE
If onything should happen to your auld mum...

JOHN
You're not old, mum, you're just forty...

ANNE
Your poor faither was only forty-three when the poverty of his childhood, and the dust of that old pottery, took him away frae us... I don't want you tae worry about me, son, for I'll take care o' meself for my bairn's sake, but if onything should happen to me, never be tempted into the sojerin'.

JOHN
Indeed I won't, mum. Sweir tae God, I won't. I would never kill onyone who did me no harm. I never even liked playing at soldiers... I like reading books and I like learning things... the stars and animals and fish... the birds. That sort o' thing.

ANNE
I'll tell you something, John. Now, that your dad isn't with us onymore, I'm going back tae my weaving job at the Auldhouse Factory, an' I'm goin' tae skimp an' save, so that I can send you and your brother tae Glasgow University. You're bright enough lads, and some day, ye'll maybe make fine school teachers… It'll be a struggle an' a sacrifice, but some day, your auld mum will be proud of you… (THE TWO OF THEM EMBRACE, A SPONTANEOUS ACT OF BOTH) I had a dream last night, John…

JOHN
Tell me it, mum!

ANNE
I dreamt that Robert Thomson, the grandson of Robert Burns cam' doon the road from Auldhouse, your faither used tae speak to him often, and he had a message to you frae the great bard hiself…

JOHN
For me, mum?

ANNE
Aye, son, for you. I dreamt he told me that the spirit of his granda would remain in Scotland for countless generations, and that with courage and study, you might one day arise tae the same plain of greatness as Wallace and he. That you would know the same loneliness and suffering, but that you would carry on in your era a message tae Scotland for the brotherhood o' man. Puir bairn, on what small shoulders rests such a mighty task!

JOHN
Don't worry, mum, I'm game.

ANNE (CUDDLING HIM)
Aye, son, the Glasgow laddie is aye game!

(End of Act 1, Scene 2)

ACT 1, SCENE 3

(ENTER HEADMASTER OF POLMADIE SCHOOL, WEARING CAP AND GOWN. HE IS A VERY DOMINANT, MOROSE MAN. WALKS UP AND DOWN FOR A MOMENT, CHIN IN HAND. ANOTHER TEACHER PASSES HIM.)

TEACHER
Good morning headmaster.

(A NOD FROM THE HEAD BUT NO REPLY UNTIL TEACHER IS ALMOST OFF-STAGE).

HEAD
Oh, just a moment, Harvey!

TEACHER (RETUMING QUICKLY)
What is it, Mr Gourlay?

HEAD
Tell me, Harvey!

TEACHER
Yes, Mr Gourlay.

HEAD
What would you think, Harvey, of a soldier who brought his rifle and bayonet into church service?

TEACHER
Oh, it would be highly irregular, sir. After all, sir, the church is the temple of God, a haven of peace, a sanctuary.

HEAD
Well said, Harvey! What do you think then of the pupil in your class who left this… this…this lethal weapon behind him in the kirk pew yesterday? (HE DRAWS FROM HIS POCKET A CATAPULT, HARVEY CANNOT HELP LAUGHING) It's no laughing matter, Harvey.

TEACHER
But it's hardly lethal, sir.

HEAD
I wouldn't be so sure, Harvey. About a week ago as I was walking along the lane, some boy hidden behind one of the middens, some boy with one of these… these… these weapons of terror let fly a large chestnut at me. I can tell you, Harvey, there was quite a swelling right here.

TEACHER
A conker on the bonker, sir.

HEAD
Don't be facetious, Harvey! You find that boy and send him to me.(HARVEY GOES TO

WALK OFF) and Harvey…

TEACHER
Yes, sir?

HEAD
Would you tell Miss Lauder I would like to see her?

TEACHER
Very well, sir. (GOES OFF)

HEAD (TAKING OUT A TAWSE)
Now I have the panacea
That all the culprits fear,
That sets the young ones
Shaking in their shoes.
Its powers are inherent
For it is the great deterrent,
It's the certain sure
Corrector of abuse.
When a boy, he tells a lie,
Use the strap,
When he wavers in the eye,
Use the strap,
When he's forty seconds late,
Or loitering by the gate,
Don't let your wrath abate,
Use the strap.
Now you aren't very wise,
If you think to civilise
By using methods
Gentle, calm and mild,
But revert to cave-man's laws
Of the angry tooth and claws,
And our very first wee victim
Is the child.
When a boy, he blots his jotter
Though he thinks you are a rotter,
Use the strap,
Though it makes you sound a fool,
When you talk such gibberish drool,
'To be kind is to be cruel',
Use the strap!

(MAKING HIS EXIT) Oh, thank God, for the advancement of education and refined cruelty. That Lochgelly harness maker was one of mankind's greatest benefactors. There should be a statue put up to him in George Square. (EXIT AS JOHN MACLEAN AND A BOY ENTER)

JOHN (HIS ARM ON THE BOY'S SHOULDER)
I heard you were in some trouble with Mr Gourlay, last week, Willie.

WILLIE
Aye, sir… it's like this sir. I wis late tae school… I get up at five to dae the milk round but that morning I slept in…

JOHN
Oh, you do the milk round, do you? Is your father laid off or something?

WILLIE
My faither's deid, sir. He died when I wis three an' I'm the eldest so I have tae help my ma… We live in a wee room, sir, a single-end they cry it, and oor James has a wrackin' cough all night, sir, he coughed, and my maw had tae get out o' bed to gi'e him the inhaler… so I couldna get tae sleep 'til mornin' and I wis an hour late on my rounds wi' the milk.

JOHN
How many live in the room, Willie?

WILLIE
Five of us, sir. My brother and two cousins she has tae keep… their Ma's in hospital.

JOHN
You'll not have much breakfast before school, Willie?

WILLIE
I love Sundays, sir. Sundays is great. My ma gets ribs an' cabbage frae the Saltmarket. But maist mornings I've a plate o' purritch…

JOHN
Here, Willie, take this wee poke o' sandwiches! Come on Willie, take them! I'm lunchin' out today

(WILLIE HESITATINGLY TAKES THEM. JOHN PUTS HIS HAND ON THE BOY'S HEAD)

JOHN
You're a good lad, Willie a good laddie. Already a worker at the age of ten. And I'll tell you

something, Willie.

WILLIE
Yes, sir?

JOHN
Always help your mother, and be loyal to the class you belong to—the workers. They're the real people, the salt of the earth. Remember that, Willie.

WILLIE
Yes, sir.

(EXIT WILLIE, AND JOHN IS ABOUT TO GO WHEN THE HEADMASTER COMES IN A FLURRY)

HEAD
Oh, oh, just a moment, Mr Maclean… (DRAWING HIM FORWARD TO FRONT STAGE) I have a few things to say to you…Never in the history of Polmadie School have we involved ourselves in the political arena…That, Mr Maclean, is the position! It's the duty of the politicians…

JOHN
Come to the point, Mr Gourlay!

HEAD
To the point? Yes. Hmm. Of course. Yes, of course, I am not concerned in the least about your personal politics Mr Maclean, but it has come to my attention… it has been brought to my attention, that you are advocating some very radical views in the local press.

JOHN
Such as?

HEAD
Such as the Housing conditions… Tell me, Mr Maclean, what has housing and education got in common? Your role is in education, is it not?

JOHN
We work in a school-house… don't we, Mr Gourlay, and if the plumbing or heating is bad, that affects our education, doesn't it?

HEAD
If that happens we notify the authorities. The authorities attend to that, Mr Maclean.

JOHN
And if they don't, you notify them again with more urgency. In other words you pressurise them into action. Well that precisely is what I am doing with the general housing conditions and problems in Pollokshaws, Mr Gourlay.

HEAD
But outside your teaching duties, Mr Maclean.clearly outside your teaching duties! Let these people of the tenements take care of themselves...

JOHN
But they can't, Mr Gourlay, they can't. That's the point. Quite a number of them can't even read or write. They live, if anyone lives, in the City of Dreadful Night. Can I see a wee boy, a pupil of mine, live in an over-crowded single-end, fatherless, and up at five in the morning to a milk round, and not be moved either as a human being or a teacher. After the final bell sends them scurrying home, Mr Gourlay, we are locked out of their lives, as remote from them as a distant planet. What right have we then to add to their misery, to badger and bully, to train like circus animals? And train for what, Mr Gourlay? To knock the spirit out of them, or make them as brutal as the system, to make cannon-fodder for some bloody war, to bayonet or be bayoneted? Is that what it's all about, Mr Gourlay? Is that what Glasgow University trained us for? Is that our role?

HEAD
This is preposterous... this is shocking, Mr Maclean. I never dreamed you held such violent opinions...

JOHN
Surely, sir, you can see the violence is on your side. Surely you can see that?

HEAD
Enough. I've heard enough. These... these socialist opinions will be your undoing.

JOHN
I'm glad you equate Socialism with ordinary kindness and humanity, sir.

HEAD
Enough I said. The School Inspectors have an excellent report on your work in the classroom, but I still have to answer to certain members of the School Board regarding your activities.

JOHN
So they've engaged you to spy on my politics, have they?

HEAD (SHARPLY)
Mr Maclean! Not another word. We'll let the matter rest at that for the moment. You may

go. Goodness me, what's the world coming to? That kind of talk undermines authority... promotes anarchy. I could understand it coming from an eccentric street orator like the Clincher, but from a graduate of Gilmorehill? My God, the world must surely be coming to an end! I heard too about your antics in Greenock during the holiday term...

JOHN
My antics?

HEAD
Call it a propaganda campaign then! When most teachers are more than relieved to find themselves recuperating their minds and bodies in some pleasant highland village or coastal resort, where do we find our young Mr Maclean, but down among the carcasses and offal of some Greenock slaughter-house... not very edifying... for a teacher...

JOHN
Less edifying for those who had to consume the meat from that unhygienic cesspool—The Greenock Jungle! And before I left Greenock, what d'you think, Mr Gourlay? The local authority had initiated an investigation, a Health Inspector was to be appointed... and with the assistance of Mr Allan, a good Christian, Mr Gourlay, the local Presbyterian minister no less—a Greenock Housing Committeewas formed... So indeed, Mr Gourlay, if you are honest, you might say that the holiday did everyone concerned the world of good... except the profiteers, of course.

HEAD
Listen, Maclean!

JOHN
I'm listening.

HEAD
You and I went to Glasgow University. We're proud, of course, of our alma mater. Of course we're proud. Let us not debase those high ideals with the politics of the sordid slums. I have to maintain a discipline of both pupils and staff in this school. Already this morning I have had words, sharp words, on the subject with Mr Harvey and Miss Lauder. She refuses point blank to use the belt. Says that life inflicts too much punishment on these children already.

JOHN
She's right, you know.

HEAD (EXPLODING)
She's what?

JOHN
She's dead right. What d'you or I know of the real background of these bairns, how much they endure in their home surroundings, how many meals a day they get, how many fathers out of work, or dead, how many beatings they get, or neglect through poverty and illness? Which of us really know the inner, trembling hearts of these children? Which of us Mr Gourlay?

(End of Act 1, Scene 3)

ACT 1, SCENE 4

(CLINCHER, WEARING HIS LUM HAT AND SWALLOW-TAILED COAT, PERCHED ON A SOAP-BOX AT THE CORNER OF GLASGOW GREEN. SPEAKING TO THE AUDIENCE. A POLICEMAN BEHIND HIM TAKING NOTES.)

CLINCHER
Ladies and Gentlemen, I stand before you, and not behind you. (LOOKING OVER HIS SHOULDER) like our friends, the Glasgow polis spies… and unlike the Glasgow magistrates, I have nothing to hide. Let me tell you about these same magistrates, folk. They made Jamaica Bridge twelve feet too narrow, but to make up for the mistake, they threw themselves a
banquet. Aye, folk, the Glasgow Baillies'll go down in history for their great ability in getting themselves big feeds. And these same Baillies haven't much liking for me, folk. I wonder why. (POINTING OVER HIS SHOULDER) They've instructed the polis not to laugh at any of my quaint remarks. Anytime they feel like laughing, they're to go up a close and do it. (ENTER JOHN MACLEAN AND JAMES MACDOUGALL, HIS FRIEND) I came to the city of Glasgow, ladies and gentlemen, in nineteen canteen, about three years afore the Pope left Partick, and when I discovered that the world ended at Govan Cross, there wasn't any sense in me going any further. Ladies and gentlemen, this city of ours is not, as it is called, the second city in the great Empire of the Brits. It is decidedly the first in many respects. It is the first in (a) Overcrowded, filthy, abominable slum tenements.(b) That great social boon, tuberculosis, that leaves less mouths to feed. (c) The mighty profits made from our world renowned ship-building industry and the little returned to the people of Glasgow. (d) The number of nit-wits, jack-asses, toadies and creeps that pose as magistrates in that noble edifice called the City Chambers. And that's only the start of the list, ladies and gentlemen. How dare they call us the second city in the Empire? How dare they?

HECKLER (FROM THE STALLS)
Question time, Clincher. What I need to know…

CLINCHER
What you need to know, friend, is when to keep that great orifice in the lower half of your

cranium shut. The gap there is almost, though not quite as big as the one in your brain. But never mind, I've been speaking for an hour, so shoot your question… (HE COMES DOWN OFF THE SOAP BOX AND MOVES TO THE FRONT OF STAGE. WALKS UP AND DOWN, THEN TURNS HIS BACK AS HE WALKS BACK TO UPTURN THE SOAP-BOX AND PUTS HIS NEWSPAPERS, 'THE CLINCHER' IN IT. HE HAS A LARGE PLACARD ON HIS BACK READING 'KISS ME UNDER THE MISTLETOE', AND A MISTLE TOE IS PINNED TO THE TAIL OF HIS COAT. HE RETURNS TO STAGE FRONT.) Come on then. Let's have the first question!

FIRST HECKLER What I want to know is this! Can a French polisher become a naturalised British citizen?

CLINCHER
Listen to him, folks! The last time I saw a mouth like his, it had a hook in it. Can a French polisher become a naturalised British citizen? As much chance as you have of becoming a gentleman.

SECOND HECKLER Should a blind man have to pay rates for stair-head?

CLINCHER
Another genius in the audience, folks. You should join your friend and then the pair of you should apply to join the Glasgow Polis. You're just about the right standard for acceptance. I'm sure you all heard of the polis-man that found the dead horse in Sauchiehall Street and carried it doon to Hope Street, because he couldn't spell 'Sauchiehall'. Well, these same polis-men have harassed me since I took my message to the streets of Glasgow. Will your big newspapers publish what I have to say? Will they hell! So I publish my own paper, 'The Clincher' and the Baillies instructed the polis to harass me. I've been through thirteen polis stations without having my hair cut. Then not getting results that way, they classify me as a lunatic, but sure Glasgow is one big lunatic asylum and the Clincher is its head-keeper. I've been through all the asylums—Woodilee, Gartnavel, Gartcosh—you name them, and still come out intact, just as daft as I went in. This trick-cyclist in Gartcosh, by God, he was the queer one, was nearly out of his mind, trying to find the silver cell that I told him was in my brain. I told him that Shakespeare and Burns and Shelley had silver cells in their brains too, and he just gawked at me with his mouth open like that French polisher in the front row there. And to save me from further harassment, I had to get an eminent physician in the city to sign me a certificate proving I was sane. Hands up how many of you in the audience can prove you are sane? None? Watch out or your relations can lock you away! I am proud to boast that I, The Clincher, am the one and only certified sane man in the city of Glasgow.

(SONG)
I ramble the streets of old Glasgow,
Where the braw hielin' polis-man struts,

And because I jist say whit I'm thinkin',
They aw try tae make oot I'm nuts,
It's nuts tae wash oot in public,
Aw the old linen that stinks,
But I tell them tae take a good piddle,
Cause the Clincher jist says whit he thinks!!!
BE GOOD TAE YER GRANNY AN' GIE 'ER
MAER WHISKY!!

(HE PICKS UP HIS SOAP BOX AND EXITS FOLLOWED BY THE POLICEMAN.)

JOHN (MOVING FRONT WITH JIMMY MACDOUGALL)
He's the shrewd old customer… he knows what's going on behind locked doors… Says quite a bit but knows even more.

JIMMY
What started him off, John?

JOHN
He came in from Old Killie, Kilmarnock, about thirty years ago… A carpet weaver flung on the scrap heap. He started a barber's shop in George Street and invented this thing called 'Oleaginous'…

JIMMY (SMILING)
Olea-what?

JOHN
Oleaginous. I looked it up in the dictionary. Olive oil, pure and simple olive oil… He added some green dye to it… now they all do it, and sell for half-a-crown sixpence worth of the original… There's capitalism at work, pure and simple, Jimmy… That sums it up. He called it, Petrie's, Alex Petrie's his name… 'Petrie's Golden Petals'… You should read the label he wrote for it… 'Once rubbed on your head, it not only creates a halo, but restores to your memory thoughts long hidden from your tears'. Powerful stuff, indeed!

JOHN:
His first row with the Baillies came when he was shaving their great big whiskers… He'd soap and lather them and maybe get one side of their face done when along'd come a fire engine… the Clincher couldn't resist fire engines… and off with his apron and out into the street in hot pursuit, leaving some proud Magistrate half-shaved, and literally foaming at the mouth…

JIMMY:
So the poor Clincher had, I suppose, to bear the brunt of their impatience at all the ten-

ants complaints, every deputation and delegation to the Chamber's corridor...

JOHN:
That's exactly what happened. They left their wrath with him and took their custom elsewhere... (ENTER A GRIM-FACED GOSPELLER, CARRYING A SANDWICH BOARD, 'PREPARE TO MEET THY GOD'.) Good Lord, what's this?

GOSPELLER:
The Day of Wrath is at hand! Armageddon is nigh! Oh my dear brothers, my dear friends, have you been washed in the blood of the lamb?

JOHN
Listen, friend, I've seen more than my share of lamb's blood down in that dirty Greenock slaughter-house.

GOSPELLER
Have you been saved, friends? Have you seen the light?

JOHN
Aye, pal, we've seen the light all right—the bright dawn of Socialism that lights the human consciousness, free from humbug and hypocrisy.

GOSPELLER
Put not your trust in worldly affairs, brothers...

JIMMY
Naw, leave all that to the boss class and they'll fairly muck things up...

JOHN
ever mind, Jimmy! Listen. (PUTS HIS ARM ON JIMMY'S SHOULDER AS THEY BEGIN TO MOVE OFF.) We'll do some meetings, outdoor meetings in the Border Country, and then we'll return to Glasgow and start a campaign that'll shake the city...

GOSPELLER
The Day of Wrath is coming.

JOHN
Aye, friends, it's coming all right.

(End of Act1, Scene 4)

ACT 1, SCENE 5

(JOHN MACLEAN AND AGNES WOOD TOGETHER).

AGNES
What a meeting, John! Hawick has never before heard or seen the like. I could almost feel the Armstrangs, and the rest, all the old Border reivers, stirrin' in their graves.

JOHN
I'm glad, now I came to Hawick, (PUTS HIS ARM AROUND HER GENTLY) and if our public meetings were good, meeting Nan Wood was a special bonus indeed.

AGNES
I sat in the audience enthralled with your face lighting up with anger and indignation at the tyranny of it all. What like is your mother, John?

JOHN
The finest, bravest I know. It's many years since my father died and he and my sisters bore the burden of seeing my brother and I through Glasgow University, both of us you know are teachers…

AGNES
Where does your brother teach, John?

JOHN
Poor fellow, he's far from home, in South Africa. The poverty we endured when my father left the pottery on account of his health, made him an easy victim of T.B. like thousands of other poor folk in Glasgow and elsewhere. He thought South Africa's climate might help, but I'm afraid he's still doing poorly. He was a good brother to me, always gave me good advice. 'Don't waste this short life, John,' he used to say. 'Get a purpose and dedication as soon as you can. Treat it seriously.' he said.

AGNES
You certainly did that, John. I like that wee vertical cleft on your forehead… That denotes a deep thinker…

JOHN
Oh, so you're a bit of a phrenologist as well, Nan.

AGNES (COYLY)
As well as what, John?

JOHN
A charmer!

AGNES
I bet you say that to all them bonny mistresses at the school you teach in. I'm sure you have many a good chat with one or other of them

JOHN
Oh, indeed, I do.

AGNES
There now, what did I tell you?

JOHN
I do have a good chat with them indeed about teachers' salaries and headmaster's tantrums... about square and isosceles triangles... about Plutarch and Socrates... and wee Tommy's missing school-bag.... I'll tell you straight...

AGNES
You don't need to tell me, John, I know. Whisht a moment, John, and I'll sing you a wee song!

(TUNE—THE PATRIOT GAME)
The bright dawn is breaking
O'er Scotland's fair shore,
When the people will suffer
The Tyrant no more,
When freedom alights
On the lochans and hills
With a message of hope
For the mines and the mills.
When the lassies frae Hawick
And the Inverness lad
Have at last won the right
To be happy and glad,
When no longer will tear-drops
Rub lustre from joy,
When the world is a rainbow
For each girl and each boy.
When the Red banner's raised
And firmly held high
With hearts of true courage
And a light in our eye,
Our masters long gone
Oh, the change there will be,
When Scotland has won

That great right to be free.

JOHN
Come with me, Nan, into the deep heart of Glasgow and together we will fight for that right for the people. I'm sorry, Nan, to ask you to leave these braw hills and valleys in exchange for the dank, dour tenements, but so many bairns, and so many good poor folk need our help... Nan Wood, will ye come?

AGNES
With you, John, anywhere in the world.

(End of Act 1, Scene 5)

ACT 1, SCENE 6

(A BOY PLAYING WITH THE PEERIE, AND GIRL DANCING WITH HER SKIPPING ROPE ON THE STAGE. THEN THEY PLAY HOP-SCOTCH AND SHORTLY AFTERWARDS LINK HANDS AND SING).

BOY AND GIRL
Here we come gathering nuts in May
Nuts in May, nuts in May
Here we come gathering nuts in May
On a cold and frosty morning.

(OLD FATHER TIME ENTERS STAGE FRONT. CHILDREN PLAY ON QUIETLY IN THE BACKGROUND)

FATHER TIME
I see the children at their play,
With sparkling eyes and hearts so gay,
Quite unaware that soon will come,
The hideous blare of trump and gun,
As heartless Kaiser, King and Tsar
Prepare for man's most bloody war.
I see brave Lenin to the fore
Trying to prevent this gore
And in these Islands now I see
His comrades, Maclean and Connolly
Striving hard with all their might
To get the people not to fight
Why for rich and cruel bosses
Should Europe's field be full of crosses?

MARS
But see the poor daft idiot horde
Accept the bayonet, gun and sword,
Heeding liars who declare
They fight for 'King and Country' fair,
Marching out with bated breath
To meet an ignominious death.

FATHER TIME
I see the 'form divine' in mud,
And Europe's glory drenched in blood,
Children's laughter overcast
And withered in the frightful blast.

(ALL VACATE THE STAGE IMMEDIATELY AS A HUGE EXPLOSION TAKES PLACE. LIGHTS, SMOKE, TURMOIL. DRUMS BEAT AS AVAILABLE CAST MARCH ON SINGING, IT'S A LONG WAY TO TIPPERARY.' THE REST OF THE CAST THEN MARCH OFF-STAGE, LEAVING TWO SLIGHTLY TIPSY SOLDIERS, ONE WITH A BOTTLE IN HIS HAND. SUPPORTING AN OFFICER, RUPERT BROOKE, HE BREAKS LOOSE AND AT STAGEFRONT, MELODRAMATICALLY DECLAIMS.)

RUPERT BROOKE
If I should die think only this of me,
There is some corner of a foreign field
That is forever ENGLAND.
There is in that rich earth,
A richer dust concealed,
A dust that ENGLAND bore, shaped, made
aware...

GLASGOW SOLDIER (COMING FRONT STAGE. HOLDING UP HIS HAND TO CHECK BROOKE)
Stop, stop, haud it. Did you write that yersel? Those glaring inaccuracies!

RUPERT (INDIGNANTLY)
Glaring inaccuracies?

GLASGOW SOLDIER
Aye. Take that first line for a start! What is it?

RUPERT
If I should die think only this of me...

GLASGOW SOLDIER
Aye. Do you only want to be remembered dying for England? And did you never do any other effen good in your life? Did you never run ony messages for your maw, or get your old man a pint, or kiss some bonny lass in the moonlight? Well, if ye didn't you're better effen deid. And that bit aboot the corner of a foreign field being forever England. My God, hasn't John Bull's colonial appetite diminished when he's satisfied with the corner of a field... If he had been satisfied with that in the first instance there wouldn't be half the bloody wars in the world. What do you say, Paddy?

PADDY (PUTTING HIS HAND UP)
Gospel true! Me hand to God!

LASGOW SOLDIER
Forever England? You'll notice, Paddy, he's no claiming any of it for Scotland or Ireland.

PADDY
Greedy thing!

GLASGOW SOLDIER
And then that bit aboot there is in that rich earth a richer dust concealed. Whit d'ye think aboot that, Pat?

PADDY
Poorly. Very poorly. In fact I don't think much of it at all.

GLASGOW SOLDIER
I don't think the French would either... After all his nibs here is callin' his dust richer than the dust of all the great Frenchmen and women that ever were buried in French soi—Voltaire, Moliere, Joan of Arc, Louis Pasteur, you name them. That's a bit over the score, Paddy... eh?

PADDY
Bejasus, it is that. I would say it was surely lamentable. Lamentable. Here, ossifer, have a swig.

RUPERT
I don't touch the stuff...

GLASGOW SOLDIER
I could tell that by the crap you write. As Rabbie used to say, 'whisky and Freedom' gang together. Noo there wis a real poet for ye. None o' your jingo codswallop aboot Rabbie.

But never mind. What made you jine up, Paddy?
PADDY
I didn't jine up. I wus hi-jacked.

GLASGOW SOLDIER
Hi-jacked?

PADDY (HOLDING HIS HAND UP)
Gospel true. Hand to God. I wus hi-jacked… There I wus, a quiet, dacint, sensible, peaceable fella, drinkin' wan night in this wee pub, Shanahan's in Cashel town, a stone's throw from Tipperary…

GLASGOW SOLDIER
That's the place it's a long way tae… ?

PADDY
Aye, that's it! I had taken a bellyful o' porter… an' I wus as p… p… puggled as a newt, when this recruitin' sergeant…

GLASGOW SOLDIER
Frae the Black Watch?

PADDY
I don't know to this day where the hell he came from but he says, says he, you'll get Home Rule for Ireland when it's over, if ye join, an' he gives me a shillin' for another drink, an bejasus' I didn't know another thing 'till I woke up in the barracks o' Clonnel, dressed up in these khaki falderals, with a bayonet in me hand to stick in some poor mother's son I never seen in me life…

GLASGOW SOLDIER (BITTERLY)
Your country needs you. It never needed me all these years I wis on the parish… Poor little Catholic Belgium occupied by the Huns. As the sensible fellow over the water says, 'What about poor little Catholic Ireland occupied by John Bull for seven hundred years?' 'And poor little Scotland as weel?'

PADDY
Why don't we join together, Jock, an' knock the stuffin' outa them Saxon dumplings… After all, we fight all their bloody wars for them, don't we?… If we joined together an' cut England down to size, I'm certain sure, the world'd breathe wan great bloody sigh o' relief…

RUPERT BROOKE (UNABLE TO STAND IT ANY LONGER)
I say… Look here you chappies…

GLASGOW SOLDIER
As your Cockney comic says you keep your cake-Hole shut, mate! We've had enough poetry oot o' you for the present. Are ye listenin' Paddy?

PADDY
Hand tae God, I'm listenin'.

GLASGOW SOLDIER
D'ye know, Paddy, how much ma wife got workin' in the mills? A 56 hour week? D'you know how much she got?

PADDY
Naw, I never had any money in me life. A few shillings and a meal labourin' in Sheridan's farm… don't know much about money… Mebbe she'd get a pound or thirty shillings?

GLASGOW SOLDIER
Eight shillings, Paddy, a miserable, measly eight shillings. That's whit some of our best paid women folk get paid in the mills… But never mind Paddy, we'll go out and fight this war to end wars, Paddy and when we come back we'll build a land fit for heroes…

IRISH SOLDIER
Aye Jock aye, when we come back, when we come back…

(THEY GO OFF, ARM AROUND EACH OTHER'S SHOULDERS, SINGING 'IT'S A LONG WAY TO TIPPERARY… RUPERT WITH HIS LITTLE STICK SWAGGERS IN FRONT. BEFORE THEY MOVE OFF COMPLETELY, THE STAGE BECOMES DARK AND A SPOTLIGHT LIGHTS JOHN MACLEAN ON HIS ROSTRUM NEAR THE WINGS ON THE OTHER SIDE OF THE STAGE. THE SOLDIERS HALT TO LISTEN A MOMENT. POLICEMAN, AS USUAL, TAKING NOTES BUT SPOTLIGHT DOESN'T REVEAL HIM UNTIL NEAR THE END).

JOHN
Land fit for heroes to live in? War to end wars? Don't believe one single word of it comrades! After this damned war the economy of the country will be in such a bloody mess that it will take a hero to live in it, all right. Hundreds of thousands of soldiers lucky enough to survive the holocaust on the continent will have no jobs to return to. The false economy of war-time Britain will disappear with the signing of the Peace Treaty and thousands will walk the streets, not as heroes but as poor, disheartened, jobless rejects. The slumlands of Glasgow and all the other cities will remain slums, and the already greedy landlords, seeing the influx of new labour into the munitions industry, are trying desperately to increase the rents. War to end wars? That is the biggest lie of the lot. This war is but the grim beginning of a series of wars in Europe and elsewhere, as the capitalists, envious of each other's markets and territories, fight it out with voracious greed and

fury like beasts of the wild. This is not a war to end wars, comrades, this is a war to begin wars of an unprecedented, brutal scale…

ENGLISH VOICE (IT COULD BE RUPERT)
Why don't you enlist, mate?

JOHN
Enlist? I have been fighting in the army of Socialism for the past 15 years and I will tell you, friend, that is the only army worth fighting for. (AT THIS POINT SPOTLIGHT ON THE POLICEMAN WRITING THIS DOWN) God damn all armies!

(End of Act 1, Scene 6)

ACT 1, SCENE 7

(TWO LOCAL WOMEN AND MRS BARBOUR AT TUBS IN STEAMIE. SONG TO THE TUNE OF 'IF IT WISNAE FUR THE WEAVERS').

If it wisnae fur the steamie
Whit wid we do
The teeny weeny jaw box
Won't see oor washing through
We'd seldom hae a blether
An' we wouldnae hae a clue
If it wisnae for the patter
O' the steamie

Ye've heard o' wash house blues
But we're no blue at all
For its here you get the banter
On things both great and small
Tenants' rights or landlords
And relativity
You're bound to hear the answer
In the steamie

Oor talk is no' soap bubbles
Like maist MP's we know
We could dry oor claes in seconds
With that hot air they blow
We would cut them doon in stature
An aneath the flair they'd go
If we had them fur an hour

In the Steamie.
FIRST WOMAN
Steamie, aye it's a rerr wee name for it isn't it. Apart frae the steam o' the tub a poor body can let aff their ain steam withoot the fear o' being spied on like they do to John Maclean…

SECOND WOMAN
I'd like tae see them spy in here. They wouldnae hauf get a roastin'.

MRS BARBOUR He said 'twas the greedy profiteers that caused the war an' that the only cause the workers should fight for was Socialism… God damn all other armies he said.

SECOND WOMAN
An' right too. To think of all the boys oot amang they bullets an' shrapnel, dying by the thousand in the mud an' filth an' dirt o' foreign lands. My God, it's no' Christian, it's savage, it's cruel, no matter how many Bishops bless the banners… Tell us aboot Maclean, Mrs Barbour, when you saw him in the coort.

MRS BARBOUR He wis great, Jean, he wis splendid. Towerin' ower that pygmy of a Sheriff, with a mind an' a purpose of his ain, crystal clear. You should have seen yon court hoose, crammed wi' platers, an' caulkers, an' riggers, all in their workclaes an' when John Maclean appeared there wis a cheer that would waken the deid in Ingram Street Kirkyard.

SECOND WOMAN
I'd've been there masel' only wee Jimmy's doon wi' the mumps.

MRS BARBOUR
Oh, there's plenty o' chance comin' Jean, an' we'll see a lot o' that man again. They've their knife in him… The school board's ganging up on him in Govan, the landlords are wild with him takin' up oor fight against the rents increases. Listen lassies…

FIRST WOMAN (AS THE THREE WOMEN HUDDLE TOGETHER)
Aye, we're listenin', Mrs Barbour, whit wid ye have us dae?

MRS BARBOUR
We're going tae go intae every tenement and back court an' dunny in Govan an' we're going tae organise a rent strike… We're no' goin' tae pay a penny if they put the rents up…

FIRST WOMAN
A rent strike! A rent strike! But they'll jile us.

SECOND WOMAN
No they'll no'. They huvnae jiles big enough for all of us, an' if they lift Mrs Barbour like

thon Mrs Pankhurst in London, we'll march intae George Square an' make a hero outae her.

MRS BARBOUR
It won't come tae that, for listen noo. There's mair in store… We must talk tae the riveters, an' caulkers. We must take all Clydeside intae this. We must take the menfolk left, wi' us—an' if the school directors daur sack John Maclean, here's whit we'll dae. Whether they sack him or no', we'll dae it anyway. Here's whit we'll dae…

(THE SCENE ENDS IN THIS ATMOSPHERE OF CONSPIRACY)

(End of Act1, Scene 7)

ACT 1, SCENE 8

(LORNE STREET SCHOOL—17TH NOVEMBER 1915, HEADMASTER AND JOHN MACLEAN IN THE CORRIDOR).

HEAD
It is rather unfortunate that it should come to this, Mr Maclean.

JOHN
I shouldn't worry unduly headmaster. It was the old hag herself that did it, that dangerous dame—Mata Hari on the home front.

HEAD
Hag? Dangerous Dame? Mata Hari? I don't see.

JOHN
That Westminster Cow, DORA, Defence of the Realm Act. Designed at first to prise out German agents and spies, but now used almost exclusively to spy into trade union and Socialist activities. So you might say, headmaster, that this great war is being fought for a strange kind of freedom indeed. The freedom for the British Ruling class to eat both halves of the cake at the same time.

HEAD
I don't quite understand, Mr Maclean.

JOHN
What a diabolical situation for the lads in the trenches to be in, headmaster. Facing death out there while the bosses who sent them are conniving through DORA and the like to whittle away and dissolve the benefits, few though they've been, achieved during decades

of struggle prior to the war. What a dirty rotten game, headmaster. Even a child could see through it.

HEAD
Oh, I know little or nothing about politics, I just teach...

JOHN
You merely teach loyalty, love and devotion to God, the Royal Family and a British Empire that will be dissolved before the end of this century.

HEAD
In your humble opinion, might I say, Mr Maclean.

JOHN
You just teach, if you mention them at all, that the workers who produce every grain of wealth under the sun are a rabble, a mob, or as Burke called them 'the great unwashed'. That's not teaching, headmaster, that's what the old Clincher himself calls brainwashing.

(SOUNDS OF MARCHING OUTSIDE. A GREAT CROWD COMING NEARER).

HEAD
Good Heavens. What was that I heard?

(THE CROWD SING THE RED FLAG ONSTAGE. ONE VERSE).

HEAD
What on earth's happening, Mr Maclean. Has the good city gone mad?

JOHN
Never mind, headmaster, the truth will eventually come out in the washing.

(MRS BARBOUR AND HER STEAMIE' FRIENDS COME ON STAGE CARRYING BANNERS AND PLACARDS. 'NOT A PENNY ON THE RENTS'. 'F FOR THE FACTOR' AND AN EFFIGY OF A LANDLORD. BEHIND THEM A GROUP OF WORKERS FROM THE SHIPYARDS AND WITH THEM, JIMMY MACDOUGALL. MRS BARBOUR WAVES HER BANNER AT THE HEADMASTER.)

MRS BARBOUR
Aye, it'll come oot in the washin' all right. We'll see tae that. Whit dis a little nincompoop like you mean by lettin' go of a first rate teacher like John Maclean? Answer me that! Come on, tell me?

HEAD (BACKING AWAY FROM THE ONSLAUGHT)

It wasn't I… it… it was the Govan School Board.
MRS BARBOUR (SNAPPING HER FINGERS OR MAKING A RUDE SIGN)
Well that's whit I think o' the Govan School Board. A bunch o' twits, stuck-up non-entities and idiots the total of whose brains wouldnae fill a thimble. We should have a say in who has the right tae educate oor bairns…

OTHERS
Hear! Hear!

MRS BARBOUR
And I tell you this much, Mr Headmaster. John Maclean will not waste a moment longer of his breath teaching lies and nonsense about the Establishment to the bairns o' Glasgow. He'll not have to teach the curriculum as the clowns of Capitalism see it. Though 'm certain sure John Maclean never told a lie to child nor man. But from now on, John Maclean will teach the real history of the people, the struggles of the working-class to reach the red dawn of freedom. Cone on, John, come with us into George Square and lead the people of the tenements out of the City of Dreadful Night. Come on, John!

(THEY HOIST MACLEAN ON THEIR SHOULDERS AND SINGING THE RED FLAG MARCH OUT OF THE SCHOOL)

(End of Act 1)

ACT 2, SCENE 1

(A GLASGOW MAN, WEARING A BONNET AND SCARF, WALKING ALONG THE TRONGATE SINGING, HE HAS A SLIGHT DRINK IN HIM, NOT TOO MUCH).

GLASGOW MAN
I belang tae Glasgow, dear old Glesga toon.
Whit's the maitter wi' Glesga
That things are upside doon
I'm only a common old working chap
And why then all the fuss?
We'll straighten things oot
And wan day make sure
That Glesga belangs tae us!

POLICEMAN
Come on now, get a move on!

GLASGOW MAN Who dae ye think ye're pushin' ya big teuchter… I'm no' the poor old Clincher, ye cannae muck me aboot… See Tim Doran an' Bill Renton at the corner yonder! You get a move on, constable! It's you's on the beat, no' me, so you get a move on before I get John Maclean and the Clyde Workers Committee on tae ye fur intimidation, provocation and a multitudinous lot of scurrilous inferences.

(GOES OFF SINGING 'I BELANG TAE GLESGA'. POLICEMAN SCRATCHES HIS HEAD AND STARES AFTER HIM WITH BLANK BEWILDERMENT).

(End of Act 2, Scene 1)

ACT 2, SCENE 2

(ENTER BALLAD SINGER WITH SONG SHEETS).

BALLAD SINGER
I sing you a song of the famous Red Clyde,
And the city I love with devotion and pride;
The big London bosses don't like us so well,
But for all that we care, they may all roast in hell.
They brought in a law, they called it 'Munitions',
Its purpose designed to lower conditions
These con-men of London had the ball in their stride
But they reckoned without the brave folk of the Clyde.
Westminster decided our courage to test
And our working class leaders they soon did arrest,
Gallagher, MacDougall, and Kirkwood and Bell,
Wainright and Bridges and Jimmy Maxton as well.
They came in the night and they lifted Tom Clarke,
Like bandits they pounced on these folk in the dark,
Anderson and Glass, not a leader they missed
And the bold John Maclean was top of the list.
In an Edinburgh court house the good man was tried
Afraid as they were of the lads on the Clyde
For anger was rife and rebellion they dread
The slaves were arising and their banner was red.

(SPOTLIGHT ON JOHN MACLEAN IN THE DOCK IN EDINBURGH HIGH COURT, 11TH APRIL 1916).

JOHN
Yes I am an opponent of compulsory military service. I hold that the present war is a war of capitalist aggression. I believe that the British and German and French workers should refuse to die for their capitalist masters. I spoke to the crowd at a mass meeting at Nelson's

column on Glasgow Green on Sunday 30th January. I said then to the workers 'All you men are supposed to be patriots and won't use any goods of German manufacture…

STRATHCLYDE
Very commendable advice, very commendable indeed.

JOHN
Wait 'til I finish, my Lord!

STRATHCLYDE
Very well. Continue! I told the workers 'I understand you all have German alarm clocks to waken you in the morning. As patriots you cannot surely continue to use them. You should pawn them or sell them! Be sure you do it all at one time and then you will all sleep in in the morning'.

(LAUGHTER IN THE COURTROOM).

STRATHCLYDE (BANGING THE GAVEL FURIOUSLY)
Silence in court or it shall be cleared instantly. Mr Maclean, after a patient and long consideration and investigation, you have been found guilty not for the first time of contravening the regulations of the Defence of the Realm Act… to a man so intelligent and highly educated as you, it would be idle for me to dwell upon the gravity of the offence. The sentence of the court is that you should be sent to penal servitude for a period of three years…

FIRST VOICE
But, my Lord, this sentence is unjust, outrageous!

STRATHCLYDE (TO POLICEMAN)
Officer, arrest that man and charge him with contempt of court!

(POLICEMEN DRAG MAN OUT)

SECOND VOICE
I too wish to register the strongest protest against this vicious class legislation.

STRATHCLYDE Arrest him also!

THIRD VOICE
You cannot silence all of us. Are we to go back to the dreadful days of Muir and Palmer, when even Robert Burns feared transportation for speaking honestly and openly?

STRATHCLYDE
Officer, seize that man as well!

FOURTH VOICE
This is nothing but a damned police state (STARTS SINGING AT THE TOP OF HIS VOICE)
The peoples flag is deepest red
Its glory shrouds our martyred dead
Though cowards flinch and traitors sneer
We'll keep the red flag flying here.

STRATHCLYDE (BESIDE HIMSELF WITH FURY AND BANGING THE GAVEL)
Seize him! The court must be cleared. Arrest him! Clear the court! Clear the court at once! Clear the court I said!

VOICES
Cheer up, John, cheer up, don't worry John we shan't let you rot in prison.

(End of Act 2, Scene 2)

ACT 2, SCENE 3

(DUBLIN. THREE DAYS LATER. JAMES CONNOLLY SITS AT A SMALL TABLE WITH PATRICK PEARSE. THE IRISH TRICOLOUR AND THE PLOUGH AND STARS' BEHIND THEM. CONNOLLY HAS A LETTER IN HIS HAND. THE SCENE TAKES PLACE A FORTNIGHT BEFORE THE 1916 IRISH REBELLION).

CONNOLLY
I've had serious news from Edinburgh through one of our agents,

PEARSE
I didn't know you were familiar with that city, Jim… was under the impression you had lived in Glasgow though your parents were from County Monaghan…

CONNOLLY
Familiar? I knew it like the back of my hand. And well might I. I was born there. You see I was a street scavenger there too, a common or garden dustman… And here I am trying to sweep up the rubbish of Dublin Castle and the English Ascendancy in Ireland… shall I read you an excerpt from the letter?

PEARSE
Go ahead, Jim.

CONNOLLY
It's from John Leslie, an insurance agent in Edinburgh, an early comrade of mine and a founder there of the Social Democratic Federation (READS) To James Connolly, Commandant General of the Irish Citizen's Army. Dear James, Things are very serious here in

Edinburgh. Yesterday they jailed a dear comrade and friend, John Maclean, for three years. Not content with that they gave him penal servitude... Today they've jailed Gallagher, Muir and Bell and shortly it will be the turn of Maxton, McDougall, Smith and others. The suppression by this means of free speech in the West of Scotland is one of the most dangerous steps backwards for these Islands and we urge you, James, to take what measures you can in Ireland in protest.

PEARSE
Damn serious indeed!

CONNOLLY
Pearse, you know how canny I have always been about premature action?

PEARSE
Oh, none knows better than myself James.

CONNOLLY
I have cared too much for the lives of the young lads of the Citizen's army and your own Irish Volunteers as well.

PEARSE
I have always understood that and respected you for it, though at times I've disagreed. At Donovan Rossa's grave I expressed my philosophy.

CONNOLLY
I will tell you now, Pearse, the situation has changed radically with these arrests and sentences. John Bull has taken the velvet glove off to reveal the mailed fist. He has declared the Glasgow Socialists and the working class of Clydeside to be as great an enemy as the Kaiser. They are desperate to introduce conscription and even Ireland will find ourselves in Mountjoy or Kilmainham like John Maclean and his comrades and if the leadership is jailed the movement is cut off, splintered.

PEARSE
What do you propose, Jim?

CONNOLLY
The Irish Citizen's Army and the Irish Volunteers must unite in one great bid to free Ireland... We shall set Dublin aflame in one of the bravest rebellions in history. We shall be suppressed but we shall light the spark to ignite and set blazing the of John Bull's ill-gotten Empire. We shall let the world know that England is as ruthless funeral pyre to small nations as any Kaiser or Czar...

PEARSE (SHAKING HANDS WITH CONNOLLY)

James Connolly, I have waited long and impatiently on this day... name but the hour!

CONNOLLY
Ten days time. We shall march our soldiers down Sackville Street and occupy the GPO.

PEARSE
Easter Week. The resurrection—glorious symbol!

CONNOLLY
I have studied international politics for a very long time, Patrick, and I'll tell you this. Capitalism has written its death warrant by starting this war in Europe. Lenin and his party are going to end the Czar and the Russian Ruling Class in a few years time and from then on until the end of the century, country after country will break from Imperialism slowly perhaps, but the impetus will grow.

PEARSE
And little Ireland, victim of the English Bully for so long will have played its glorious part.

CONNOLLY (RAISING THE STARRY PLOUGH)
To the Irish rebellion and my Scottish comrades in jail!

PEARSE (WITH THE TRICOLOUR)
England's difficulty is Ireland's opportunity!

(SONG BY MARCHING CROWD).

We will sing a rebel song
As we proudly march along
To end the age old Tyranny
That makes for human tears
And our fight is nearer won
With each setting of the sun
And the Tyrant's might is passing
With the passing of the years.

(End of Act 2, Scene 3)

ACT 2, SCENE 4

(PETERHEAD PRISON. JOHN, ALONE PACING UP AND DOWN IN HIS CELL. HE HAS BEEN ILL).

JOHN
Brave lads! Brave lads! The Dublin boys had a go at Kitchener's great John Bull, the mighty

British Empire! Good for them! Held them for a week 'til the gun boats shelled the streets. James Connolly dead! Brave, gallant comrade, wounded in the fight, they bound him in an armchair and murdered him. Oh brave John Bull, protector of small nations. Courageous Johnny! Freedom's Champion! Upholder of human rights.

WARDER
Prisoner!

JOHN (IGNORING HIM)
…and Patrick Pearse, the poet, the dreamer, and his brother murdered too. Their great heroic mother. She gave two lovely sons for Ireland's cause… not just Ireland's, the cause of humanity.

WARDER
Prisoner, there's a visitor (EXIT WARDER)

(AGNES MACLEAN COMES IN. SHE STANDS FOR A MOMENT, SHOCKED BY JOHN'S APPEARANCE. THEN RUSHES TO HIM).

AGNES
My God, John, what have they done to you?

JOHN
Never mind about me for the moment, Nan. Tell me about yourself and the two wee lassies Jean and Nan! How are you keeping?

AGNES
We miss you, oh heaven knows how we miss you. Nine long months since they took you to Peterhead and so far away from Glasgow.

JOHN
Aye, they were afraid. Barlinnie was too near with the mood of Clydeside. They want a hostage. If I had been in Ireland they'd have shot me as well. In this sham democracy here they murder people more subtly.

AGNES (NODDING TOWARDS THE WINGS)
Shh! He's listening, John.

JOHN
Let him listen! He knows it's true. When this dirty war is over and they free the conscientious objectors, such as survive, the truth will come out. Some have died, some have committed suicide others have been knocked off their heads and in this way got into asylums. I saw these men around me in a horrible plight. Through numerous expedients I was able

to hold my own.

AGNES (PUTTING HER HAND TENDERLY IN HIS)
But at some price John, Jimmy told me all and I see it myself. My God what callous brutes to harm my good and Gentle man. Your eyes are sunken and you've lost weight. That hunger strike…

JOHN
They fed me forcibly. But tell me, Nan, there isn't long to go. About yourself?

AGNES (TRYING TO SHRUG OFF HER OWN WORRIES)
Oh I'm all right, John, just fine and the girls grow more bonny each day. You should see them in their new straw hats, and ribbons in their hair, red ribbons in their hair.

JOHN
Come on Nan, I know you're holding back. Tell me everything.

AGNES
You know it anyway. It's desperate hard. We just survive from day to day. The wee girls miss their Dad. He gives them strength and confidence and love.

JOHN
I miss them even more. Not an hour passes but I think of them and you.

AGNES
Not able to fight you fair and square, the Boss class spreads the rumour that you're a traitor, spy and German agent. They say we've German gold. They say much worse, anonymous letters. Last week I caught this crank, a spinster in Langside, outside our door. She just dropped a note. 'My three sons are dead in Flanders and all because of John Maclean. If I had my way I'd put him in the rack. I'd tear his eyeballs out.'

JOHN (NODDING TOWARDS THE WINGS)
She has plenty of friends in this establishment. I'll tell you that much, Nan.

AGNES
Last week they took the poor daft creature to Gartnavel and kept her in. My God but it's hard, John. A hard, hard struggle. A world of lies and slander. Even them that go to the kirk and dream of heaven. What kind of heaven? To crown their evil they want a halo.

JOHN
My poor fond lass. Nine years ago I took her in from Hawick's green and lovely fields, its gentle murmuring brooks and hawthorns wild. I took her into this, the sordid tenements, this dirty wretched prison, this brutal bitter struggle. I lost my steady job. I could have

been a well paid Labour hack official or MP.

AGNES
When you come out of here, John, is there… is there any other way of managing? I don't want… I don't want to see my husband crucified. I don't want it John…

JOHN
Listen, Nan… every night in this wee cell, I see upon the white washed ceiling, I see the crucified of Europe… This cell becomes a battlefield…. There's nothing I wouldn't do to save the working class from the dreadful consequence of their masters' greed. I can't escape my mission, Nan. See how the poor, courageous people of Glasgow have defied the bosses. It gives me hope. It gives me hope… and, listen… I've had news from Russia… the most brilliant Marxist in Europe has crossed the German frontier and is now leading the Russian workers and peasants against the Czar and the landlords… I'll tell you, Nan, I don't know how long it will take the West, but the East is going red… a beautiful red like the great sunset of Capitalism, and the red dawn of Freedom.

(End of Act 2, Scene 4)

ACT 2, SCENE 5

(NEAR CHARING CROSS, GLASGOW. ENTER A JOLLY, BOISTEROUS, GIDDY GROUP, WHICH INCLUDES A SILLY YOUNG THING (FIAPPER), A SOLDIER GOING OFF TO THE FRONT, AND ONE OR TWO PASSERS-BY WHO HAVE GOT CAUGHT UP IN IT. A BOTTLE OF WHISKY AND SOME WAVING GLASSES. PASSER-BY SINGS THE CHORUS OF JUST A WEE DEOCH AN' DORIS. ENTER THE BALLAD SINGER OF A PREVIOUS SCENE. CARRIES A BUNCH OF COLOURED BALLAD SHEETS).

BALLAD SINGER
Buy a ballad sir? Buy a ballad, mam? Ballads for sale, a penny a sheet. Ballads of Glasgow, the old and the new. (SINGS)
I'll sing you a song
Of our sorrow and grief,
And things we endure
Past human belief;
For three bloody years,
This war has dragged on,
Poor mothers in tears
For the sons that are gone.

(GROUP IGNORES HIM. SOLDIERS MARCHES UP AND DOWN STAGE SINGING).

SOLDIER
Pack up your troubles in your old kit-bag,
And smile, boys, smile.
(GRINS LIKE A CHESHIRE CAT)
While there's a Lucifer to light your pipe
Smile, boys, that's the style
What's the use of worrying,
It's never worth your while,
So pack up your troubles in your old kit-bag,
And smile, smile, smile. (ANOTHER GRIN)

BALLAD SINGER
I'll sing you a song of Sammy and Tom
One lies at Ypres and the other at Somme
And the brave, smiling lad from Fintry or Mull—
What's left of him now,
But a poor empty skull?

(ENTER SANDWICH-BOARD MAN).

SANDWICH-BOARD MAN
Prepare to meet thy God! Prepare your soul for the Day of Wrath! (TO SOLDIER) do you know anything of the Day of Wrath, friends?

SOLDIER (WITH A GREAT GUFFAW)
Do I no' just? Kit inspection at the double in Maryhill Barracks. That bloody sergeant-major...

SANDWICH-BOARD MAN
Fire and brimstone!

SOLDIER
Aye, how did ye know? That's just whit we called him, 'Old Fire and Brimstone'. Other times we used to call him 'Old Limey Loudmouth'.

SANDWICH-BOARD MAN
What shall it profit a man if a mill-stone is tied round his neck when the Day of Reckoning is nigh?

PASSER-BY
Good Lord, this fellow gives me the creeps. Here, Mac, take a swig and, for Pete's sake, cheer up!

(THROUGHOUT THIS SCENE, THE BRIGHT YOUNG THING IS GOING ABOUT WITH A LARGE WHITE FEATHER TICKLING THE OTHERS—EXCEPT THE SOLDIER—UNDER THE CHIN).

BALLAD SINGER
I'll sing you…

SOLDIER (INTERRUPTING HIM RUDELY)
Keep right on to the end of the road,
Keep right on to the end.

BALLAD SINGER
I'll sing you a song
Of that same road as well,
From Maryhill Barracks
It leads into hell!
From here to the trenches,
Like the bayonet you bear,
It twists and it turns,
God only knows where.

FLAPPER (TRYING TO FORCE THE WHITE FEATHER ON THE BALLAD SINGER AND STAMPING HER FEET IN PETULANT RAGE).
Coward! Malingerer! Why aren't you in uniform?

BALLAD SINGER (POINTING TO HIS TATTERED CLOTHES)
Excuse me, miss, but I am in uniform, the ragged regimentals of the poor, and I've been in them since my first pair of hand-me-downs, I'm no' goin' to dress up for the first time in my life, just to get killed. And what about your ain family, miss? Your dad for instance? Is he in the Army?

FLAPPER
Of course not. Papa… darling Papa is senior manager of Bishopton Ordnance Factory… He's in the Arms Industry…

BALLAD SINGER
Oh, the Arms Industry! Arms… and legs… Excuse me sayin' so, miss, but there's hardly a portion of the human anatomy that Industry doesn't include… It's a bloody business all right… As for me, miss, I'm quite content to be on the side of John Maclean…

ALL (SHRINKING BACK FROM HIM)
John Maclean!

BALLAD SINGER
Aye, the same John Maclean!

PASSER-BY
Him that's in Peterhead Prison?

FLAPPER
A common convict!

SOLDIER
In the pay of the Huns!

SANDWICH MAN Anti-Christ... Apostate... Heretic... Heathen.

BALLAD SINGER
My God, but don't you display a fine Christian charity... Nae wunner the bishops bless the banners going into war...

SANDWICH-BOARD MAN There shall always be wars and rumours of war.

BALLAD SINGER
Aye, if the generals have their way. If the generals and the arms bosses, and the crooked statesmen have their way... A Christmas not long past, the Germans and the British rank-and-filers played football and drank and sang together in no-man's land... The pity was they didn't play extra time... an extra time that stretched out to infinity...

SOLDIER
Sorry, mate, but you're living in a pipe-dream... cloud cuckoo land... the land of never-never and make believe... The people of all countries would need to turn on them that start the war, the profit merchants and the bosses... Even one major country at war, to do that very thing, would change the murderous pattern of history. Sorry, mate, but there isn't one wee hope in hell of that happening... Not a hope in hell...

(SOUND OF DRUMS... MARCHING FEET... A TAPE BEGINNING TO PLAY, THE INTERNATIONAL...)

BALLAD SINGER
D'you think not, pal?

(TAPE'S VOLUME INCREASES, TO BE JOINED BY RECORD OF SOVIET RED ARMY CHOIR WITH A ROUSING CHORUS).

SANDWICH-BOARD MAN (EMERGING FROM THE BOARD AND GOING ON HIS KNEES)
Oh, ye of little faith, Hallelujah! Hallelujah!

(RED BANNERS APPEAR BACK-STAGE. NEWSBOY RUSHES ON STAGE).

NEWSBOY
Read all about it. Revolution in Russia! Great Revolution in Russia! The Czar is toppled! Read all about it!

SOLDIER (READING THE PAPER)
Good Lord, it's incredible... impossible... thousands of half-starved soldiers deserting the Eastern front... Russia in turmoil as workers and peasants and soldiers revolt... millions of people involved... This makes the French Revolution seem just a skirmish...

PASSER-BY (READING)
And they're going to demand an end to the war in Europe... They are calling for a Peace Agreement... a rumour too that before long they are going to make John Maclean their new Russian Consul for Scotland...

SANDWICH-BOARD MAN (STILL ON HIS KNEES)
Oh, woe is me! Woe is me! The end of the world is at hand... Armageddon has come and we are all marching in a great column through the valley of Joseph... weeping... and wailing... and gnashing of teeth...

BALLAD SINGER
What's up with this geezer? He seems to be the only one that's gnashing his molars in this place. (SLAPPING HIM ON THE BACK) Cheer up, Mac, you'll get over it. John Maclean... a Soviet Consul for Scotland... well that takes the biscuit... A Peterheid convict representing a hundred and fifty million people... that should give the 'respectable' British Government a proper red face... red face? (SLAPS THE SANDWICH BOARD MAN) Do you get it, pal? Well, they have to release John now. Coupled with the protests at home, they'll have to release him now. (RUBS HIS HANDS) Oh, my, but it's a great day for the Irish and Scotland, isn't it?

FLAPPER (WHIMPERING)
But what about my poor Papa?

BALLAD SINGER
Your poor Papa? A minute ago you were saying he was rich. Senior manager, no less, of Bishopton Arms Dump. Make up your pretty little mind, miss.

FLAPPER
But if this peace thing you talk about gets out of hand, there'll be no need for ammunition and he'll be out of a job, won't he?

BALLAD SINGER
Well now, would you believe it? You've just put it in a nut shell. He'll be out o' that job for a certainty but... but wait a minute... we might turn Bishopton into a war museum to display the Capitalist's stupidity and cruelty, and then mebbe we could make your old man

an attendant, a living fossil of the ugly establishment he used to run… On the other hand we might stuff him…

FLAPPER
Stuff my old man… oh… oh… ooh… Stuff my dear Papa…

BALLAD SINGER
Stuff him and put him in a glass case as a show piece.

FLAPPER
Ooh… ooh… ooh.

BALLAD SINGER
On the other hand, if he behaved himself, we might get him a decent sensible job in producing the explosives for the great hydroelectric dams and roadways and bridges we need for Scotland, and for quarrying the stone that we'll need for transforming the slums into decent houses for the people. And take my advice, you daft wee lassie. D'you see that white feather o' yours?

FLAPPER
My white feather?

BALLAD SINGER
Aye, your white feather. It should be pinned on the breast of every worker, who on the bosses command, sticks a bayonet in the guts of a fellow worker, no matter his nationality. But since you haven't enough feathers to go round, I'll tell you what to dae. Stick it in a vat and dye it red.

FLAPPER
Dye it red?

BALLAD SINGER
Aye, dye it red. And put it on your bonnet like a flaming crest for the next May Day march to Glasgow Green. It will be the greatest turn-out in the history of Glasgow… A hundred and fifty thousand workers will be there… I promise you that… And at the head of the march will be our own John Maclean…

SONG
I'll sing you a song
Of the famous Red Clyde
I'll shout and proclaim it,
I'll sing it with pride,
And if one I can honour,
I'll say it again,

Brave Scotland had never
A man like Maclean.

(End of Act 2, Scene 5)

ACT 2, SCENE 6

(JOHN MACLEAN'S HOME AT 42 AULDHOUSE ROAD, POLLOKSHAWS. JOHN AND AGNES TOGETHER).

AGNES

Nothing, John… nothing in the world will describe my delight in having you home with me again… I mind when I was a wee lass, the gloom o' winter held fast the hills and dales o' Hawick… Then spring came suddenly that year… the birds were singing and early flowers came… Well that's the way I feel… only better. But, John, you must rest. Take it easy for a while… for our sake and your own…

JOHN

It's great to be home with you again, Nan… but rest or ease, tell me how… since Russia's had its revolution and toppled the Czar, here in Britain they've jailed, interned the poor exiles of Russia in case they're Bolshies…. I'm the Consul for the USSR… Who else can fight for them?

AGNES

Louis Shammes, your assistant, could carry on in your absence… even for a little while, John, to give you a rest.

JOHN

Rest, Nan? That's one thing the capitalists make sure we Socialists never have, even in their prisons. I didn't want to tell you, I didn't want to worry you… but this afternoon, they've arrested Louis Shammes at our office…

AGNES

Good God… this makes it worse.

JOHN

I want to tell you something most important, Nan… Since the British Government murdered James Connolly in Ireland, many a night I've thought on it… How did brave Connolly feel leaving Norah, the wife he adored—the relentless, decent struggle of honest men and women to help their class, their brothers and sisters out of the darkness. And faced with barbarism disguised as Christianity, and their so-called 'Freedom' what chance have they?

AGNES

There are times, John, I feel terribly afraid for the children's sake. They're so young and vulnerable... For all children, Nan, all children. And that's what I want to tell you about. The future. The Russian Revolution has shaken the bosses to the core, but it has made them more alert to the dangers they face from working classes of the world... They'll go to any length, Nan, to stop it happening here or on the Continent or America... anywhere...

AGNES

From what I see happening to you, John... and what has happened in Ireland, I've nae doubts about that. Nae doubts whatever.

JOHN

It's ten years ago, Nan, since Jack London described it in his book, *The Iron Heel*, and already the rumblings of Fascism are heard in Europe... Mussolini is building up his team of gangsters in Italy. Fascism isn't a mere political party with a sadistic kink in it. It's the bosses iron fist to keep the working classes in slaver... and it'll spread to other countries... On Christmas last in Peterhead, I had a nightmare.

AGNES

No surprise, the way they treated you. Doctors, my foot!

JOHN

I was reading Einstein the week before, and it gave me some picture of the immense strides and leaps that science will make in the near future... I dreamt this Christmas night that the boss-clan had put a raving maniac in charge of defeated Germany, and that with the help of Krupps and others, he built up a huge arsenal and an army and plunged the world into a war, worse, Nan, worse than the present one...

AGNES

Oh, heaven forbid, John, heaven forbid! What future would the children have?

JOHN

I'm going to fight that happening, Nan. With the help of modern science misapplied, future wars will be devastating, and Capitalism, Nan, as we know too well, is a ruthless, barbaric beast. I've got to warn and brace the Scottish working class... We can, in Scotland, advance to Socialism a thousand times faster than in England... Ireland is severing the first link in John Bull's tottering Empire... Soon it will be India, Cyprus, Africa and the rest... England is sadly a nation of flag-waving, self-opinionated dupes... as the Clincher describes them—the brain-washed Brits... Scotland should go it alone, Nan, and even then we'll not be that much alone. Why should Scottish lads have to die for John Bull in Ireland or anywhere else? It breaks my heart every time I read the war casualty list in The Herald.

(DURING THIS SPEECH TWO SINISTER FIGURES HAVE APPEARED IN THE BACKGROUND AT EACH CORNER OF THE STAGE. THEY ARE DRESSED IDENTICALLY AND BOTH CARRY NOTEBOOKS IN WHICH THEY WRITE WHAT IS BEING SAID).

FIRST POLICE SPY
We are returning to you letters written from your Consul office. The Post Office has instructions not to deliver such letters. The Post Office also has instructions not to allow any correspondence to be delivered to your office.

SECOND POLICE SPY
The British Government does not recognise such a Consulate.

JOHN
Oh, but this is rare. The 'freedom loving democrats' are showing themselves up in their true colours.

FIRST POLICE SPY
Did you or did you not, John Maclean, make statements to large audiences at Glasgow, Shettleston, Cambuslang, Lochgelly, Harthill and numerous other places?

JOHN
Well, you should know, I saw you often enough lurking in the shadows with that hang-dog look of yours.

SECOND POLICE SPY
Did you or did you not state at these meetings that the workers should down tools and create the Revolution?

FIRST POLICE SPY
Did you or did you not state that the Clyde district had helped to win the Russian Revolution, that the revolutionary spirit on the Clyde was ten times stronger than it was two years ago?

SECOND POLICE SPY
That the workers of the Clyde should take control of the City Chambers, and retain hostages…

FIRST POLICE SPY
That they should take control of the post offices and the banks…

SECOND POLICE SPY
All this has been recorded against you, Mr John Maclean, and we are arresting you on a

charge of sedition.

JOHN
You see the way it's going, Nan… They sit in their comfortable bungalows in Bearsden and Whitecraigs and care not a jot for the poor wee tenement children of Glasgow…

VOICE OF A GLASGOW POET
I see in the back streets of Glasgow
A child with a beauty her own
Akin to a lonely white flower
Mid clefts in the rock there had grown.
Years passed, I returned to that back street,
The child in her beauty was gone,
And there stood a poor haggard creature
In a place where the sun never shone.

JOHN
Goodbye, Nan, my lovely lass, and once again our polis friends on behest of those who sent them, we know who sent them, create misery… Nan, my precious comrade, they'll hound us further… Take the wee children back to Hawick, and give them the chance of the Spring you knew in the days of youth. I'll fight them, lass, don't worry. We'll fight and win!

(PETE SEEGER'S SONG OF SACCO AND VANZETTI'S TRIALS. SACCHO'S LETTER TO HIS SON).

'Be good to your mum, Distract her on the discouraging way, Bring her on wee walks to gather flowers, etc.'

(LIGHT FOCUSED ON OTHER SIDE OF THE STAGE TO THAT WHICH JOHN, POLICE SPIES AND AGNES HAVE MADE THEIR EXIT. SPOTLIGHT ON LORD STRATHCLYDE ON THE JUDGE'S SEAT ONCE MORE, DOING A BIT OF BURLESQUE IMMEDIATELY PRIOR TO THE FAMOUS 1918 TRIAL. REMOVING AND REPLACING HIS WIG SEVERAL TIMES).

(End of Act 2, Scene 6)

ACT 2, SCENE 7

(COURT HOUSE).

STRATHCLYDE
(SONG OR RECITATION)

If I didn't have a wig,
People wouldn't think me big,
The poor and honest true man
Would look on me as human,
Unbecoming to my call,
Sure that wouldn't do at all,
Though some of them may chortle,
I must never seem quite mortal,
While this quaint device I use,

See them shiver in their shoes,
I couldn't be a pompous prig
If I didn't have a wig
If I didn't have a wig,
Sure I couldn't do my gig.
If I didn't crown my pate,
Now they wouldn't think me great,
If I didn't wear this screen,
Ah, my dandruff might be seen,
How could I sentence fair
With a head of common hair,
And, dear me, they'd be appalled
If they found that I was bald,
I'd be classed a mere old pig
—If I didn't have a wig.

(PULLS THE WIG OFF AND STARES AT IT CONTEMPTUOUSLY).

But they could make them less absurd looking. couldn't they? A bit more flowing and graceful decorum. They give you the impression that they ran short of materials... a war-time economy... regulation issue or something... Nothing they remind me more of than some frowsy housewife that's forgotten to take out her curlers, in the fish-queue. (BANGS THE GAVEL) It's hard to look grave and profound wearing this thing, but for ten thousand a year, it's worth having a try... Bring on the prisoner.

COURT SARGEANT (SHOUTING)
Bring on the prisoner... John Maclean!

(CALL ECHOES DOWN THE CORRIDOR).

STRATHCLYDE (BURYING HIS HEAD IN HIS HANDS)
My God... not him again! (ENTER JOHN MACLEAN, STANDS ON BOX STAGE FRONT) Mr. Maclean, do you object to any of the jury? Do you object to any particular juryman?

JOHN
I object to all of them.

STRATHCLYDE
That's highly irregular, Mr Maclean, highly irregular.

JOHN
If I may say so, the whole proceedings are highly irregular. I refuse to plead guilty or not guilty and I will conduct my own defence.

STRATHCLYDE
Very well then. We'll call the first witness.

SARGEANT
Call the first witnes… Special Constable Knox…

(ENTER SPECIAL CONSTABLE KNOX. STANDS ON BOX)

FIRST SPECIAL CONSTABLE
I was on duty that day in Glasgow Green when the prisoner was haranguing his audience…

STRATHCLYDE
The prisoner was what?

FIRST SPECIAL
Haranguing. It means he was… he was… how shall I put it… He was speaking to the audience in quite a loud and forceful way…

STRATHCLYDE
Just like I'm doing to you?

FIRST SPECIAL
Quite, my Lord.

STRATHCLYDE
Then why didn't you say so in the first place… I want no circumlocution in this court… For the juries sake, I want no use of repetition, tautology, or superfluous ambiguities… no big words either. Do you understand?

FIRST SPECIAL
Quite, my Lord.

STRATHCLYDE (ASIDE)
That's funny, for I don't. (ALOUD) Never mind. Proceed.
FIRST SPECIAL

As the prisoner was speaking I was keeping these mental notes in my head.

STRATHCLYDE
Where else could you keep them? Unless in your pocket, of course. (ASIDE) Jolly witty today, old chap, carry on, witness…

FIRST SPECIAL
And I heard the prisoner state clearly all the expressions to be found in the indictments… (STANDS DOWN QUICKLY FOLLOWED BY SECOND SPECIAL CONSTABLE).

SECOND SPECIAL
I too was taking mental notes…

STRATHCLYDE
These mental notes. Were you taking them in shorthand?

SECOND SPECIAL (OPEN-MOUTHED)
Beg your pardon, my Lord?

STRATHCLYDE
Oh never mind, Proceed!

SECOND SPECIAL
And I heard the prisoner state exactly the expressions… The prisoner was standing on his soap box about twelve feet from his audience and if you drew a line…

STRATHCLYDE
I'm going to draw the line right now. What are you? A maths teacher?

SECOND SPECIAL (BEAMING)
No, my Lord, but I was in the Murder Squad for a time. They measure everything there.

STRATHCLYDE (ASIDE)
They didn't measure intelligence when they accepted you into it. But tell me, witness, why were all you big, burly men just taking mental notes?

SECOND SPECIAL
Oh, the crowd was with him, my Lord. They held his view a hundred per cent. They'd have throttled us…

STRATHCLYDE
Really? So you were afraid.

SECOND SPECIAL
Well… no… my Lord. What shall I call it—judicious? And we have six more special constables as witnesses also…

STRATHCLYDE
Well, Mr Maclean, you are accused of Sedition, a very serious charge indeed. Have you put all of your case?

JOHN (BOLD AND CLEAR)
I am a Socialist, and have been fighting for and shall always fight for an absolute reconstruction of Society for the benefit of all. I have nothing to retract. I have nothing to be ashamed of... I act square and clean for my principles. No matter what your accusations against me may be; no matter what reservations you keep at the back of your head. (HE TURNS TO FACE THE AUDIENCE FULL FRONT) My appeal is to the working class. They and they alone can bring about the day when the world can be one brotherhood, on a sound economic foundation... I am not here as the accused but the accuser of Capitalism, dripping with blood from head to foot!

STRATHCLYDE
It would be fruitless for me to go into the niceties of this or that legal point. You are obviously a highly educated and intelligent man, and realise the thorough seriousness of the offence you have committed. Without retiring, the Jury have found you guilty and today, the sentence of this Court is that you be sent to penal servitude for five years.

JOHN (CLENCHING HIS FIST ABOVE HIS HEAD)
Keep the struggle going boys! Keep it going!

(STAGE BECOMES ALL DARK; THAN A SPOTLIGHT ON LENIN WHO STANDS ON ONE OF THE HIGHER BOXES).

LENIN
The World Working Class Revolution began with individual heroes representing with supreme courage all the honest elements of a 'Socialism which had been largely corrupted into Chauvinism. Maclean, Liebknecht and Adler are among these heroes, the great forerunners of Socialism! Men of the highest principle.

(End of Act 2, Scene 7)

ACT 2, SCENE 8

(BUCHANAN STREET STATION. ALL THE CAST ARE ON THE STAGE).

FIRST WOMAN
What time did you say the train was due, Mrs Barbour?

MRS BARBOUR
He's due in the 4.30 frae Aberdeen... Aye, this platform, Jeannie... Ma God, where did ye get a hat o' thae dimensions... You're blockin' ma view...

SECOND WOMAN
Oh, I got it specially for the occasion... The hail toon's turning oot' an' they're goin' tae see Jeannie MacFarlane at her best...

FIRST WOMAN
Did ye ever see sich crowds in George Square? Them poor statues'll have corns an' blisters wi' all they folk standin' on their toes...

MRS BARBOUR
Ah, weel, they stood on a few toes in their time, didn't they? I hope the train comes in soon. Some poor folk have been here for hours, since morning...

FIRST WOMAN
Just for the glimpse of John Maclean... That's whit he means tae the Glasgow folk... There never wis another like him in this city... not even blessed Mungo himsel'...

MRS BARBOUR
That's him comin' noo, Jeannie, that's him comin' (A GREAT CHEER GOES UP) That's him at the windae wi' his wife, Nan...

SECOND WOMAN
Oh my, but he's awfu' peely-wally wi' that prison life... The poor man's been in an' oot that often...

(CHEERS AS JOHN IS CARRIED SHOULDER-HIGH ON TO THE PLATFORM).

VOICES
Speech, John, speech!

(SOMEONE PROVIDES A BOX FOR HIM TO STAND ON).

JOHN
I'm not going to say very much. It's been a long journey but worth every mile of it to see the warm, friendly, honest face of old Glasgow again. We fought the bosses in war, and we'll fight them in peace. They sought to jail us, gag and silence us... they invented sleekit laws to do that very thing, but they failed miserably. There's hardly a single soul on Clydeside that doesn't see through their dirty game, and if the rest of Britain was half as awake as the Red Clyde, we'd make short shrift of this class-ridden humbug society... But don't be down-hearted, comrades, in the long and bitter struggle! As Rabbie said, 'It's comin' yet for a' that! Three cheers then, all of us, for the Revolution!

(CHEERS. THE CROWD SING THE JOHN MACLEAN MARCH AS THEY CIRCLE THE STAGE OR FORM AS PRODUCER WISHES. AFTER THE MARCH SONG... A SPOTLIGHT ON AN ENLARGED PICTURE OF JOHN MACLEAN).

VOICE
For five more years, this courageous and brilliant working-class fighter devoted his entire being to the struggle for peace and Socialism, until from his very intensity of effort, and the harsh suffering he endured during his prison sentences, he died at the age of 44.

END OF PLAY

THE WEAVER LADS

CHARACTERS

Jamie Blue	Ballad-singer/narrator
Tam Brice	Calton weaver
Jamie Foy	Calton weaver
James Finlay	Rich Glasgow merchant
Kirkman Finlay	His son. A principal character in play
Annie Brice Tam's wife.	Calton bleacher lass
Alexander Richmond	Government agent recruited by Finlay
Henry Home Drummond	Solicitor General for Scotland
Francis Jeffrey Defence	Lawyer for the weavers
Andrew McKinlay	Calton Weaver. Prisoner in 1817
John Campbell	Witness in 1817
Old Hawkie	Famous Glasgow Street character.
Feea	Famous Glasgow street urchin
Andrew Hardie	Glasgow weaver
Margaret McKeigh	Andrew's sweetheart
James Hardie	Justice of the Peace
James Turner	Government spy in 1820
Dougal Smith	Weavers' union leader
Buffoon	Tory die-hard
Nichol H Baird	Kilsyth yeoman
Widow Hardie	Andrew's mother
Caretaker	Attendant at cemetery
Andrew White	One of the 1820 weavers
Peter Mackenzie	Glasgow historian

Lord President of the 1820 court.
Court Clerks. Weavers, Mourners.

ACTS AND SCENES

ACT 1 SCENE 1 The Calton in Glasgow
ACT 1 SCENE 2 The Calton in Glasgow
ACT 2 SCENE 1 Kirkman's mansion in Queen Street
ACT 2 SCENE 2 High Court of Judiciary in Edinburgh
ACT 3 SCENE 1 Glasgow Cross and High Street
ACT 3 SCENE 2 Germiston in the Garngad District. Glasgow.
ACT 3 SCENE 3 Glasgow Cross

ACT 4 SCENE 1 Henry Drummond's mansion at Blair Drummond.
ACT 4 SCENE 2 The High Court in Stirling
ACT 4 SCENE 3 Margaret McKeigh's living room in Glasgow
ACT 5 SCENE 1 Duncan's book shop in the Saltmarket, Glasgow
ACT 5 SCENE 2 Outside the house of Mr Reddie, Town Clerk
FINALE: Under monument to Baird and Hardie, also headstone to the Calton Weavers. Replicas in wood of both on stage, surrounded with trade nnion banners

ACT 1, SCENE 1

(JAMIE BLUE (BALLAD SINGER) AT GLASGOW CROSS).

Song: THE CALTON WEAVERS

As I went in by Glasgow city,
My weaver friends I was glad to see.
But ere I came by Brigton Cross,
I heard some news might daunton me.
Calton Weaver, Calton Weavers,
bonnie lads we'll see nae mair,
you gave your lives for workers' freedom
and in your glory we all share.
Glasgow is a braw wee city,
sitting on the banks of Clyde
Famous folk that we might boast of,
but the weavers are our pride.
Tyrants slew the Calton Martyrs,
in an Abercromby grave they lie,
but heroes in the name of Freedom,
never, ever, ever, die.

(THE YEAR IS 1787 IN THE CALTON DISTRICT OF GLASGOW. TWO YOUNG WEAVERS, TAM AND JAMIE, STAND AT THE STREET CORNER. THEY ARE POORLY DRESSED, NOT MUCH BETTER THAN THE HODDEN GREY).

TAM
I'm wonderin', Jamie. Where will it all end?

JAMIE
It fair maks ma blood boil!

TAM
When I came in frae Tarbolton wi' my faither ten year ago. I wis only a laddie o' fifteen,

but the Clyde and the toon o' Glesga were a real wunner tae look at… the great wide street at the Tron, all thae curious piazzas at the Cross… the windin' Highgait up tae the great Cathedral; the great Greenlaid oot wae its fine paths and the river Clyde itself as clear as a wimplan burn. Aye, I had high hopes. Ma faither had pride in the weavin' and he taught me. But noo, sad tae say, I don't live in the Calton… like mony anither—starve in the Calton!

JAMIE
Sma' wunner indeed, they cry the looms the four posts o' poverty, for that's what they've become for maist o' us.

TAM
Noo, look at Davie Dale. They say he came in fae Ayrshire wi' little gear tae his name and look at him noo, wi' his mills, an' his fine hoose in Charlotte Street, an' there's others o' his kind. They say…

JAMIE
Aye, but for every one that arises in this ill-divided world of oors, there's a thousand in need. We a' cannae be Davie Dales for there wouldn't be a bale o' yarn spun in Scotland, or the coal dug, or the ships made.

TAM
Nor a house built. Not long ago, I mind folks looked up tae the weavers. We had a bit o' independence; we could feed an' clothe oor families decently. But noo we're expected tae live on air.

JAMIE
Tell you this Tam; I had a strange dream the ither night. I dreamt the Commission Agent, Wilson, here in the Calton.

TAM
I ken him too weel.

JAMIE
I dreamt that he came into the hoose wi' a commission to weave as much material.

TAM
That'll be the day!

JAMIE
As much material as would make a new suit of clothes for some Arabian Emperor.

TAM
Tell me seriously, Jamie!

JAMIE
Whit?

TAM
Had you a good dram afore you went tae sleep that night?

JAMIE
No' a drap, Tam. No' a drap. An' the funny thing wis I took Wilson seriously, an' I just went on producin' length after length o' cloth, but Wilson just kept on shakin' his heid, an' I sensed that no matter how fine the yarn was, or how lang the weary hours, Wilson wid never be satisfied. I knew there was something daft aboot it a'. But could I mak it oot?

TAM
That wis nae dream Jamie. It was a nightmare reflectin' aw yer worries. But talkin aboot Emperors. Here's one o' them in person! Say nothin' Jamie and listen.

(ENTER FINLAY AND HIS SON, KIRKMAN. THOUGH THE TOBACCO LAIRDS ARE MORE THAN A DECADE PAST THEIR PRIME, FINLAY SENIOR WEARS THE SCARLET CLOAK, WHITE BREECHES AND COCKED HAT OF THAT 'SUPERIOR' GENTRY. HE EYES THE DOWN-AT-HEEL WEAVERS WITH SUSPICION AND DISDAIN. THEY ARE PART OF BURKE'S 'GREAT UNWASHED').

FINLAY
There's something underhand going on, my boy. I can sense that!

KIRKMAN
You mean these men, father?

FINLAY
Yes, I do! When I see these idlers and vagabonds hanging about street corners, I know they are up to no good. Conspiring I would say. Some mischief against their betters. Yes! Just look at the cut o' them.

KIRKMAN
Father?

FINLAY
What is it boy?

KIRKMAN
Are these the ones wouldn't follow your drum to save the American Colonies from the rebels out there?

FINLAY
Heavens, no! These sorts of riff-raff were mere bairns at the time. I can tell you, lad, you'll need to brush up your history. I must say, by your marks, you're quite behind in your class. I think laddie, that in the business world you're intended for; you'll have to rely on your wits more than any book learning. Study both friend and foe, then beat them all to it!

KIRKMAN
These two men are watching us, father.

FINLAY
Oh, I know fine what's in their minds. The merchants have asked them to accept a thirty per cent cut in wages and they are resentful and vicious. They've already cut the webs of the blacklegs, the weavers that accept the cuts. There's trouble brewing among these hot-heads. I can tell! We'll need more troops in Glasgow soon. These radicals have no respect for authority, law and order! By Jove, we'll teach them a lesson!

(EXIT FINLAY AND SON)

TAM
That's how much he understands oor position, Jamie.

JAMIE
Or is he deliberately blind? Finlay has shares in some of the big merchant hooses himself. He surely knows the new machinery of the spinning jennies has made a bottle-neck that the slower looms haven't caught up wi'. We make a bare livin' wage but they want us to work sixteen hours a day tae earn the same siller that ten hours work would hae got us previously. Well, they're not on Tam. They're jist not on!

(FINLAY AND HIS SON RETURN. TAM SEES THEM).

TAM
Here's his nibs again. I wunner whit the heck's goin' on here.

JAMIE
Let's draw back into the shadows a bit.

(TAM AND JAMIE GO OFF STAGE)

FINLAY
I wonder what's keeping the fellow, I'll tell you lad, the common rabble is fast losing any respect they had for their superiors. Why only last year some scurrilous rhymer in Mauchline by the name of Burns had verses printed that encourages that sort of thing,

and another man in Paisley. a weaver himself, had been circulating nasty squibs against the mill-owners.

KIRKMAN
I didn't know that weavers could write, father?

FINLAY
That's the basic trouble with them—they're reading too much, both at the looms and in their spare time. They're educating themselves; they're getting big ideas of equality and justice. Shortly they'll want to take over the place. What the blazes is keeping this damn fellow? (SEES HIM COMING). Ah, here he comes.

(ENTER BLACKLEG).

BLACKLEG
(LOOKING AROUND CAUTIOUSLY. HE CARRIES A PACK) I'm sorry, Mr Finlay, but I saw these two neebours hangin' aboot the corner, and I jist thought I'd play it safe. We a' know, Mr Finlay that discreesion is the better pairt o' valour an' its' wiser tae be safe than sorry...

FINLAY (VERY IMPATIENTLY)
For God's safe, cut that silly babble and down to business!

BLACKLEG (OPENING HIS PACK AND TAKING OUT SOME CLOTH)
That's as may be, Mr Finlay, but I'm no goin' to be seen talkin' tae a merchant in Calton without some kind o' cover up. Isn't this the fine stuff I'm sellin' you Mr Finlay? As good as the best frae Paisley or France?

FINLAY
Yes, yes, yes, but get on with the news!

BLACKLEG
I did as ye telt me sir, I tried to get as mony weavers tae work on in spite o' the ithers. Some of the strikers wanted tae burn the looms. They call us black-legs. They were that angry but the cooler wans made them keep their heids. I'm afraid Mr Finlay, oor side cannae keep it up much longer. Ma ain loom in the back-shed is stripped tae the wood. I'm jist left wi' the spare loom in the back room o' the hoose.

FINLAY (TAKING OUT HIS PURSE AND FURTIVELY SLIPPING SEVERAL GOLD COINS TO THE BLACK-LEG) Good man! Don't waste a minute! Go and tell your friends to keep it up! Resist these radicals! Resist them everywhere! Spread rumours!

BLACKLEG
Whit kind o' rumours, Mr Finlay?

FINLAY
Aren't they trouble-makers, heathens, radicals, revolutionaries, spies from the Continent, agents from that infernal democracy across the Atlantic, and always, always, ungodly? Remember that! This rabble rebels, not just against the State and the glorious Constitution, but against the Almighty himself! You'd better go me and tell your friends to hold out! There's help coming. Assure them of that. Good day.

(FINLAY AND SON MAKE THEIR EXIT. THE BLACKLEG STAYS FOR A MOMENT GREEDILY COUNTING HIS BRIBE, UNTIL HE HEARS THE VOICE OF ANNIE, THE BLEACHER LASS SINGING, AS SHE DRAWS NEARER. EXIT THE BLACK-LEG. ENTER ANNIE WITH A BACKET OF LINEN)

ANNIE (ANNIE IS SINGING AS SHE MOVES ACROSS STAGE)

(SONG: THE GALLANT WEAVER)

Where Cart rins rollin' tae the sea,
by many a flower and spreading tree.
There lives a lad, the lad for me,
he is a gallant weaver.
O' I had wooers aught or nine,
they gied me rings and ribbons fine,
and I was fear'd my heart wid tine,
and I gied it tae the weaver.

My daddy signed my tocher-band,
to gie the lad that has the land
but to my heart I'll add my hand
and gae it tae the weaver.
While birds rejoice in leafy bowers,
while bees delight in opening flowers,
while corn grows green in summer showers,
I'll love my gallant weaver.

(THE TWO WEAVERS CREEP OUT FROM THE SHADOWS AND TAM, WHO IS ANNIE'S SWEETHEART, GIVES HER A SUDDEN PECK OF THE CHEEK. SHE JUMPS WITH SURPRISE, ALMOST DROPPING THE BASKET OF CLOTHES).

Oh, Tam Russell, weel I never. You almost frightened the life oot o' me. whit are the pair of ye'daein', skulkin' like thieves in the shadows?
TAM (POINTING IN THE DIRECTION OF THE TRON STEEPLE)
We were jist earwigging' on the honourable 'baccy Baron, and I can tell you Annie, Jamie and I learned a few things tae whit we might call out mutual advantage! And where have you been?

ANNIE
Doon on Glesga Green, past Airn's Wall, bleaching these bits. Where else?

JAMIE
Sae, ye've got a new lumber.

ANNIE
Whit's that ye're sayin'. Whit new lumber?

TAM
She better no, I can tell you that!

JAMIE
This fellow you're singin' aboot. He comes frae the river Cart. That's oot by Paisley. Tam here is frae Camlachie Burn.

ANNIE
I never heard anybody puttin' Camlachie in a song yet. Whit would it rhyme wae fir a start!

TAM
Whit beats me is how anyone can sing sae gaily in daurk times like these. Annie is one o' the few who can dae it.

ANNIE
Dae ye want me to go into sack cloth and ashes and wear a greetin' face o' the time, on account of the hard times? Or maybe jist jump in the Clyde like a poor lost soul? Somebody maun be cheery; for God knows it's the sad tales I hear doon on the bleachin' green ayont the Well. Mither's tales o' wee ailin' hauf-nourished bairns, carried in wee plain boxes to the kirk-yaird in Abercrombie Street! In truth if I didn't at times find some sort o' cheer I'd be hert-broken myself.

TAM (PUTTING HIS ARM ROUND HER)
Dinnae fash yourself lassie. Though the merchants and magistrates are ganging up on us, you and I'll soon be married when the bright day comes!

JAMIE
Aye, when the bright day comes!

(END OF ACT 1, SCENE 1)

ACT 1, SCENE 2

(STAGE IS STILL IN DARKNESS AND INNER CURTAIN DRAWN. SPOT ON JAMIE BLUE AT LEFT OF STAGE. (HE IS READING FROM A BROADSHEET).)

JAMIE
Neither the merchants nor the authorities, nor the use of blacklegs could force the Calton weavers to accept the wretched conditions the masters were intent on forcing on them. In September 1787, the magistrates, representing the employers, arrived in the Calton to press the weavers to submit. These civic dignitaries were not in office by popular consent; in fact the population of Glasgow at the time was almost 70,000 and only a mere twenty to thirty very wealthy tycoons had the right to vote.

(VOICE INTERRUPTS JAMIE'S SPEACH SHOUTING 'HOLD IT! HOLD IT'. ENTER JAMES FINLAY, DRESSED AS IN SCENE 1, HE WALKS UP TO JAMIE BLUE).

FINLAY
That's how you see it, my dear fellow. These trouble-makers were engaged in unlawful assembly.

JAMIE
Aye, and who made it unlawful? Certainly the people had no say in your law making: it was imposed by the law lords and a corrupt Parliament.

FINLAY
Careful what you say sir! There are folk got the gallows and the hulks for less treasonable remarks.

JAMIE
So what? Does that make them untrue? Crowds gathered, hundreds of weavers in particular, to protest against hunger and injustice.

FINLAY
It was a mob, I tell you. Out to destroy the town of Glasgow.

JAMIE
Utter nonsense! Unarmed citizens against thousands of troops and their guns, billeted in and around Glasgow?

FINLAY
The chief magistrate had no option but to have the Riot Act read to that uncontrollable mob.

(SPOTLIGHT ON SECTION OF THE DEMO CARRYING PLACARDS OF PROTEST AND JEERING AT THE AUTHORITIES. AN OFFICER IS SEEN READING THE RIOT ACT AND THE JEERING INCREASES).

JAMIE
The chief magistrate had another option. He could have told these poor hungry people that he and his associates would return immediately to the Council House in Trongate and there examine with genuine compassion the grievances of these hard working people. He could have, with his men and troops, retired in safety to Glasgow and from the huge profits made annually from the growing industries, he and his fellow merchants could have come to some fair settlement with the harassed weavers. Instead he chose the murderous path!

(OFFICER READS LAST PART OF THE RIOT ACT AND THE TROOPS OPEN FIRE AT POINT BLANK RANGE. A GOOD NUMBER OF MEN FALL ON THE STAGE. SOME CRAWL OFF WOUNDED BUT SIX LIE THERE, DEAD).

FINLAY
The lower classes had to be taught a lesson!

JAMIE
And it is a lesson that the lower classes—as you call them—have never forgotten! That fellow countrymen and avowed christians, could have them shot down in cold-blooded ruthlessness. That men whose ancestors had engaged in the same struggle against oppression, in this, one of the bonniest lands in Europe, had now stilled the voices and closed the eyes of good brave men; made widows of their wives, and left their children fatherless! Without the weavers ye wouldn't be clad; your beds would have no covering; your windows no curtains. What lesson have you taught us then? A lesson of class hatred and oppression that will endure until a real Glasgow, one of equality and common sense, arises on the banks of the Clyde. Amid the gloom and the grief, I'll prophecy this: when all the rich mausoleums, tombstones and monuments in the burial sites in the city are forgotten, a green grave in the Calton will remain in the hearts of the people!

(SONG; THE WORK O' THE WEAVERS).

(END OF ACT 1, SCENE 2)

ACT 2, SCENE 1

(YEARS LATER. IN THE PARLOUR OF KIRKMAN FINLAY'S MANSION IN QUEEN STREET, GLASGOW. KIRKMAN, THE SON OF JAMES. IS NOW A GROWN MAN. DRESSED IMMACUTELY. HE HAS A SHREWD. FLORID FACE. A LARGE PORTRAIT OF HIS FATHER, IN HIS TOBACCO LORD'S REGALIA LOOKS DOWN FROM THE MANTLE-PIECE. KIRKMAN IS STUDYING THE PORTRAIT AS THE CURTAIN OPENS).

KIRKMAN
Not a dissimilar situation at all. Is it father? I remember that walk with you in the Calton those many years ago. I remember your fine words of advice. 'Wits more than book learning'! 'Study friend and foe alike and beat them all to it'! Well sir, I haven't done badly. Not badly at all! Several of the largest mills in Scotland; partnership with David Dale; shares in New Lanark; ships on the Clyde. a mansion here, a castle in Dunoon—and wait for it father—Provost of Glasgow and a seat at Westminster! No' bad, father, for a laddie behind in his class! No' bad at all! (MOVES TO WINDOW) I can see my statue in George Square yet!

(MAID APPEARS AT DOOR)

MAID
The visitor has arrived sir, at the back door, and he's holding the boy, Feea.

KIRKMAN
The boy Feea?

MAID
Yes, sir. the poor street waif. The gentleman thinks Feea was following him, sir, but he wasn't sir. He'd only be lookin' for a stable or an outhouse tae sleep in. We a' know him sir.

KIRKMAN
Tell the gentleman to let the boy go immediately and to come here.

MAID
Yes, sir. (EXITS).

KIRKMAN
What a ridiculous creature, afraid of his own shadow! A great pity I need his services at all, but he's most useful, indeed essential at present. Afterwards we can ship him off.

(ENTER RICHMOND. HE IS TALL, LEAN AND LANTERN-JAWED. WEARS A CLOAK AND BROAD BRIMMED HAT. HE IS SELF-EDUCATED AND WELL SPOKEN, A VERY CUNNING PERSON).

Ah, there you are Richmond. Forget about the boy, he knows nothing of our business; a street Arab, one of the small casualties of circumstance. Sit down and let me hear what you have to say!

RICHMOND (SITTING DOWN. HE WEARS A FROWN).
I am very angry, Mr Finlay, I feel like terminating the whole business.

FINLAY (GOES TO CABINET AND POURS OUT TWO GLASSES OF CLARET).
Angry?

RICHMOND
Yes, very angry. You had the men arrested and thrown in prison without consulting me! My name will be worse than mud in Glasgow, My wife and I and our poor children will have to flee the city.

FINLAY
You will be taken care of. I haven't done badly by you so far. Have I? I helped to get the Outlaw Bill lifted on you in 1813 to allow you back into this country. Didn't I? I promoted you from a common weaver to the position of Commission Agent with premises in the Trongate. I spoke for you with Robert Owen for a responsible post in his New Lanark experiment. I gave you money!

RICHMOND
All for what ends, Mr Findlay? You told me I had a free hand and that you would consult my opinion before any of the weavers were arrested. At New Year I gathered them at Leggat's tavern in Tradeston. They had scarcely signed the Oath in the Old Wynd saloon when you had them arrested! Not a word; not a message to me.

FINLAY
I will be quite straight with you Richmond.

RICHMOND
Please do!

FINLAY
I am quite certain that in the event of informing you that arrests were imminent, you might have circumvented those arrests, and that Treasonable Oath which these men signed would have been disputed when it was read in the House of Commons. There is the grave possibility that the Suspension of the Habeas Corpus Act would not have been passed and the Whigs would have had a field day to further the Reform Movement! Do you know Mr Richmond that very oath, signed by these men, which you delivered into my hands, was the very one which was read aloud by Lord Sidmouth in Parliament and won the day for us Tories? Do you know Richmond, that with your invaluable assistance, not only has Trade Unionism and workers' combination received a deadly rebuff, but the daft, untimely, irresponsible demands for a wider franchise has been postponed at least for decades, if not killed entirely! Could I allow such important measures to rely upon the whim or choice of any individual? Even your good self?

RICHMOND
It was no whim, Mr Finlay; some quite innocent people have been arrested.

KIRKMAN
Their innocence of guilt will be proved shortly in the High Court in Edinburgh.

RICHMOND
Not Glasgow?

KIRKMAN
Not Glasgow! The prejudice of the West Country is notorious. You and your family will take up secret residence in Edinburgh, Mr Richmond. The financial arrangements will be attended to by Mr Reddie, the chamberlain. Everything will be provided for. I have spoken to Lords Sidmouth and Castlereagh about the exceptional services you have been rendering to the government and both of them agree that you shall be recompensed fully. In Edinburgh you will provide the Procurator Fiscal and the police with all the important information at your disposal.

RICHMOND
Before I go, Mr Finlay, I would dearly like to know....

FINLAY
Yes?

RICHMOND
Your ultimate objective! You surely aren't after the mere imprisonment or death of these unfortunate creatures? What is behind it all?

FINLAY
Ultimate objective? what else, Mr Richmond, but law and order and the continued safety of state and church? What nobler aspirations?

RICHMOND (GOING TOWARDS DOOR)
I somehow feel there is something else.

FINLAY
Just leave as you came Mr Richmond. And pray don't be so suspicious, like you were with that daft waif, Feea.

RICHMOND
And I have another great fear, Mr Finlay; that this Edinburgh Court business will be bungled!

FINLAY
Bungled? What absolute nonsense! You have paranoiac fears of everything. Steady your nerves my good man!

RICHMOND
Good day! Will Mr Reddie be in his office?

FINLAY
Yes. All arrangements have been made between us and the Edinburgh police. There is an envelope with details and money in his office. Better catch the first coach tomorrow morning at the Black Bull Inn. There shouldn't be too many inquisitive folk. Good day Richmond! Cheer up! You have done Glasgow some great service! (HE RINGS FOR MAID)

MAID
Yes, sir?

FINLAY
See my friend to the door! (EXIT RICHMOND AND MAID) A kittle customer! But no match for his betters! Ultimate objective! Wouldn't he just like to know!

(END OF ACT 2, SCENE 1)

ACT 2, SCENE 2

(THE SCENE IS SET IN THE HIGH COURT OF JUSTICIARY. EDINBURGH. 19TH JULY 1817. PRESENT: ANDREW MCKINLAY, A CALTON WEAVER IN THE DOCK, FRANCIS JEFFREY, DEFENCE LAWYER, SOLICITOR GENERAL HENRY HOME DRUMMOND FOR THE CROWN).

DRUMMOND (FROM THE INDICTMENT)
Andrew McKinlay, weaver, the Calton district, Glasgow. You are charged with High Treason on the third section of the Act of Treason, passed in the reign of our most gracious majesty, George the Third which states, inter alia, that every person who shall administer, or cause to be administered, any Oath or engagement intending to bind the person taking the same to commit any Treason or Murder, or any Felony punishable by Law with death, shall on conviction Thereof, by due course of law, be adjudged guilty of Felony, and shall suffer death as a Felon without benefit of clergy. We charge that you, Andrew McKinlay, did, upon the 15th February last, 1817, in the tavern of Mr. Robison's, Gallowgate, Glasgow, administer this secret oath of Treason, which did bind, or did purport to bind the persons taking the same, to commit Treason by effecting, by physical strength, the subversion of the established Government, Laws and Constitution of this
country.

JUDGE
Andrew McKinlay, do you plead guilty or not guilty?

ANDREW
Not guilty, my Lord.

JUDGE
Call the first witness! (VOICE: JOHN CAMPBELL) (Enter Campbell)

FRANCIS JEFFREY
I object your Lordship, to John Campbell being called as a witness.

JUDGE
What are your grounds for objection?

FRANCIS JEFFREY
We, the defence lawyers for the prisoner, Andrew McKinlay have been obstructed by the Crown in obtaining both the identity and the access to this Crown witness. When, as the law provides, we were eventually told his identity, we were obstructed in reaching him in order to hear and judge the credibility of his evidence. He was not confined in a civil jail, but a military fort, Edinburgh Castle. Upon our application to the Fort Major, we were told that no access whatever could be given. This man is merely a witness shut up in the Castle of Edinburgh, to be hatched until ready to give evidence, but who he is or what he is, is not to be known until he is produced in the witness box.

DRUMMOND
My Lord, it was the business of the Panel to have applied to the Court for the liberty to see this witness. The Lord Advocate had merely refused his consent but told the Applicants to apply to the Court. At all events, the objections against Campbell had come too late, and, if there was anything in it, it ought to have been argued before going to trial.

FRANCIS JEFFREY
I can prove my Lord, that there was a peremptory and positive refusal to allow the Defence access. Suppose the Lord Advocate put in his list of witnesses, 'John Campbell, now locked up in my cellar' and refuses admission to him, is it possible to suppose that this person could be examined as a witness?

JUDGE
Objection over-ruled! Application should have been made to the Court. And to be candid, Mr Jeffrey I rather suspect you know well the legitimacy of this witness. But whatever your motives, I will ask John Campbell to enter the witness box and take the oath. (CAMPBELL DOES SO).

CLERK
Raise you right hand. Do you swear by Almighty God that any evidence you will give will be the truth, the whole truth and nothing but the truth?

CAMPBELL
I do.

CLERK
What is your full name?

CAMPBELL
John Campbell.

CLERK
You are presently domiciled with your wife in Glasgow?

CAMPBELL
Yes.

CLERK
Where are you from originally?

CAMPBELL
Symington, Ayrshire.

CLERK
What is your occupation?

CAMPBELL
I am a weaver mechanic and I have been a peace-officer.

CLERK
Have you received any reward, or promise of reward, for being a witness and giving your evidence?

CAMPBELL
I have! (CONSTERNATION IN COURT) Yes my Lord! I have been offered inducements in prison to attempt to make me a witness against Andrew McKinley. I was apprehended on the 22nd February last along with the prisoner in the dock. There was no warrant or cause assigned. Mr Salmond, acting Procurator Fiscal, at first attempted to persuade me into an admission of guilt. He said I had subscribed tae the Treasonable Oath in Leggat's Inn on New Year's Day. 'John' he said 'I have six men who will swear that you took that Oath, and you are sure to be hanged'. I refused to cooperate with him. Shortly afterwards, I was removed tae Edinburgh Castle. Here I was visited by Mr Drummond who told me my name was on the list of witnesses against McKinlay. He tried every inducement to get me to support the indictment. He said he would try and get Lord Sidmouth to find a post for me in the Customs and Excise. He said he would get me a passport to the Continent and money to travel with. Sir William Rae, the sheriff was in my cell at the time when Mr Drummond wrote down his promise of assistance. He wanted Sir William to sign it also as a witness to the promises made. The Sheriff warned me not to in front to Mr Drummond, and refused to have anything to do with it himself.

LORD ADVOCATE
Remember Campbell that you have been on Oath and that the Clerk of the Court has

taken down an accurate record of your statement! Will you read it and sign it?

CAMPBELL
I will.

FRANCIS JEFFREY
My Lord, may I now propose as corroboration for Mr Campbell's rather, rather revealing, statement about the machinations of our principled associates, the Crown lawyers, we call upon Sir William Rae, Sherriff of Edinburgh.

LORD ADVOCATE
On no account, your lordship, is this necessary. In consequence of the grave disappointment I have experienced in the turn which this evidence has adduced, I could not possibly receive a verdict which my former impressions had led me to expect. I therefore cannot take up valuable time of the Judge and the Jury in going further into a discussion which could be beneficial to neither the country nor the panel. I leave it therefore to the Jury to return a verdict of not guilty or not proven as they see proper.

FRANCIS JEFFREY
After the very candid and judicious admission which the Public Prosecutor has made of the utter failure of the case it would be inexcusable in detaining the court with any argument or observation.

JUDGE
Very well. Will the Jury please retire for their verdict. (JURY GO OUT BUT RETURN IN SECONDS) Have you reached a verdict?

FOREMAN
We have your Lordship.

JUDGE
Is Andrew McKinlay, weaver of the Calton, Glasgow 'not guilty' or 'not proven' of the charges against him?

FOREMAN
Not proven, my Lord.

JUDGE
Andrew McKinlay, you have been found not proven by this High Justiciary Court of Edinburgh and you are free to go.

(MCKINLAY GOES INTO THE WELL OF THE COURT AND THANKS FRANCIS JEFFREY FOR HIS SHREWD DEFENCE, THEY ARE JOINED BY THE SMIL-

ING JOHN CAMPBELL, WHO THROWS HIS ARMS AROUND HIS LIBERATED FRIEND).

MCKINLAY
I cannae thank ye enough John. I got your message in the tobacco roll ye passed on an' I let Mr Jeffrey read how Drummond was drilling ye. My God ye had some pairt tae act in front o' that man.

CAMPBELL (LEAVING WITH HIS ARM ROUND MCKINLAY)
We had tae beat them at their ain game, Andra, but at least we had the truth on our side. Sometimes though, in that lonely cell, I aft times wunnered how I could cairry on the act that I wis on their side. An' then I thought o' Shakespeare of all people. 'A' the world's a stage and a' the men and women merely players. They have their exits' (TURNS TO HIS FRIEND) and this, Andra is ours! (THEY LEAVE TOGETHER).

DRUMMOND (HE IS LEFT ALONE IN THE COURT)
It makes me think of Lord Neville's remark during the administration of Pitt. 'Don't draw the trigger until you are sure to kill!'. Next time, I will be sure. You can bet your life on that!

(END OF ACT 2)

ACT 3 SCENE 1

(GLASGOW CROSS IN THE YEAR 1820. THREE YEARS AFTER ANDREW McKINLAY'S TRIAL IN EDINBURGH) (JAMIE BLUE AND THE MOST FAMOUS, OLD STREET CHARACTER OF GLASGOW, HAWKIE, ARE CHATTING TOGETHER AT THE CROSS WITH A SMALL AUDIENCE GATHERED AROUND THEM. JAMIE IS DRESSED FAIRLY ORDINARY BUT HAWKIE IS WEARING THE BLUE-GOWN, THE 'OFFICIAL' GEAR OF THE LICENSED CITY OF GLASGOW MENDICANTS. YOUNG FEEA, THE WAIF, IS SKIPPING UP AND DOWN THE CAUSEY WITH WILD DELIGHT).

JAMIE BLUE
It's a wheen ago since I saw ye, Hawkie.

HAWKIE
It must have been aboot the year eighteen-canteen, Jamie; the year afore the High Wind and the Short Corn, the year after the mad rush tae the Sugarally Mountains. And where are ye livin' yersel, Jamie?

JAMIE
I'm living, scraping a living, in Nae Man's Land. That's hauf way between Glesga an' the highly pugnacious kingdom o' Pollokshaws.

HAWKIE
Are they still sufferin' ye oot in The Shaws, after that sang ye wrote aboot the queer folk? What about givin' us a few verses of your immortal rendering?

VOICES
Aye, Jamie. Let's hear 'The Queer Folk'.

HAWKIE (TO CROWD)
Let ye hae 'The Queer Folk'? Do ye no think there's enough queer folk among ye' already?

VOICE (IN LOUD PROTEST)
Naw!

JAMIE BLUE
Tell ye whit. I'll let ye hear 'The Queer Folk' after Hawkie explains his rig-oot! That eye-dazzlin' regalia he's wearin'. Come on Hawkie. Gie's the low-doon!

HAWKIE
Weel folk, it's like this. I've aye yearned tae be an official beggar since ma mither apprenticed me tae that pick-the- louse of a tailor. Him that let me fa' off the ironin' table frae want o' sleep stichin' duds for fairmers' gets from Ballochmyle tae Balloch. It turned me intae a cripple. But the city o' Mungo, Glesga, has recently honoured me for educatin' its citizens for mony years, and presented me wi' this blue gown, an' makin' me an official beggar! Last year I starved unofficially and this year I starve officially! Every stane o' flesh I lose is weighed in a proper Tron weighin' machine, recorded and approved. Like the Provost himself, I have a badge of office! Like maist o' you wastrels, I'll gang intae a pauper's grave, but they'll keep the blue-gown for some other silly bugger! But dinnae fash yerselves, when I go, I'll come back tae haunt Glesga for a century or twa yet!

(ENTER ANDREW HARDIE AND HIS SWEET-HEART, MARGARET, HAND IN HAND).

JAMIE BLUE
There's a brave few years left in ye still, Hawkie.

VOICES
'Queer Folk in The Shaws' Jamie!

JAMIE BLUE
A' right then. Have it your ain way!

(SINGS)

Who never unto The Shaws has been,
has surely missed a treat.
For wonders there are to be seen.
which nothing else can beat.
The folks are green, it's oft been said,
of that you'll find no trace,
There's seasoned wood in every head
and brass in every face.
Look smart and keep your eyes about,
their tricks will make you grin.
The Barrhead coach will take you out.
The folks will take you in!

(CHEERS FROM CROWD).

HAWKIE
It's like this ye see. Pollokshaws is waging an undeclared war against Glesga. It wants to retain its independence. No' to be absorbed into oor growing slum lands o' Gorbals and the like. Jamie here, frae whit I gather, lives in a meadow 'a tween the two districts. Being a plebeian at heart, he's firing a broad-side on behalf of' the toon folk.

MARGARET (TO ANDREW)
Look at the wee lad wi' the skippin' rope. I never saw anyone so lithe and agile!

ANDREW
That's Feea. the stray wain o' the city. All the bairns know him. The poor lad has lived in these streets for years. Maist folk are kind tae him. but there are some who taunt him. He's a hairmless laddie and whit an acrobat! I hear he can throw a ba' owre Nelson's Monument on the Green and catch it before it lands. He can leap the Saltmarket and dive intae the Clyde frae the Stockwell Brig.

MARGARET
Will we daunder doon the Saltmarket tae the Green, Andrew?

ANDREW
What day is this?

MARGARET
The second of April, eighteen-twenty...

ANDREW
I thought maybe it was the first of April, All Fools Day—but anyway let's dae something daft!

MARGARET
Like what?

ANDREW
Like holding up the Gallowgate and the Eglinton Barracks, disarming the troops and declaring a free Scotland!

MARGARET
Just the two of us. We'd surely end up in the Parliamentary Road Asylum!

ANDREW
A right apt street they picked for an asylum. Tell ye what. We'll visit my old grandfather in Toonheid. Whit d' you say Margaret?

MARGARET
As you wish. (THEY LINK ARMS AND GO UP HIGH STREET. THE CROWDS AT THE CROSS HAVE DISPERSED) I'd so glad you've left the Army, Andrew. You'll never know how much I missed you all that time. I'm happy you're back at the weaving, though I know there's no' much siller in it. Maybe, someday, it'll be on the mend.

ANDREW
Sad tae say, Margaret, every few years bring a crisis; the wages fa' or else we're oot o' work completely. The last couple o' years has been a scunner, I don't understand economics much, but the system seems a never ending road o' peaks and troughs; boom and crash. No one could plan for a future in a set-up like that. The weavers are a' sick tae a man o' it. But whit can be done? Whit's the road oot?

MARGARET
I feel the same mysel' at times, and then I try tae pray and hope.

ANDREW
Look Margaret. Look at the corner o' Duke Street. there's folk gathered aroon the postbox at the corner. I wunner whit they're gawking' at? Let's hurry! (THE COUPLE GO UP TO THE POST BOX. ANDREW SQUEEZES BETWEEN A FEW PEOPLE AND STARTS READING ALOUD A PROCLAMATION ON THE WALL) 'Friends and countrymen! Rouse from that torpid state in which we have been sunk for many years, we are at length compelled from the extremity of our sufferings and the contempt heaped upon our petitions for redress, to assert our rights at the hazards of our lives; and proclaim to the world the real motives, which, if not misrepresented by designing men, have reduced us to take up arms for the redress of our common grievances. The enormous public meetings held throughout the country…'

JAMES HARDIE, JUSTICE OF THE PEACE (PUSHING HIS WAY THROUGH

THE CROWD AND TEARING THE NOTICE DOWN)
How dare you read aloud this seditious literature?

ANDREW
How dare you sir, tear the bill down. I'm putting it back.

JAMES HARDIE
I have every right to prevent you from reading such treason. I am Mr. James Hardie, Justice of the Peace in Anderston.

ANDREW
Anderston? Is that right? Are ye no' far travelled then? (TAKING MARGARET'S HAND) Come on lass, let's get awa' frae this mandarin. (A FEW YARDS AWAY A MAN SIDLES UP TO ANDREW).

MAN (A GOVERNMENT AGENT PROVOCATEUR)
I see you are interested in this affair. Do you live in the vicinity?

ANDREW
Not far frae here. I live in the Drygate.

MAN
Well don't miss the meeting in the Townhead on Tuesday. We need good men to be there.

ANDREW
You can count on me. (MAN EXITS).

MARGARET
I don't like this at all, Andrew. I'm afraid. Don't do anything foolish, I need you so much. It may be a trick. Remember whit we said about All Fools Day?

(END OF ACT 3, SCENE 1)

ACT 3, SCENE 2

BALLAD SINGER
At Germiston on the fourth of April,
a band of weavers, they gathered there.
They proudly swore they're chains to sever,
or tae old Glasgow return nae mair.
Young Andrew Hardie, they chose their leader.
an honest lad wha plied the loom.

(SCENE: GERMISTON. DISTRICT, A HALF MILE NORTH OF GLASGOW CROSS. IN THE BACKGROUND SEVERAL FACE EACH OTHER IN A CIRCLE. THEY ARE FOR THE MOST PART, WEAVERS. THE AGENT, TURNER, IS ADDRESSING THE MEN).

TURNER
The Secret Committee of the Provisional Government has just received positive information that the great Insurrection has already commenced in England. And as a signal of this, the coach from Carlisle will not arrive in Glasgow tomorrow. (CHEERS) The company here assembled will march to Condorrat, where you will be joined by another large body of men. Then on to our objective, the great arms factory at Carron, where the workers have struck and are eager to deliver to you stacks of real arms and ammunition. Yes, even cannon guns. (LOUD CHEERS).

DOUGALD SMITH
I have been asked to take command of this party. But tell me, Mr Turner, where are the hundreds promised to us from Anderston and other districts?

TURNER
Some of them will find separate routes to join up at Condorrat. Of that you may be sure.

DOUGALD SMITH
I wish I could be! How on earth could a handful o' men with pikes an' muskets face up to a company o' dragoons, or even the yeomanry, on the way tae Carron? We'd a' be slaughtered!

TURNER
There'll be no troops to confront you on the march to Carron.

DOUGALD SMITH (SUSPICIOUSLY)
An' tell me how'd you know that?

TURNER
Many of the soldiers are for reform, just like yourselves. In England there are mass desertions from the army to the radical cause.

DOUGALD SMITH
For all you say, I still smell a rat. I'm no gonna lead the lads to their death. I don't forget the spy Richmond, three years since.

VOICE
Coward!

DOUGALD SMITH
Call me what you will. Reason guides me!

ANDREW
Let's no quarrel. I canna see all the works striking, all the troops in Eglinton and Gallowgate barracks, all the proclamations on the walls, all the general tension; if there isnae somethin' fannin' the flames of revolution! If we fail, out of suspicion or whatever, to seize this chance tae assert oor rights, how could we ever ease our conscience or claim tae be true sons o' Wallace an' the fearless patriots of Scotland!

TURNER
Nobly said! Well, Smith?

DOUGALD SMITH
I'm still no' convinced. Too many lives are at stake! And whit about our wives and bairns?

TURNER
You decline the leadership of a gallant band?

DOUGALD SMITH
I dae! I dinnae ken whit's goin' on?

VOICE
Me too! (AN ANGRY UPROAR).

ANDREW
Let there be nae rancour! We're a' volunteers. Anyone wha feels like oor delegate has the right tae withdraw. There's nae compulsion. (A NUMBER OF MEN LEAVE THE RANKS).

TURNER
Well, that's settled. We'll need to pick a leader in lieu of Smith.

VOICES
Andra Hardie! Andra Hardie!

TURNER
Yes indeed, and who better. I understand, Mr Hardie, that you have some military experience? Form the men up and proceed to Condorrat. Here's this half-card. A man called Baird will meet you there with the other half of the card to match this. He shall assume leadership there, with you as second-in command. The Provisional Government will take note of your services.

ANDREW HARDIE
I dae this with nae desire for ony reward but the freedom of Scotland. Scotland free frae wealthy oppressors and tyrants!

(THE WEAVERS MARCH OFF LEAVING TURNER AND SMITH AND THE MEN WHO OPTED OUT. STANDING A DISTANCE FROM THE OTHERS, TURNER SLOWLY SKULKS AWAY. DOUGALD SMITH AND THE OTHERS WATCH HIM).

DOUGALD SMITH
You'll notice he's no leading them to capture the Carron Iron Works. Oh, no! He's needed for whit he cries 'liaison'. Glesga wid lose a' links wid the great revolution if it wisnae for Mr Turner. I can tell ye this lads, I'm mair than a little suspicious o' that yin and his cronies. I wish tae God that Andra Hardie an' the ithers had heeded me. I wish they had.

(END OF ACT 3, SCENE 2)

ACT 3, SCENE 3

(ENTER THE BELLOWING BUFFOON IN THE SHAPE OF HUMPTY DUMPTY DRESSED TO THE FRONT OF THE EGG WITH THE UNION JACK AND ON HIS HEAD, A TILE HAT WITH THE PIRATE'S FLAG, SKULL AND CROSS BONES ON IT. HE HOLDS HAWKIE BY THE EAR WITH ONE HAND AND JAMIE BLUE WITH THE OTHER BUFFOON).

BUFFOON
I caught these two loafers at Glasgow Cross. (TWEAKS HAWKIE'S EAR) Where did I catch you?

HAWKIE
Ouch! At Glasgow Cross.

BUFFOON (TO JAMIE BLUE)
And where did I catch you?

JAMIE BLUE
At Glasgow Cross.

BUFFOON
They were singing revolting ballads and handing out seditious literature. (He lets go of the two men). Now isn't that disgusting for true born loyal Scotsmen. Sorry, I mean North Britons! His gracious and royal and most honourable Majesty, King George IV came to visit Edinburgh in this most glorious year of his reign 1820. He came to visit Edinburgh (aside) he wouldn't touch Glasgow with a ninety foot pole! He came to honour Edinburgh

with a view of his portly physiognomy. And our royal bard, Sir Walter Scott wrote a lovely song of servile welcome. And do you know, and do you know what? A disgraceful weaver by the name of Sandy Rodgers had the nerve and the cheek as well, to write a combustible parody on it! (HE CATCHES JAMIE BLUE'S EAR AGAIN). And do you know what I caught this fella, this street mendicant doing? Singing! He was singing that vile parody. Come on! What were you doing!

JAMIE BLUE
Singing.

BUFFOON
All right then. Let the good folk hear what you were singing. (HE PUSHES JAMIE BLUE WHO MOVES FORWARD).

JAMIE BLUE
An' I'll tell you this. I'm no one bit ashamed of it. (HE SINGS BOLDLY).

Sawny, now the king's come,
Sawney, now the king's come.
Kneel and kiss his precious bum,
Sawney, now the king's come!
In Holyroodhouse, lodge his snug,
And butter weel his sacred lug.
Wi stuff wad gar a Frenchman ugg
Sawney, now the king's come!
Tell him he is great and good,
An' comes fae Scottish royal blood
Tae yer hunkers, lick his fud
Sawney, now the kings' come!
And if there's in St James' Square,
Ony thing that's fat and fair,
Treat him nightly with such ware,
Sawney, now the king's come.
Show him a' your biggings braw,
Our castle, college, brigs and a',
Your jail and royal forty-twa,
Sawney, now the king's come.
An' when he rides Auld Reekie through,
Tae bless ye wi' a kingly view
Greet him wi your 'Gardyloo'
Sawney, now the king's come!

BUFFOON
No wonder his Royal Majesty wouldn't come near Glasgow with such abominable treason

circulating the arteries of the city.

HAWKIE
If you want my opinion, Royal George was shipped tae Scotland by Lord Sidmouth tae rally all the true blue Tories an' toadies of this bartered land. In my opinion, 'twas naught but a showy circus of the idle rich tae taunt an' cow the millions of poor in their desperate need!

BUFFOON
But who would heed or ask the opinion of the likes of you? An ailing creature of the God-forsaken wynds and dunnies in the lower depths of Glasgow!

JAMIE BLUE
Oor day will dawn!

BUFFOON
God forbid!

JAMIE BLUE
We have a better chance of that happenin' than you camels have of climbin' through the eye of a needle!

BUFFOON (PUTS HIS HANDS TO HIS EARS)
I know what's botherin' you pair. It's the breakin' o' the strike and the Radical Wet Wednesday has you in the dumps. Imagine the nerve and audacity of a handful of ragged, half-starved weavers of Glasgow and Strathaven taking on the might and glory of the British Army. The victors at Blenheim and Waterloo!

HAWKIE
What about Peterloo? You were very brave there as well, mowing down defenceless women at a peaceful demonstration! Brave men on horseback wi' flashin' sabres. Heroes, indeed! (TO THE REAR OF THE STAGE, THE BAREFOOT FEEA ENTERS WITH A WHEEL BARROW).

BUFFOON
Tell me where are your weavers that set out for Carron-side? Where are they now? I'll tell you where they are, rotting in the dungeons of Stirling Castle! And like all conspirators against law and order, it's the right place for them! (AS THE BUFFOON IS RANTING AWAY, HAWKIE MAKES A SIGNAL FOR FEEA TO BRING THE WHEEL BARROW BEHIND THE FOOL. WHEN HE DOES SO, HE TILTS THE BARROW, WHILE JAMIE AND HAWKIE PUSH THE BUFFOON INTO IT).

FEEA
Will we dump him in the Clyde, Hawkie?

HAWKIE
Naw! Naw! Scum floats to the surface an' we want tae keep oor good old Clyde clean. We'll find a dirty puddle for his sort!

(END OF ACT 3, SCENE 3)

ACT 4, SCENE 1

(SCENE: THE STUDY OF HENRY HOME DRUMMOND'S RESIDENCE AT BLAIR-DRUMMOND, NEAR STIRLING. JULY 1820. JAMES HARDIE J P AND HENRY DRUMMOND ARE IN DEEP DISCUSSION).

DRUMMOND
All the prisoners have been returned to Stirling Castle from Edinburgh where they were detained for the convenience of the Crown lawyers. The trial as you know, is set to be here in Stirling on the 13th July, in about ten days' time. I am glad, Mr Hardie, to offer you the hospitality of Blair-Drummond for as long as you care to stay.

JAMES HARDIE
I feel privileged indeed to be in such fine surroundings. A very pleasant change from the suburbs of Anderston in Glasgow.

DRUMMOND
Besides, I have some important points to discuss with you. I would like you to remain here until the trial of Baird, Hardie and the others is over. By the way, you are not in any way related to the Hardie in the dock?

JAMES HARDIE
Good heavens, no! Not in any way, Your Alsatian hound might, broadly speaking, be related to the wolf! To tell you the truth Mr Drummond, the common surname that the prisoner and I hold, is something of an embarrassment to me. I am ashamed that a Hardie could be involved in such criminal, treasonable activities.

DRUMMOND (SMILING).
Of course! Please excuse my referring to it at all. You understand that I will not be appearing as a Crown lawyer in Stirling?

JAMES HARDIE
Yes.

DRUMMOND
Sir William Rae has been chosen as Lord Advocate to be assisted by an able English barrister, Mr Sergeant Hullock. (RISING AND PACING THE ROOM). Ever since that

debacle with the witness, Campbell, three years ago in Edinburgh, there has been an uncomfortable stigma, a certain distrust, hanging over me. Lords Sidmouth and Castlereagh are determined this time to ensure conviction and execution of the prisoners. There is to be no bungling on this occasion. And I would like to assure you that I am as anxious as the noble Lords to see this case through to its proper conclusion. Behind the scenes a little, I am assisting the Crown in vindicating my absolute loyalty. The conviction of these prisoners is most vital to me.

JAMES HARDIE
And every bit as important to me, sir. You have my complete assurance Mr Drummond!

DRUMMOND
And confidence?

JAMES HARDIE
And confidence. I was assured by the most prominent men in Glasgow that I could reveal all that you wished to know. In return Mr Drummond, I know that you will later use your good influence to assist me realise a certain ambition I have treasured for years.

DRUMMOND
But of course Mr Hardie, or may I call you James? That goes without saying, I had you brought to Blair-Drummond several days before the trial because we have several things to discuss and I learned that you are the recipient of valuable information. I understand you know the names of agent provocateurs in Glasgow?

JAMES HARDIE
Yes. Three of them live in my own district, Anderston. Their names are Craig, King and Turner. Another man Lees is English spoken and most likely recruited in the Fleet Prison.

DRUMMOND
Where are they now?

JAMES HARDIE
Safely abroad. Most likely at Cape Town, South Africa, and well paid.

DRUMMOND
Were any of them ever in the hands of the Glasgow Police?

JAMES HARDIE
Yes, Craig was, for a short time. He was drilling his dupes at night on the Sauchiehall Road when one of his men's pike broke a street lamp. The men scattered, but the police caught Craig and took him to the prison in Anderston. He was already charged when I reached the station, but the next morning I saw Mr Houldsworth.

DRUMMOND
Mr Houldsworth?

JAMES HARDIE
The manufacturer and chief magistrate of Anderston.

DRUMMOND
Why James? Why should you see him?

JAMES HARDIE
Under no circumstances did we want these agents detained. They were to proceed unhindered and indeed, I might say assisted. I saw Mr Houldsworth and assured him that Craig was, how should I put it, one of ours! He was fined five shillings by Mr Houldsworth and because Craig had no money on him at the time, the magistrate paid the five shillings out of his own pocket.

DRUMMOND (LAUGHING)
The magistrate paid out of his own pocket? By Jove, that's comical indeed. Worthy of a Fielding or a Smollet novel. Eh?

JAMES HARDIE
I didn't see much humour in it at the time. I found it a perfect nuisance. Why fine him at all?

DRUMMOND
You know who printed the treasonable proclamation?

JAMES HARDIE
Yes, we know who printed it; where it was delivered; and the numbers involved in its distribution. In fact, it was Craig and Lees arranged and paid for its printing. It was distributed from one of their houses in my district, Anderston. That's why I was up so early that Sunday morning, Mr Drummond. I knew everything that was going on, especially in my own district. That morning I extended my surveillance to the east of Glasgow, about two miles or so from Anderston. And, of course, all the districts were plastered with proclamations calling everyone to strike and revolution.

DRUMMOND
Who wrote the proclamation?

JAMES HARDIE
I cannot say for certain, but is uncannily like the 'Treasonable Oath' of our friend Richmond. The phrasing is so similar.

DRUMMOND
Continue, James with your travels to the East of Glasgow that Sunday morning.

JAMES HARDIE
I knew that there would be no uprising in Anderston.

DRUMMOND
How did you know that?

JAMES HARDIE
All ostentation. Display, lights burning at night, leaflets being delivered and pike handles and heads. It was too much, too overt and everyone was suspicious. In the back streets of Brigton and Duke Street, I sensed there was the more likely source of revolt. So I made eastwards. My hopes were rewarded. I found a bunch of men, mostly weavers, gathered eagerly around the Proclamation.

DRUMMOND
And as Justice of the Peace, you rightly forbade them to read, let alone heed, seditious literature?

JAMES HARDIE
One of them, Andrew Hardie, the prisoner, turned on me quite angrily, more or less told me to proceed on my business. I gave him as good in return and provoked him into retorting that his blood would need to be shed before I'd be allowed to take down the Proclamation. Then I was jostled on to the street. Here was the kind of stalwart Craig and King and the others needed!

DRUMMOND
Who jostled you into the street?

JAMES HARDIE
There were several of them. I just cannot exactly remember.

DRUMMOND
Was the prisoner one of them?

JAMES HARDIE
Most probably. He was the one who expressed most opposition to my tearing down the notice.

DRUMMOND (SHAKING HIS HEAD)
In a court of law, you will need to be much more specific, James, or the case won't hold.

You will have to declare under oath that the accused seized you by the lapels or caught you by the middle and ejected you, a Justice of the Peace, off the Glasgow pavement. Nothing, but nothing less, will do James, if you do not wish to be a discredited witness. My arch enemy, Jeffrey is defending Hardie, and take it from me James; he will make you appear a perfect idiot if you show the least sign of wavering inconsistency. I learned all this to my cost in 1817, a lesson for which I have paid dearly. Have a stroll in the orchard James, and think it over! I have another witness to see shortly. (JAMES HARDIE RISES TO LEAVE).

JAMES HARDIE
I'll take a stroll as you suggest, Mr Drummond. But rest assured, on the day I shall not be found wanting.

DRUMMOND
Oh, before you go James, since you have placed such open-hearted confidence in me, I think it only my duty to repay you in some small measure. You mentioned earlier some sort of treasured ambition you entertain. Well, James, speaking recently to Mr Kirkman Findlay, in Glasgow, he mentioned, if I remember correctly, some sort of vacancy which might occur in the police supervision of that city. Yes?

JAMES HARDIE
That is perfectly correct, Mr Drummond. The present Superintendent of the Glasgow Police is coming on in years. He could, if the powers that be see fit, he could be, well, retired gracefully on superannuation. And, well, I don't see any reason why not!

DRUMMOND
Nor I, James. Nor I! For your zeal for law and order against the rampaging reformers, you have behaved admirably. I hear you dragged some of the scoundrels, posing as respectable citizens, out of bed and clamped them in jail; then their houses were ransacked for secret correspondence! That will shake the ruffians!

JAMES HARDIE
The Glasgow Police are too easy going; they need discipline.

DRUMMOND
I'll vouch for this, Mr Hardie, you'd fit the bill admirably!

JAMES HARDIE
Indeed sir! We badly need some fresh blood! (HE EXITS).

DRUMMOND (STARTLED)
Fresh blood? Oh, yes, I see what you mean. Yes, indeed, we could so with more of that! (HE RINGS FOR SERVANT).

SERVANT
Yes sir?

DRUMMOND
Should a young man of the Kilsyth Yeomanry, a Mr Nichol Hugh Baird arrive, would you show him in.

SERVANT
He has already arrived, sir.

DRUMMOND
Show him here straightway then! (ENTER NICHOL H BAIRD, A SLIM. RATHER NERVOUS YOUNG MAN OF HIGH PERSONAL CONCEIT. DRUMMOND SHOWS HIM TO A CHAIR AND TAKES AN ARMCHAIR FACING HIM). I want you, Mr Baird, to put yourself completely at ease in my company. I can assure you that our conversation shall proceed no further than this room. The Crown Lawyers have informed me that you were wavering in your evidence against the Radical conspirators? That you even tried to flee the country to escape going into the witness box?

NICHOL BAIRD
I'm... I'm somewhat confused, sir. I... I don't know what to do!

DRUMMOND
Your precognition stated that you confronted ten or twelve weavers on the road and they demanded your arms. That you bravely answered that you would not give them your pistol, but willingly, let them have, if they dared, its contents. What has made you waver, Mr Baird? I swear I must know the answer to this!

NICHOL BAIRD
It... it was... it was the men in the Company, sir!

DRUMMOND
In the Kilsyth Yeomanry?

NICHOL BAIRD
Yes. Yes, sir!

DRUMMOND
Why?

NICHOL BAIRD
They must, they must have heard something sir. When I first told them that I had confronted the weavers single-handed, they were so proud of me! But now, they no longer

believe me. They say that local farmers didn't see me on that road at all! They laugh and jeer and call me 'Hercules' and 'Jack the Giant Killer'!

DRUMMOND
I'm warning you, Mr Baird. You'd better go into that witness box and stick to your precognition. Otherwise you may find yourself in the dock! You are not surely going to allow yourself to be cowed by your comrades and ignorant farmers? Are you? You have committed yourself to the side of the law and you must stand by it.

NICHOL BAIRD
I was boasting sir… and my conscience, sir… my conscience!

DRUMMOND
Damn your conscience! Your freedom's in jeopardy, I warn you! You wanted to flee the country. Did you fear that friends of the weavers would threaten your life? Well, what if I assure you that after you have given your evidence, you will be given safe passage to North America, where I believe you have friends! You will also be given money to assist you there, and no disclosure to a soul of your whereabouts. Out there you can begin a new life away from your jeering comrades.

NICHOL BAIRD (TEARFULLY)
Oh, thank you! Thank you sir!

DRUMMOND (RISING AND PUTTING HIS TWO HANDS ON BAIRD'S SHOULDERS, HE RAISES HIM TO HIS FEET).
Pull yourself together, man. Go into that witness box in Stirling and face that Judge and Jury like a bold British Yeoman! You need fear no consequences. Do you understand?

NICHOL BAIRD
I… I'm so relieved, sir.

DRUMMOND
Off you go! I will assure the Crown of your resolution.

(BAIRD SALUTES AND MAKES HIS EXIT. DRUMMOND RINGS FOR HIS SERVANT AND INSTRUCTS HIM TO BRING A BOTTLE OF CLARET, POURS HIMSELF A LARGE GLASS).

Baird and Hardie versus Hardie and Baird! What a strange, almost unearthly coincidence! It sends a weird shudder down the spine. The great family of man! My God, what a cynical world you created with plenty of scope for us sinners!

(END OF ACT 4, SCENE 1)

ACT 4, SCENE 2

(AS ANDREW HARDIE AND THE OTHER PRISONERS WERE NOT IN THE DOCK TO MAKE ANY STATEMENTS, THE DEVICE OF A DIVIDED STAGE BY THE USE OF LIGHTING ARRANGEMENTS HAS BEEN USED. ONE PART OF THE STAGE, TO THE RIGHT, REPRESENTS THE HIGH COURT AT STIRLING ON THE 13TH JULY 1820. A SMALLER SECTION, STAGE LEFT, REPRESENTS ANDREW HARDIE'S CELL IN STIRLING CASTLE, WHERE, STILL IN IRONS, HE IS WRITING A LETTER TO HIS FRIENDS, AT THEIR REQUEST, FULLY DESCRIPTIVE OF THE EVENTS OF THE FATEFUL MARCH FROM GERMISTON IN GLASGOW TO THE FATEFUL 'BATTLE' OF BONNYMUIR. THIS LETTER IF SUBSTANTIALLY THE SAME AS HARDIE'S DECLARATION, WHICH WAS READ IN COURT BY THE CROWN, WITH A DIFFERENT EMPHASIS BY THEM, OF COURSE.) THE JUDGES, THE CROWN LAWYERS, MR SERGEANT HULLOCK, (BARRISTER), FRANCIS JEFFREY IN DEFENCE. MR KNAPP. CLERK OF ARRAIGNS).

FRANCES JEFFREY
My Lords, I wish to lodge an objection. I have nothing personal against Mr Sergeant Bullock, barrister, who has been sent from England to assist the prosecution, but I do not think he is competent to practise in the Scottish Court.

LORD PRESIDENT
It has not been without due consideration that Mr Bullock is being received in this Court. The Treaty of the Union between Scotland and England has assimilated the two countries, excepting the Laws. However, by that same Treaty, it was settled that the Law of Treason, and since, the Union, the distinction of English and Scottish advocates have ceased with reference to Courts of this description. Mr Hullock, therefore, is perfectly entitled to practise here. Objection overruled. Would the Clerk of Arraigns read the indictment!

MR KNAPP
That the prisoner Andrew Hardie, is accused of four counts of High Treason:
FIRST: That he did compass and imagine the death of His Majesty the King, a count which includes nineteen overt acts of Treason.
SECOND: That Andrew Hardie did levy war against the Crown forces.
THIRD: That Andrew Hardie did compass and intend to depose the King from the Style, Honour and Kingly name of the Imperial Crown of this Realm; with the same overt acts as in the first count.
FOURTH: That Andrew Hardie did compass to levy War against the King in order to compel him to change his measures.

LORD ADVOCATE
Gentlemen of the Jury, it will not be necessary for me to go back far previous to the ter-

rible events of the 5th April at Bonnymuir. It is, however fitting that I should notice that betwixt the night of Saturday, the 1st of April and Sunday morning the 2nd, there was posted up, all over the town of Glasgow and in various parts of the adjoining country, an address to the inhabitants of the United Kingdom, containing matters of the most treasonable nature. A copy of this abominable document is laid before you, and I will call as an early witness, a respectable Magistrate of Glasgow, Mr James Hardie, Justice of the Peace, who will swear on oath that he saw the accused, Andrew Hardie, eagerly absorbing with others, the contents of that pernicious and treasonable document. I call on Mr James Hardie as witness.

CLERK
Mr James Hardie, (JAMES HARDIE GOES TO WITNESS BOX AND CLERK HANDS HIM BIBLE) do you swear by almighty God that you shall tell the truth, the whole truth and nothing but the truth?

LORD ADVOCATE
Are you Mr Hardie, one of his Majesty's magistrates in Glasgow?

JAMES HARDIE
I am.

LORD ADVOCATE
I would like you to describe for the benefit of the Jury, what exactly transpired.

JAMES HARDIE
I was in Duke Street, in Glasgow, on Sunday morning, April 2nd, A crowd attracted my attention,. Among them I saw the prisoner. The people were looking at a placard on the wall which the prisoner was reading aloud. I was so placed that I could see that the prisoner was reading it word for word exactly. I pressed through the crown with the intent of pulling it down. I was prevented by the prisoner who jostled me off the pavement and seized me by the collar. I told the prisoner that it was an improper, illegal paper. He immediately demanded my authority. I told him that many persons in Glasgow knew I was a Magistrate. The prisoner then said that before he would allow anyone to take the placard down he was prepared to shed the last drop of his own blood. I made another attempt to remove the placard, but I was prevented by the prisoner with the assistance of others. Four or five persons were involved but the accused was the most active.

LORD ADVOCATE
Thank you Mr Hardie.

FRANCIS JEFFREY
Are you really a Magistrate of Glasgow, Mr Hardie?

JAMES HARDIE
I am.

FRANCIS JEFFREY
Come, come, Mr Hardie. Let's have your real function. Are you a real Magistrate of the town Council?

JAMES HARDIE
Well. No. I am, however, a Justice of the Peace, and I have rendered the Magistrates of Glasgow, long and loyal service.

FRANCIS JEFFREY
I am sure you have. That is all. Mr Hardie.

(SPOTLIGHT ON ANDREW HARDIE WRITING HIS LETTER FROM STIRLING JAIL).

ANDREW HARDIE
My Dear Friends, Stirling Castle, 1st August 1820. I will not trouble you with an account of my imprisonment, but shall close this letter with a few observations on my trial and witnesses. The first in order, is Mr Hardie. It is not at all necessary that I should give you the sum of his evidence. I do not deny preventing him from taking down the Bill, without asking his authority for doing so; neither shall I mention the abusive language he gave to me, nor what I said to him. But as I have a good and just God to answer, and to whom I must give answer and to whom I give account of my actions in a very short time, I hope you will form a more favourable opinion of me, that I would tell no lies. He says that I seized him by the collar, and drove him off the pavement twice, but it is very strange that I mind all that passed and cannot charge my memory with doing so! The next I shall mention is Nichol Hugh Baird!

(SPOTLIGHT SWITCHES TO LORD ADVOCATE).

LORD ADVOCATE
My next witness is Nichol Hugh Baird of Kilsyth Yeomanry.

CLERK
Mr Nichol Hugh Baird! (BAIRD GOES INTO WITNESS BOX)

LORD ADVOCATE
Where do you reside?

NICHOL HUGH BAIRD
Kelvinhead, but I am presently in the Kilsyth Yeomanry.

LORD ADVOCATE
Will you describe for the benefit of the jury what happened on the 5th April last?

NICHOL HUGH BAIRD
I was on duty with the troops at Falkirk in April last and had leave of absence on the fifth of that month. On my road to Falkirk I overtook a dozen or so men who... who planted themselves across the road and obstructed my passage. One of them, Hardie, the accused, stepped forward and I asked him to divide the road with me, to let me pass. He answered that he would be damned if he would. They then demanded my pistol.

LORD ADVOCATE
And what, Mr Baird, was your reply?

NICHOL HUGH BAIRD
I instantly drew my pistol and presented it at them. I said I would rather give them the contents of it. I then rode back to Kilsyth.

LORD ADVOCATE
Thank you, Mr Baird.

(SPOTLIGHT SWITCHES BACK TO ANDREW HARDIE IN STIRLING JAIL).

ANDREW HARDIE
This Nichol Hugh Baird of the Kilsyth Yeomanry Cavalry actually swore that he met ten of us on the road; that we demanded his arms and he in return presented his pistol to us, saying he would give us the contents before he would do so. In the name of common-sense what would tempt this coxcomb to swear such a notorious lie as this—to face and frighten, ten or twelve unarmed men—he is worthy of being classed with Sir William Wallace. I am astonished, after such a feat, he did not petition the Officer of the Hussars to fight the whole of us at Bonnymuir himself. But he had done enough for one day! But the truth of the matter is this. We never saw him on the road at all! He had got notice of our approach, and putting more trust in the swiftness of his horse than in his own valour, or either turned or hid himself until we passed. I understand there are about twenty people who could testify that he did not pass until we were off the road altogether. I told one of my counsel it was altogether lies. My suffering country! As I am within view of being hurried into the arms of my Almighty Judge, I remain under the firm conviction that I die a martyr in the cause of truth and justice, and in the hope that you will succeed in the Cause which I took up arms to defend! May God send you a speedy deliverance from your oppressors!

(SPOTLIGHT RETURNS TO LORD ADVOCATE).

LORD ADVOCATE
I have nothing further to do but now pronounce sentence of death on all prisoners pres-

ently convicted of High Treason in this Court. In the instances of Andrew Hardie and John Baird, this sentence will be carried out in the town of Stirling on the 8th of September 1820. May the Lord have mercy on your souls!

(END OF ACT 4, SCENE 2)

ACT 4, SCENE 3

(MARGARET McKEIGH'S HOME IN TOWNHEAD, GLASGOW. A SMALL, SIMPLE WORKING-CLASS RESIDENCE. MARGARET, WHO WAS ALWAYS A BONNY, FORTHRIGHT LASS, WORTHY OF SUCH AN HONEST AND COURAGEOUS MAN AS ANDREW HARDIE, IS NOW TRANSFORMED BY HER INTENSE ANGUISH OVER THE MANY MONTHS SINCE APRIL INTO A WOMAN OF TRAGIC BEAUTY. IT IS SEPTEMBER 9TH, 1820. A SLOW MOURNFUL BELL RINGS IN THE STREET OUTSIDE. A LETTER IS LYING FOLDED ON THE TABLE. MARGARET WIPES THE TEARS FROM HER EYES AND TAKES THE LETTER UP TO READ. THE VOICE OF ANDREW HARDIE READING THE LETTER).

Stirling Castle, 7th September 1820.

My dear and loving Margaret,

May providence send his ministering angels and soothe you with the balm of comfort! O, may they approach the beauteous mourner and tell you that your lover lives—triumphs—lives, though condemned, lives to a nobler life. My dear Margaret, I hope you will not take this as a dishonour that your lover died for his distressed, wronged, suffering and insulted country; no my dear Margaret, I know you are possessed of nobler ideas than that, and well do I know that no person of feeling or humanity will insult you with it. I have every reason to believe it will be the contrary. I die firm to the cause in which I embarked, and yet we are outwitted and betrayed, yet I protest, as a dying man, it was done with a good intention on my part. But well did you know my sentiments on that subject long before I was taken prisoner. No man could have induced me to take up arms to rob or plunder. No, my dear Margaret, I took them for the restoration of those rights for which our forefathers bled, and which we have shamefully allowed to be wrested from us. But I trust that the innocent blood which will be shed tomorrow, in place of being a terror, will awaken my countrymen, my poor, suffering countrymen, from that lethargy which has so over clouded them! You will give my dying love to your father and mother, James and Agnes, Mrs Connell and Jean Buchanan. At the expense of some tears, I destroyed your letters. Again farewell, my dear Margaret, may God attend you still, and all your soul with consolation fill, is the sincere prayer of your most constant and affectionate lover while on earth. Andrew Hardie.

(MARGARET, WHO SITTING AT A SMALL TABLE WHILE READING THIS, BREAKS DOWN AND CRIES. A FEW SECONDS LATER A KNOCK COMES TO THE DOOR, AND DRYING HER EYES, SHE LETS IN ANDREW'S MOTHER,

THE WIDOW HARDIE; HER FRIEND ANNIE BRICE (THE BLEACHER LASS FROM THE CALTON, NOW 52 YEARS OF AGE). THE WIDOW HARDIE, THEN ANNIE, EMBRACE MARGARET).

ANNIE
God knows an' I know what the pair o' you are goin' through. I lost my ain Tam, thirty three years ago this month. Aye, god knows what it's like. I was nineteen at the time. The same age as yourself, Margaret.

WIDOW HARDIE.
Annie's been the great comfort to me Margaret. Not only the noo, but through the lang years. We first met down at the Green by Airn's Well. At the bleachin' wisn't it Annie? An' us singing merrily, ye'd think we hadn't a care in the world, or a dark cloud tae shroud our life wi'! Annie dear, tell the Lass whit happened tae yer sweetheart. It'll maybe lift oor minds frae Andra for a moment.

ANNIE
I mind weel, my Tam and his best freen, Jamie, staunin' as large as life at a corner o' the Calton. 'Dinnae fash yersel' lass' says he. 'You and I will be married yet when the bright day comes.' Three days later, the massacre in the street. The shoutin' and the screamin', an' the guns blazin' frae the sojers, and the magistrates roarin' them on! There wis nae bright day comin', unless it was at the end of a rainbow. Tam went doon in a daurk pool o' blood. Ithers were killed on the spot. Tam was made a cripple an' he died that winter. That mony, mony years ago noo!

WIDOW HARDIE
Aye, it's mair than thirty years. After that there was 1803, 1807. 1812, 1814, right up tae noo. An' for the hand-loom weavers, It's been a life o' hell and high water, with hardly a year o' rest or respite! I mind them all. And God knows this is the worst yet. If it wisnae for the help and comfort we gi'e each ither we'd be starvin', crawlin' brutes. The ministers hae no time for us but tae draw sweat and blood frae oor poor sinews. Is that a letter frae Andrew, Margaret?

MARGARET (LIFTING THE LETTER BUT KEEPING IT CLOSE TO HER)
It is Mrs Hardie. It's his last letter forever!

ANNIE
I would treasure it Meg, for that lad of yours was the salt of the earth. One in a million.

MARGARET
I know that Annie, and I'm so glad you and Mrs Hardie came. I wis feelin' kind o' sad and lonesome. (ANNIE CUDDLES HER).

WIDOW HARDIE

Oh. I can tell you this. I'm no goin' tae sit back and grieve at whit the flint hearted murderers did tae ma braw laddie. I'm goin' tae show up the scoundrels if I hae tae walk the pavements of Glasgow till my dyin' day. The lyin' newspapers cried him a low born idle conspirator; a product of the red republican alley ways o' the Clyde; a man who could scarce read! But I've kept every single letter he wrote frae the stinkin' dungeons. An' if I have to search the world itsel' I'll find a man tae publish them and show everybody the kind a' lad he wis! And I wunner' lass, could you make me a copy o' that letter frae Andra?

MARGARET

Oh, Mrs Hardie, I'd be only too pleased an' happy. I'd gie ye this one, only I want to treasure it and keep it close to me.

WIDOW HARDIE

Naw. Naw. A copy 'll dae fine. I want the weaver poet, Sandy Rogers, over in the Drygate to take a look at the letters first. He knows a man with a print shop in Howard Street. Aye! They think they've downed us women folk as weel, under the weight o' sorrow, but 'twas us gave life tae oor sons! And by all the merciful Jesus, we hae a bitter, bitter score to settle!

(END OF ACT 4, SCENE 3)

ACT 5, SCENE 1

(SCENE; A BOOKSHOP IN THE SALTMARKET, GLASGOW. IT'S OWNER, JAMES DUNCAN, IS CLEANING THE SHELVES WHEN RICHMOND, THE SPY, ENTERS. ALTHOUGH DUNCAN HAS HEARD OF RICHMOND'S ACTIVITIES, HE HAS NEVER SEEN HIM BEFORE. RICHMOND BROWSES THE BOOKS. IT IS LATE AFTERNOON OF THE 9TH FEBRUARY 1821).

DUNCAN

Can I help you sir?

RICHMOND

I see you have the latest on political economy?

DUNCAN

We try to keep up to date, but it's not easy. Most of the important publishers are in London. Are myou interested in some particular author or title?

RICHMOND

No. No. I just thought I'd take a look. In fact I came into your shop for a receipt stamp.

Do you stock them?

DUNCAN
Of course! What value do you require?

RICHMOND
Do you have a ten shilling stamp?

DUNCAN
A shilling one?

RICHMOND
No! Ten shillings, I said!

DUNCAN (SURPRISED)
Oh, I'm afraid I don't have a stamp of that high value in stock. I think you will have to try the larger bookshop, Brash and Reid, up the street at Glasgow Cross. It's just a few yards up. I'm sorry.

(RICHMOND FROWNS AND LEAVES THE SHOP. A FEW MINUTES LATER A WEAVER, LIVING NEXT DOOR, RUSHES INTO THE SHOP).

WEAVER (EXCITEDLY)
Mr Duncan! Mr Duncan! What in God's name is he doing in your premises? You shouldn't be seen with him, Mr Duncan. If word gets aroon that you're hob nobbin' wi Richmond, you're a ruined man!

DUNCAN (STARTLED)
Richmond? Was that Richmond?

WEAVER
Aye, Mr Duncan. Him that just left your shop. That was Richmond the spy. The scoundrel that got Andra McKinlay o' the Calton, framed on a treason charge, four years ago. An' then helped, frae Edinboro', to set up the agents in Glasgow to carry on the dirty work, that ended in oor lads being hanged in Stirling! Him and his friend were drinkin' o'er at the Globe Tavern. I saw him frae the winda' an' then he crossed the road alane.

DUNCAN
So that's the infamous Richmond? He came in here for a ten shilling receipt stamp. That covers no less than a thousand pounds upwards!

WEAVER
Good God! A thousand punds! Maist o' us is slavin' for three or four shillings a week. We

couldnae earn than sort of money for fifty or sixty years honest work. We jist couldnae! That wis Richmond's blood money, Mr Duncan. The creepin' Judas Iscariot has the nerve tae come back tae Glasgow tae collect the blood money for his foul deeds in the city! The brass neck o' the villain. He must be stopped Mr Duncan! He must be stopped!

DUNCAN (PUTTING ON HIS COAT).
I don't know about stopping him, but we must find out where his loot is coming from. I sent him to Brash and Reid's for the stamp. If I hurry he might still be there. The Chronicle newspaper office is a few doors away, so I will collect my friend MacDougall, the journalist, from there, to act as a witness. Would you look after the shop, Sandy?

WEAVER (AS DUNCAN LEAVES).
Nae bother at a'! Hurry, Mr Duncan. Hurry an' the weavers o' Glasgow will bless you for discoverin' the source o' the blood money! (Alone at the shop door). I never dreamed I'd see the day when Richmond, that creepin' spy, would be spied upon himsel'! I never thought I'd see the day!

(END OF ACT 5, SCENE 1)

ACT 5, SCENE 2

(GLASGOW CROSS, THE FIGURES OF JAMES DUNCAN AND RAB MacDOUGALL STANDING IN THE SHADOWS. A GLASGOW WARPER, WHITE, A COLLEAGUE OF RICHMOND'S STANDS AT THE DOOR OF BRASH AND REID'S. IT IS A COLD DAY AND AS RAB MacDOUGALL HAD ONLY A LIGHT JACKET, HE SHUFFLES IMPARTIENTLY IN THE COLD).

RAB
What the hell is keeping him?

DUNCAN
He's probably browsing through the books to evade any suspicion that he's in a hurry to grab his ill-gotten gains. Besides, from what I observed in my own shop, he has an irresistible desire to parade his enormous knowledge. He'll be giving old Reid a profound lecture on David Hume or Adam Smith, no doubt. But the way, who's the tubby gentleman standing at the door? Do you know him, by any chance?

RAB
That's a canny dicey customer called White, a warper from King Street, round the corner. In Richmond's less palmy days in Glasgow they two used to drink together in 'The Globe'. Ah! Here he's a coming out now to join his greasy friend.

DUNCAN
Look at him. He walks upright as if the gods of heaven smiled on his dark infamy. No

thought now for the decent men, his fellow weavers, he cast into the dark dungeons of Glasgow, Edinburgh and Stirling for weary months of heart breaking anguish. Nor the mothers, wives and hungry bairns. Such villains are the disgrace, the plague of any city. Come on, Rab. Let's follow them!

(WHITE AND RICHMOND WALK ROUND THE SHADOWED STAGE. SYMBOLISING THE STREETS OF GLASGOW, RAB AND DUNCAN FOLLOW AT A DISTANCE. RICHMOND OCCASIONALY CASTS A FEARFUL GLANCE OVER HIS SHOULDER, EVENTUALLY HE AND WHITE MOVE OFF-STAGE).

RAB (COMING TO CENTRE STAGE, AN AMAZED LOOK ON HIS FACE)
Jamie! Jamie!

DUNCAN
What is it Rab? What is it?

RAB
Did you see the house the pair of them went into? That's Reddie's place! Reddie, the Town Clerk of Glasgow. I don't believe it! I just don't believe it!

DUNCAN
Are you sure Rab? Are you sure?

RAB
More sure than my job on the Chronicle if I write an exposure of this. It's almost incredible Jamie. Oliver and Castles and the other spies and agent provocateurs responsible for Waterloo and the Cato Street conspiracies, were recruited from the Fleet and other prisons, but here we have the highest authorities in the City of Glasgow involved!

DUNCAN
Reddie, the Town Clerk, he's a friend of Kirkman Finlay!

RAB
His right hand man!

DUNCAN
Will Finlay be with Reddie and Richmond?

RAB
I doubt it very much. Kirkman Finlay is too cute a customer for that. After the revelations in London, I believe that canny gent will keep himself as much out of the picture as possible! He'll let Reddie do his dirty work.

DUNCAN
Ah, Rab, I'm beginning to see, I'm beginning to see the inner workings of it all. It's not so

intricate, when you come to think of it. I'll put it this way. Why did the Government of the day move heaven and hell to send Thomas Muir of Huntershill into transportation and his eventual death?

RAB

We all know, Jamie. It was to kill the Reform Movement in its infancy so that the corrupt boroughs and place-men would remain in office.

DUNCAN

As they did, Rab. As they did! And Lords Sidmouth, Castlereagh and the others, want that system to remain. And our 'friend' Kirkman Finlay is their chief agent in Glasgow to ensure that! But what, Rab, is to be Finlay's return for his fine services? Our brave Kirkman is too shrewd a business man to risk all this foul intrigue for nothing. Think back, Rab. Think back five years ago. Just five years ago, the year before McKinlay's arrest and the so-called 'Treasonable Oath'!

RAB

Five years ago? 1816?

DUNCAN

Aye, what great momentous event happened in Glasgow that year, Rab?

RAB (IT SUDDENLY DAWNS ON HIM)
The ship! Good Lord, the ship! Finlay's ship!

DUNCAN

Aye! Indeed! Finlay's ship! 'The Earl of Buckingham'! It took to the High Seas. Finlay's powerful cronies allowed him to trade wi' India. A first since the Act of Union in 1707 and a triumph for Finlay. This was his reward! Gold a plenty for him and his kind!

RAB (PULLING DUNCAN TO THE SIDE).
There's someone in Reddie's house approaching the window. But there's no sign of anyone coming out. Do we need further proof, Jamie?

DUNCAN

Yes. I'd like to know if Reddie himself is entertaining Richmond.

RAB

Wait a moment then! I think I have a ruse that might work. There's a police friend of Richmond's that used to come over from Edinburgh in the old days. I'm sure his name was Brown. You stay here Jamie.

(RAB GOES TO REDDIE'S DOOR AND KNOCKS. SERVANT COMES TO

DOOR).

SERVANT
What is it, sir?

RAB (BOLDLY)
Is Mr Richmond here?

SERVANT
Mr Richmond? There is no gentleman of that name here.

RAB
Yes, there is! He came here a considerable while ago and I am waiting to see him!

SERVANT
Very well, stop a little and I shall enquire.

(EXIT SERVANT).

SERVANT'S VOICE
There is a gentleman at the door, sir, waiting to see Mr Richmond.

REDDIE
Mr Richmond! Mr Richmond? Who is here that wants Mr Richmond?

RAB
I want him very particularly; I am one of his friends from Edinburgh!

REDDIE
Oh, very well, I will send him down to you in a minute. (EXIT REDDIE).

RICHMOND (COMING TO DOOR)
Who can be wanting me?

RAB
Mr Richmond. I am sorry to disturb you, but a friend of yours, a Mr Brown from Edinburgh, is very anxious to see you at The Globe Tavern in the Saltmarket.

RICHMOND
Tell him I will be down in a little.

RAB
Very well. Good evening to you, Mr Richmond (RICHMOND CLOSES DOOR. RAB

RETURNS TO DUNCAN IN THE SHADOWS).

DUNCAN (SHAKING RAB'S HAND GLEEFULLY). You don't need to tell me a thing. I saw and heard everything. What a pair of scoundrels. Have no doubt all Glasgow shall hear of this.

(END OF ACT 5, SCENE 2)

FINALE

(SEVERAL YEARS LATER. AT SIGHTHILL CEMETERY. WOODEN PAINTED REPLICA OF THE MARTYRS MONUMENT, TO THE LEFT OF STAGE. ANDREW WHITE STANDS NEAR MONUMENT, AWAITING THE ARRIVAL OF THE REMAINS OF BAIRD AND HARDIE FROM STIRLING IN THE AGREED TRANSFER BY THE AUTHORITIES AND THE MONUMENT COMMITTEE. THE CARETAKER APPROACHES ANDREW).

CARETAKER
I'm sorry sir, but only relatives an' very close friends can attend the burial.

ANDREW
Oh?

CARETAKER
Such are my instructions, sir.

ANDREW
Frae what source,. Might I ask?

CARETAKER
The high heed yins.

ANDREW
Certainly no the relatives! One might think they'd hae some say in the matter! Even though the brave lads have been dead mauny's a long year, their memory still frightens the life oot o' them that fear the truth.

CARETAKER
I know whit you mean sir, but I can tell you I'm acting on instructions frae the Commissioner of Police himself, Mr James Hardie.

ANDREW
Oh, that pleasant fellow! Is he still on the go? An' tell me, who advised him? It wisnae

Kirkman Finlay or Richmond or they Edinburgh lawyers, by any chance?

CARETAKER
Good heavens, no! Richmond bolted frae Scotland tae London, lang ago! An' Kirkman Finlay, he's gone oot o' politics completely!

ANDREW
No' before time!

CARETAKER
He retired tae his big estate and castle at Tower Point, doon by the Holy Loch at Dunoon.

ANDREW
Tae enjoy his ill-gotten gains frae all the wage slaves o' the Deanston Mills and the hauf starved natives in the tea plantations o' Bangladesh and India. I suppose he never got ower the guilty suicide of his friend, Lord Castlereagh, or the threatened impeachment of that other villain, Sidmouth? Tell me sir, if you know, whit happened tae that prime perjurer, Nichol Hugh Baird?

CARETAKER
Oh, he shot his bolt too! Like Richmond and several others. Tae the back woods of America I heard!

ANDREW
Tae bring the benefits of white civilisation tae the Indians nae doubt. Tae teach them tae cheat and lie, wi' the Bible in one hand and Machiavelli in the ither. Or maybe wi' the great bravado he showed at Carronside, he'll crush, single handed, ony revolt o' the slaves!

CARETAKER
All I know sir, is that the authorities absolutely refused tae allow a public funeral for Baird and Hardie.

ANDREW
I know that.

CARETAKER
You know?

ANDREW
Yes. Indeed! It winnae fur nothin' that after execution o' the two lads at Stirling an' their burial there, six sentries were posted there night and day frae September tae middle o' October tae mak' sure nae Glasgow sympathisers took their remains back to this city wi' honour. That wis lang years ago a' despite the slow, small measures o' reform, the authorities

are still afraid of the voice o' the people! Working class martyrs are dangerous folk. That's why they're kept oot o' establishment history books and hidden under mountains o' useless information an' royal rubbish. We werena' lang in Australia afore we heard all aboot it.

CARETAKER (CURIOSITY GREATLY ARISEN)
Australia? Were you a friend of the deceased?

ANDREW
I wis mair than a friend. I was a dear comrade. I wis only sixteen when I shouldered that prood pike on the road to Bonnymuir. The last of the jailed prisoners tae tak' a fearful fareweel o' Andra Hardie. I clung tae him till they wrenched us asunder. Then I was transported in chains in the foul hulks tae the convict settlements of Australia. the ithers settled there. some o' them married; ithers brought their wives oot from Glasgow. Their pardons came at long last. Noo, they're amongst the maist respected citizens of Australia, no' the chained convicts of an ignominious day. Their sons and daughters will bring credit and glory tae the land that gied refuge to their hunted fathers and exiled mothers.

CARETAKER (DELIGHTED)
It's Andra White, isn't it? I heard o' you. Shake hands, Andra. Shake hands! (THEY DO SO) I'm so proud to do just that. A bit foolhardy tae tak' that lang and dangerous road to Bonnymuir, maybe, but a brave wee laddie for a' that. A bonnie, game wee laddie! Ah. here's some of the mourners comin'. I'd best attend tae them.

(ENTER SEVERAL OF THE CAST INCLUDING WIDOW HARDIE, ANNIE BRICE. MARGARET McKEIGH, JAMIE BLUE, OLD HAWKIE, FRANCIS JEFFREY. ANDREW WHITE GOES FORWARD TO MEET THEM AND JOIN HANDS WITH MRS HARDIE AND MARGARET McKEIGH. ENTER JAMES DUNCAN AND PETER MACKENZIE, THE HISTORIAN OF GLASGOW).

WIDOW HARDIE
I cannae' thank ye enough, Mr McKenzie, for publishin' Andra and John's letters frae Stirlin' an' helpin' tae bring aboot this day and their vindication!

PETER
I had to do my duty, Mrs Hardie. I mysel' was deceived partially, jist for a time, mind ye! But they letters fairly opened my eyes tae the spy system that Glasgow suffered those mony years frae the die-hard Tories. Needless tae say, the pamphlets spread like wild fire all owre the city. If the gates here had been open tae the general public, the crowds would have reached tae Glasgow Green! Ah. Here's my friends, Jamie Blue and Old Hawkie. How's the town hospital treatin' ye, Hawkie?

HAWKIE
Almost as bad as the jail, Peter. they only let you oot for cheery occasions like funerals.

PETER
This is an occasion nae man'd like tae miss. A proud and memorable day.

ANDREW WHITE
It is that! I mind weel those years lang syne. Our hearts were steeled by the courage and callous fate o' the Calton Weavers o' 1787. Then the sufferin's o' Andra McKinley and his comrades in the dungeons in 1817. Oor march tae Bonnymuir wis not only for reform, but for the real freedom o' the workin' people. We still hae a lang, lang way to go, but the spirit of Baird and Hardie an' the Calton lads, and their braw, brave wimen folk is there tae guide us! And nae matter how lang or daurk or difficult, that day will surely dawn!

WIDOW HARDIE
For this I gave my son.

MARGARET McKEIGH
For this I gave my love.

(THE SCREEN AND SIDE CURTAIN OPEN TO THE CALTON MARTYRS STONE ALSO A HOST OF TRADE UNION BANNERS, REAR STAGE).

SONG: THE ROAD TAE BONNYMUIR.

END OF PLAY

NOTES

A Parody: Based on the well known poem by Joyce Kilmer.

Bonnymuir: The poem was recited at the Martyrs' Grave, Sighthill Cemetery in 1973.

Children of the Night: With an appended note in the archive: 'In a world very rich (for some) it is estimated that after 2000 years of so-called Christianity, there will be 100,000,000 homeless destitute children'.

Glen Masson: Based, apparently, on a true story as noted in *Glasgow Cross and Other Poems*: 'This poem describes the sad fate of an orphaned lad from Mull, who ran away from various foster homes on the mainland in an effort to return home to his island. The discovery of the unidentified bones led to a Government enquiry.'

Holy Cliff's Prayer: Printed with the note appended: 'dedicated to Cliff's fan, Tom Brown, the bloated windbag in the Daily Discord [aka *Daily Record*].'

John Cairney's Prayer: Dated 28th October 1987. John Cairney is a noted Scottish actor best known for his dramatised portrayal of Robert Burns on television.

On Balladier Bridge: Written in 1999 with the manuscript note: 'This is more of a song than a poem. it needs a beautiful Gaelic tune with the poignancy of *The Cuilean* or *Roisin Dubh*. Though written in the English language it is essentially Irish in feeling and thought. As close to James Clarence Morgan that I will ever strive. Like a poor fluttering moth to a bright burning candle.' Dromore is a small town in County Down.

Ora Pro Bonis: Published in *The United Scotsman*, February 1973.

Poison Pen: Written under the pen name Sebatino McGlame which Anderson sometimes employed in the 1970s.

Shy Couple: Written under the pen name Sebatino McGlame.

Song of a Spud: Dated 9th March 1976.

The Billionaire's Wife: The manuscript notes: 'reportedly based on on a true case reported in the *Daily Record*'.

The Blackberry Man: In 1986, a broadsheet featuring this poem with an illustration by John Gagahan was produced in a limited edition of 250 copies.

The Green Hills of Monaghan: Jim Friel notes that, in answer to the suggestion that there is a lack of County Monaghan songs, Anderson noted that there are many Gaelic songs from the county, and penned this in response.

The Malapropist: Written under the pen name Sebatino McGlame.

The Moonlighter: Printed as a broadsheet entitled 'Scotia Ballads, number 2' with the note: 'For those who don't know, the Glasgow moonlighter is not an uncommon form of exit from a house, when the factor, the HP hounder, etc become too much for the poor, oppressed tenant. The flitting is done in the wee sma' hours o' the mornin'.

The Orra Man: An orra man is a general farm worker skilled in a multitude of tasks.

The Polis o' Argyll: Recorded in the 'Ding Dong Dollar' songbook and album.

The Scabs of Nottingham: This refers to the miners' strike of 1984-85. Unlike in other parts of the country, many of the Nottinghamshire miners continued working.

The Spectre Inspector: Written under the pen name Sebatino McGlame.

The Stash Me Father Wore: Printed with the note appended: 'This song was composed and sung by Pope Paul when he was a communist prisoner in Poland. A full plenary indulgence will be granted to soloists and choristers who sings this gentle hymn'.

The Sunbright Flower of Peace: Anderson notes in an interview that this poem was translated into 'several languages'. However, no such translations have been found.

The Wee Folk: Dated 1972

The Workers Millennium: Dated December 1999. A handwritten note appended to the broadsheet refers to the third last line 'the continuation of brainwashing in the schools since we were infants'.

Waukrife—a Pectoral Encounter with Nessie: 'Waukrife' is a Scots term meaning unable to sleep.

A Ballad of Red Clyde I: Broadsheet appended with the following notes: 'Corra Linn—waterfall on the Clyde; hairst—harvest; bield—shelter; cottar—peasant farmer; biggings—houses (outhouses); hodden grey —poverty; mirky—dark; Haukenfield—Glasgow district beside Clyde Ironworks; thole—bear.' 'Purly' Wilson was a Radical weaver hanged at Glasgow Green in 1820 who is reputed to have invented the purl stitch in knitting.

A Song for the Glasgow Irish: Dated 16th March 1999.

A Song of Paddy's Market: The famous market on Shipbank Lane was open for around 200 years before its closure in 2006.

Glasgow Streeet Characters: Anderson contributed a piece on the Glasgow Clincher to Radio Clyde. It is not clear whether it was ever broadcast but he planned another programme featuring songs written in Glasgow entitled 'Songs of the Clyde, with a brief sketch of their authors'. It was to include: *Logan Braes*, by John Mayne; *Robin Tamson's Skiddy*, by Alexander Rodger; *My Highland Laddie*, by Mrs Grant of Laggan and *Wee Willie Winkie*, by William Miller.

Johnny and the Starlings: First published in *The Voice*, Easterhouse community newspaper. Recalls one of several attempts to rid Glasgow city centre of its massive starling population that dirtied its historic buildings.

Let Glasgow Flourish!: Broadsheet appended with the notes: "Let Glasgow Flourish' is part (in my opinion, the main part) of the City's motto. Molendinar, a small stream, running into the Clyde at Glasgow. The Fisher's Yett is a still older name for Saltmarket. The Bell o' the Brae is the place where, legend has it, Wallace confronted Edward I. Bishop Wishart crowned Bruce at Scone; he suffered long imprisonment for it and was released in the exchange of prisoners after Bannockburn. Prebends were the large parishes within the diocese of Glasgow. Rafts: the Clyde was so shallow in the vicinity of the city that imports had to be ferried into the Broomielaw, the quay, on rafts.'

Old Scotia: Mentions by name many of the folksingers and characters who frequented the Scotia Bar in the 1970s.

Pioneerville. Ha! Ha! Written in 1981. Interviewed in 1977, Anderson responded to a question about Garthamlock: 'How do you see the future for Garthamlock?'. 'Like many another housing scheme, we are at present at the cross-roads, Garthamlock could be made into a pleasant little towns hip, or it could, on the other hand, be allowed to degenerate into a spiritless dump, I hope the Glasgow Corporation do not proceed with their plan to build more houses here when already there are hundreds of empty houses both in Garthamlock and adjacent districts. It seems quite senseless to me. The new housing scheme at Craigend has taken over the green fields between Garthamlock and Ruchazie to the west of us. Surely the Corporation could leave us a bit of green belt that is left. The £300,000 improvement project will be a big benefit, but it needs to be speeded up. Auchenlea Park will be a pleasant addition, but we need more shops and other amenities. Vandalism is still going to be one of our big problems and will only be stamped out by the co-operation of the authorities and all the tenants, but I still think that the housing schemes could be 're-deemed' even at this late hour. However, it will require a major operation.' The Anderson family later moved to the new houses at Craigend.

Rab's Impression of the First Sunday Opening of the Victoria Bar. The editor of this volume was attendant at this occasion, but it was notable for an unusual occurence. The opening took place on the day after the clocks went back by one hour. The editor had, unfortunately, put his clock *forward* by one hour and was astonished to arrive at the Victoria Bar, two hours too early, to find the bar closed and the streets deserted.

Song of the Vicky Bar. Dated December 1979. The editor of this volume was inspired enough by this song to pen his own version:

Til The Victoria Bar.

  Weel-warn braken-doun auld bar,
Yuir yellow-pentit neat surroun,
Lik straikit lichtening in a haar,
Gars ye be seen frae aa aroun,
  Yuir muckle mirrors on the waa,
That like the dell ir evir wi us,
Wad cannilie induce us aa,
To see oursels as ithers see us.

  Ayont yuir door stauns weel-faured makars,
Speiran aye o poet's quairs,
Wha tell thir tale til onie takers,
An sell thir ain weel-warkit wares.
  May ye be hird abune the thrang,
Ye base-begotten unkennt bards,
Ye screive yuir sune-forgotten sang,
An weave yuir testament wi wards.

  The loons ir knockan doun the drams,
An haudan up the bar,
Wha deal in alcoholic dwaums,
An see the warld thro uisqueba,
  Ye wadna ken, ye drunken billie,
Ye droukit fule, ye canna ken,

Fur if ye kennt ye luikt as sillie,
By Gode! ye'd nevir drink agin,

  An aye thir will be bonnie callants,
Wad bless our lugs wi plaisant souns,
The couthie croun o auld Soots ballants,
An cantie tirl o hieland tunes.
  Whiles owre yon crouselie liltan trills,
Malr lofty thochts hae risan,
To rectify aa Scotia's ills,
Gin ither folks wad only lissan.

  Wan Rabbie saw twa brigs o Ayr,
He kennt the ane wad pruve the better,
The auld stane brig stuid solid thir,
Thro rain an snaw an stormy weather.
  So wi ye! Victoria Bar,
Wan ithers faa til dust,
Ye'll dree the blasts o tim an wear,
An gang out nane the warse.

Where is the Glasgow That I Used to Know?: Dated March 1995.
Ya Bass. The Tongs, the Fleet and the Brigton Billy Boys were notorious Glasgow gangs. Sir Percy Sillitoe was the Chief Constable of Glasgow (and later head of M15) who promised to clean up the streets. 'Ya Bass' was a gangland slogan meaning 'you bastard[s]'.
Squibs, Skits And Epitaphs. Political characters through the seventies to the nineties mentioned in this section of the book are too numerous to discuss in detail.
The Hero of Hospitality Inn. Based on an actual incident which took place on 6th June 1993. The 'hero' is Jim Friel, Anderson's great friend.
Two of a Kind: Dated 5th June 1981.
The Rose and the Thorn. Based on the career of Madeleine Smith, notoriously tried for murder of her lover in 1857. The verdict was not proven although she was almost certainly guilty. Anderson takes a sypathetic view of her plight.

INDEX OF NAMES

Allan, Willie 159
Anderson, Donald 21
Barbour, Mary 307, 335–339, 360–365
Beaton, Willie 165
Behan, Dominic 13, 21, 27, 35–36
Benn, Tony 202
Blair, Tony 22, 180, 182–183, 186, 190
Blake, William 71
Blythman, Morris (Thurso Berwick) 14, 16–17, 37
Bogle, Eric 21
Broderick, Mick 18, 32, 158
Brogan, Benedict 27
Brooke, Rupert 307, 331–333
Brown, George 22, 111, 117, 174, 185
Brown, Tom 413
Buchan, Janey 22, 183, 189, 191
Buchan, Norman 22, 188
Burns, Robert 14–15, 20, 29, 33, 38, 66–67, 69, 128, 313–315, 317, 325, 341, 368
Cairney, John 22, 66–67, 69, 136, 413
Campbell, Ian 18
Churchill, Winston 56, 58, 77, 187
Connolly, Billy 18
Connolly, James 307, 307–362, 342–345, 353, 425
Cook, Robin 180
Coyle, Stephen 35
Damer, Seán 27
Dewar, Donald 22, 183
Donnelly, Michael 32, 34,
Feeney, Peter 159
Ferguson, Reverend R 39
Foot, Michael 202
Franco, Francisco 60
Friel, Jim 14, 34, 192, 413
Gagahan, John 413, 416
Gaitskill, Hugh 183
Gallacher, Willie 18, 38
Goebbels, Joseph 72, 111
Gray, Alasdair 32, 37
Greig, John 17–18
Grimes, Jimmy 19, 32, 158–159,
Hardy, Andrew 17, 51, 142, 182
Hardy, Keir 182

Harman, Harriet 180, 194
Harvey, Tam 18–19, 158, 158
Healey, Dennis 202
Henderson, Hamish 14–18, 23–24, 26, 29, 34, 39, 60
Hume, Alex 184
Imlach, Hamish 18, 159
Jackson, Glenda 180, 194
Johnstone, Arthur 38
Kavanagh, Patrick 15–16, 28–29
Keir, Harry 29–30, 34
Kelman, James 23, 32, 37
Kilmer, Joyce 413
Kincaid, John 14
Kinnock, Neil 184
Kitson, Alex 176
Kyle, Danny 18
Lally, Patrick 184–202
Lally, Patrick 22, 33, 143–144, 168, 180–182, 184, 191, 197
Laurie, Cy 18, 165
Lewis, Gary 25, 35
Liddell, Helen 180
MacDiarmid, Hugh 14
MacDonald, Tom 34
MacGill, Patrick 29–30, 34, 419
MacGonagall, William 26
Maclean, John 25, 29, 33, 35–36, 39, 307, 313–315, 320–324, 328, 330, 334–343, 346–352, 355, 357, 359–361
MacLeod, Colin 23
Major, John 187
Makem, Tommy 13
Marshall, Billy 27
Martyn, Jon 18
Maxwell, Robert 180, 184
Mayne, John 414
McCabe, Brian 27
McCann, Stevie 180
McCarthy, Joseph 60, 111
McCulloch, Frank 18
McDougall, Carl 24
McGinn, Janette 29, 38
McGinn, Matt 29, 34, 36
McGrath, John 36
McGrath, Tom 29
McGregor, Gerry 18, 32
McLaughlan, Brendan 21, 32, 38

McLay, Farqhuar 23
McMillan, Roddy 14, 29
McNulty, Pat 18, 29
McVicar, Ewan 17, 25, 30, 39
Miller, William 34, 414
Mitchell, Ellen 27
Monaghan, Tommy 181
Morgan, James Clarence 413
O'Hanlon, Fergal 13
Paterson, Gavin 35
Pearse, Patrick 307, 342–344
Petrie, Alexander (The Clincher) 26, 29, 149–151, 303, 307, 323–326, 338–339, 354, 414
Reagan, Ronald 23, 60, 116, 173, 198
Reid, Jimmy 22, 182, 188
Relich, Mario 27
Richard, Cliff 22
Richards, Sheila 14
Robertson, George 175, 180
Robertson, George 175, 180, 185
Robeson, Paul 14
Rodger, Alexander (Sandy) 26, 34, 414
Russell, Bertrand 30
Sands, Bobby 18, 100, 104
Scanlan, Hugh 200
Scott, Walter 20, 313, 388
Short, Clare 22, 182
Sillitoe, Percy 169, 416
Simon, Joey 37
Smith, John 186–187, 191
Smith, Madeleine 416
Stevenson, Gary (see Gary Lewis)
Thatcher, Margaret 128–136, 420
Thatcher, Margaret 20–21, 113, 128, 136, 178–179, 195–196, 201
Todd, George 14
Wilson, 'Purly' 414
Wilson, Brian 175
Wilson, Harold 22, 111, 193
Wilson, Jamie 51
Yeats, William Butler 78, 81
Young, James 22

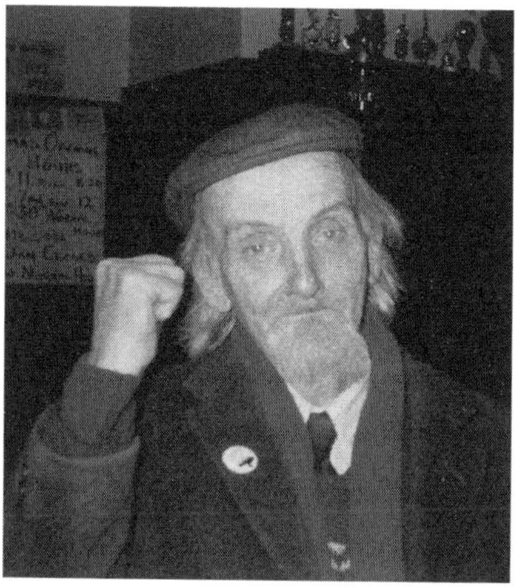